The Vietnam Experience

The False Peace

1972-74

by Samuel Lipsman, Stephen Weiss,
and the editors of Boston Publishing Company

Boston Publishing Company/Boston, MA

Boston Publishing Company

President and Publisher: Robert J. George
Vice President: Richard S. Perkins, Jr.
Editor-in-Chief: Robert Manning
Managing Editor: Paul Dreyfus
Marketing Director: Jeanne Gibson

Senior Writers:
Clark Dougan, Edward Doyle, David Fulghum, Samuel Lipsman, Terrence Maitland, Stephen Weiss
Senior Picture Editor: Julene Fischer

Researchers:
Jonathan Elwitt, Sandra W. Jacobs, Michael Ludwig, Anthony Maybury-Lewis, Carole Rulnick, Nicole van Ackere, Robert Yarbrough

Picture Editors:
Wendy Johnson, Lanng Tamura
Assistant Picture Editor: Kathleen A. Reidy

Picture Researchers:
Nancy Katz Colman, Robert Ebbs, Tracey Rogers, Nana Elisabeth Stern, Shirley L. Green (Washington, D.C.), Kate Lewin (Paris)

Archivist: Kathryn J. Steeves
Picture Department Assistant: Karen Bjelke

Historical Consultants:
Lee Ewing, Stuart A. Herrington, Tad Szulc
Picture Consultant: Ngo Vinh Long

Production Editor: Kerstin Gorham
Assistant Production Editor: Patricia Leal Welch

Editorial Production:
Sarah E. Burns, Pamela George, Gordon Hardy, Dalia Lipkin, Theresa M. Slomkowski

Design: Designworks, Sally Bindari
Design Assistant: Sherry Fatla

Business Staff:
Amy Pelletier, Amy P. Wilson

About the editors and authors

Editor-in-Chief *Robert Manning*, a long-time journalist, has previously been editor-in-chief of the *Atlantic Monthly* magazine and its press. He served as assistant secretary of state for public affairs under Presidents John F. Kennedy and Lyndon B. Johnson. He has also been a fellow at the Institute of Politics at the John F. Kennedy School of Government at Harvard University.

Authors: *Samuel Lipsman*, a former Fulbright Scholar, received his M.A. and M.Phil. in history at Yale. *Stephen Weiss*, an American historian, has M.A. and M.Phil. degrees from Yale. He is a former fellow at the Newberry Library in Chicago. Messrs. Lipsman and Weiss have coauthored other volumes in *The Vietnam Experience*.

Historical Consultants: *Lee Ewing*, editor of *Army Times*, served two years in Vietnam as a combat intelligence officer with the U.S. Military Assistance Command, Vietnam (MACV) and the 101st Airborne Division. *Stuart A. Herrington*, a lieutenant colonel in the United States Army, was a military intelligence officer in Vietnam. He is the author of *Peace With Honor?* and *Silence Was a Weapon*, two books about his experience in Vietnam. *Tad Szulc* spent twenty years as a political, diplomatic, and foreign correspondent for the *New York Times*. The author of over a dozen books, he has also been a contributing editor for the *New Republic* and a member of the editorial board of *Foreign Policy*.

Picture Consultant: *Ngo Vinh Long* is a social historian specializing in China and Vietnam. Born in Vietnam, he returned there most recently in 1980.

Cover Photo:

President Richard Nixon honors the last American combatants to come home—the 653 POWs—at a reception at the White House on May 24, 1973. The prisoners' return was perhaps the United States's only tangible gain as a result of the January 1973 cease-fire, which was to be virtually ignored by both Communist and GVN forces.

Library of Congress Catalog Card Number: 85-072265

ISBN: 0-939526-15-8

10 9 8 7 6
5 4 3 2

Contents

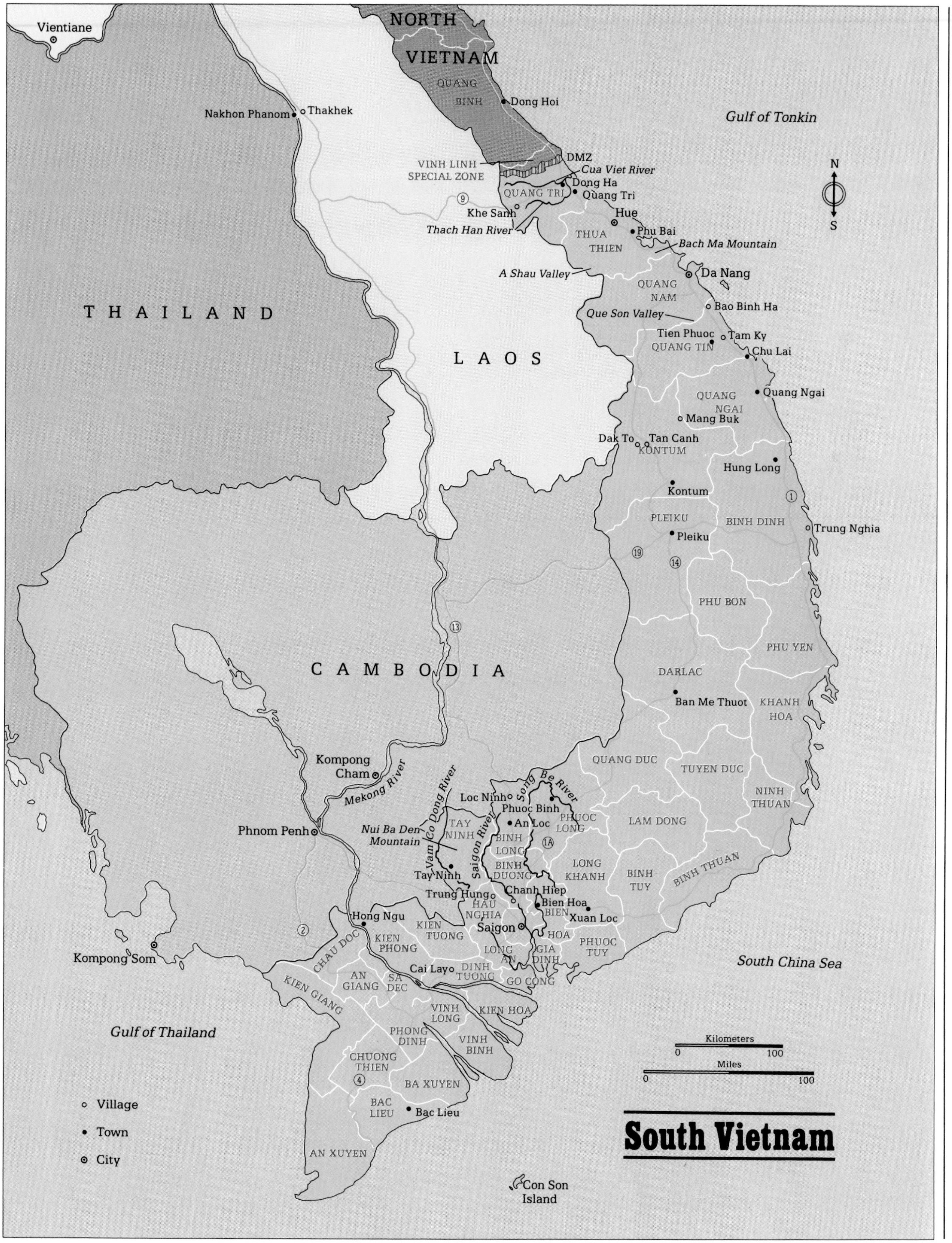
South Vietnam
Vientiane
NORTH
VIETNAM
QUANG
BINH
Dong Hoi
Nakhon Phanom
Thakhek
Gulf of Tonkin
VINH LINH
SPECIAL ZONE
DMZ
Cua Viet River
Dong Ha
QUANG TRI
Quang Tri
9
Khe Sanh
Hue
Thach Han River
THUA
THIEN
Phu Bai
Bach Ma Mountain
A Shau Valley
Da Nang
QUANG
NAM
Bao Binh Ha
THAILAND
Que Son Valley
Tien Phuoc
Tam Ky
QUANG TIN
Chu Lai
LAOS
QUANG
NGAI
Quang Ngai
Mang Buk
Dak To
Tan Canh
KONTUM
Hung Long
Kontum
1
PLEIKU
Pleiku
BINH DINH
Trung Nghia
19
14
PHU BON
13
PHU YEN
CAMBODIA
DARLAC
Ban Me Thuot
KHANH
HOA
Kompong
Cham
Mekong River
Co Dong River
Song Be River
QUANG DUC
TUYEN DUC
NINH
THUAN
Loc Ninh
Phuoc Binh
An Loc
PHUOC
LONG
LAM DONG
Phnom Penh
Nui Ba Den
Mountain
Vam
TAY
NINH
Saigon River
BINH
LONG
1A
BINH
DUONG
LONG
KHANH
BINH
TUY
BINH THUAN
Tay Ninh
Trung Hung
HAU
NGHIA
Chanh Hiep
Bien Hoa
BIEN
HOA
Xuan Loc
Hong Ngu
KIEN
TUONG
Saigon
2
CHAU DOC
KIEN
PHONG
LONG
AN
GIA
DINH
PHUOC
TUY
Kompong Som
Cai Lay
DINH
TUONG
AN
GIANG
SA
DEC
GO CONG
South China Sea
KIEN GIANG
VINH
LONG
KIEN HOA
Gulf of Thailand
PHONG
DINH
VINH
BINH
CHUONG
THIEN
4
BA XUYEN
Kilometers
0
100
Miles
0
100
Village
Town
City
BAC
LIEU
Bac Lieu
AN XUYEN
Con Son
Island

"Peace Is at Hand"

"The four-sided conference," the Harvard professor wrote of the Paris negotiations to end the Vietnam War, "should be looked upon primarily as a plenary session to legitimize the work of two negotiating committees. . . . Hanoi and Washington would discuss mutual withdrawal and related subjects. . . . Saigon and the NLF would discuss the internal structure of South Vietnam."

The Harvard professor was Henry Kissinger, and his words suggested what became known as the two-tiered, or double-track, approach to the Vietnam negotiations. The strategy was designed to separate the military issues of the war from an ultimate political solution for South Vietnam's future. Kissinger wrote the essay in the fall of 1968 as advice for whomever would have the responsibility for conducting these negotiations in the newly elected Nixon administration. By the time they appeared in the January 1969 edition of *Foreign Affairs*, Nixon had appointed Kissinger to be his national security adviser and his words

had become, in effect, a public memorandum to himself.

Kissinger's article contained a wealth of advice and warnings for the negotiations with the North Vietnamese as well as the South Vietnamese:

It would be difficult to imagine two societies less meant to understand each other than the Vietnamese and the American.

The traditional style of American diplomacy was also likely to cause problems with Saigon:

When agreement seems imminent, American diplomats suddenly go into high gear to gain the acquiescence of the ally. He in turn feels tricked by the very intensity and suddenness of the pressure while we are outraged to learn of objections heretofore not made explicit. This almost guarantees that the ensuing controversy will take place under the most difficult conditions.

But no matter what happened, Kissinger warned: "There is clearly a point beyond which Saigon cannot be given a veto over negotiations."

For three and one-half years Henry Kissinger tried to heed his own advice and reach an agreement with Hanoi that would end the fighting in Vietnam. His attempts, however, resulted only in disappointment, frustration, and defeat. Then on June 20, 1972, the White House received a reply to a note sent to Hanoi the previous week inviting the Communists to resume secret negotiations in Paris. The response was short but to the point: "The DRV side, clothed by its goodwill, agrees to private meetings." It suggested July 13 as the date of the proposed session. Kissinger

Preceding page. *South Vietnamese President Nguyen Van Thieu kneels in prayer amid the rubble of the La Vang Cathedral near Quang Tri City in September 1972.*

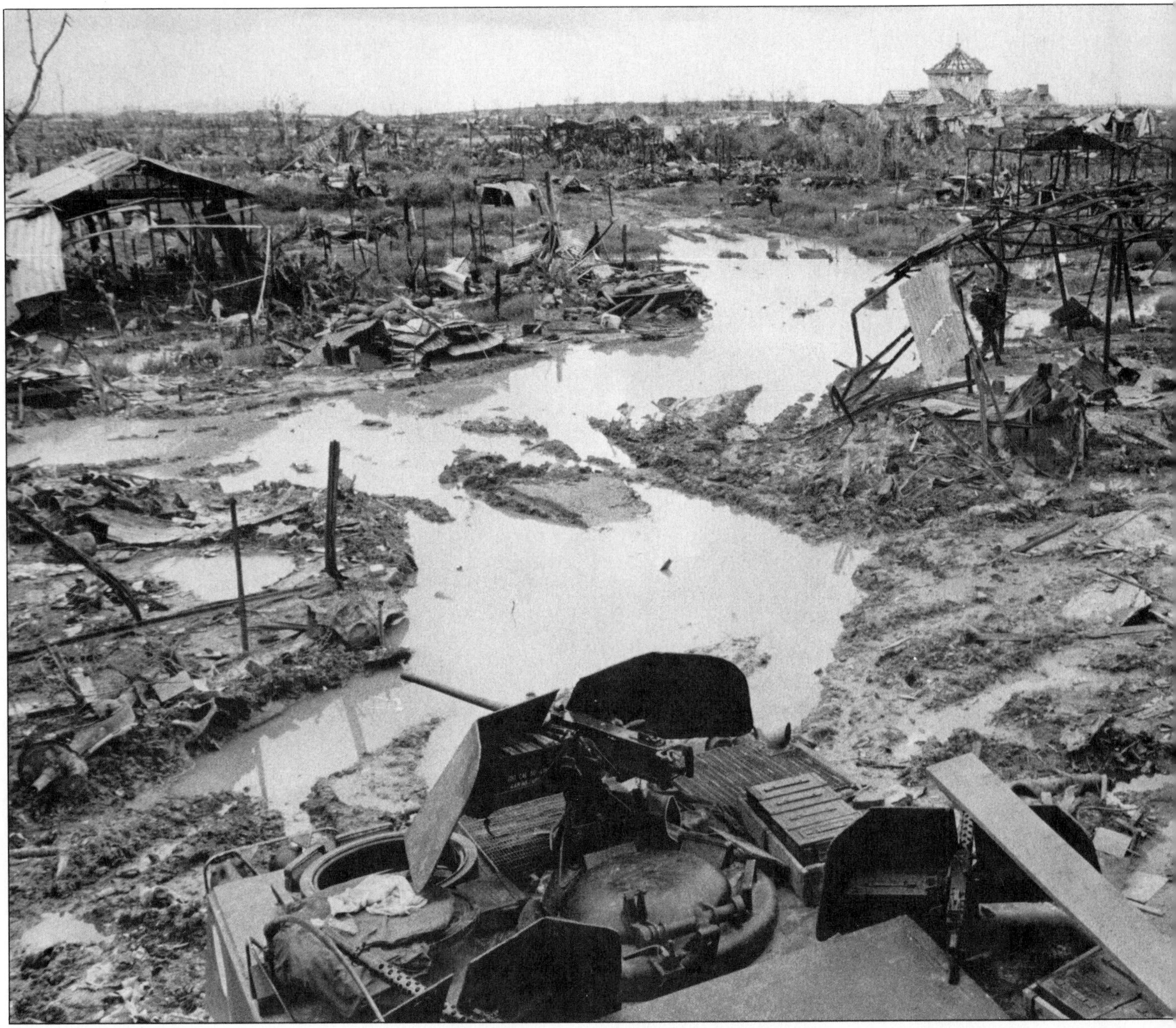

quickly responded, and the two sides settled on July 19 as the date of their rendezvous.

Kissinger was hardly startled by Hanoi's response. In fact, he expected it. But most Americans, had they been aware of the secret exchange of diplomatic messages, would have been shocked, for in the early summer of 1972 peace seemed more distant than ever.

Previous peace negotiations, both public and private, had failed because neither Washington nor Hanoi felt able to compromise on two key issues. From the vantage point of Washington and Saigon the withdrawal of U.S. troops had to be coupled with a simultaneous withdrawal of North Vietnamese troops from South Vietnam. This North Vietnam refused to consider, since such a step would leave what remained of the southern Vietcong seriously outgunned and outmanned by the ARVN.

For its part, North Vietnam insisted that President Thieu be removed from power in Saigon and a coalition government take his place. As a matter of both principle and strategy the United States would not take responsibility for ousting Thieu. Hanoi's position, in fact, rejected Kissinger's basic, two-tiered bargaining premise by refusing to separate political and military questions.

In the hope of breaking the stalemate and in the knowledge that compromise would be necessary to reach any agreement, the United States softened its position. First privately in October 1971 and then publicly in January 1972, the Nixon administration advanced peace proposals that called upon the U.S. to withdraw its troops from the battlefield while not mentioning an NVA withdrawal. By implication they could remain. This implication was made explicit in a proposal Kissinger conveyed to Soviet President Leonid Brezhnev during a secret conference in Moscow in late April. Kissinger now waited for Hanoi to bend.

Between the April message to Brezhnev and the affirmative North Vietnamese response in June, momentous events took place. The Communist Easter offensive (see chapter 7, in *South Vietnam on Trial*, another volume in "The Vietnam Experience") stalled under the weight of American B–52 bombing and the surprisingly determined resistance by South Vietnamese defenders. American aircraft—this time B–52s—also systematically attacked North Vietnam for the first time since the bombing halt of 1968, while other American aircraft closed North Vietnam's ports and inland waterways with thousands of deadly mines. Despite these actions against their ally, the Soviet Union and the People's Republic of China barely whimpered in protest. When Richard Nixon's scheduled summit meeting in Moscow in late May not only proceeded without delay but proved to be a major success, Hanoi realized that it was internationally isolated.

The not-so-secret meetings

Kissinger met with the North Vietnamese on three occasions in July and August 1972. Telling the Communists that he could no longer keep his travels a secret, Kissinger gained agreement that the two sides would announce each meeting but without public comment. Privately, Kissinger told Nixon, "They were as positive ... as we could expect if they do want to settle." Kissinger noted a friendlier attitude on the part of the North Vietnamese; they were more willing to show appreciation for the famed Kissinger wit. One of his assistants noticed that the quality of the snacks served by the North Vietnamese hosts showed steady improvement, from egg rolls on July 19 to fruit and cookies on August 1, and reached a comparatively epicu-

While diplomats negotiate in Paris, the battle in South Vietnam rages on. Here Quang Tri City, once the home of 850,000 people, lies in ruins. Fighting leveled the city in 1972.

rean height on August 14 when wine and rice cakes appeared. What Kissinger found was an evolving change of strategy in a badly divided North Vietnamese Politburo that, Kissinger believed, would bring even tastier delicacies to the snack table at future negotiating sessions.

The unity of the North Vietnamese had never wavered when it came to their national objective of "liberating" South Vietnam and reuniting the country. Disagreements within the ruling body, always difficult for U.S. intelligence to ferret out with precision, had pertained only to the means of achieving these goals. In the summer of 1972 the Politburo split into two factions and would remain divided until the very end of the war. Although the two sides were often called "doves" and "hawks," that distinction can be misleading. Rather, the division lay between those who wanted to pursue North Vietnam's goals more cautiously and those who argued for more aggressive action. The failed 1972 offensive forced the Politburo to consider a change in strategy, and by the end of the summer of 1972 the "doves" had emerged with a slim majority.

The proof for Kissinger's analysis came a month after the August 14 meeting in Paris, not from Hanoi during the negotiating session on September 14 but from the Provisional Revolutionary Government (PRG), the administration of the National Liberation Front. Conceding that "there exist in South Vietnam two administrations, two armies and other political forces," the PRG argued that a solution to the war must involve "mutual respect and mutual non-elimination." This was the first hint from the Communists that they would no longer insist on the ouster of President Thieu, a signal that they were finally anxious to conclude an agreement.

When Kissinger again met with the North Vietnamese in Paris on September 26, the Communists went a step further. They dropped their demand for a coalition government (even one that included President Thieu was unacceptable to the U.S.) and instead proposed a "Provisional Government of National Concord" whose only function would be advisory and whose only responsibility would be to arrange elections for the postwar South Vietnam. Kissinger made a noncommittal response to North Vietnam's newest proposal, saying that he wanted to study it overnight. North Vietnamese earnestness was demonstrated by serving shrimp and caviar.

Along with their new proposal of substance on September 26, the North Vietnamese asked for Kissinger's assent to a schedule by which the two sides would complete a peace agreement. The schedule confirmed Kissinger's analysis of North Vietnamese strategy, and he agreed to it in principle.

North Vietnam wanted to sign a treaty on October 30, one week before the American presidential elections. Kissinger had reasoned as early as late July that the North Vietnamese had given up all hope that the dovish candidacy of George McGovern could defeat Richard Nixon's

reelection bid in November. The enemy would be anxious to settle before the election. Hanoi knew Nixon as a hard-line president, and the Politburo feared the actions Nixon might take with a new mandate. Finally, Hanoi also believed that Nixon, himself, would be anxious to end the war before facing the American public at the polls.

The North Vietnamese were decidedly wrong on this last point. Nixon's pollsters had informed him that his lead over George McGovern was insurmountable and that a late peace agreement would not add to his plurality. On the contrary, such a treaty would of necessity represent a compromise and might cost him votes among the extreme right. Nixon thus privately cautioned Kissinger that there was no need to produce an agreement prior to election day.

Kissinger now had to convince Nixon that the election day deadline was not to be used against the administration but rather offered the best fulcrum for squeezing additional concessions out of Hanoi. Kissinger also warned Nixon that waiting until after the election posed its own dangers, since the negotiations "would have to be pursued without a deadline on Hanoi." Moreover, support on Capitol Hill to end the war through legislation was growing. Finally, he told Nixon, "we might not even be able to count on Soviet and Chinese acquiescence indefinitely."

Kissinger's arguments proved persuasive to Nixon. "He accepted the foreign policy rationale." It was in the nature of the Nixon-Kissinger relationship, however, that the president did so, "not without reminding me that it was really against his political interests," as Kissinger recorded in his memoirs.

With his approach to the negotiations approved by the White House, Kissinger carefully contained his excitement when responding to North Vietnam's September 26 proposal the following day. He now knew that a settlement was imminent. As the session on September 27 ended, the North Vietnamese suggested that the next meeting be scheduled for October 7. Attempting to turn the time pressure up ever so slightly, Kissinger countered with the suggestion of October 8. If the Communists were to keep to their schedule, they would have three weeks to meet all of America's remaining objections.

Breakthrough

When Kissinger returned to the secret negotiations on October 8, the first thing he noticed were two thick green folders in front of Le Duc Tho, special adviser representing the North Vietnamese government in the secret talks and a member of the Politburo at least since 1955. Tho had joined the peace negotiations in 1969 when the Nixon administration invited Hanoi to send a senior official to conduct secret talks with Henry Kissinger. According to Averell Harriman, the American negotiator with whom Le Duc

Tho had some preliminary discussions in 1968, "Talking to him was like talking to the head of the Soviet Government. . . . He could make decisions on the spot."

As Kissinger listened carefully on October 8 to Tho's restatement of North Vietnam's bargaining position outlined in the September 26 session, his eyes never left the green folders in front of Tho. The morning session droned on without progress and was adjourned for lunch. At 1:00 P.M. Tho entered the room where the American delegation was dining and suggested a longer break, until 4:00 P.M. As the minutes passed, the American delegation was "preoccupied, tense over what was to come," as Kissinger recollected.

At precisely 4:00 the meeting resumed. Tho did not waste time. He began, "I think we cannot negotiate in the way we are doing now" and handed Kissinger the green folders. Tho proceeded to outline their contents: nine points that were to become the basis for the Paris Agreement on Ending the War and Restoring Peace in Vietnam.

Tho began by suggesting that the United States and

North Vietnam reach an agreement to solve the military questions. On the political future of South Vietnam, "we shall only agree on the main principles." Tho characterized the political problems as "the most thorny, the most difficult" and suggested that they not be permitted to prolong the negotiations.

What Tho presented was a proposal, not for a Government of National Concord as advanced on September 27 but an Administration of National Concord, charged with "organizing" ill-defined general and local elections. The two administrations in South Vietnam, the Saigon government and the PRG, would remain intact, as would their armies. Furthermore, this Administration of National Concord, which would consist of members of the two sides in the civil war and mutually agreeable representatives of South Vietnam's uncommitted "third force," would operate

An ARVN soldier races through the ruins of Xom Suoi, thirty-five kilometers north of Saigon. Anticipating a cease-fire, both sides scrambled for strategic positions in October 1972.

Special Adviser Le Duc Tho, the chief North Vietnamese negotiator at the peace talks, waves to the press corps. Tho proved to be a brilliant, if infuriating, negotiator.

on the principle of unanimity. It could accomplish nothing without the assent of President Thieu.

Tho had more to offer: He dropped the demand that the United States cease all aid to the Thieu government and proposed the "replacement of armament," a means by which the United States would be able to extend continued military assistance to Saigon and Hanoi would be free to resupply its forces.

The proposal also incorporated further clauses that had either been proposed by the United States or previously agreed upon:

- A cease-fire in place would immediately follow the signing of the agreement.
- American POWs would be returned concurrent with the withdrawal of U.S. troops. Tho even promised that POWs held by the Pathet Lao would be returned.
- Infiltration of new NVA troops into the South would end.
- The U.S. would extend postwar economic assistance to North Vietnam, as originally offered by President Johnson.

There were some missing elements. The U.S. had ceased to demand a withdrawal of NVA troops from South Vietnam and Tho did not mention them. Although he had previously offered to remove northern soldiers from Laos and Cambodia as part of a settlement, he was now silent about their status. Finally, he maintained that North Vietnam could not negotiate cease-fires in Cambodia and Laos because of the "principle of noninterference in these countries." They were sovereign states.

Tho concluded his presentation by reminding Kissinger that his proposal was essentially the American peace plan:

This new proposal is exactly what President Nixon has himself proposed: ceasefire, end of the war, release of the prisoners, and troop withdrawal. ... And we shall leave to the South Vietnamese parties the settlement of these [political] questions.

At the conclusion of Tho's presentation Kissinger immediately requested a recess. He embraced his assistant Winston Lord and said, "We have done it." He remembered it as "my most thrilling moment in public service."

For the next three days Kissinger and Tho engaged in marathon sessions to convert Hanoi's nine points into legal language acceptable to the United States. The Administration of National Concord no longer was "required" to reach a political settlement within ninety days but only charged to "do their utmost." It was rechristened the National Council of National Reconciliation and Concord (NCNRC). The replacement of military equipment was placed on a "one-for-one" basis, rather than Hanoi's proposal for "equality," which would permit the Communists to build up their force in the South until it reached the level of South Vietnam's.

The North Vietnamese refused to compromise on other issues. They would not discuss the withdrawal of even some of their troops from South Vietnam, arguing that South Vietnam was not a foreign country to them. The status of Laos and Cambodia proved to be a thorny issue. Tho refused to place within the text of the agreement any mention of the other Indochinese countries, because North Vietnam was not empowered to negotiate on their behalf. The two sides agreed to express their commitment as separately stated "understandings." They agreed that all foreign troops would be withdrawn from Cambodia and Laos, and Tho stipulated that NVA troops would be considered "foreign" in that context. Kissinger pressed for a commitment for a cease-fire in the two countries. Tho would only promise a cease-fire in Laos, within thirty days after the signing of the agreement. He would not commit North Vietnam to any cease-fire in Cambodia, arguing that "Hanoi's influence on the Cambodian Communists was not decisive." Kissinger admits that he was "skeptical." In his memoirs, however, he reluctantly concluded that "it turned out to be one occasion when Tho was telling the truth."

The most difficult problem, however, turned out to be the status of the civilian political prisoners held by Saigon, many of them Vietcong political cadres. Tho's October 8 proposal called for the simultaneous release of these prisoners with the American POWs. Kissinger "saw no possibility of Saigon's releasing the core of the Viet Cong guerillas" and refused to link the fate of American POWs with "our ability to persuade Thieu to release Viet Cong prisoners." Le Duc Tho objected, "as well he might," as Kissinger pointed out, because "it in effect left all South Vietnamese Communist prisoners in Saigon's jails."

Despite these problems, when a sixteen-hour session begun on October 11 ended at 2:00 A.M. the following day an agreement was virtually complete. The status of the political prisoners remained unresolved; wording on North Vietnamese commitments in Laos and Cambodia was incomplete; and a precise formula for continued U.S. assistance to South Vietnam was still required. On October 12 Kissinger boarded an airplane for Washington to report to President Nixon. Before leaving he agreed upon a second schedule with Le Duc Tho:

October 18: Kissinger travels to Saigon for consultations with President Thieu.
October 21: All U.S. bombing of North Vietnam ceases.
October 22: Kissinger arrives in Hanoi to initial the agreement.
October 31: Formal signing in Paris.

The schedule would provide Kissinger with an opportunity for his greatest public relations spectacle, greater even than his secret trip to Peking in 1971. On October 21 he would feign illness in Saigon, only to appear miraculously in the enemy's capital to proclaim the peace.

At the White House, the president ordered steak and wine to celebrate the agreement. After discussions with Kissinger, Nixon sent a cable to the North Vietnamese informing them that he consented to the draft, provided that four changes of wording were made. Kissinger proceeded to brief other top administration officials in the Pentagon and State Department, while State Department lawyers looked over the text and translation of the agreement. On October 17 Kissinger again left Washington for a brief layover in Paris, where he intended to work out the remaining language in the agreement. His next stop was to be Saigon.

When Kissinger departed Paris on October 12, he had left behind several members of his staff to work with North Vietnamese counterparts in what were called "technical talks," designed to reach agreement on the still disputed points and to produce a series of protocols that would further elaborate the manner of carrying out the agreement: the planning and timing of prisoner releases and U.S. troop withdrawal, the methods by which both sides could equip their allies, the composition and size of the international peace-keeping force, and other arrangements for executing the agreement. When Kissinger returned to Paris on October 17 he found progress on virtually all fronts but still no complete agreement. Leaving Paris the next day, Kissinger cabled Hanoi with proposed language for all areas of dispute. He warned the North Vietnamese that he would not proceed to Hanoi unless the agreement was final. On October 18 he landed at Saigon's Tan Son Nhut airport; his first meeting with Thieu was scheduled for 11:00 A.M. the following day.

The puppet unbound

Arriving on schedule at the presidential palace, the American delegation was kept waiting fifteen minutes by President Thieu. Ushered into the president's military operations room, they found themselves surrounded by maps, reports, and telephones directly linking Thieu to his corps and division commanders. Kissinger handed Thieu a personal letter from Nixon urging him to assent to the agreement. Nixon's letter ended:

Dr. Kissinger, General Haig, and I have discussed this proposal at great length. I am personally convinced it is the best we will be able to get and that it meets my absolute condition—that the GVN must survive as a free country. Dr. Kissinger's comments have my total backing.

Thieu read the letter without comment.

Kissinger handed him a copy of the draft agreement, in English, since no reliable Vietnamese translation was yet available. Thieu's first words were to announce that his adviser, Hoang Duc Nha, would serve as translator for the meeting, despite the fact that everyone present was fluent in English. As Kissinger began to summarize the contents of the agreement for the group, he noted that Nha's translations required only half the time of his comments. When he questioned Nha on the matter, the American-educated adviser responded, "I am a master of contraction."

Kissinger's summary continued for an hour. At its conclusion Thieu raised only peripheral questions: What were the modalities for signing the agreement? Was the agreement essential to President Nixon's reelection? (Kissinger told him, no.) In the opinion of Ambassador Ellsworth Bunker and Kissinger, Thieu seemed reconciled to the inevitable. The meeting adjourned to give Thieu's staff an opportunity to study the draft.

Precisely what Thieu knew about the draft agreement prior to that meeting has remained a source of controversy ever since. What everyone, including Kissinger, later agreed upon, however, is that the American government had deliberately misled him.

In a series of cables at the end of July and in a personal visit to Saigon in early August, Kissinger informed Thieu of America's basic negotiating position. Thieu specifically objected to a "stand-still ceasefire," and a tripartite electoral commission, which he viewed as a disguised coalition government. Thieu, according to Kissinger, "doubted that Hanoi would offer a ceasefire." Kissinger not only failed to inform Thieu that he thought an agreement in the near future quite likely but further "agreed [with Thieu] that Hanoi would probably not give up its political demands." Kissinger thus, according to his own memoirs, left Thieu with the impression that whatever he agreed to was unlikely to result in a final settlement.

Other observers subsequently learned from American and South Vietnamese sources of other exchanges during the August discussions with Thieu not recorded by Kissinger. According to Allan Goodman, a political scientist affiliated with the Hoover Institute, Kissinger led Thieu to believe that the Nixon administration's apparent willingness to compromise was only "for domestic political purposes, but that Hanoi's intransigence would be punished after the election." The journalist Arnold Isaacs reported that Kissinger "engaged Thieu in fanciful pipe-dreaming about possible ARVN amphibious landings in the North," a discussion that Kissinger alludes to in his memoirs. Whatever the truth of these allegations it is abundantly clear that Kissinger (1) knew of Thieu's objections to several key provisions of any settlement, including a standstill cease-fire, the continuing presence of NVA troops in South Vietnam, and any electoral commission; (2) knew that these provisions were acceptable to both Hanoi and Washington and either already were or soon would be placed on the negotiating table; and (3) knew that they would form the basis of an agreement that would likely be reached by November.

As the pace of events accelerated in September and October, Kissinger purposely refused to inform the South Vietnamese president fully. Kissinger later offered two reasons for his decisions, reasons that, in fact, are mutually contradictory. On the one hand Kissinger argues, like Le Duc Tho, that the final settlement merely incorporated previous peace proposals made by President Nixon with President Thieu's approval. Thus, he argues, he already had Thieu's assent. At the same time Kissinger maintains that he *knew* that these very same provisions were unacceptable to President Thieu. He feared that if he informed Thieu of the status of the negotiations that the South Vietnamese leader would leak them to the press and then publicly denounce them. Such a maneuver would sabotage the rapid progress being made in Paris and suggest to the North Vietnamese that they were being tricked by Washington. Furthermore, according to Hanoi, both sides "agreed to be responsible for the concurrence of their respective allies." This was the foundation for the two-sided secret negotiations and was never disputed by Kissinger or any other American official.

During the October meetings in Paris Kissinger did dispatch some cables to Ambassador Bunker in Saigon with information to be passed on to Thieu. On October 8 he reported that "the other side may surface a ceasefire proposal during these meetings." In fact, they had already done so. He admitted this much only to explain why he felt it was "essential that Thieu instruct his commanders to move promptly and seize the maximum amount of critical territory." On October 11, after agreeing with Le Duc Tho to the scheduled October 31 signing of the agreement and an immediate cease-fire, Kissinger offered the most curious circumlocution to Saigon: "At this juncture I see no chance of ceasefire in time frame shorter than two weeks." On October 12 his hints were somewhat stronger: "They appear ready to accept a ceasefire in place in the near future."

Thieu was therefore not without justification in feeling deceived by the Americans when he finally received the text of a nearly completed agreement on October 19. Nor was he merely feigning outrage when he actually read the agreement only to discover that Kissinger had negotiated on behalf of the South Vietnamese government provisions he, Thieu, had already rejected.

Kissinger's position in Saigon was made even more difficult by the "good" news he received at Ambassador Bunker's residence on the evening of October 19. From Washington he learned that Hanoi had accepted without change all of his proposed language on the outstanding issues. Nixon cabled Hanoi with his view that "the text of the agreement could be considered complete." However, he added that he wanted firmer language on three matters pertaining to Laos and Cambodia that were not to become part of the actual text of the agreement but, rather, secret "understandings." "While we were at it," as Kis-

Kissinger and the Vietnamese

When Richard Nixon and his national security adviser, Henry Kissinger, assumed office in January 1969, they optimistically believed that they could achieve a negotiated settlement to the Vietnam War within a year. The basis of this optimism was not so much a "secret plan" to end the war (though Nixon claimed that he had one) as a germinal concept or idea of how the war would end. The road to peace, both men believed, lay through Moscow. With a combination of belligerence and inducements directed at the Soviet leaders, a carrot and stick approach, they believed that they could lead the Russians to force Hanoi to negotiate on American terms.

When a breakthrough in the Paris negotiations finally came, the one year had stretched into four, but Soviet pressure on the North Vietnamese Politburo did, in fact, play a major role. It had required persistent cajolery and threats on the part of the Americans to achieve this goal. Even then the frustrations did not end, for both Vietnamese parties proved to be even more tenacious in negotiating when the chips were down than they had been in the empty talks of the previous four years.

It was in the mind and spirit of Henry Kissinger that the effects of this frustration were most keenly felt. His memories of the period of intense negotiations in the second half of 1972 he described as "a most painful" period, an assessment that becomes abundantly clear in a careful reading of his memoirs. Most statesmen use their memoirs as a means to cleanse the historical record of their less admirable behavior. While many observers would argue that Kissinger's memoirs, in general, are no exception, his account of the peace negotiations is in many respects remarkably frank. Writing five years after the event in the coolness and detachment of his study, Kissinger's pen fairly seethes in resentment, directed in equal measure against his North Vietnamese enemies and his South Vietnamese allies.

In conducting secret negotiations with the North Vietnamese, Kissinger and Nixon requested that Hanoi nominate a high official empowered to act on behalf of the government. In Le Duc Tho the Politburo selected one of its own members, a man whom Kissinger described as "dignified" and "composed" with "impeccable" manners who "served his cause with dedication and skill." Despite the acknowledgement of these qualities, Kissinger routinely referred to his negotiating partner with the condescending nickname of "Ducky."

If he was scornful of Tho, Kissinger was downright vicious in remembrance of the North Vietnamese interpreter, Nguyen Dinh Phuong. In calmer moments Kissinger described Phuong as an "excellent" interpreter. Yet, in his memoirs he repeatedly mocked the North Vietnamese's mispronunciation of English words. Phuong used the British pronunciation of the word "schedule" but accented the second syllable so that he repeatedly said, "shed*yule*." He softened the "g" in prolong so that the word came out as "prolongue." It is particularly ironic that this brand of humor came from a man whose own foreign accent was often imitated and the object of unkind witticisms.

More telling was Kissinger's repeated use of the word "insolent" in describing the North Vietnamese. The word itself suggests disobedience to a recognized authority, a servant–master or child–parent relationship. Use of the term does not reveal any recognition by Kissinger of a relationship among equals, usually a prerequisite for fruitful negotiations.

Much of Kissinger's frustration was a result of the refusal by the North Vietnamese to play the role assigned to them in his larger theory of the international balance of power. In one revealing phrase he suggested that Hanoi was "too egotistical to think of foreign policy in terms of an international system." It seems not to have occurred to Kissinger that the leaders of a small, underdeveloped nation would be more concerned with their own national survival than with conforming to the geopolitical theories of the American national security adviser.

As irritated as Kissinger became with the North Vietnamese, his most savage blows were saved for the South Vietnamese allies. While he may well have felt cause for resenting Thieu's attitude toward the peace negotiations, he repeatedly identifies the South Vietnamese president's attitudes with Vietnamese racial traits. According to Kissinger's memoirs, he was the target of "the elusive tactics Vietnamese reserve for foreigners." He reports that Thieu irritated him with his "cultural arrogance" and "characteristic Vietnamese opaqueness."

Kissinger would ultimately indicate some grudging respect for the South Vietnamese president and the difficult position he occupied in Saigon. But he was less charitable with Thieu's cousin and confidant, Hoang Duc Nha. Superficially, Nha should have appealed to Kissinger: He was educated in the United States and thoroughly Americanized. According to Kissinger, however, he "had retained from his Vietnamese background only an infinite capacity for intrigue." Fortunately for Kissinger, intrigue was not exclusively an art of the Vietnamese; his own fame rested greatly on his own "infinite capacity" for using that age–old tool of the diplomat.

This is not to suggest that important cultural differences between Americans and Vietnamese do not exist. The recognition and understanding of such cultural patterns is often a necessary step for the successful negotiator. But rather than accepting the Vietnamese on equal terms and using their national traits as a tool in his diplomacy, Kissinger arrived at generalizations that only deepened his frustration and brought little honor to the country he represented.

singer put it, Nixon requested a new schedule that would delay the halt in the bombing of North Vietnam and the national security adviser's arrival in Hanoi by forty-eight hours. It was the third schedule to which the United States had committed itself.

Without delay Hanoi accepted the formulations on Cambodia and Laos. Nixon responded that North Vietnam had "satisfied all points." The United States was firmly committed to signing the treaty on October 31.

Kissinger met with Thieu again on the morning of October 20. As in his previous encounters, Thieu seemed morose but ultimately willing to sign an accord. Kissinger agreed to meet with Thieu's advisers the following morning, to be followed by an afternoon session with Thieu himself.

In the morning session South Vietnamese Foreign Minister Tran Van Lam proposed twenty-three changes. Now in possession of a Vietnamese translation of the agreement, the South Vietnamese noted several problems. The proposed National Council of National Reconciliation and Concord was described in English as an "administrative structure." The North Vietnamese had cleverly used a word that, while an acceptable translation of the word "administrative," gave it a stronger connotation of "governmental authority." The South Vietnamese objected to the implication of a coalition government. North Vietnam had also used its standard translation for "American serviceman," one that, according to one Vietnamese official, "any kid on the street could tell Dr. Kissinger meant 'dirty Yankee soldier.'" Such examples greatly reduced South Vietnamese confidence in Kissinger's negotiating skills and provoked Thieu to remark that "Kissinger must have been tricked by Tho."

Still reeling from this meeting with Thieu's advisers, Bunker and Kissinger learned first that the afternoon session with the president would have to be delayed and then that it was canceled. The two Americans retired to the ambassador's residence for the night to await a showdown the following morning. At 9:00 P.M. the telephone rang. Thieu wished to speak with Bunker. "Nearly hysterical," as Kissinger described him, he accused Bunker and Kissinger of organizing a coup against him. He ordered the Americans to desist. Among the chief plotters he numbered an American army officer and two-tour-veteran of the Vietnam War, General Alexander Haig, Kissinger's chief of staff.

On Sunday morning, October 22, Kissinger met with Thieu again, expecting a major confrontation. But by now Thieu had collected himself. He restated his objections. They centered on the continued presence of NVA troops in South Vietnam, the composition and functions of the NCNRC, and the failure to define the DMZ as a "political boundary" separating two sovereign states. Kissinger handed Thieu a letter from Nixon, cabled to Saigon the previous evening:

Were you to find the agreement to be unacceptable at this point and the other side were to reveal the extraordinary limits to which it has gone in meeting the demands put upon them, it is my judgment that your decision would have the most serious effects upon my ability to continue to provide support for you and for the Government of South Vietnam.

While tough sounding, Nixon's letter was actually a bluff. The president had already ordered Kissinger not to coerce Thieu into agreement: "It cannot be a shotgun marriage," he wrote. Pointing to the approaching presidential election, he expressed his preference for dealing with an "indignant Hanoi" than with a "preelection blow-up with Thieu."

Thieu concluded the meeting "with some dignity," as Kissinger recalled it, and promised a final response to the Americans when their meeting resumed at 5:00 P.M. In the meantime he wanted a final discussion with his advisers and leaders of the National Assembly.

Kissinger called the afternoon session "the most bizarre." Only Bunker and Kissinger sat on one side and Thieu and Nha on the other. Thieu chose to speak in Vietnamese. He frequently burst into tears. At the corresponding place in his translation Nha's own tears would begin to flow. Thieu accused the United States of "conniving" with China and the Soviet Union to sell out South Vietnam. He sketched a history of betrayal on the part of the United States that stretched back to the earliest days of the Nixon administration. He completely rejected the treaty and offered a total of 129 textual changes, all "essential" to the agreement. At the end of the meeting Kissinger called Washington with the bad news: "Thieu has just rejected the entire plan or any modification of it and refuses to discuss any further negotiations on the basis of it."

The following morning Kissinger paid a final farewell visit and boarded a plane for the return trip to Washington. Summing up his four days in Saigon, Kissinger would write in his memoirs that "Thieu developed a bitter hatred of me." It was hard for Kissinger to disguise the fact that the feelings were reciprocated. More than a decade later the two men had not met again.

Before departing Saigon Kissinger worked out with the White House the necessary steps for explaining the breakdown to Hanoi. Kissinger advised the president to stop all bombing of North Vietnam on schedule and as promised, arguing that Hanoi was not responsible for the impasse in Saigon and should not be further punished. Nixon, however, agreed to a halt only in northern North Vietnam, sparing Hanoi and Haiphong. Kissinger also suggested that all bombing in support of the South Vietnamese army within South Vietnam be suspended as a sign of American displeasure with Thieu's intransigence. Nixon rejected the advice. He had no intention of implying at this time that he was willing to conclude a separate peace with Hanoi.

More painfully, Kissinger had to inform the North Vietnamese that he would not be arriving in Hanoi to initial the agreement. Hoping to arrive in Washington before Hanoi could respond to the news, Kissinger arranged for the cable to reach Hanoi after his departure from Saigon and while airborne. Without specifically mentioning that Saigon had refused to sign the agreement, Kissinger told the North Vietnamese leadership:

The DRV side is aware of the fact that the constant U.S. position has been that it will not impose a unilateral solution on its allies and that it will move ahead only on the basis of consultation. . . .

The President reiterates his firm belief that an agreement is obtainable in the very near future. It is essential that the DRV and US sides mutually explore existing difficulties in the same spirit of good will which has characterized discussions thus far.

clear his condition for any cease-fire: a complete withdrawal of NVA forces from South Vietnam. In his only potentially conciliatory phrase, Thieu declared, "We should make preparations so that if a cease-fire takes place, now or in a few months, we will not be in a disadvantageous position."

What Thieu did not tell his nation was that he had already begun to make such preparations even before Kissinger's visit to Saigon. Under American prodding, the South Vietnamese president had ordered his commanders to seize as much territory as possible in the final weeks of October. This did not deter Thieu from denouncing Hanoi for having issued the same orders to its commanders.

South Vietnamese intelligence captured a COSVN di-

The bombshells explode

Kissinger was well aware that Hanoi's next step might be a public disclosure of all that had transpired in the previous two weeks. His only hope for silence from the North was that the Communists' sense of urgency in concluding an agreement had not diminished. But when "the bottom fell out," as one Kissinger aide put it, it fell not in Hanoi but in Saigon.

Scarcely had Kissinger returned to Washington than Thieu began to release to the press portions—not with scrupulous accuracy—of the proposed agreement. For instance, he stated that North Vietnam had demanded that the U.S. "stop providing South Vietnam with all kinds of support." About the political clauses of the treaty, Thieu alleged that "the entire southern administration resign, not just 'Mr. Thieu' individually." That evening Thieu publicly denounced the agreement on national radio and made

Members of the South Vietnamese government march toward the presidential palace on October 27, 1972, to demonstrate their opposition to a coalition and support for Thieu.

rective ordering Communist guerrillas to capture as many hamlets as possible in the days preceding the cease-fire. They struck on October 20. The operation was designed to place as many as 10,000 political cadres in administrative positions by the time of the cease-fire. When the cease-fire was canceled, almost 5,000 Communist soldiers and many cadres were either killed or captured.

This chain of events proved to be too much for Hanoi to bear. Fearing that they had been tricked by Kissinger into exposing their cadres for arrest by Thieu, Radio Hanoi broadcast its version of the events in Vietnamese, French, and English. The broadcast summarized the draft agreement, "accurately" in Kissinger's words, on the basis of the nine-point proposal Tho had made in Paris on October 8.

It did not broadcast a precise transcript of the agreement, but it did reveal the schedule agreed to by the U.S. and the continued postponements Kissinger had requested and received. It released Nixon's letter calling the agreement "complete" and demanded that the U.S. keep its promise and sign the agreement in Paris on October 31.

Kissinger was awakened with news of the North Vietnamese broadcast and rushed to confer with Nixon. The two men decided that Kissinger would give the American version of events at a hastily assembled news conference that morning. Kissinger would reaffirm the basic framework of the agreement, defend Saigon's right to request changes, but caution America's ally against any major revisions. What Nixon and Kissinger were unable to decide in advance were the national security adviser's exact words. He would speak extemporaneously. Thus, only one paragraph into his talk Kissinger uttered the words that were to "haunt me from then on." "Peace is at hand," he said. Le Duc Tho later riposted, "Peace is at the end of a pen."

Hanoi did not respond immediately to Kissinger's request to select a date for the "one more negotiating session . . . lasting no more than three or four days" to settle the "six or seven very concrete issues . . . that can easily be settled," as Kissinger phrased it in his press conference. On November 4, three days before the American presidential election, Hanoi proposed a meeting in Paris on November 14. Kissinger had invited North Vietnam "to meet . . . on any date of their choice"; still there was the inevitable skirmishing over timing until both sides agreed to return to Paris on November 20.

The delay was not at all displeasing to Richard Nixon. He had several business matters to attend to during the interlude. The first, and most important, was to secure the historic landslide reelection that polls showed would be his. The snag in the negotiations did not seriously jeopardize his victory but might well diminish his plurality. Kissinger's "peace is at hand" statement was designed to blunt such a reaction. It worked. The statement, as Kissinger recorded it, "after a moment of stunned surprise, produced jubilation nationally." Even George McGovern, Nixon's opponent, seemed to be caught off guard and expressed his "relief" that peace in Vietnam was finally near. Three days later he changed his mind, "puzzled as to why the settlement comes in the closing hours of this campaign." In those final days on the campaign trail he pressed the issue, accusing Kissinger of "misleading the people of this country. . . . Peace is not at hand, it is not even in sight."

But for George McGovern it was far too late. His vacillation on even this, the final straw for him to grasp in the contest, seemed to symbolize his entire campaign. On November 7 Richard Nixon defeated him with an unprecedented plurality of votes, carrying more states than any candidate before him.

The two presidents

Solidly reaffirmed in power, President Nixon then bent to the task of handling his temperamental counterpart in Saigon, President Thieu. Relations between Kissinger and Thieu had so deteriorated that the president's chief adviser was no longer of much use in seeking agreement between the two allies.

The first step was to regain Thieu's confidence. Implementing a plan that General Creighton Abrams had outlined to Thieu while accompanying Kissinger to Saigon during the October talks, the Pentagon now began to rush an arsenal of weapons to the South Vietnamese armed forces under the code name Enhance Plus. Operation Enhance, carried out in mid-1972, had been designed to restore South Vietnamese stockpiles to their levels prior to the enemy's Easter offensive. Enhance Plus was designed to increase them further, providing a higher base upon which the U.S. would be able to replace Saigon's weapons, one for one, following the cease-fire.

Tan Son Nhut Air Base and Saigon's harbors soon backed up with the newest flow of American aid. Nearly 300 fighter and transport planes and 277 helicopters made their way into South Vietnamese inventories. In addition to the aircraft, South Vietnam received nearly 200 tanks and armored personnel carriers, fifty-six artillery pieces, and nearly 2,000 trucks. The remaining U.S. and Korean forces serving with the Vietnamese also began to hand over the equipment they intended to leave behind. To avoid the clause in the peace agreement that required the U.S. to "dismantle" its bases upon quitting South Vietnam, the Americans signed a "memorandum of understanding" on November 2 that deeded to the South Vietnamese the rights to those bases.

The effect of the build-up is symbolized by one statistic: By the end of 1972 South Vietnam possessed the world's fourth largest air force. It remained to be seen, however, how well and how wisely South Vietnam would be able to use the sophisticated additions to its arsenal.

President Nixon intended the aid to be an unmistakable signal to both Saigon and Hanoi, and lest it be misunderstood, he simultaneously dispatched General Haig to Saigon with a personal letter for delivery to President Thieu on November 10.

Nixon began his letter by expressing his dismay with Thieu's public disavowal of the agreement and promised to improve on some of the provisions most annoying to Saigon. The U.S. would attempt to strengthen the clause on the DMZ to "emphasize the distinctive character of South Vietnam" as a separate country. Kissinger would attempt to find some formula for a mutual reduction in forces on

A South Vietnamese airman paints his country's flag on a C-130 transport plane, one of hundreds of aircraft the U.S. gave to South Vietnam from October 1972 to January 1973.

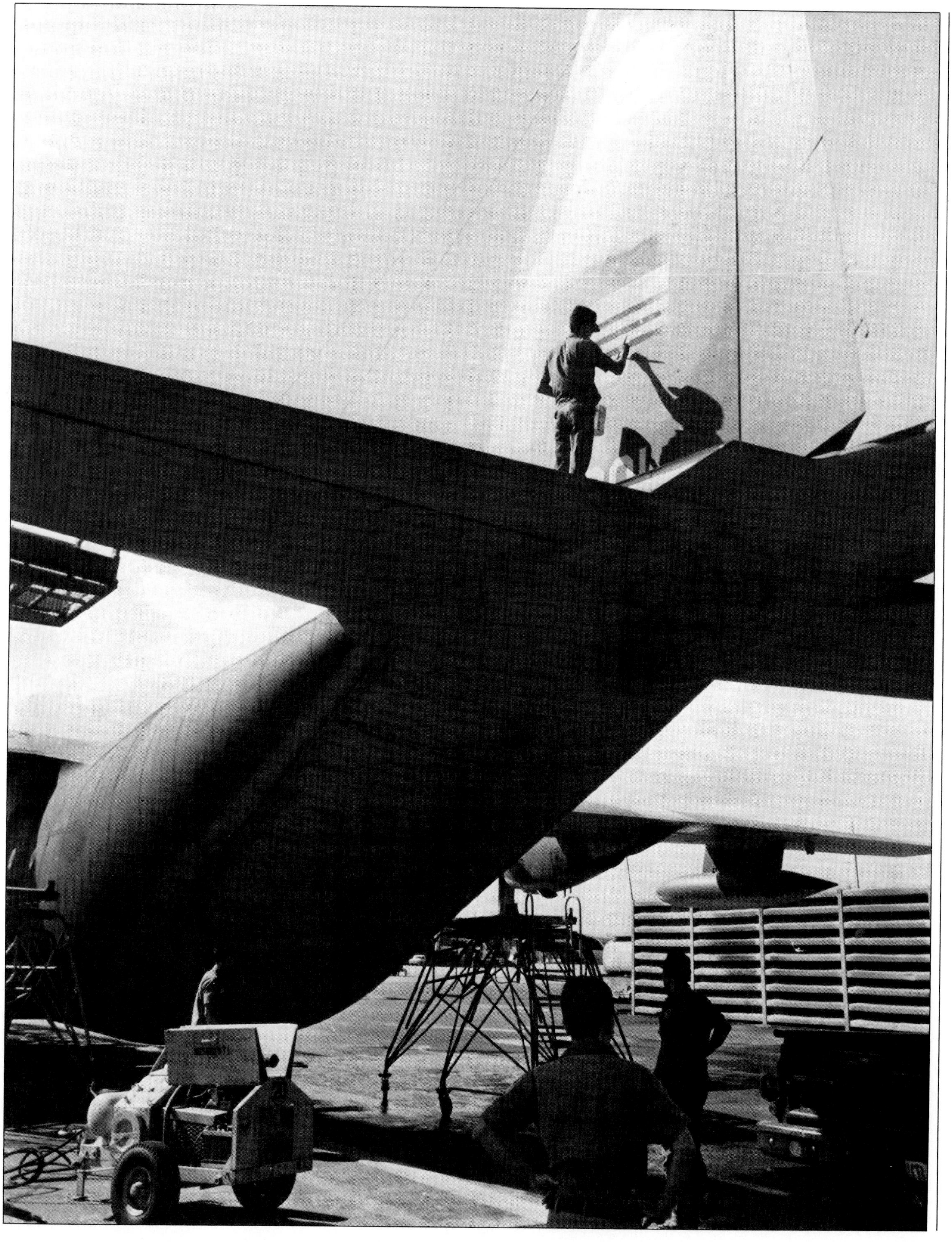

both sides and guarantees of a partial NVA withdrawal from South Vietnam. Nixon further asked for Thieu's cooperation, inviting him to express some priorities among the 129 proposed changes in the agreement.

Nixon ended the letter with a threat and an inducement. He wanted Thieu to proceed "under no illusion, however, that we can or will go beyond these changes in seeking to improve an agreement that we already consider to be excellent." If, however, Thieu signed the agreement, Nixon was willing to make assurances:

But far more important than what we say in the agreement . . . is what we do in the event the enemy renews its aggression. You have my absolute assurance that if Hanoi fails to abide by the terms of this agreement it is my intention to take swift and severe retaliatory action.

Thieu responded to Nixon's letter in his second meeting with Haig on November 11. According to Kissinger's account, "he . . . flatly turned down our suggestion to establish priorities among the textual changes he sought. He insisted on *all* of them." He even spelled out the precise terms under which he would accept a withdrawal of North Vietnamese forces. Another round of letters and a meeting between Thieu and Ambassador Bunker produced only the most negligible progress. Thieu limited his proposed modifications of the treaty to sixty-nine items, "leaving almost no paragraph of the draft document untouched," Kissinger lamented, as he prepared to travel again to Paris for what he hoped would be the last round of negotiations.

By this time Kissinger's relations with Thieu were not the only ones to suffer. "Relations between Nixon and me now were wary and strained," he recalled in his memoirs. There were several reasons for the difficulties.

Kissinger had earlier noted a tendency for Richard Nixon to become morose and depressed rather than elated in the period of recovery following a great victory. His landslide election proved to be no exception. Kissinger remarked that Nixon "withdrew even more, even from some of his close advisors. . . . It was as if victory was not an occasion for reconciliation but an opportunity to settle the scores of a lifetime."

Kissinger vs. Nixon

When *Time* magazine named Henry Kissinger and Richard Nixon jointly as "Man of the Year" in 1972, it identified the foreign policy of the United States as the result of a close partnership between the two men. Behind this teamwork, however, lay a complex personal relationship. While admiring each other's skills, the two men were leery of each other; their relationship was cemented more by mutual need than mutual trust. This aspect of their partnership became clear upon the publication of their respective memoirs. They frequently disputed each other's version of events, arguing over the origins of important foreign policy decisions, motivations for adopting particular actions, credit for achievements, and even interpretations of petty bureaucratic infighting. Nowhere are these discrepancies more dramatically revealed than in their discussions of the inspiration for the Christmas bombing of North Vietnam, shown below. While both men officially view that campaign as a heroic moment in their collaboration, each, ironically, accuses the other of having pressed for the final escalation of the war. Declassification of White House documents may some day resolve this particular discrepancy. But the relationship between Richard Nixon and Henry Kissinger will long remain a conundrum for students of history to ponder.

Kissinger:

He [Nixon] sent another cable suggesting that I interrupt the talks after all, on the pretext of giving the negotiators an opportunity to consult their principals. In that case he would authorize a massive air strike against North Vietnam during the recess. This was not my preference. I favored resumption of the bombing of the twentieth parallel only if the talks broke down altogether, and we had not yet reached that point.

—*White House Years,* pg. 1,421.

Nixon:

Kissinger considered that we now had two options open to us. Option One would be to break off the talks at the next meeting and dramatically step up our bombing while we reviewed our negotiating strategy in order to decide what kind of agreement we would be prepared to accept with and without the South Vietnamese. This was the option Kissinger favored. . . . I strongly opposed breaking off the talks and resuming the bombing unless it was absolutely necessary to compel the enemy to negotiate.

—*RN: Memoirs of Richard Nixon,* pg. 721.

Beyond personal strain, the opinions of Nixon and Kissinger began to diverge on the text of the agreement itself. Kissinger later described as "pure fiction" the reports that Nixon's "sharp legal eye spotted loopholes" in the treaty. Still, two issues clearly began to trouble Nixon: He wanted a stronger statement requiring respect for the DMZ and he wanted wording in the agreement itself on a cease-fire in Cambodia and Laos, an issue on which the DRV had only been willing to commit itself to a verbal understanding.

Nixon's final instructions to Kissinger revealed the president's frame of mind. He was not optimistic and ordered Kissinger to "discontinue the talks" at the first sign of North Vietnamese intransigence. Kissinger was to remember this as "the darkest and perhaps most malevolent frame of mind of [Nixon's] Presidency."

The return to Paris

Le Duc Tho arrived first in Paris and his preliminary remarks to newsmen at Le Bourget, a military airport near the French capital, were not encouraging. Tho doubted whether the U.S. was now "really serious" about concluding an agreement. As evidence, he cited the deliveries of "a great number of aircraft and tens of thousands of tons of weapons" to South Vietnam, as well as the "ferocious bombing" of North Vietnam by B-52s. Tho later privately told some members of the U.S. negotiating team that the delay in signing the peace document had eroded Politburo support for the agreement. As the author of that agreement, Tho reported that he was now under suspicion by his fellow members of the Politburo who feared that Kissinger had tricked him. As a result, Tho told the Americans, he could not "show flexibility in the negotiations" and would have to return frequently to Hanoi for instructions on how to proceed.

Kissinger did not help matters with a tactical mistake he made as the first negotiating session opened on November 20. Upon concluding his opening remarks, the American negotiator placed on the table all sixty-nine of Saigon's proposed changes. Kissinger later described the list as "preposterous," adding that "it went . . . far beyond what we had indicated both publicly and privately." In addition, Kissinger proposed forty-four additional changes on behalf of the U.S. While admitting that he had made an error in judgment, Kissinger explained that they were only "for the record," so that the transcript of the negotiations would show that the U.S. had faithfully transmitted all of Saigon's concerns to the North Vietnamese.

As a matter of fact the list of American objectives at the renewed negotiations was small in number, if not in importance. There were four major goals:

- to negotiate a strong statement defining the DMZ as an international, political boundary and barring any military movement across it;
- to gain a commitment for at least a token withdrawal of NVA forces from South Vietnam;
- to write the commitment to an Indochina-wide cease-fire into the text of the agreement; and
- to agree to a strong international force capable of supervising and enforcing the cease-fire.

In addition to these major issues, Kissinger also wanted to resolve the translation problems that appeared in the original document and to arrange a procedure accept-

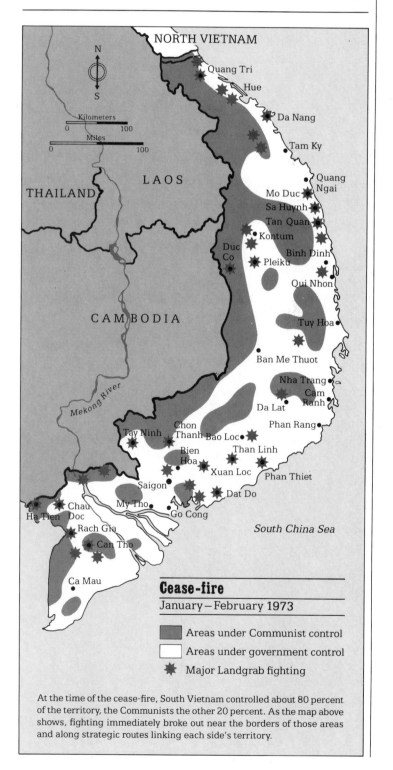

NORTH VIETNAM
N
S
Kilometers
0
100
Miles
0
100
Quang Tri
Hue
Da Nang
Tam Ky
Quang Ngai
LAOS
THAILAND
Mo Duc
Sa Huynh
Tan Quan
Kontum
Duc Co
Binh Dinh
Pleiku
Qui Nhon
CAMBODIA
Tuy Hoa
Ban Me Thuot
Nha Trang
Cam Ranh
Da Lat
Mekong River
Phan Rang
Tay Ninh
Chon Thanh
Bao Loc
Bien Hoa
Than Linh
Xuan Loc
Phan Thiet
Saigon
Dat Do
My Tho
Go Cong
Chau Doc
Ha Tien
Rach Gia
Can Tho
Ca Mau
South China Sea
Cease-fire
January–February 1973
Areas under Communist control
Areas under government control
Major Landgrab fighting

At the time of the cease-fire, South Vietnam controlled about 80 percent of the territory, the Communists the other 20 percent. As the map above shows, fighting immediately broke out near the borders of those areas and along strategic routes linking each side's territory.

able to Saigon for all parties to sign the agreement. For its part, Saigon refused to sign any document that also carried the signature of its enemy, the PRG.

When the negotiations resumed on November 21, Hanoi's reaction was predictable. It denounced Kissinger's tactics and gave him a taste of his own medicine, which only served to provoke a tantrum by the American negotiator. "On behalf of the PRG," it withdrew a concession made in October. It now demanded that Vietcong political prisoners be released simultaneously with American POWs. This threatened the entire agreement, since freedom for the POWs was the single most important objective of the U.S. in the negotiations. Kissinger would only link their release with the withdrawal of American troops.

The negotiations in November lasted for five days, ending on November 25. According to Kissinger the North Vietnamese were deliberately stalling, making a con-

Henry Kissinger and Le Duc Tho share a relaxed moment outside the Paris villa where many of their meetings took place. The villa was owned by the French Communist party.

cession one day, only to rescind it the next. Kissinger, meanwhile, was bombarded with a series of conflicting cables from Nixon. At one point Nixon wrote, "We have no choice but to reach agreement along the lines of the October 8 principles." But the very next day the president instructed Kissinger to "interrupt the talks" so that he could "authorize a massive air strike against North Vietnam." In the welter of conflicting advice, Kissinger finally asked for a recess in the talks. Tho and Kissinger agreed to renew them on December 4. On December 3 American intelligence discovered a disturbing development. Schoolchildren were being evacuated from the city of Hanoi.

The talks resumed on schedule on December 4 and lasted a record ten days, ending on December 13. There is considerable disagreement over what transpired during that period. Kissinger's version suggests that Hanoi continued the tactics of November, holding out concessions only to raise new objections or withdraw previous commitments. Kissinger surmised that Le Duc Tho "was willing to risk a break-off in the talks." Reporters learning some of the details of the sessions from Kissinger's aides were not so convinced. Some progress was clearly made. Most of the translation problems were resolved. The phrase describing the National Council of National Reconciliation and Concord as an "administrative structure" was simply deleted. Tho also agreed to return to the original text with respect to Vietcong political prisoners.

But Tho refused to compromise on most of the United States's major issues. He could not define the DMZ as a political boundary since that would be the equivalent of moral surrender in the war. The Communists were fighting precisely because they believed Vietnam to be one country. Nor would Tho promise in a written, legal document to arrange cease-fires in Laos and Cambodia; they were sovereign nations and he could not speak for them. Again, however, he gave verbal assurance of a cease-fire in Laos and again, reiterated that Hanoi had lost control of Cambodia's Communist forces. Tho also refused to make any mention of NVA forces in the text of the agreement. Finally, on the international supervisory force, to be called the International Commission of Control and Supervision (ICCS), Hanoi proposed a token force of 250 to 500 men, while Kissinger demanded a far larger force, 7,500.

Faced with this impasse, Tho and Kissinger met again on December 13. Tho had a previous commitment to brief the Kremlin's leadership on the negotiations and to engage in diplomatic consultations. The two men agreed to "keep in contact" and to resume the negotiations if the remaining issues could not be resolved by diplomatic channels. Kissinger left Paris that evening for Washington. Tho flew to Moscow the following morning. On December 18 American B-52 bombers attacked Hanoi and Haiphong in the most intensive bombing campaign of the war. The Pentagon code-named the operation Linebacker II. To the world it became known as the Christmas bombing.

America again at war

Of the three major escalations of the war ordered by President Nixon, his motives for ordering the renewed bombing of North Vietnam's principal cities remain most shrouded in mystery. On this occasion, unlike his incursion into Cambodia in 1970 or the bombing and mining of North Vietnam in Operation Linebacker I in May 1972, Nixon made no dramatic television appearance to explain his decision and rally public support. Kissinger would later write, "If I admired Nixon's decision [to order the bombing], I was less enthusiastic about his refusal to explain it to the public."

In his memoirs Kissinger offered such a justification, defending the bombing as a response to "an apparent North Vietnamese determination *not to allow the agreement to be completed.*" While Kissinger's explanation is admittedly conjectural, there is little doubt that Hanoi was in no hurry to complete the agreement. There are several reasons why Hanoi may have wanted to delay the signing, and all of them probably affected the Politburo's decision.

Hanoi, after all, had made concession after concession during the fall in the hopes of signing an agreement prior to the November elections in the U.S. Deliberateness, however, was the method of negotiation preferred by the Communists, and after the American election there was no longer any incentive for them to speed up the process. Moreover, the Politburo believed that further delays would exacerbate disagreements between Washington and Saigon. With American expectations for peace reaching a fever pitch following Kissinger's "peace is at hand" declaration, Nixon might even be forced to sign a separate peace with Hanoi and the PRG, leaving Thieu odd man out.

Finally, Hanoi felt compelled to match the build-up of ARVN stockpiles. American intelligence noted a vast quantity of war materiel beginning its way down the Ho Chi Minh Trail into South Vietnam. The North Vietnamese later said that the materiel had been sent from the U.S.S.R.

A residential district in Hanoi ruined by a B–52 raid against an adjacent railroad yard during Operation Linebacker II. Such collateral destruction fueled a worldwide outcry.

in the fall but detained by the Chinese for several months. Lacking the transport and cargo aircraft of the United States, Hanoi's resupply effort would be much lengthier. Hanoi's delaying tactics may have been designed to allow them to complete their own "Enhance Plus" program.

While it does seem clear that Hanoi was willing to postpone the signing of an agreement, this does not prove that the Communists would not "allow the agreement to be completed" at all. Furthermore, the Communists' dilatoriness was more pronounced in November and the December impasse was a result of honest areas of disagreement. To gain further concessions from North Vietnam on these issues would require patience on the part of the U.S.

But patience was a luxury that Richard Nixon could no longer enjoy in December 1972. Hanoi had negotiated under a strict, self-imposed schedule in October, and now it was Nixon and Kissinger who were forced to adopt a similarly rigid deadline of their own making. For psychological reasons, at least, Nixon desperately wanted the peace agreement concluded by the day of his second inauguration. Having won election in 1968 on the promise to end the war in Vietnam, he had only until then to make good that pledge. In addition, both Kissinger and Nixon wanted to begin the second term with Vietnam as history. They would then be able to continue to pursue their foreign policy goals without the internal divisions that had marred the first four years in office.

Aside from such psychological reasons, concrete factors also began to overwhelm Nixon and Kissinger. The Ninety-third Congress would convene on January 3, 1973. Elected simultaneously with Nixon's landslide victory on November 7, the new Congress was considered by both the president and Kissinger to be even more dovish in its sentiments than its predecessor. Kissinger was convinced that a clear antiwar majority would emerge in the new Congress. In November, Kissinger cabled Bunker instructing him to "point out composition of our new Senate to Thieu. *No matter what happens* there will be fund cutoff."

Unfortunately for the administration, the new Congress would have an early opportunity to do just that. For the previous six months, the Pentagon had actually been building up its forces in Southeast Asia in order to conduct the bombing campaign against the North that Nixon had ordered in May. Thus, even while the administration was announcing further withdrawals of American troops from South Vietnam as part of its Vietnamization program, the total number of American troops committed to operations in Southeast Asia was actually increasing. Almost 40,000 additional American troops went to Thailand, Guam, and to the naval fleet off the coast of Vietnam. This more than offset the 20,000 servicemen withdrawn from South Vietnam.

The cost of maintaining this "augmentation force," as it became known, totaled over $4 billion by midautumn and was straining the Pentagon budget. Defense Secretary

Melvin Laird, who had advanced the Vietnamization program primarily in order to reduce Pentagon spending in Vietnam so that other defense priorities could be met, insisted that the president request a supplemental defense appropriation from Congress to pay for the "augmentation force." Nixon persuaded Laird, whom he had kept in the dark about the state of the negotiations, to wait until January. But Laird, whose powerful friends on Capitol Hill gave him considerable leverage within the administration, could not be put off any further. Among the first messages that Nixon would have to send to the new Congress was a request for the $4 billion. Both Kissinger and Nixon were convinced that Congress would seize the opportunity simply to write the United States out of the war.

Thus, when Kissinger returned from Paris on December 13, both men felt that decisive action would have to be taken. The following day, Kissinger cabled Hanoi with an ultimatum: The United States threatened that "grave con-

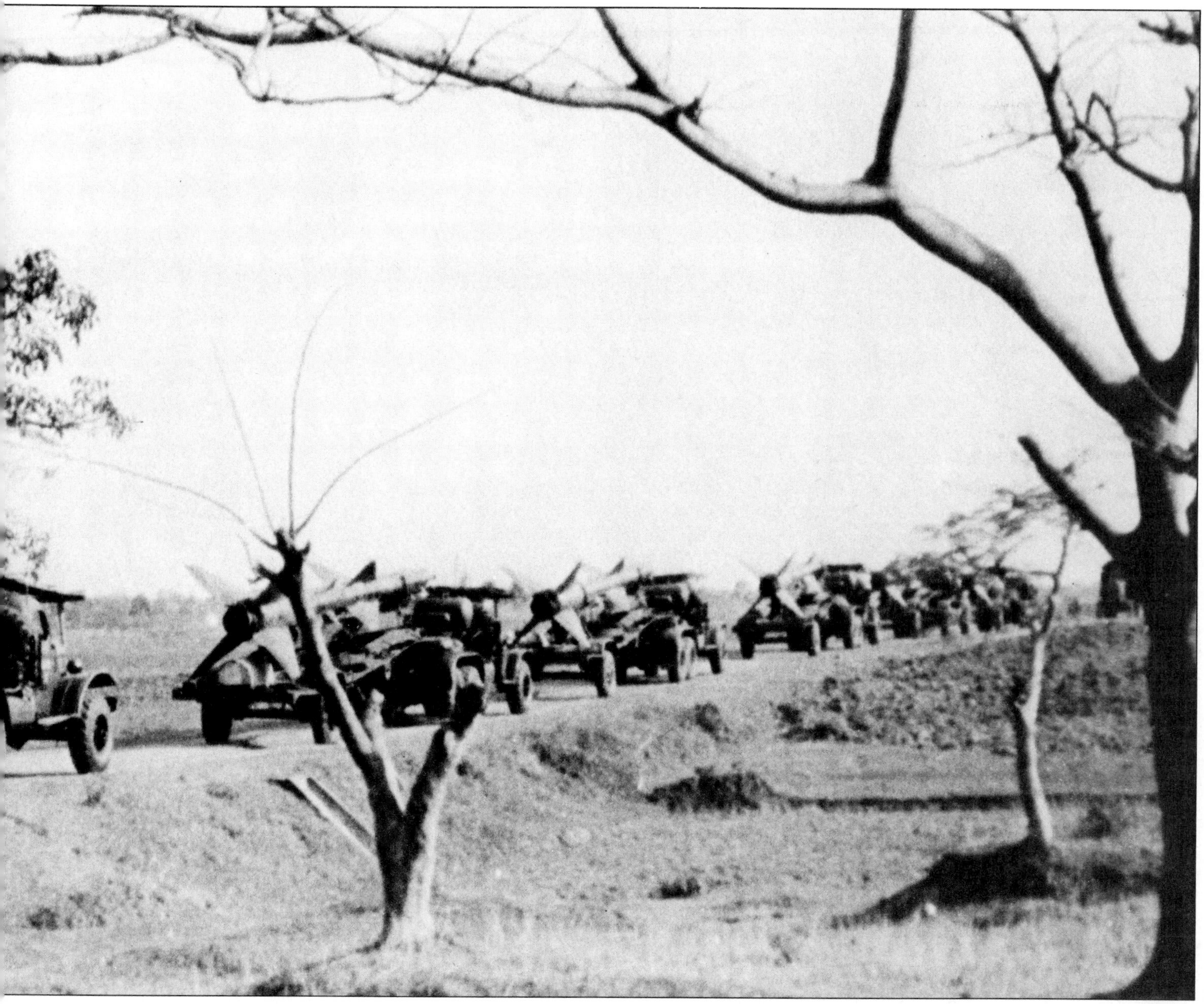

sequences would follow if serious negotiations did not resume within seventy-two hours," although North Vietnam had not "walked out" of the peace talks and had never indicated that it was unwilling to continue the negotiations. The three days passed with no response from Hanoi, and on December 17 Nixon ordered another mining of Haiphong Harbor and the renewal of the bombing in northern North Vietnam. (For a full account of Operation Linebacker II and the domestic and international reaction to it, see chapter 7 of *Rain of Fire*, another volume in "The Vietnam Experience.")

Eleven days later, on December 29, the bombing ended as abruptly as it began, again with no word of explanation from President Nixon. The White House simply announced that Dr. Kissinger and Le Duc Tho would resume negotiations in Paris on January 8. When later asked at a press conference whether the bombing had succeeded, Kissinger coyly responded, "I will say that there was a deadlock in the middle of December and there was rapid movement when the negotiations resumed on January 8. These facts have to be analyzed by each person for himself."

A convoy of SAM rockets in North Vietnam moves towards South Vietnam in December 1972 in response to the South Vietnamese build-up.

Did the bombing work?

Kissinger's implied conclusion was widely shared by the American people, who felt that a major show of American military power had forced Hanoi back to the negotiating table and permitted the rapid conclusion of the peace talks. The "facts," however, that Kissinger asked "each person" to analyze "for himself" suggest a much more ambiguous sequence of events.

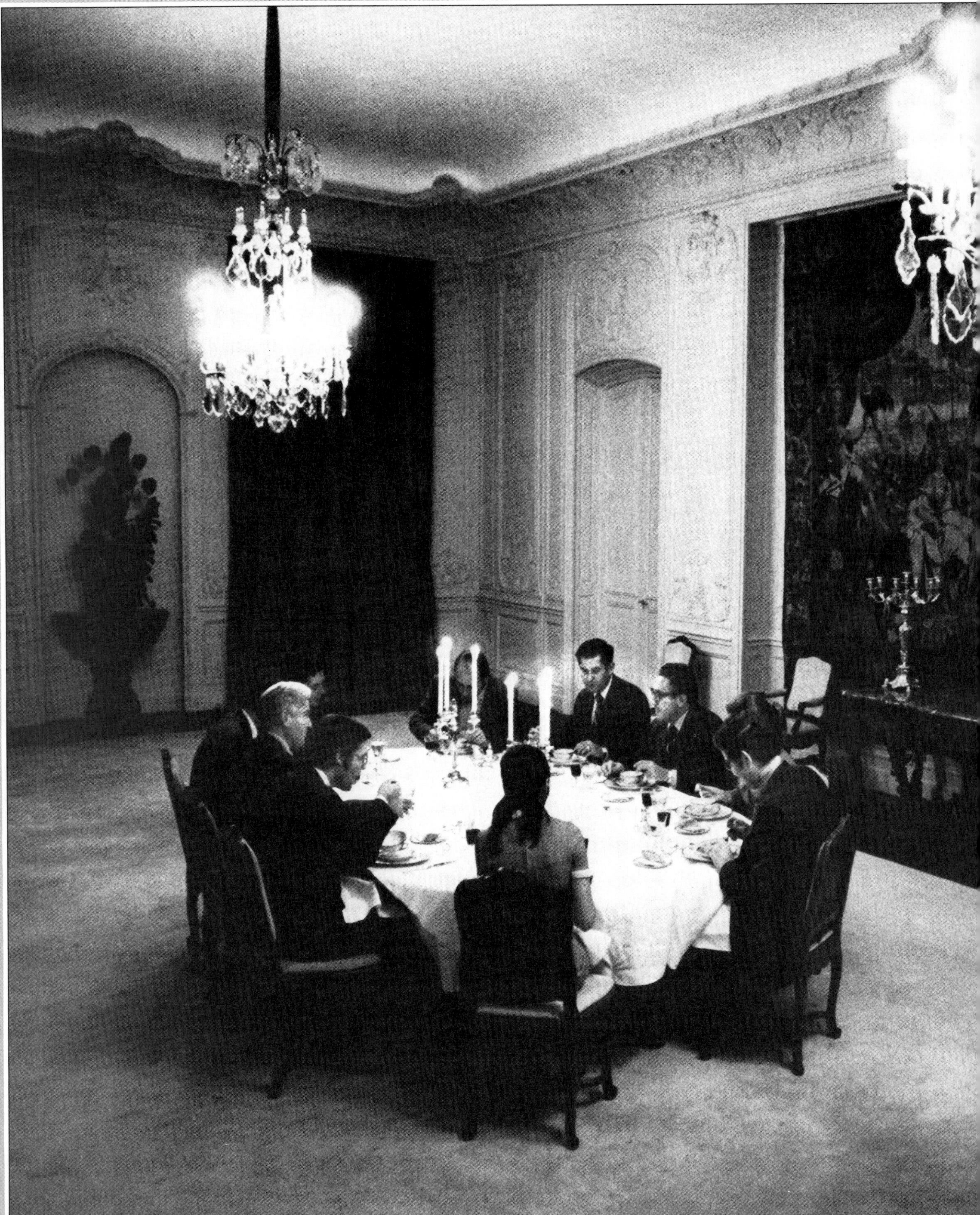

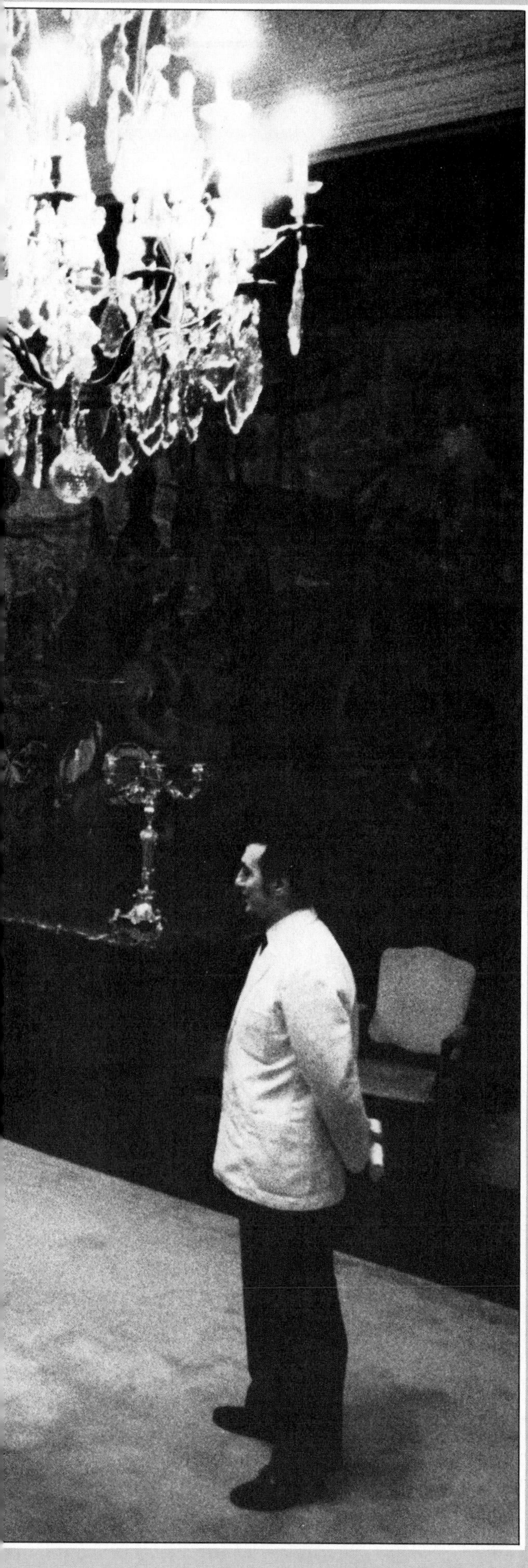

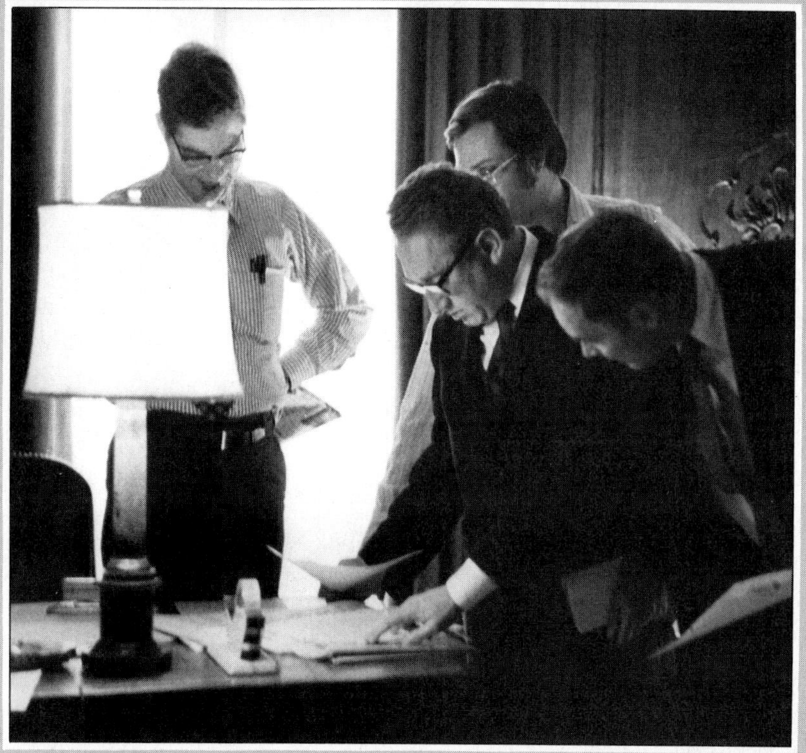

Above. *Kissinger and his chief of staff, General Alexander Haig (right), pore over documents. Behind Kissinger stand his two assistants, Peter Rodman (left) and Winston Lord.*

Left. *Kissinger and his staff take a break from their labors to dine at the ambassador's residence. Seated across from Kissinger is Deputy Assistant Secretary of State for East Asian and Pacific Affairs William Sullivan.*

Kissinger in Paris

The opulent residence of the U.S. ambassador to France was a second home to Henry Kissinger and most of his senior staff during the autumn of 1972. Long days and even longer nights of hard work kept Kissinger and his staff busy as they raced first to achieve an agreement with the North Vietnamese in October, and then to break the deadlock in negotiations in November and December.

Hanoi responded to the Kissinger ultimatum of December 14 on December 26, after eight days of concentrated B–52 raids. The Politburo reminded Kissinger and Nixon that they had not walked out of the negotiations and that North Vietnam maintained a "constantly serious negotiating attitude," as Kissinger demanded in the cable. However, Hanoi rejected the "ultimatum language" in the American message and would not return to Paris until the bombing ended. Kissinger and Nixon proceeded apace, exchanging messages with Hanoi to determine the scheduling of future sessions should Hanoi maintain its "constantly serious negotiating attitude." When all of the preliminaries had been decided, the U.S. cabled its satisfaction to Hanoi and Hanoi confirmed its "constantly serious negotiating attitude" and willingness to resume talks once the bombing ended. The following day, December 29, Nixon ordered the bombers grounded.

The problem with the American ultimatum was that there was no concrete step that Hanoi could take to show compliance. North Vietnam was willing to resume serious negotiations if the bombing stopped; the U.S. was willing to stop the bombing if serious negotiations followed. Both sides simply agreed to agree. The true test of the bombing campaign's effectiveness can thus not be measured by the resumption of talks in Paris but by their substance.

Before Kissinger could keep his appointment with Le Duc Tho, the United States still had its recalcitrant ally in Saigon to deal with. Fearing that President Thieu would see the bombing campaign as a signal that the peace agreement was dead, Nixon sent Alexander Haig back to Saigon on December 19. He carried with him Nixon's most strident letter yet to the South Vietnamese president. In his own handwriting, Nixon added the concluding paragraph:

I have asked General Haig to obtain your answer to this absolutely final offer on my part for us to work together in seeking a settlement along the lines I have approved or to go our separate ways. Let me emphasize in conclusion that General Haig is not coming to Saigon for the purpose of negotiating with you. . . . You must decide now whether you desire to continue our alliance or whether you want me to seek a settlement with the enemy which serves U.S. interests alone.

Thieu's response was hardly what Nixon and Kissinger had hoped for. Although he now withdrew his objections to the political clauses of the agreement, he still insisted on a withdrawal of all NVA troops from South Vietnam. After consulting with Kissinger, Nixon decided that, if necessary, he would sign a separate agreement with Hanoi.

Once the bombing halt was announced, Nixon renewed his demands on Thieu. He promised to raise the question of North Vietnamese troops but told Thieu frankly that "the result is certain to be once more the rejection of our position." Nixon then continued, "Accordingly, if the North Vietnamese meet our concerns . . . we will proceed to conclude the settlement. The gravest consequences would then ensue if your government chose to reject the agreement and split off from the United States."

But Nixon concluded on a more hopeful note, assuring Thieu of "continued assistance" if he decided "to go with us." Finally, Nixon committed the United States to "respond with full force should the settlement be violated by North Vietnam."

In response, Thieu again put forward his complaints and asked Nixon to instruct Kissinger to present them in Paris. But, as Kissinger noted in his memoirs, "he did not say he would refuse to sign."

As Nixon's letters to Thieu indicated, the American president was in a far different frame of mind in early January than in mid-November. Then he had told Kissinger to

Despite negotiations, the war continues. A South Vietnamese personnel carrier crew on its way to relieve a besieged firebase runs for cover after hitting a land mine, December 1972.

be a tough negotiator and break off the talks at the first sign of problems. An open break with Saigon was to be avoided at all costs. In contrast, Nixon's final instructions in January revealed a willingness to conclude an agreement at virtually any price. Kissinger quotes Nixon as "urg[ing] me to settle on whatever terms were available. Belying his imagemakers, he even said he would settle for the October terms." Thus disarmed, Henry Kissinger departed Washington for Paris and his climactic meeting with Le Duc Tho.

Peace is at hand

Once the two sides returned to the negotiating table, rapid progress was made. By the end of the second session, on January 9, Kissinger was able to cable Washington with good news. Noting that it was Richard Nixon's sixtieth birthday, Kissinger reported:

We celebrated the President's birthday today by making a major breakthrough in the negotiations. In sum, we settled all the outstanding questions in the text of the agreement.

In describing the final sessions of the negotiations, American and North Vietnamese versions stand in direct contradiction. Both sides assign all credit to their opposites for ending the deadlock. Both sides claim they would have settled for the final text of October. A review of the issues that caused the deadlock in December reveals that both parties had some reason to make their claim but suggests that the American team had given up more than it gained, as Nixon had, in fact, instructed:

- DMZ: a clear victory for North Vietnam. The seventeenth parallel was defined "as provided for" in the Geneva accords, continuing the ambiguity that permitted the DRV to justify its presence in South Vietnam. The clause also specifically stated that the DMZ was "not a political or territorial boundary."

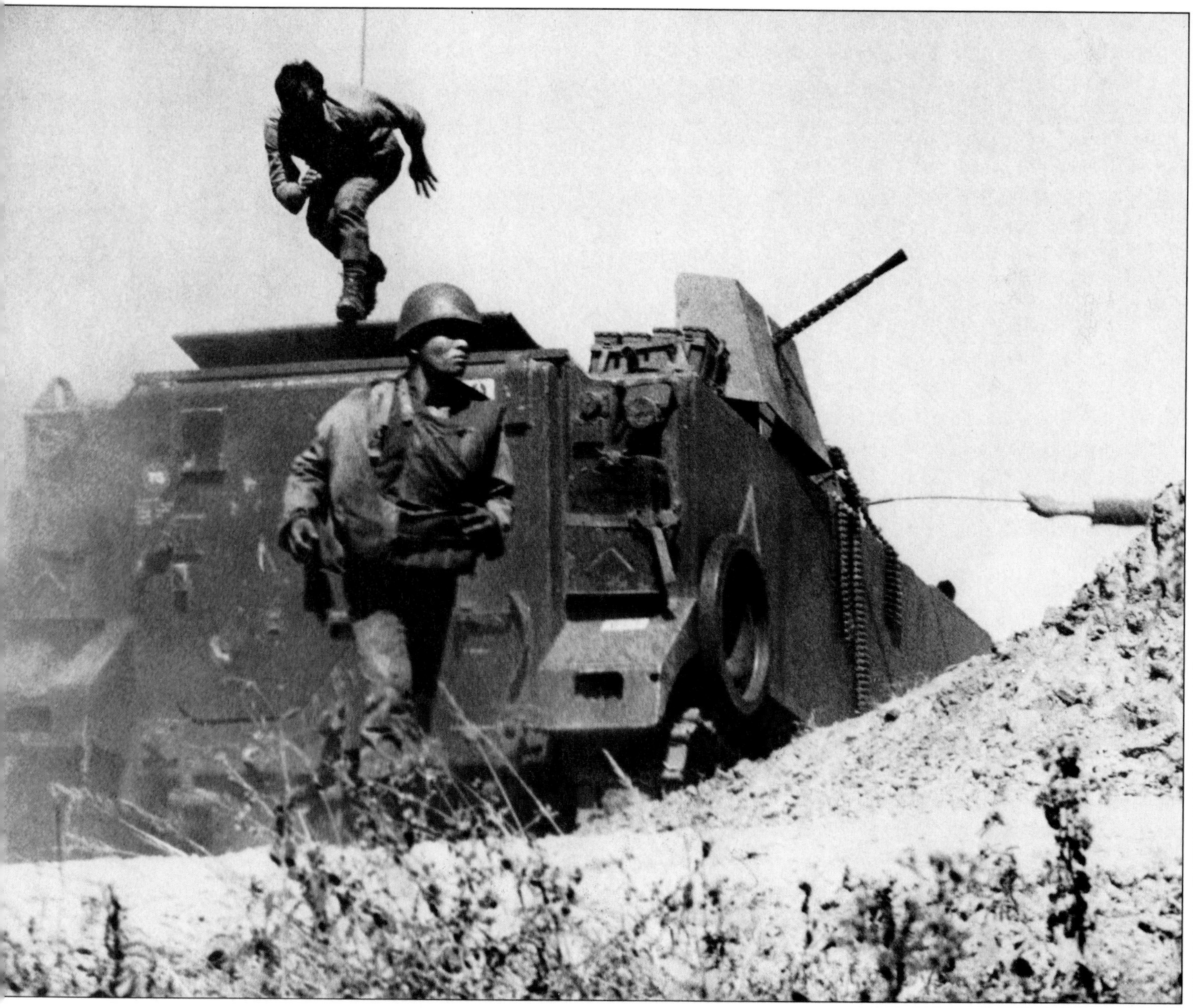

- Withdrawal of NVA troops from SVN: a poor compromise. The NVA troops were not mentioned once in the agreement, although Kissinger secured a verbal commitment, another "understanding," that North Vietnam would make a token withdrawal of 30,000 troops.
- Indochina cease-fire: North Vietnamese position upheld. No mention of an Indochina-wide cease-fire appears in the final agreement. Again Kissinger had to accept Tho's "understanding" that a cease-fire would be arranged in Laos and his claim that his government could not carry out a commitment in Cambodia.
- Size of ICCS: mathematical compromise. As the last outstanding issue, Kissinger suggested that the two sides simply "split the difference" and agree on a force numbering 1,160 people. As a matter of principle it was hardly a victory for Kissinger since North Vietnam's goal was to keep the force small.

A few other changes, actually already agreed upon in November or December, were also incorporated into the final text. The National Council of Reconciliation and Concord lost its adjectival description as an "administrative structure." North Vietnam returned to the October draft language on release of South Vietnamese political prisoners; their release was not linked with the return of U.S. POWs.

The United States did, however, win one unequivocal victory in the final negotiating sessions: the modalities of signing an agreement. Thieu would not have to sign the same document as the PRG. Reprising the same game of musical chairs that ended the deadlock over the shape of the negotiating table in 1969, the U.S. and North Vietnam agreed that they would each sign two copies of the peace agreement and their respective allies would sign different copies.

More than a decade after the war neither North Vietnam nor the United States had released the complete text of the October agreement, making a detailed analysis of the differences between the two versions impossible. Kissinger later said that some minor changes in language gave an advantage in nuance to the South Vietnamese and American side. But the diplomatic product of the negotiations in November and December, of the bombing campaign over North Vietnam, and of the final sessions in January was meager indeed. When asked by one of his assistants why he had not pressed Hanoi for more concessions, Kissinger answered in exasperation, "Look, you don't understand my instructions. My orders are to get this thing signed before the inauguration."

Before leaving Paris, Kissinger and Tho agreed to a fi-

Peace is at hand. On January 27, 1973, the agreement to end the Vietnam War is signed in a formal ceremony at the Hotel Majestic in Paris.

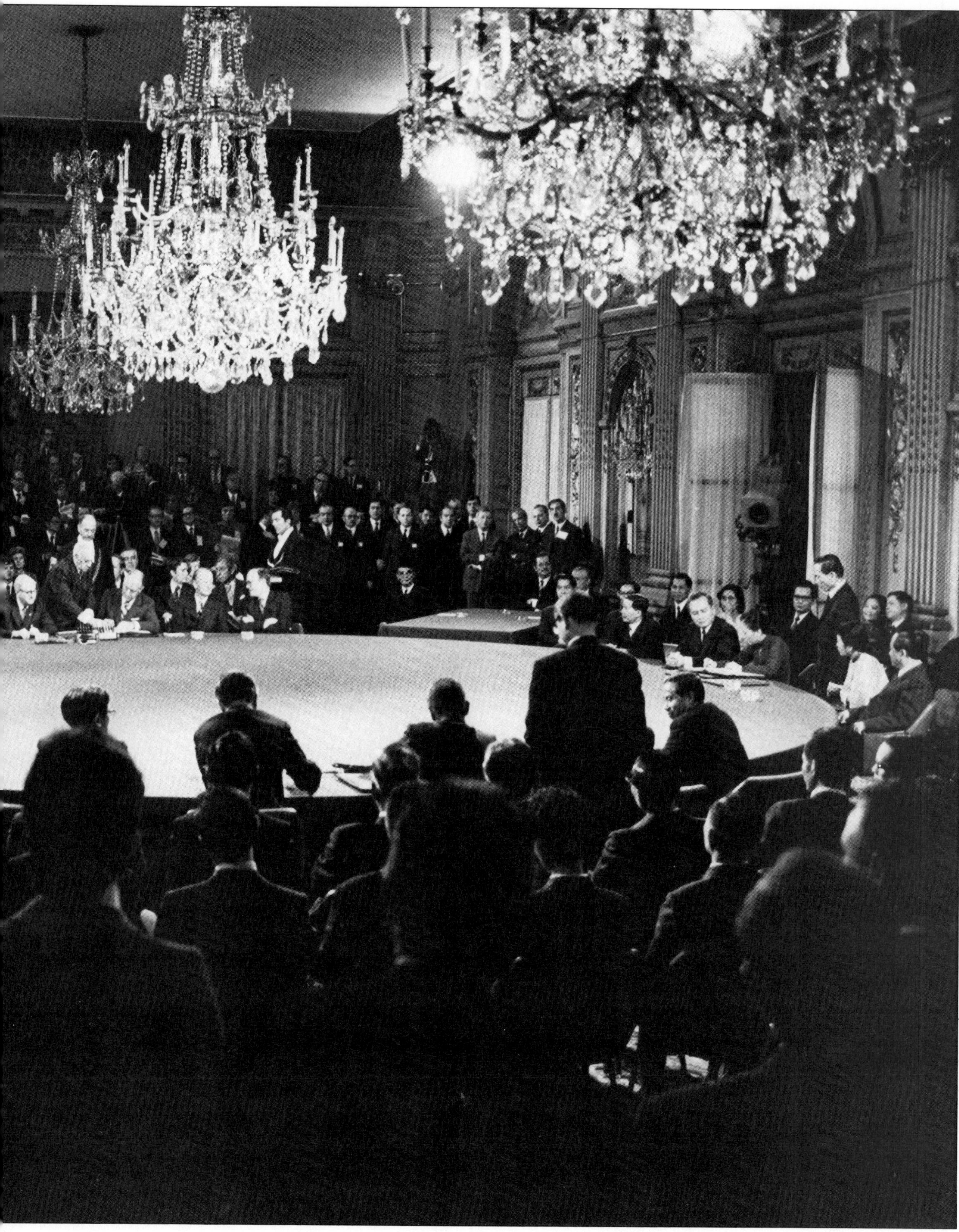

nal schedule for signing the agreement. Both sides would indicate their approval of the text by initialing the pact on January 23, three days after the inauguration. The agreement was to become a legally binding document with the formal signing ceremony on January 27.

By Saturday, January 13, Kissinger could declare the agreement "once again complete." Also in place were four protocols on the modalities of carrying out the treaty: arranging the cease-fire, returning the POWs, international supervision of the agreement, and clearing the mines from North Vietnamese waters.

After four years of sterile negotiations, the Paris agreement had, in reality, been worked out in four days of talks in October and two days in January. The speed with which the languid negotiations had been concluded may have seemed surprising, but the reason was simple: For their own different reasons, both Washington and Hanoi had come to believe that reaching a peace agreement was imperative.

The role of American air power in halting the 1972 Easter offensive convinced Hanoi that the removal of the remaining American troops in South Vietnam was a prerequisite to ultimate victory. In addition, improved American relations with the Chinese and Soviet Communist superpowers had added uncertainty to Hanoi's ability to ensure a steady flow of military assistance. In order to maintain a battlefield equilibrium, the withdrawal of the American force thus became an even greater imperative. To achieve that objective the North Vietnamese had to separate it from the goal of removing Thieu from power.

The policy of détente also led the Nixon administration to make further concessions for the sake of an agreement. Nixon's promise to the American people of a "generation of peace" depended on a "structure of peace" constructed out of improved relations between the United States and both Russia and China. While considerable progress had been made toward that grandiose goal during Nixon's first term in office, the war in Vietnam had become the major roadblock to the historic breakthrough that both Nixon and Kissinger sought. Moreover, the domestic support for Nixon's foreign policy depended on a sense of steady progress in disengaging America from Vietnam. The Vietnamization process, however, had reached a point where the remaining troops might well have to stay in Vietnam indefinitely, while the POWs languished in North Vietnamese prisons. Only a signed agreement could extricate the administration from the problem.

The view from Hanoi, as could be expected, and from Washington, with less reason, brushed aside the needs and sensitivities of the South Vietnamese government. As so often happened during the war, Saigon was caught squarely and uncomfortably in the middle of decisions in which it did not participate. The Nixon administration had made up its mind: It would gain Thieu's approval of the agreement—or sign without him.

It was thus not with a great deal to show for his efforts that Nixon again dispatched Haig to Saigon with another letter for President Thieu on January 16. Nixon told Kissinger, "Brutality is nothing. You have never seen it if this son-of-a-bitch doesn't go along, believe me." The text of his letter scarcely differed in tone:

I have therefore irrevocably decided to proceed to initial the Agreement on January 23, 1973 and to sign it on January 27, 1973 in Paris. I will do so, if necessary, alone. In that case I shall have to explain publicly that your Government obstructs peace. The result will be an inevitable and immediate termination of U.S. economic and military assistance....

But Thieu still refused to give up. He requested "one more" negotiating session. In a flurry of diplomatic exchanges, Nixon issued an ultimatum: He required Thieu's assent by January 20 or he would proceed alone. On January 20 Thieu replied that he would send Foreign Minister Lam to Paris—to conduct the final round of negotiations. Nixon ignored the reply, only extending his deadline until noon on January 21. Finally, Thieu relented. Lam would sign the agreement on January 27.

The war in Vietnam was, if anything, not lacking in historical ironies. It was therefore fitting that the signing of the peace agreement should witness its own. On January 22, less than twenty-four hours before Henry Kissinger and Le Duc Tho initialed the text of the Paris agreement ending the war in Vietnam, a war that to millions of Americans had become known as "Lyndon Johnson's war," the thirty-sixth president of the United States died of a heart attack at his ranch in Texas. That a peace agreement had at last received the approval of all parties had not yet been publicly announced. But President Nixon, in mourning Lyndon Johnson's death, informed the nation that he had privately communicated the fact to the former president prior to his death. Lyndon Johnson, it seemed, would rest in peace.

* * * *

At 9:00 P.M. on January 27, 1973, NVA rockets struck the war-torn town of An Loc in South Vietnam's Binh Long Province. The ink had scarcely dried on the Paris agreement, signed one hour earlier in an elaborate ceremony by U.S. Secretary of State William Rogers and his counterparts from North and South Vietnam and the Provisional Revolutionary Government. Eleven hours after the rockets hit the town an in-place cease-fire throughout Vietnam was scheduled to go into effect. One of the enemy shells struck the compound of Lieutenant Colonel William B. Nolde, the senior American adviser to the province chief. According to the Pentagon's official casualty statistics, the forty-three-year-old father of five children was the last American to die in combat in Vietnam.

The funeral procession of Lieutenant Colonel William B. Nolde winds its way to Arlington National Cemetery.

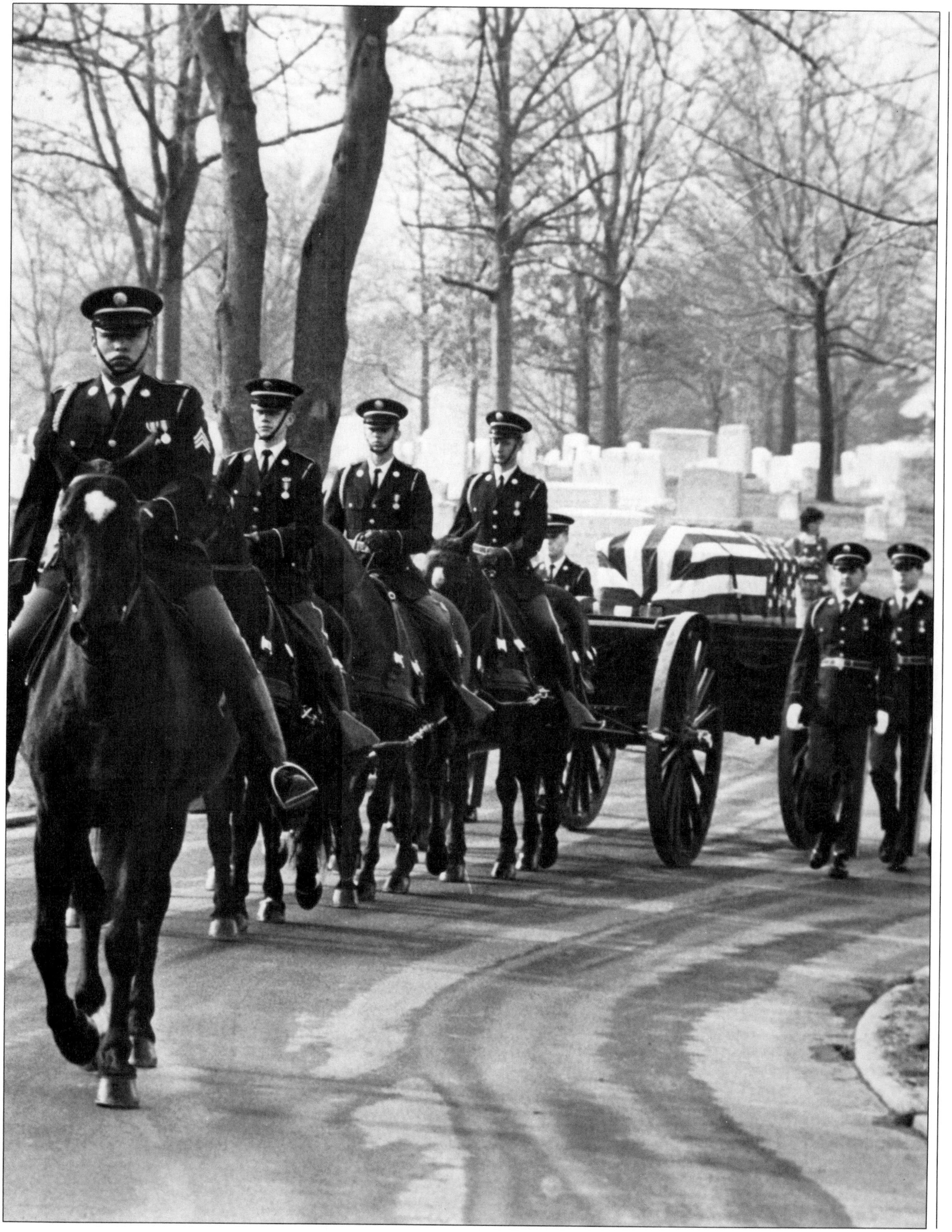

Cease Fire!

Along the Thach Han River, running through the
rubble that was once the city of Quang Tri, a
fierce artillery duel raged throughout the night of
January 27-28, 1973. As they had done virtually
without interruption ever since September, when
an exhausted ARVN recaptured the capital of
Quang Tri Province but could advance no farther,
North Vietnamese regulars on the northern bank
of the river lobbed rockets and artillery shells into
ARVN positions to the south. The South Vietnamese answered with their own heavy guns. As
dawn broke on the morning of January 28, the firing continued unabated. Slowly the hands of a
clock in Paris moved toward the hour of cease-
fire—2400 hours Greenwich Mean Time, 8:00 A.M.
in Saigon. For a few minutes after 8:00 the firing
continued. Then there was an eerie silence.

South Vietnamese Marines peered warily over
the edge of their bunkers in time to see a huge
yellow, red, and blue flag of the PRG rise over
the enemy positions. Then to their amazement,

they saw a few NVA regulars stand up. A few Marines followed them and extended a tentative wave. The enemy soldiers returned the gesture. Peace had come to the Thach Han River.

But what transpired at the Thach Han River was to remain a lonely exception, for peace had not come to South Vietnam. In fact, the very conditions that made a true cease-fire possible in Quang Tri City explained why the fighting continued without interruption throughout the rest of Vietnam. In Quang Tri two conventional armies stared at each other across a natural border. An easily discernible front line marked a boundary between the territory under control of the respective forces.

Elsewhere in South Vietnam the scene was dramatically different. Conventional armed forces operated in conjunction with guerrillas; opposing lines and areas of control shifted with each sunrise and sunset; few areas could be labeled 100 percent secure. In such a situation a cease-fire was predictably hopeless. As one ARVN division commander described the problems:

When it came time to determine the extent of control for each side in those contested areas, no one would admit to the presence of the other because frequently no one was there. In certain villages and hamlets both sides had their own governmental apparatus, one of them public, the other underground. Who in that case would be able to ascertain which belonged to whom and on what grounds?

Tragically, the only way to ascertain "which belonged to whom" was to fight over it.

In the hamlet of Trung Hung near Bien Hoa an old man, speaking French to a reporter so that government soldiers would not understand him, described the "last minutes" of the war in his home village. "The liberation side was in the hamlet before the cease-fire. They considered this their territory and they put up their flags." The next morning, the Saigon government moved to reclaim control. "The hamlet was attacked by government airplanes," the old man related. "As you can see, all the buildings were destroyed." It was a bitter beginning of the "era of peace" for the people of Trung Hung.

Preceding page. *South Vietnamese soldiers jubilantly celebrate the new "era of peace" as a cease-fire takes effect throughout their country on January 28, 1973.*

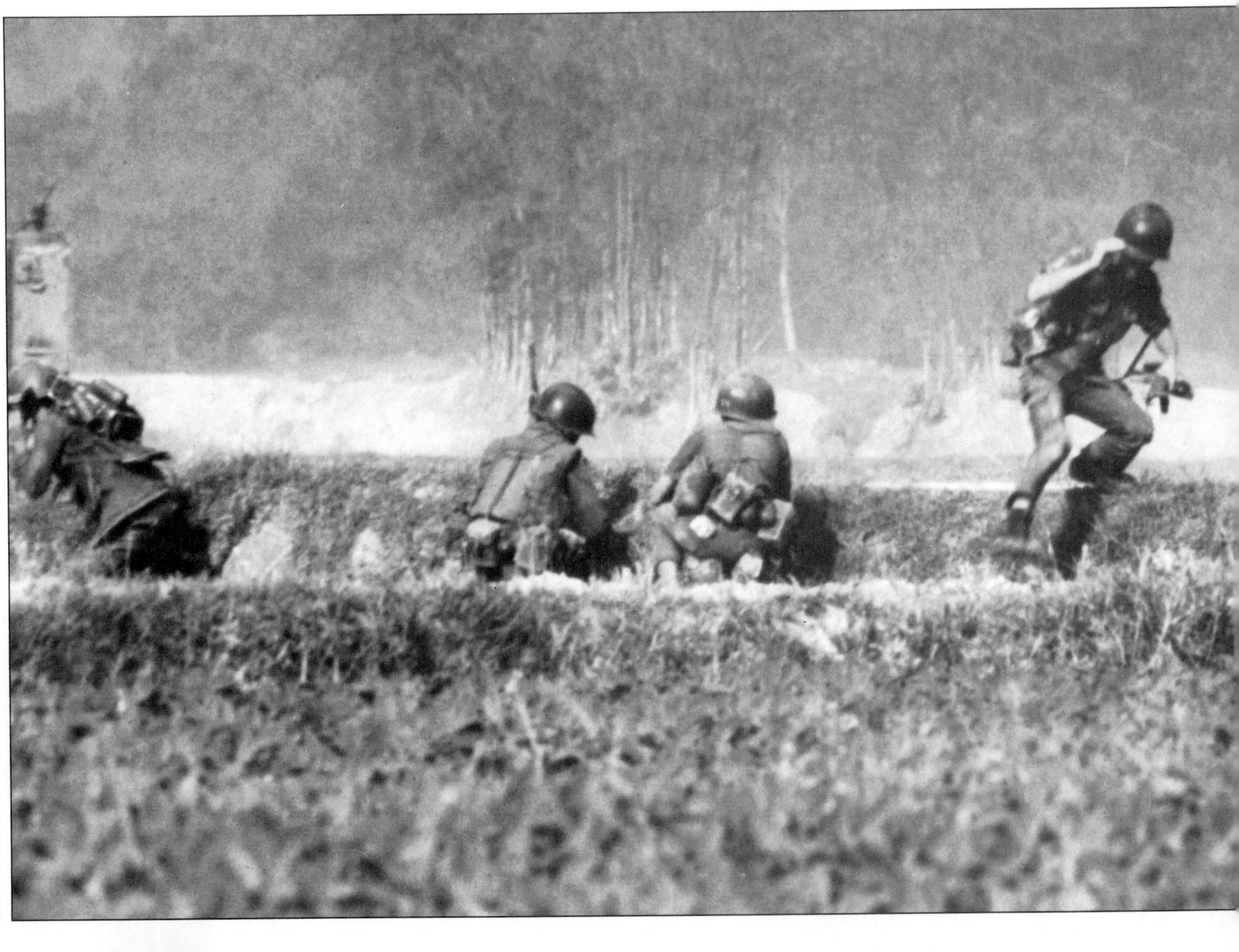

Much the same scenario occurred in the village of Chanh Hiep, thirty kilometers north of Saigon. There, Communist cadres had entered the village at 3:00 A.M. and awakened the population with loudspeakers proclaiming the village "liberated." By dawn the villagers could hear the sounds of advancing ARVN soldiers. As 8:00 approached, many looked nervously at their watches. At precisely 8:00 A.M. President Thieu's voice proclaimed the cease-fire from villagers' radios. "We should not believe that the Communists will respect the cease-fire. Believing this is a naive and erroneous attitude," he told his people. "Any Communists who penetrate into the hamlets and villages must be shot dead on the spot," Thieu ordered. Through it all South Vietnamese 105MM howitzers continued to pound suspected Communist positions around Chanh Hiep. Said one South Vietnamese sergeant, "This war will never end."

The shoe was on the other foot at the mouth of the Cua Viet River in Quang Tri Province. There on the eve of the cease-fire South Vietnamese Marines attacked Communist strongholds in an attempt to deprive the enemy of the valuable port. Marine advances were short-lived as NVA artillery and infantry attacks, continuing after 8:00 A.M., drove the Marines southward.

All of these battles were part of a larger pattern of attack and counterattack that became known as Landgrab '73. Like the previous landgrab in October 1972, both Communist and Saigon forces reacted to the approaching cease-fire by ordering their units to gain control of as much territory and as many hamlets and villages as possible prior to 8:00 A.M. on January 28. If all went well, members of the International Commission of Control and Supervision would then certify each side's gains under the terms of the Paris agreements.

The Communist campaign differed only slightly from the strategy used during the aborted October landgrab. Instead of attacking three or four days prior to the cease-fire, they coordinated their movements for the very eve of the truce. Otherwise, they repeated their errors. Rather than concentrate their attacks on a few well-chosen loca-

Landgrabbing. In spite of the cease-fire, ARVN troops battle near Tay Ninh City on January 28, 1973, as Communist soldiers try to cut off a road.

tions, the Communists spread their forces thin and attacked over 400 hamlets. But the ICCS was not yet ready to take its positions in the field, and South Vietnam followed with its counterattacks unhampered by international observers. Within two weeks after the cease-fire went into effect, Saigon had reclaimed virtually every one of those hamlets; only 23 remained contested.

President Thieu adopted a somewhat different strategy for South Vietnam's Landgrab '73 campaign. In control of most of the country's populated areas, Thieu's objective was to regain control of lost territory. In a special meeting of his National Security Council on January 21, 1973, he issued orders "to regain as much of our territory as possible during the ceasefire period." To this end ARVN units "located forward posts in areas . . . claimed by the Communists." This would provide him with a legitimate excuse for "defending" these outposts in enemy territory even after the cease-fire.

The landgrabbing did not make for an auspicious beginning of the cease-fire. In purely legalistic terms the Communist attacks during the night prior to the cease-fire were permissible and the government counterattacks a violation of the cease-fire. But such standards put South Vietnam in an extremely unfavorable position. As during most of the war, South Vietnamese troops were largely in a defensive posture, guarding the areas under their control. In normal circumstances, Communist attacks could gain them only temporary control of villages. It would have grossly misrepresented the balance of power on January 28 to grant the enemy permanent control only because they had attacked prior to the 8:00 A.M. deadline.

This was but one example where legalistic compliance with the Paris agreement conflicted with the spirit of its provisions. If the Communists had law, but the South Vietnamese justice, on their side during Landgrab '73, the situation would as often be reversed as the treaty went through its tortuous and tortured existence.

Restoring the peace

The cease-fire was only one, if perhaps the most important, provision of the accords signed in Paris on January 27. In all the Agreement on Ending the War and Restoring Peace in Vietnam, as the treaty was entitled, consisted of twenty-three articles, divided into nine chapters. Virtually every article was to become the object of disputed interpretation, which even the most careful reading of the text does little to resolve.

Article 1 recognized the "independence, sovereignty, unity, and territorial integrity" of Vietnam as defined by the 1954 Geneva agreements. Both Saigon and Hanoi could justify almost any action they took on the grounds that they were merely upholding their own interpretation of this article.

Articles 2 to 7 form Chapter II, covering the "Cessation of Hostilities—Withdrawal of Troops." These articles called for a cease-fire both in South and North Vietnam and provided for the withdrawal of U.S. forces, including all uniformed advisers, as well as for the dismantling of U.S. bases.

Chapter III, consisting only of Article 8, stipulated the exchange of all military POWs, obliged each side to provide all possible information on the fate of the missing and the dead, and called for the two South Vietnamese parties to negotiate the release of any prisoners held for political reasons.

Articles 9 to 14 formed Chapter IV, "The Exercise of the South Vietnamese People's Right to Self-Determination," which spelled out the manner in which the Saigon government and the PRG would arrive at a political settlement to the conflict. Of principal importance, Article 12 required the two South Vietnamese parties to "do their utmost" to establish the National Council of National Reconciliation and Concord "of three equal segments" and operating on the "principle of unanimity." The NCNRC would then be directed to form local councils on the same basis and to agree to general and local elections. Chapter IV also' instructed the South Vietnamese factions to agree on steps to "reduce their military effectives."

Article 15 of Chapter V reiterated many clauses of the Geneva agreement, calling on both sides to respect the DMZ. Like Article 1, it made no effort to resolve conflicting interpretations of the Geneva accords.

Chapter VI's four articles established the institutions whose duty it was to enforce the agreement. First, a Four-Party Joint Military Commission (JMC) was established, consisting of all four signatories to the agreement. Operating under the principle of unanimity, the Four-Party JMC was responsible for arranging the exchange of POWs and the withdrawal of American troops, as well as overall observance of the cease-fire. The Four-Party JMC was to exist only sixty days, until all POWs were returned and American troops withdrawn. It would then be succeeded by a Two-Party JMC formed by Saigon and the PRG. It was to continue the work of its Four-Party counterpart but also discuss the return of political prisoners and the reduction in forces.

Article 18 established the ICCS. Consisting of representatives of four countries, Canada, Hungary, Indonesia, and Poland, the ICCS was designed to enforce all provisions of the treaty when the Two-Party and Four-Party JMCs could not reach agreement.

The Paris agreement also called for the convening of an International Conference on Vietnam to include the major powers that had participated in the Geneva Conference of 1954. Underneath the vague charge given this conference to "guarantee" the agreement, lay the hope that great-power diplomacy could be brought to bear on the Vietnamese parties. But the conference was never held.

Chapter VII reiterated the 1954 and 1962 Geneva

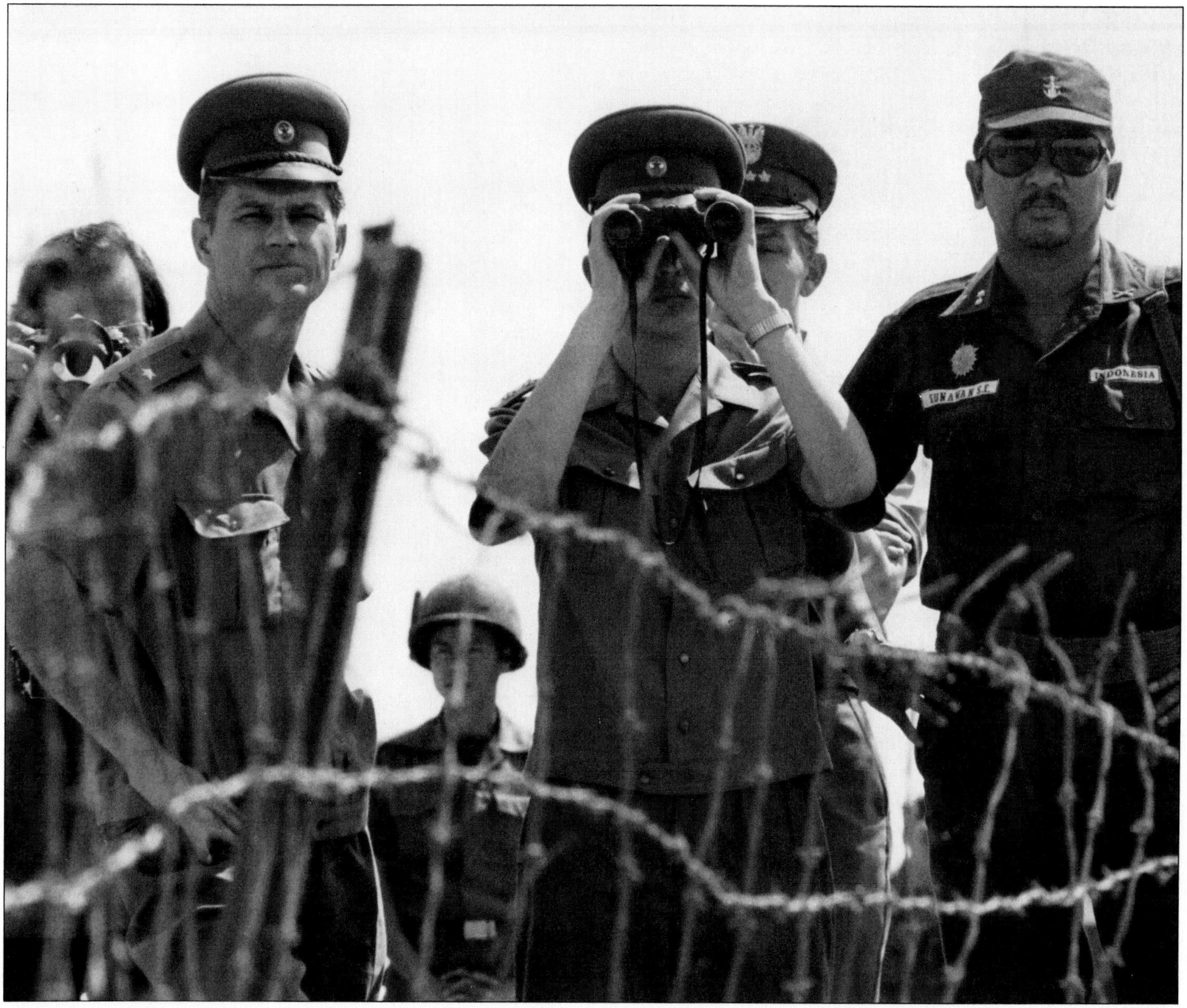

Members of the ICCS look on helplessly as an artillery battle rages near Quang Tri City on February 6, 1973. Heavy fire forced the observers to turn back from the action.

agreements with respect to Cambodia and Laos. In addition, it required all foreign troops to be withdrawn from the two countries and called for "respect for each other's independence."

Chapter VIII's two articles, 21 and 22, proved to be among the most controversial of the agreement. The former called on the U.S. to aid in "healing the wounds of war" by contributing to "postwar construction of North Vietnam and throughout Indochina." With this aid serving as a foundation, Article 22 urged the U.S. and DRV to establish "a new, equal and mutually beneficial relationship."

The agreement ended with Article 23, which declared the provisions of the treaty to be "in force" when all parties had signed.

That the cease-fire had been repeatedly violated during the landgrabbing campaigns did not come as a surprise. As early as October 1972, Kissinger had warned that fighting would continue as the two sides "tested each other." His hope was that the early fighting would taper off as the Communists and Saigon adopted "less brutal means" to settle their difficulties. A cease-fire, it seemed, was something that would have to evolve, like the anticipated political solution to South Vietnam's problems.

South Vietnam's position at this time seemed to be very strong. Most observers and the U.S. military credited the government with control of more than 90 percent of the population and at least 80 percent of South Vietnam's territory (see map, page 21). The combined efforts of America's Enhance and Enhance Plus programs had restored to the South Vietnamese armed forces the level of materiel and manpower they had enjoyed prior to the Communist 1972 offensive, and beyond. In addition, continued bombing by American B-52s throughout South Vietnam during

Landgrab

It became known as the "war of the flags" as government and Communist forces battled for control of South Vietnam's villages after the cease-fire. The flag represented political control of an area each side hoped would be recognized by the International Commission of Control and Supervision. But with the ICCS hopelessly ineffective from its inception, the display of flags served only as another reason for each side to continue the fight.

Backed by ARVN artillery, South Vietnamese soldiers attempt to retake a village near Cu Chi, recently occupied by the Communists, and bring down the PRG flag.

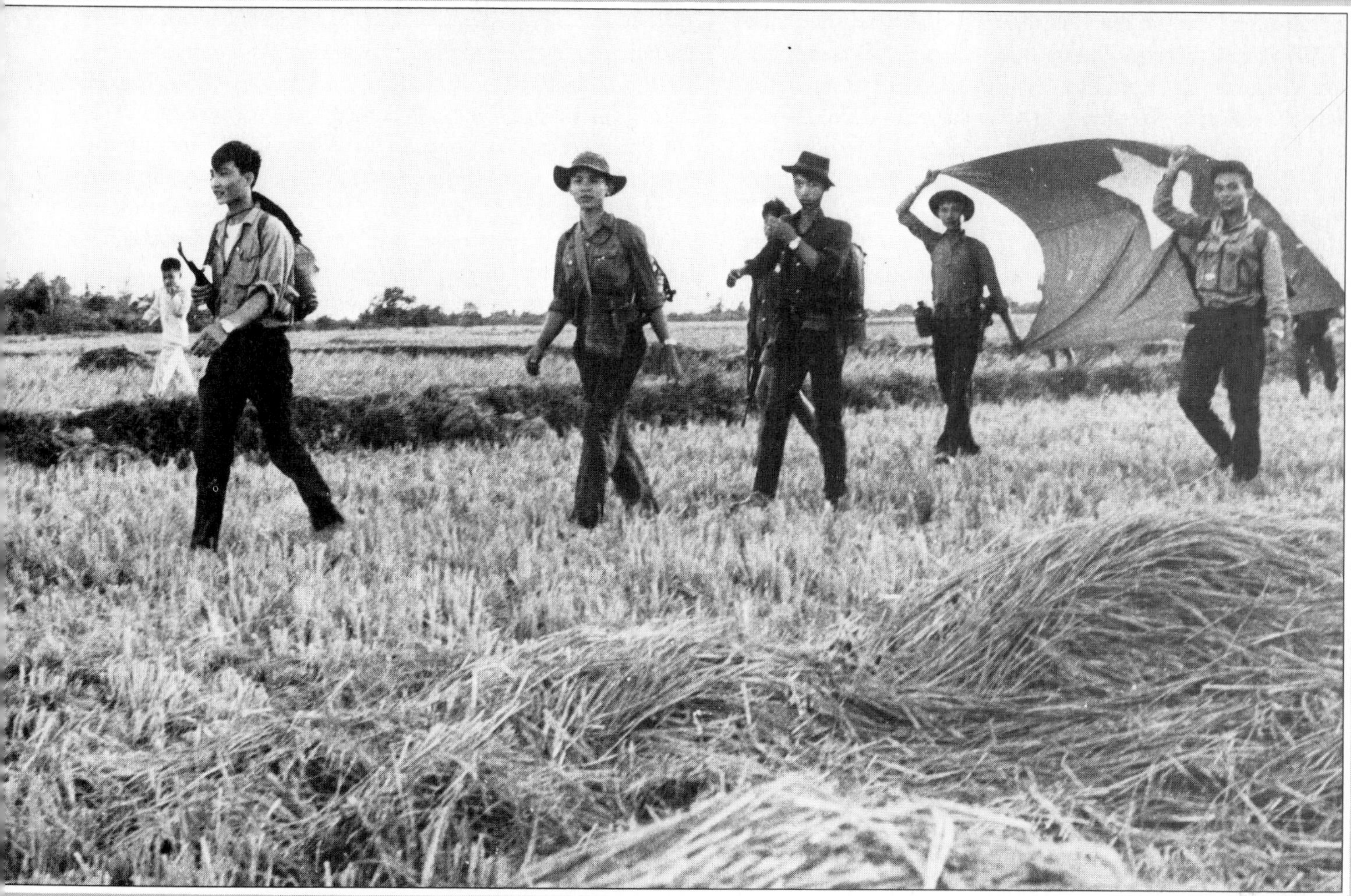

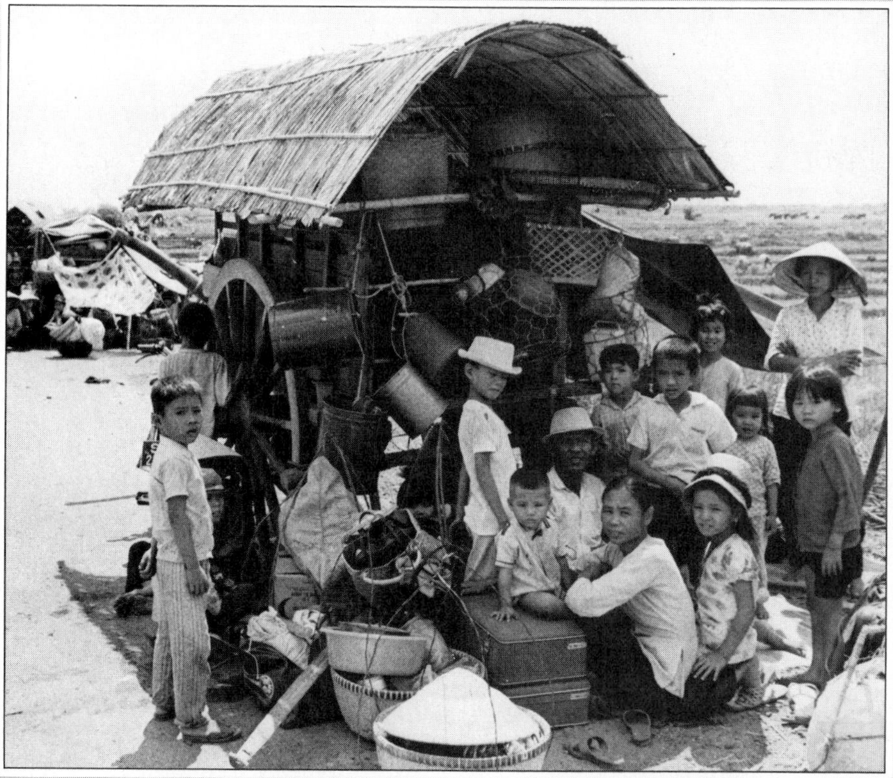

Vietcong cadres emerge from hiding in a village near Cai Lai, south of Saigon, to show their flag and gain recognition of their control of the area.

Endless war. Peasants flee their homes along Highway 13 as government and Communist troops battle for control of the road.

the fall of 1972 and the Christmas bombing of North Vietnam itself had limited the Communists' ability to match the RVNAF's rejuvenation. The new American ambassador to South Vietnam, Graham Martin, had good reason to cable President Nixon in Washington with the optimistic assessment that "we have every right to confidently expect that the GVN can hold without the necessity of U.S. armed intervention."

But the North Vietnamese were not without their assets as well. Their two greatest gains at the conference table had been the withdrawal of American forces from South Vietnam and a tacit recognition of their control over the country's remaining 10 percent of the population and 20 percent of the territory. They were now in a position to develop and consolidate their control of this territory, without the danger that their efforts would be undone by American bombers. The American Defense Attaché Office, the successor to MACV as the headquarters of the residual U.S. military force in South Vietnam, echoed Martin's prognosis that the South Vietnamese armed forces "could probably hold their own against the force the North had." But the DAO also added, "The military balance in South Vietnam was close to even." Whether this stalemate would result in peace and political accommodation or more war would be determined by the strategies that each side adopted to make the Paris agreements work to their own advantage.

Hanoi and the "Third Vietnam"

Within weeks of the signing of the Paris agreement, Henry Kissinger believed that Hanoi's strategy had become clear: They would simply ignore the provisions of the agreement they had signed in Paris. In his memoirs he concluded, "There can be no doubt that Hanoi's illegal infiltration of military equipment and personnel started almost immediately, proved decisive, and antedated all the alleged breaches of the Paris accords by Saigon."

There was considerable evidence to support Kissinger's theory. Even before the cease-fire, American intelligence noted a steady increase in the flow of military supplies down the Ho Chi Minh Trail, a flow that barely paused for the January 28 signing of the treaty, which allowed continued infiltration of materiel only on a one-for-one replacement basis. A portion of what the Communists brought into South Vietnam after that date was thus legal, but it is clear that they went far beyond the permissible.

At the time of the signing of the agreement, South Vietnam possessed a vast numerical superiority in both armor and artillery. Within three months, however, the Communists had surpassed their enemy in tanks and armored personnel carriers and almost caught up in the number of heavy guns. In both cases Hanoi had doubled or even tripled the stocks on hand at the beginning of January.

Other elements of the NVA build-up were not so clearly

violations of the agreement but greatly enhanced the enemy's military capabilities. The construction of newer and improved roads and the extension of a petroleum pipeline, it might be argued, were intended for civilian purposes but clearly had a war-making potential. Ironically, the North Vietnamese had Henry Kissinger to thank that such construction was not prohibited by the treaty. Wanting to ensure that South Vietnamese army engineers would be able to keep roads open and aid in South Vietnam's economic recovery, the agreement specifically exempted these activities from the proscribed list of purely military activities.

But of all the North Vietnamese actions in the early months of the cease-fire, none was so ominous as the increase in Communist antiaircraft defenses, particularly in I Corps. To the ten NVA antiaircraft regiments stationed in Quang Tri Province at the end of 1972, the North Vietnamese added three more by the end of April. This increase in enemy antiaircraft power posed a special threat to the South Vietnamese, since the American military strategy they inherited required almost total control of the skies. It was therefore not surprising that the American delegation to the JMC chose to make this aspect of the North Vietnamese build-up the subject of its protest.

But as happened so often in this war in which the propaganda battle could be as important as events on the battlefield, the American delegation chose the wrong target.

They focused their attack on the build-up of SAM missile sights in the Khe Sanh area, perhaps believing that the very name Khe Sanh would awaken the American public to enemy violations. On February 26, South Vietnamese General Du Quoc Dong and U.S. Major General Gilbert Hume Woodward, head of the American delegation, accused the North Vietnamese of introducing SA-2 missiles into the area, offering photographic evidence for their accusation. The head of the Vietcong delegation responded for the Communists, since the North Vietnamese would not acknowledge the presence of their troops south of the DMZ. General Tran Van Tra accused the United States of "trying to rekindle the war" and claimed that there had been no movement or redeployment of Vietcong forces since the cease-fire began.

As far as Khe Sanh was concerned, he was probably correct. The DAO later admitted that the American members of the JMC who protested the build-up at Khe Sanh "were not sure about the conclusion to be derived from the evidence." And South Vietnamese Major General Nguyen Duy Hinh, commander of the 3rd ARVN Division based in MR1, wrote after the war, "As of the beginning of 1973 [i.e., prior to the signing of the Paris agreement], Khe

---

While fighting continues south of the DMZ, North Vietnam celebrates a peaceful May Day in Hanoi in 1973 and displays its newest military hardware.

Sanh base was protected by the 263rd SAM regiment." Fighting the wrong battle at the wrong time may have cost the Americans a propaganda victory, but it did not change the basic fact: The NVA was greatly expanding its antiaircraft defenses in defiance of the Paris accords.

The difficulty of the American delegation in pinning down the enemy's violation of the cease-fire agreement at Khe Sanh reflected a deeper problem with Kissinger's analysis of the NVA build-up. Where Kissinger wrote that this resupply effort "started almost immediately," he should have written, "started even before the agreement went into effect." According to the interpretation of some Americans in Saigon, the Communist build-up was a response to the American Enhance Plus program. One American officer admitted, "They're just doing the same thing we did. Only they don't have C-5s so they couldn't quite meet the deadline." By continuing their infiltration of arms and equipment beyond the deadline, the North Vietnamese were in violation of the letter of the agreement, but the situation may have been analagous to the South Vietnamese response to Communist landgrabbing. The journalist Arnold Isaacs wrote:

> Just as the Saigon command felt justified in technically violating the ceasefire in order to recapture territory it regarded as rightfully under its control, the North Vietnamese may have felt that their buildup of men and supplies after the truce was also legitimate, since it restored the intended battlefield equilibrium.

There was other evidence to suggest that Kissinger's analysis may have been overly simplistic. The drivers in the convoys of trucks hauling the new war materiel into South Vietnam must have been surprised by the traffic they encountered going in the opposite direction. What they met was not the usual string of empty flatbeds returning to North Vietnam but a stream of NVA soldiers returning north of the DMZ. Hanoi was keeping a pledge that Le Duc Tho had made to Henry Kissinger. Article 13 of the Paris agreement only required the two parties to engage in "discussions" about "steps to reduce their effectives," but in one of their "secret understandings" Tho promised the Americans that the NVA would withdraw approx-

"Peace to the village" proclaims the banner at the entrance to Vietcong-controlled Huu Dinh in February 1973. A degree of peace returned to such villages after the cease-fire.

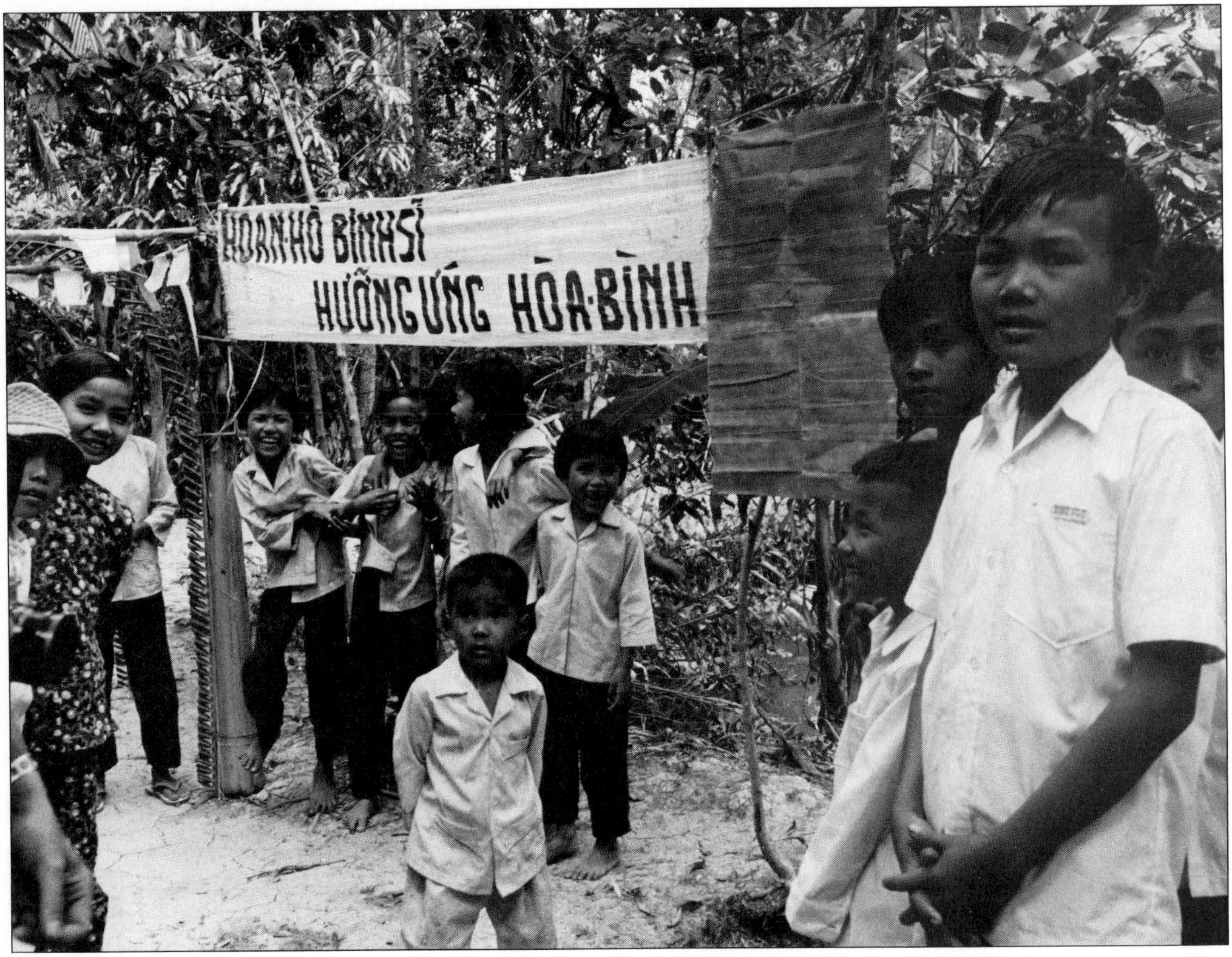
HƯỞNG ỨNG HÒA·BÌNH

imately 30,000 troops from South Vietnam as a token of "good faith." By June 30, the DAO reported that at least two enemy divisions, the 308th and the 312th, and parts of a third division, the 320B, had been redeployed back into North Vietnam. The level of mistrust between the two sides was so great, however, that the DAO did not see the movement as a "good faith" effort by the enemy. Instead, it reminded Washington that "both divisions have had sufficient time to refit and could be redeployed back to South Vietnam if needed."

This two-way North Vietnamese traffic on the Ho Chi Minh Trail was a reflection of continued divisions within the Communist Politburo. The "hawks" had not disappeared after the signing of the Paris agreements and they now pressed for aggressive military action. Southerners like Pham Hung, head of the Central Office for South Vietnam (COSVN), saw a policy of caution as little more than an abandonment of the goal of liberating South Vietnam. He was joined by the military representatives in the Politburo, Defense Minister Vo Nguyen Giap and his chief of staff, General Van Tien Dung. Both men were predisposed to settle the conflict with guns, not talk.

But these "hawks" were still a minority in the Politburo as the "doves," or more cautious members, led by Truong Chinh and Le Duc Tho, with the support of Le Duan, dominated the deliberations. Their primary objective was to consolidate the area under Communist control, to create a base from which Saigon could be undermined, to form their own South Vietnam, the "Third Vietnam."

In typical North Vietnamese fashion, the views of the minority were not merely brushed aside but incorporated into national policy. The very name that the Communists gave to the new era ushered in by the signing of the Paris agreement suggested this amalgamation: "Peace in War." Evidence of what the North Vietnamese would emphasize, and thus of which faction held the upper hand in Hanoi, was revealed not in slogans but in the actual orders issued to troops and cadres serving in the South.

When American intelligence analysts received a copy of Directive No. 2/73 issued by COSVN in late January,

Supporters of the Saigon government show their colors, as ordered by President Thieu, in a government-controlled village northeast of Saigon.

they had their first glimpse of the new Communist strategy. The directive unambiguously ordered that "military units were to play a secondary role in support of the political efforts of the cadre." These "political efforts" were designed to (1) motivate the population, (2) develop mass movements, (3) reform and strengthen the Communist infrastructure, and (4) adapt the procedures of the armed forces to the new situation. A subsequent directive, No. 3/73, issued by COSVN in June, showed that the Communist strategy had not changed. It reiterated the policy and goals of the earlier directive and further ordered all troops and cadres "to strictly observe the ceasefire."

Strict observance of the cease-fire was an important element in the Communists' strategy. They hoped to create a climate of peace within the country that would persuade refugees to return to their homes, many in PRG-controlled areas. Furthermore, they hoped that a longing for peace would create desertions from ARVN as soldiers, drafted for terms as long as twenty years, decided that in peacetime their presence in the armed services was no longer needed.

Communist propaganda emphasized its side's compliance with the cease-fire, and even the American DAO wrote in its classified report to Washington that the Communists were, in fact, doing so. In June the DAO reported that while "communist forces have been ordered to react strongly to any GVN 'nibbling operations' ... generally speaking enemy actions in the past month have been defensive, designed to hold and improve PRG control in communist occupied areas."

The CIA reported that Communist civilian technicians and political cadres had largely replaced NVA regulars on the Ho Chi Minh Trail leading into South Vietnam. As many as 30,000 of these civilians made the trek during the first months after the cease-fire. Their task was to "build roads, farm communes, and cities [sic], and to organize and run a governmental structure."

What united all of these actions into a coherent strategy was a single goal: to prepare the Communists to compete with the Saigon regime in the political struggle provided for by the Paris agreements and, if this failed, to be ready to strike back decisively at any moment. As they did so often during the course of the war, the Politburo refused to permit a choice of one option from restricting future actions. In this case, the steps taken to enhance their political position in South Vietnam could later serve as the foundation for renewed military aggressiveness. The construction of highways and petroleum pipelines might help to improve the standard of living of civilians in the areas under Communist control but would also serve as the logistical infrastructure for future fighting. The withdrawal of three divisions from South Vietnam would satisfy Kissinger's demand for a token reduction in forces but would also give the NVA time to refit and retrain these units. Thus, the North Vietnamese decision to emphasize the political

struggle did not exclude preparations for a new military offensive. In the meantime, however, North Vietnamese strategy was designed to do precisely what Kissinger had hoped, to funnel the long-standing objective of liberating South Vietnam into "less brutal means."

Why would the North Vietnamese, after nearly thirty years of warfare, suddenly turn to a strategy of political struggle? There were several compelling reasons, and together they were sufficient to persuade a slender majority of the Politburo. Above all, such a strategy offered an opportunity for a "cheap" victory in the South. Ever since the Tet offensive of 1968 the major burden of fighting the war in the South had been borne by northerners, in blood, money, and in enduring the bombing of the United States. With the agreement signed, many in the Politburo wanted to reorder their country's priorities, putting reconstruction of the North ahead of liberating the South. A political strategy offered the opportunity to do so without entirely abandoning their compatriots south of the DMZ.

Furthermore, North Vietnam's allies in Moscow and Peking had informed Hanoi that it could no longer count on a blank check for military assistance. One of the great accomplishments of Henry Kissinger's evolving relationship with the Communist superpowers had been to secure such a promise in 1972. In exchange, Kissinger offered the Soviet Union the promise of receiving "most favored nation status" in its trading relationship with the U.S. This would reduce the cost of Soviet goods in the U.S. and pave the way for greatly expanded commerce between the nations. The Defense Intelligence Agency later confirmed that the Russians and Chinese had kept their promise. While Hanoi's patrons continued to provide some military assistance to the DRV, it was insufficient to mount an offensive.

This North Vietnamese strategy, however, depended on one very important imponderable. They had to reach some agreement with President Thieu on how the political process would evolve. However, as Kissinger had pointed out to Thieu in their stormy October meetings, the principle of unanimity meant that he possessed an absolute veto over any political program for South Vietnam's future. With the agreement reluctantly signed, Thieu chose to exercise that right.

Saigon and Thieu's "Four No's"

If Kissinger seemed convinced that Hanoi would not abide by the provisions of the Paris agreement, he also had no illusions about what Saigon's strategy would be. "The root fact," he wrote in his memoirs, "was that Thieu and his government were not ready for a negotiated peace."

They preferred to continue the military contest rather than face a political struggle. As Bunker said on August 31, [1972,] when he, the President, and I met in Honolulu to review the bidding: "They fear that they are not yet well enough organized to compete politically with such a tough, disciplined organization."

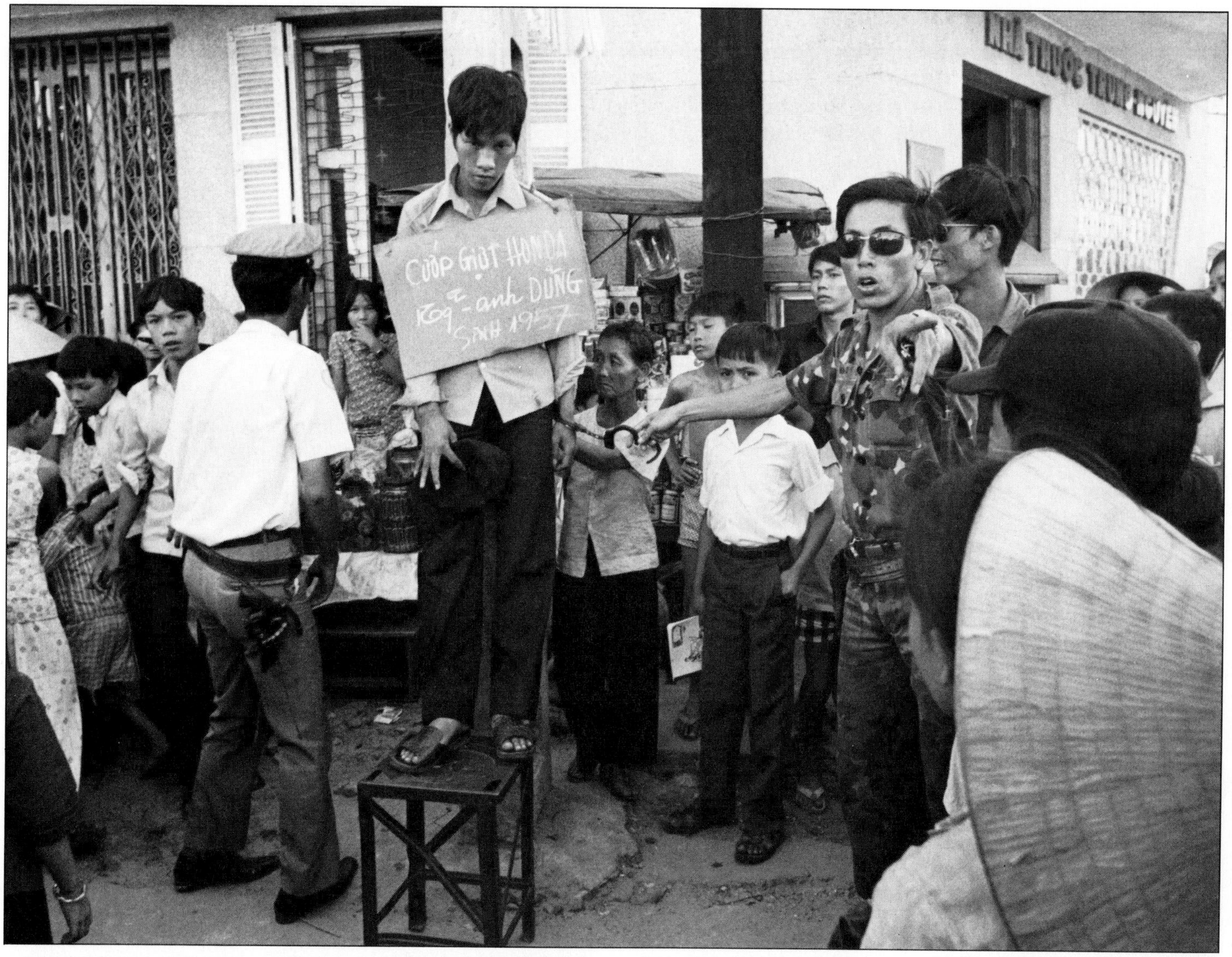
CƯỚP GIỰT HONDA
anh DŨNG
SINH 1957

An accused Communist sympathizer is displayed in Da Nang as part of Thieu's roundup of enemies in September 1972.

Thieu did not wait for the signing of the peace accords to undercut any possible political solution to South Vietnam's conflict. Using the powers granted to him when martial law was declared following the Communist Easter offensive, Thieu promulgated, without action by the National Assembly, a series of decrees designed to eliminate his non-Communist opposition within South Vietnam. Silencing these independent voices of dissent would serve his purposes in two ways. First, the Paris agreements called for a role by Vietnam's "third force," the non-Communist opposition. By eliminating the spokesmen and organizations of this "third force" he could claim that none existed. As a corollary, he could claim to speak for all of non-Communist South Vietnam in his discussions with the PRG.

Thieu first moved against the opposition press and its political parties. He forced all newspapers to post large monetary bonds to guarantee any fines levied for printing stories "harmful to the national interest." Few non-government newspapers and magazines were able to afford the bond, and as a result twenty-nine opposition periodicals were forced to shut down their presses. Two months later, in November, Thieu instituted stringent requirements for any organization to qualify for recognition as a political party and thus earn the right to compete in elections. The new decree required any aspiring political group to open branches in cities and provinces throughout the country and to win substantial electoral support in assembly elections. The decree effectively destroyed parties with only a limited geographical base and, in effect, left Thieu's New Democratic party without opposition.

Thieu's next target was opposition leaders, both Communist and non-Communist. PRG propaganda charged Thieu with waging a "white terror campaign" during the fall of 1972 in which "tens of thousands" of dissidents were arrested. One U.S. news account placed the number of those arrested in the final three months of 1972 at 20,000. While this figure was probably an exaggeration, the crackdown on Thieu's opponents was very real.

Realizing that all of these political arrests might be nullified by the provision of the Paris agreement that required the release of political prisoners, Thieu ordered a subtle change in South Vietnam's law of detention. That law had until then permitted detention without trial for political prisoners during wartime. With a cease-fire approaching, Thieu issued Decree Law 020 on November 25, 1972, changing the term "wartime" to "until law and security are completely restored." Moreover, Thieu began charging some political detainees with petty criminal activity, such as violating identity card laws. This deprived them of the status of political prisoners as defined by the peace accords and permitted Thieu to continue their detention as common criminals. In all, Thieu released only about 5,000 political prisoners under the terms of the Paris agreement, while Amnesty International estimated that he held 200,000.

Finally Thieu abolished hamlet and village elections, thereby undoing one of his most important reform initiatives. Arguing that many of the elected officials were Communists, Thieu ousted those elected by the villagers themselves and replaced them with appointments made by his military province chiefs. It was a curious argument by Thieu, because it suggested that elections conducted by his own administration and widely publicized by the United States as "fair" and giving "legitimate voice" to the Vietnamese peasants had resulted in widespread victories by the Communists. While the Vietcong and their sympathizers had undoubtedly won some of these elections, Thieu just as obviously exaggerated both the extent and the threat to security. Rather, his design was to eliminate anyone with an independent base of support.

The result of Thieu's autumn maneuvers—the epithet "repression" was probably not unduly harsh—was paradoxical. Most observers believed that Thieu had succeeded in "consolidating" his rule and was in his strongest position ever. On the other hand, he had reduced his base of support even further.

When Thieu then summarized his policy in the post-cease-fire era, it was hardly surprising that it turned out to be no more than a reiteration of the "Four No's" he had unveiled in 1969. The Four No's, as the official U.S. Army history of the Four-Party JMC noted, were not only "essentially negative … even uncooperative, policies" but directly violated many of the provisions of the cease-fire.

The first "no" was "no negotiating with the enemy." This policy made it impossible to carry out the business of the Four-Party JMC and sabotaged any efforts to realize the political provisions of the agreement. In the end, according to the army history, it "hindered American efforts to help the South Vietnamese themselves."

The policy of "no Communist activity in South Vietnam" directly violated Article 11 of the agreement, which required all parties to "ensure the democratic liberties of the people" including "freedom of political activities." For their part, neither did the Communists grant political freedoms in their areas of control, as required by Article 11.

"No coalition government" was Thieu's notice that he would do nothing to establish a National Council of National Reconciliation and Concord.

The fourth "no," "no surrender of territory to the enemy," refused to acknowledge what the Paris agreement guaranteed, the recognition of PRG hegemony in areas under its control. According to the Americans on the JMC, it "made it impossible for the commission to establish respective areas of control or bring about a ceasefire."

The Four No's were rational only to a government dedicated to avoiding a political settlement of the war and equally certain of the constancy of American military support. Such assistance would be essential for maintaining South Vietnam's enormous defense burdens. But they were not the only policy available to South Vietnam, and some of Thieu's closest advisers urged him to consider other alternatives.

Thieu's kinsman and minister of information, Hoang Duc Nha, who had proven himself so vexing to Kissinger in October, issued a warning to Thieu. Educated in the United States as an engineer, he was wholly unsentimental in his appraisal of the American character. "The Americans are traders," he told his uncle. "They'll sell you out if you can no longer assure them profit." Nha urged Thieu to attempt some accommodation with the PRG as well as to chart a more independent course in foreign policy.

Thieu rejected Nha's advice, as well as a plan advanced by General Tran Van Don, on February 7, 1973, to form a "peace government" in Saigon. Under Don's proposal, Thieu would remain as president but would "delegate all power to negotiate [with the PRG] to a new prime minister," presumably Don himself. Don formed a potential cabinet to carry out his plan, which included a call for the neutralization of South Vietnam. He even claims to have kept the American embassy informed of his thinking. His plan got nowhere in the presidential palace and Don blamed Thieu as "the main obstacle to peace."

Obstacles to peace

The only political strategy that Thieu did adopt was one that denied any legitimacy whatsoever to the PRG, a policy he carried out from the moment a Communist delegation to the Joint Military Commission arrived at Saigon's Tan San Nhut airport. They were met by South Vietnamese immigration officials requesting that they fill out disembarkation forms, a formality that would establish them as foreigners on South Vietnamese soil. The Communists naturally refused and were denied permission to leave the plane, even to eat or use rest room facilities. Throughout the night the stalemate continued, until Ambassador Bunker intervened the following morning and effected a compromise. Thieu permitted the Communists to deplane but only as a one-time exception to his country's immigration laws.

Such petty harassments followed the Communist delegates wherever they went. They were relegated to an isolated compound at Tan Son Nhut's Camp Davis and held under armed guard, "for their protection." They looked and felt like prisoners. As the JMC tried to establish regional field teams throughout the country, Thieu provided substandard housing and equipment for his Communist "guests." Some of the structures even lacked roofs. More serious trouble developed when government-inspired rioters pelted Communist delegates with stones and bricks at regional sites in Ban Me Thuot and Hue. An American delegate to the JMC team at Ban Me Thuot recalled seeing "the Secretary to the Province Council signalling people to come forward" at the beginning of the riot.

In his heavy-handed way, Thieu was trying to dramatize a very real animosity on the part of many South Vietnamese to the Communist delegates. The result, however, was to sabotage the JMC. Hanoi and the PRG refused to man additional regional committees and kept those in existence deliberately under strength. Without Communist cooperation it became virtually impossible to investigate cease-fire violations.

The impotence of the JMC virtually assured that the ICCS would not be able to carry out its functions. The ICCS was hamstrung from the outset by the principle of unanimity that permitted the Polish and Hungarian Communist contingents to veto any investigation likely to embarrass their allies. The South Vietnamese could use more subtle means because the ICCS was entirely dependent upon them, as host country, to provide logistical support and security. ARVN simply refused to do so when it was inconvenient. General Hinh admitted that ARVN "might . . . cause delays or feign 'technical troubles.' "

The Canadians, remembering their impotence in the International Control Commission established by the Geneva Agreement of 1954, especially bristled at their ineffectiveness. They complained that they could only investigate incidents within walking distance of their compounds. It was not long before the Canadian members of the ICCS gave those initials a more earthy meaning: I Can't Control Shit. In July the Canadian government threw up its hands in despair and withdrew its member-

U.S. soldiers try to protect North Vietnamese delegates to the Four-Party JMC during a government-sponsored riot in the city of Hue on February 25, 1973.

ship from the ICCS. It was replaced by Iran, then still a staunch U.S. ally.

The situation in Vietnam hardly produced a background conducive to productive discussions on South Vietnam's political future between the Saigon government and the PRG. These formal negotiations, mandated by the Paris agreement, opened in the Paris suburb of St. Cloud on March 19, 1973. According to the agreement, the two sides were to establish the NCNRC and develop a plan for elections within ninety days. As one observer pointed out, "It quickly became apparent that even if they had ninety years, they wouldn't have been able to do so." The meetings continued for thirteen months, during which time the two sides could not even agree on an agenda. With no substantive talks transpiring inside the meetings, both parties took their plans to the public.

The PRG presented a rather elaborate plan for South Vietnam's future. There was to be full freedom of movement and political activity, including the legalization of the Communist party, leading to the establishment of village-level NCNRCs. These local committees would conduct elections for a national assembly instructed to write a new constitution for South Vietnam. The Communists favored a strong parliamentary system rather than a government dominated by the president. Realizing that they could not garner the necessary majority of votes to elect a president, they hoped thereby to maximize their strength as a significant minority party in the parliament. Under the PRG's optimistic thinking, their power, influence, and legitimacy would rapidly increase under these conditions and ultimately result in Communist domination of South Vietnam's government.

Thieu naturally rejected his enemies' plan. Hoping to gain in these discussions what Henry Kissinger could not accomplish in Paris, he argued that there could be no political freedom in South Vietnam until every last NVA soldier left his territory. Only then would he consent to open elections. But his electoral plan differed sharply from the PRG's. He insisted that the first step be a nationwide referendum by South Vietnam's citizens on whether they wanted any change in the constitution. Arguing that the Saigon constitution had been approved by the voters in the 1966 elections, Thieu maintained that the discussions in Paris could not sweep aside the system without a referendum. The PRG refused to accept that constitution since it had been enacted in elections in which Communist participation was prohibited. It maintained that the Paris agreements had inaugurated a new political era and that South Vietnam should start with a clean slate.

Both sides could justify their proposals on principle. Thieu's was legalistically correct; South Vietnam did have a constitution with established procedures for amendment. The Communist proposal, ironically, was closer to the spirit of democratic theory, beginning, as it did, with grassroots elections. But principle was not what motivated

either side. Both parties realized that Communist strength lay in its local organization and discipline, while Thieu's consisted of his centralized national power, largely imposed by the ARVN. The PRG and Thieu, in turn, each placed on the table proposals that simply took advantage of their own strengths. Thieu wanted a single "yes-or-no" vote that he could most easily manipulate. The referendum would not even be on the popularity of his own rule but rather on the constitution. The PRG wanted to fragment South Vietnam's political system into countless minority parties and interest groups. With the only strongly disciplined organization in the country, it felt confident that the resulting political chaos would work to its advantage.

The proposals of both sides, however, remained merely propaganda tools. The NCNRC was never established; the NVA did not withdraw from South Vietnam; full political freedom was never granted; and no elections ever were held. All that was left for the two sides was to fight to the bitter end.

"A new, equal relationship"

The capstone to Henry Kissinger's diplomacy during the fall of 1972 was to be the first official visit by a representative of the American government to the Democratic Republic of Vietnam. The purpose of the trip was, according to Kissinger, "to encourage any tendencies that existed to favor peaceful reconstruction over continued warfare" and "to stabilize the peace insofar as prospects of American goodwill could do so." For Kissinger, landing at Hanoi's Noi Bai airfield on February 10 was "the equivalent of stepping onto the moon." He was quick to learn that however exhilarating such a landing might be, the moon remained a desolate place.

Three topics dominated the three days of discussion: North Vietnam's obligation to provide information on U.S. MIAs, America's obligation to provide financial assistance to the DRV, and the responsibilities of the two countries to bring about cease-fires in Cambodia and Laos. The nature of the discussions and the extent of the disagreement not only showed the vast gulf of misunderstanding that still divided the two countries and made the creation of the "new, equal relationship" posited in the Paris agreements impossible but also revealed some of the basic theoretical problems in the text of the agreement itself.

The discussions concerning MIAs and postwar reconstruction aid were unhappy ones for both sides. Kissinger came prepared to offer Hanoi $3.25 billion in aid over five years. But he immediately informed Hanoi's leaders that such aid would be given only if Hanoi proved more forthcoming on information concerning MIAs. The Communists immediately turned the tables, saying that such information could only be purchased through economic aid.

Kissinger was outraged, realizing that the MIA issue was one of great emotion to the American people. He castigated the North Vietnamese for holding a "purely humanitarian" responsibility hostage to dollars. Captain Stuart Herrington, a member of the American team responsible for the MIA negotiations, termed Hanoi's stance "bartering for bones."

To Hanoi, however, the situation was exactly reversed. They always believed that the American bombing had been contrary to international law and therefore criminal. The American foreign aid was nothing less than "reparations," a humanitarian gesture to compensate the North Vietnamese for the suffering they had endured under the American bombardment. Nor could the Communists resist noting that many Americans were missing in action because of their participation in the bombing. As Senior Captain To, one of Herrington's North Vietnamese counterparts, explained:

Of course we have information on many of your MIA personnel, and in some cases even the remains of your pilots we shot down . . . . But why should we give them to you for nothing? Your government has done so much damage to our people and our land that it must pay.

It was clearly an issue whose justice depended upon where one stood. As Captain Herrington thought to himself, "Had I been a North Vietnamese, I would undoubtedly have agreed with Captain To."

In reality, the positions of both countries were contrary to the Paris agreement. North Vietnam had an *unconditional* responsibility to resolve the cases of MIAs. Equally without condition was the U.S. promise to provide Hanoi with economic assistance. In a tactic that ran counter to his normal negotiating procedures, Henry Kissinger had been careful to create no "linkages" in the Paris agreement, except for the provision that tied American troop withdrawal to release of the POWs. That is, each article of the agreement presented one or more parties with unconditional responsibilities, duties to be carried out irrespective of the actions of other parties. Kissinger's thinking was that the peace would not be "clean" and that if the faithful execution of each provision were tied to the fulfillment of another part of the agreement, the whole plan would fall apart like a house of cards, or in the case of Indochina, a line of dominoes.

The result, however, was that there was little incentive for any side to live up to the commitments it had made in signing the agreement. Even if one party failed to carry out its own responsibilities, this would not relieve its opponents of the burden of carrying out theirs. Had, for instance, the DRV and the United States agreed from the outset to link financial aid to cooperation in resolving the cases of MIAs, both sides would have had an incentive to carry out the terms of the agreement. In the end, Congress provided the linkage that Kissinger avoided. It voted to deny Hanoi any assistance until the MIA situation was resolved. More than ten years after Kissinger's trip to Hanoi, both sides continued to periodically exchange the same

arguments made in Hanoi in February 1973 with no greater success.

Kissinger's discussions concerning Laos and Cambodia followed the same path, even if the immediate result was somewhat more productive. Article 20 of the Paris agreement called for both Hanoi and Washington to end all military operations in Laos and Cambodia and to withdraw their troops. By "secret understanding," Kissinger and Tho committed their countries to using all their influence to create cease-fires in the two countries. Implementation of Article 20 was to be unconditional for each side, depending on neither a cease-fire agreement nor the actions of its enemy. When Kissinger demanded that Hanoi withdraw its troops from its two neighboring countries, Hanoi injected a full cease-fire as a prerequisite. Hanoi, in turn, demanded that U.S. bombing of Cambodia and Laos be discontinued. Kissinger now told Hanoi that such a cessation would be conditional upon the withdrawal of the NVA. As in the MIA-aid discussion, both sides had established conditions outside of the text of the Paris treaty. But instead of colliding on principle, both sides decided that the practice of *Realpolitik* was more in their interest.

Peace in Indochina

The signing of the Paris agreement on January 27 had not brought even the pretext of a cease-fire to Laos. On January 28 the Pentagon announced that it would continue its B-52 strikes over that country. Anticipating that a cease-fire agreement was imminent, Communist Pathet Lao troops attacked government positions in the towns of Nam Yen, Moung Phalene, and Thakhek. Heavy fighting continued through the first week of February as Henry Kissinger made his way to Hanoi. One week later, on February 21, the Pathet Lao and Laotian government signed a cease-fire agreement.

The agreement did not signal a true peace for Laos, but the conditions were promising. The civil war in Laos had never created the intense hatreds and animosities that characterized the fighting in Vietnam and Cambodia. The relationship between Prince Souvanna Phouma, leader of the Royal Laotian Government, and Souphanouvong, head of the Pathet Lao, seemed to symbolize the nature of that war. They were half brothers who addressed each other with respect and dignity. Although the suffering and damage of battle were very real to those affected, the ebb and flow of war had taken on a lazy, almost stylized, quality. In the rainy season, when American bombers were least effective, Communists would overrun the Plain of Jars, only to be driven out once the skies cleared. If one knew the date, one knew who controlled the plain. All the while, Vientiane, the capital, retained its peaceful calm. The people of Laos, John Kenneth Galbraith once remarked, "have not learned to kill each other like the civilized nations."

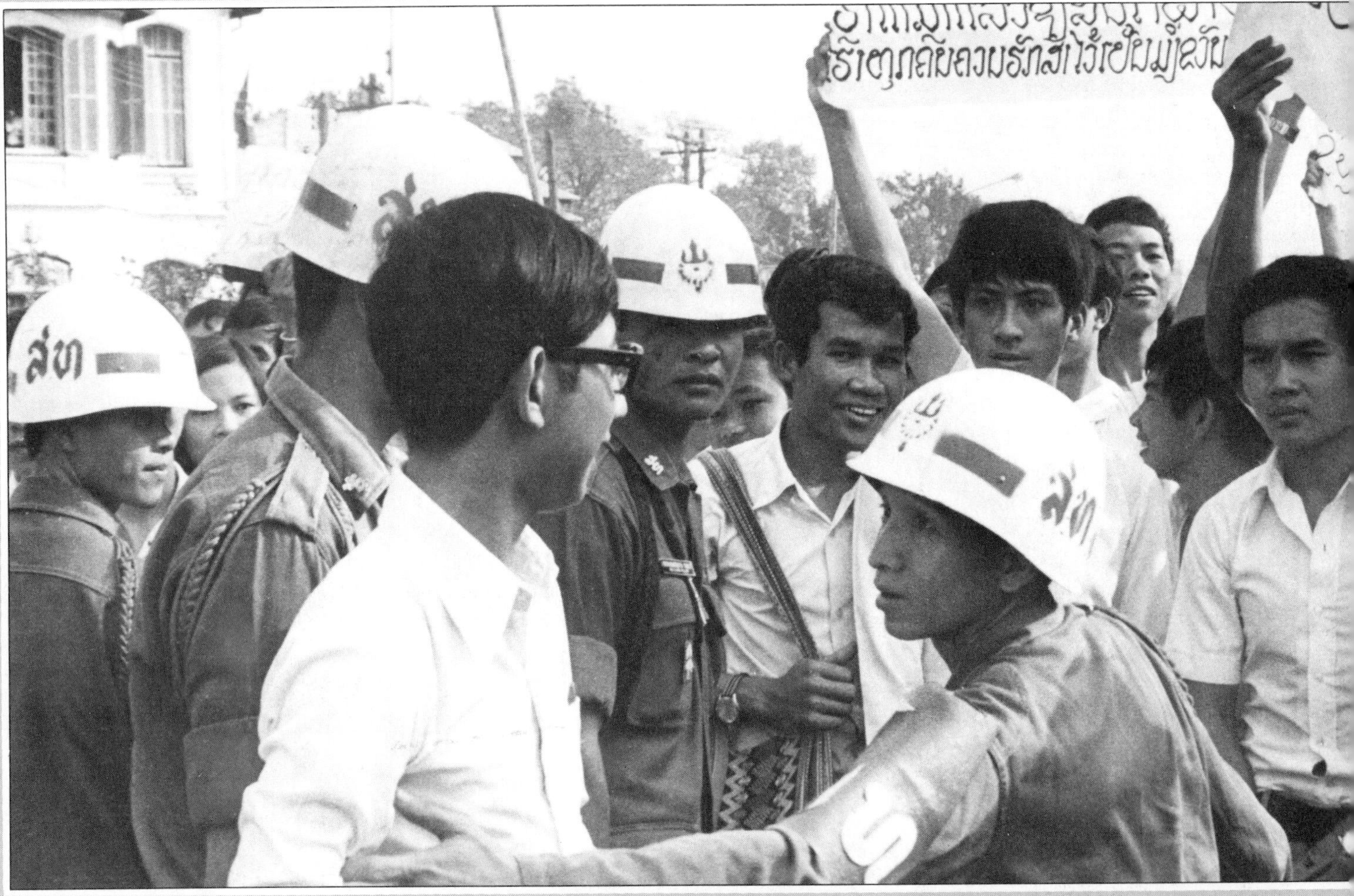

Peace in Laos; Peril in Cambodia.

Laotian students (above) celebrate the announcement of a cease-fire in their country on February 22, 1973, while Prince Souvanna Phouma and Pathet Lao delegates (far right) show their mutual pleasure at the prospect of peace in Laos. Meanwhile, President Lon Nol of Cambodia (right) sits imperiously in Phnom Penh's presidential palace as war continues to ravage his country.

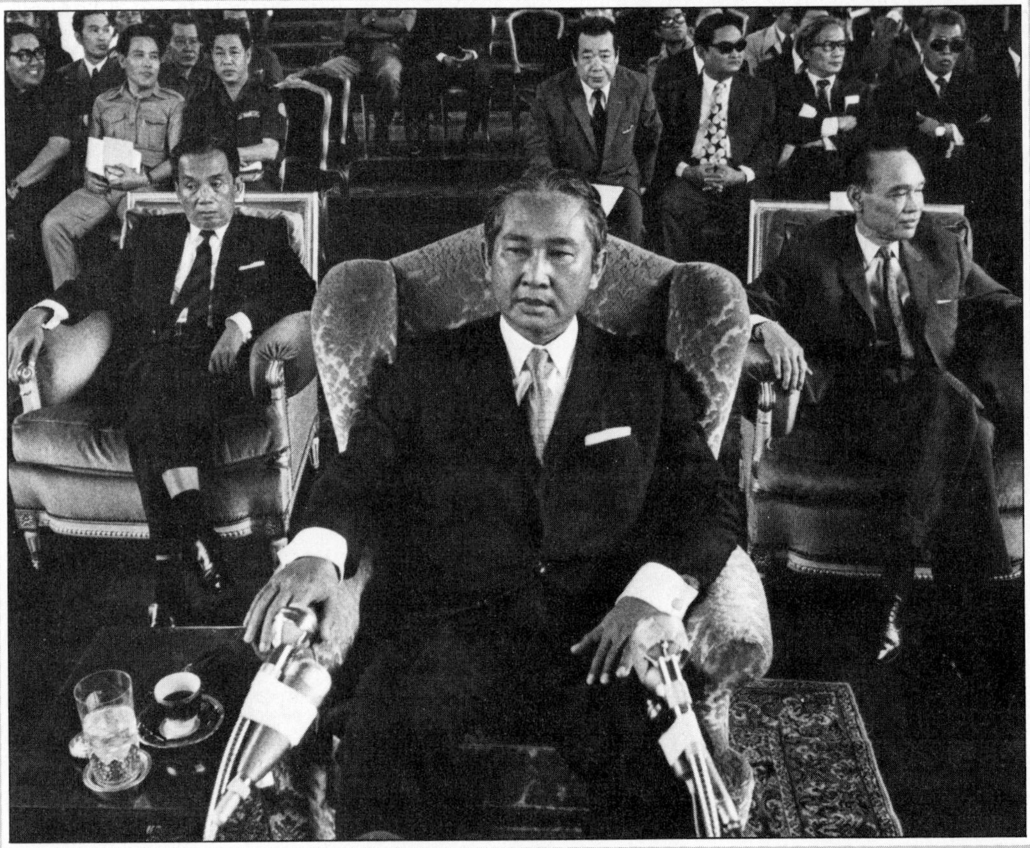

With Hanoi firmly in control of the Pathet Lao, it only took a single word to arrange the cease-fire of February 21. One day later the U.S. announced that it would cease bombing Laotian territory. In characteristic Laotian fashion, the cease-fire agreement was bereft of any peace-keeping machinery. Fighting continued sporadically, and on two occasions, once in February and again in April, American B-52s flew missions in support of the Laotian army. But by the end of April, fighting had virtually ended. Negotiations for a coalition government continued at a languid, Laotian pace. But by mid-1973 Laos, of all the Indochinese countries, had reason to look optimistically to the future.

The outlook in Cambodia, on the other hand, was probably the most dismal in Indochina. Cambodian Prime Minister Lon Nol, acting according to the script written for him by Henry Kissinger, offered a cease-fire to his Khmer Rouge opponents as soon as the Paris agreement was signed. America halted its bombing of Cambodian territory. But, having already shrilly criticized the North Vietnamese for negotiating with Kissinger, the Khmer Rouge declined, calling Lon Nol's offer a "most despicable conjurer's trick intended to mislead national and international public opinion." On February 9 the U.S. bombing campaign in Cambodia resumed.

Within weeks it became clear that Le Duc Tho's words of caution to Henry Kissinger, that Hanoi could not control the Khmer Rouge, had been true. According to Prince Sihanouk, nominal head of the Khmer Rouge exile government, the insurgents demanded that the troops of their erstwhile ally, North Vietnam, leave Cambodian soil. By midsummer the number of NVA advisers serving with Khmer Rouge forces had declined from 45,000 to 3,000. NVA soldiers did not actually leave Cambodia. They merely redeployed in the North Vietnamese sanctuaries along the Cambodian–South Vietnam border. Inevitably clashes broke out between the two Communist armies; North Vietnam had come to view the border area as de facto Vietnamese territory.

The Khmer Rouge obviously felt that it could afford the conflict with Hanoi. Although the North Vietnamese had virtually created the Khmer Rouge army, by early 1973 the insurgents seemed only weeks or months from total victory on their own. On February 3 they cut the link between Phnom Penh and Kompong Som, the country's only deep-water port. By mid-February cargo ships could navigate the Mekong River from Saigon to Phnom Penh only at grave risk. On February 23 Communist forces closed to within five kilometers of the capital.

It soon became clear that only American bombing was saving the Lon Nol government. In six months of bombing during 1973, the U.S. dropped more than 250,000 tons of explosives on Cambodia, more tonnage than had been delivered on Japan in all of World War II. Under American air cover, Cambodian troops were able to push the insurgents back to twenty-nine kilometers from Phnom Penh, but the improvement was only temporary. By April 4 all land routes to the capital were cut and when five vessels successfully navigated the Mekong with a supply of petroleum, it was the first fuel the city had received in two weeks. The only reliable resupply route left to the government was an American airlift. On April 30 Lon Nol and his family left the country for a "brief rest." No one was certain whether he would return.

Victory for the Khmer Rouge seemed inevitable, then, when on June 30, 1973, Congress cut off all funds for bombing Cambodia and the bill was reluctantly signed by President Nixon. The bombing halt would become effective after six weeks, on August 15. All that the Khmer Rouge forces that encircled Phnom Penh had to do was wait and the capital would be theirs.

Only for some reason, they did not. In one of the first visible signs of the insanity that was to mark Khmer Rouge rule of Cambodia, the insurgents decided to attack Phnom Penh in the face of America's last bombing blitz. As they massed for attack, the Khmer Rouge battalions were literally massacred by B-52s. Already in June the U.S. Air Force estimated that it had killed 10,000 Communist troops and wounded another 10,000. And the heaviest bombing was yet to come. Still the Khmer Rouge troops tried to advance. Finally, on August 10, what remained of the insurgent force began to withdraw from the environs of Phnom Penh. The capital had been saved. But when the American bombing ended on August 15, it was clear that the B-52s had bought Phnom Penh only time and not security.

Son of cease-fire

The press widely described it as a déjà vu. When Henry Kissinger and Le Duc Tho returned to Paris for a series of meetings in late May and early June little had changed in Indochina. Ostensibly they were meeting to arrange for the international conference on Indochina called for in Article 19 of the Paris agreement. In reality they were back to square one: trying to secure a cease-fire. As Kissinger arrived in Paris, Saigon announced the statistics behind the grim reality. Since January 27, 25,000 combatants from both sides and 5,000 civilians had been killed in battle. A representative of Thieu's government was present as well, providing a deeper sense of déjà vu. He commented on arrival, "the South Vietnamese government is not going to sign any document."

In his *Foreign Affairs* article of January 1969, Kissinger had offered two possible paths to a political agreement on South Vietnam's future. "It could take place formally on the national level," he wrote. "Or, it could occur locally . . . where even now tacit accommodations are not unusual in many areas." With the "formal" route clearly roadblocked, Kissinger used the May and June sessions to further the possibility of "tacit accommodation."

Kissinger noted that the Two-Party JMC was not functioning. The problem was that Communist delegates "were virtually under South Vietnamese house arrest," according to Kissinger, and therefore were unable to supervise a cease-fire. Kissinger suggested moving the PRG representatives "away from the towns to the demarcation lines in the jungle between the two areas of control, where in fact they were supposed to function." Le Duc Tho readily agreed, but Thieu vetoed the proposal. From his point of view, as Kissinger ruefully noted, "it would clearly separate South Vietnam into two areas of control . . . disproving Saigon's claim to undisputed sovereignty." A cease-fire required that each side recognize the control of territory occupied by its enemy. This Thieu would not do; it violated one of his Four No's.

Stymied in that effort, there was little that Tho and Kissinger could do except reiterate the provisions of the Paris agreement. For the sake of appearances a new set of adjectives was added to the text. Phrases like "do their utmost" were replaced by "as rapidly as possible." But there was no denying that the June 12 communiqué, as the final text of the Kissinger-Tho agreement was known, did little more than renew the call for a cease-fire made on January 27. With the irreverence of the helpless, American embassy staff members quickly dubbed the communiqué "Son of cease-fire."

But there was one hope. The communiqué included a call for "the commanders of the opposing armed forces at those places of direct contact [to] meet as soon as the cease-fire comes into force with a view to reaching an agreement on temporary measures to avert conflict." Kissinger was again trying to make a cease-fire work through "tacit accommodation" on the "local level."

President Thieu surprisingly accepted this clause of the final communiqué. But he then issued orders that nullified its intent. Defining local commanders only as the commanders of South Vietnam's four military regions, he prohibited lower-ranking officers from meeting with their Communist counterparts. Safely ensconced in their regional headquarters, the Corps leaders were in no better position to draw the boundaries between opposing forces than were politicians in Saigon. Kissinger's hope that local officers would reach "tacit agreements" on their areas of respective control, thus paving the way for an effective cease-fire, was once again foiled.

With the work of the diplomats virtually ended, Thieu was free to embark on his chosen course of action, "to continue the military contest," as Kissinger put it. Although the available documentation only provides glimpses of the emerging pattern, the evidence suggests an inescapable conclusion: The South Vietnamese armed forces, wanting to take advantage of their military superiority while they still had it, took the offensive.

The American Defense Attaché Office kept meticulous records of all enemy violations of the cease-fire but

The Last Campaign

by Arnold R. Isaacs

The last American battle in Indochina, like the first, was fought from the air. And like the bombing that began America's war in 1965, the 187-day air campaign over Cambodia in the spring and summer of 1973, while other U.S. military actions were halted by the Paris peace agreement, was enveloped in military, political, and moral controversy.

U.S. air strikes in Cambodia were halted at seven o'clock on the morning of January 29, twenty-four hours after the truce in Vietnam was supposed to take effect. The same day, Cambodian President Lon Nol announced what Washington termed a "unilateral ceasefire." In fact, the president's broadcast speech demanded that the Communists stop fighting while government forces reoccupied Communist-held territory; it was not so much a cease-fire offer as an invitation to the enemy to surrender. It was a preposterous proposal, in view of the government's military weakness, with no chance of being accepted. That same night, the Cambodian military command—showing something less than zealous dedication to the idea of a unilateral stand-down—asked for U.S. air strikes to resume. That request was turned down, but eleven days later, on February 9, American bombers once again began flying missions over the Cambodian battlefields.

As initially outlined in policy directives from Washington, the bombing policy was to be a limited one. U.S. Ambassador Emory C. Swank was instructed to tell Lon Nol that strikes would be authorized "to counter specific hostile acts" against government forces and would also have to be "clearly commensurate with the defensive requirements of the units under attack." Swank strove hard in the first weeks to stick to that policy, which would offer necessary support to Cambodian units under enemy pressure but would also promote the cease-fire that was the stated U.S. goal in Cambodia.

Within weeks, however, as fighting continued with no signal that the Cambodian Communists were willing to start peace negotiations, the Nixon adminis-

A Cambodian government soldier signals for his men to stay low as a U.S. F-4 bomber strikes enemy positions near Phnom Penh.

tration began to swing toward a different view. Events in Laos, where heavy U.S. bombing continued during the final round of peace talks in Vientiane, apparently led senior U.S. military commanders to believe that a similar policy might bring similar results in Cambodia, even though the two Khmer sides were not negotiating at all and the circumstances in the two countries were, in fact, completely different. "The 22 February cease-fire in Laos," said a declassified air force report on the Cambodia bombing campaign, "reinforced the theory that the concentrated application of airpower was an effective way to bring about serious cease-fire negotiations. This conclusion militated in favor of an intensified U.S. air effort in the Khmer Republic."

The U.S. military command and the Nixon administration also had another unannounced objective: to resume full-scale bombing of North Vietnamese bases and supply routes in their traditional sanctuary areas in eastern Cambodia. Those targets, located in the hinterland east of the Mekong, code-named Freedom Deal by the air force, had no connection at all with battles in Cambodia and were not conducted to support the Cambodian government as initial U.S. policy authorized. Rather, Freedom Deal strikes were meant to help South Vietnamese forces across the border in Vietnam. That was now the only possible U.S. air support, since bombing of Vietnamese territory was prohibited by the Paris agreement. On March 8, four weeks after the Cambodian bombing resumed, the Joint Chiefs of Staff proposed returning to the pre-cease-fire policy, in effect, with air strikes authorized against "VC/NVA supply routes, storage areas and transshipment points throughout FREEDOM DEAL." Though that policy would clearly skirt the spirit of the Vietnam cease-fire, it was justified, in the U.S. view, because continuing North Vietnamese infiltration of troops and supplies from Cambodia also violated the peace agreement.

The chiefs' proposal also recommended lifting the requirement that U.S. strikes supporting Cambodian troops had to be in response to specific enemy attacks. Instead, "the full spectrum of U.S. air strike forces" would be used "against targets posing a threat to friendly forces and population centers."

The new orders were issued the next day, March 9, and sortie rates immediately began to soar upward. From only 65 B-52 sorties in February, the figure rose to 1,200 in March and more than 1,900 in April—more in that one month than in the entire year of 1972. Fighter-bomber and gunship strikes also climbed sharply.

Despite the bombing, the Khmer Communist army scored success after success on the battlefields. It grew steadily in size and determination and severed its last links with the Vietnamese Communists. (The growing enmity between the two Communist partners was not yet grasped, however, in Phnom Penh, let alone Washington.) American intelligence estimated that the Cambodian insurgent force increased from 30,000 to 50,000 men between December 1972 and July 1973, even though it also claimed that during the same time 11,000 Communist soldiers were killed by U.S. fighter-bombers and an unknown additional number by B-52 raids.

The Khmer Republic army, by contrast, continued to sink into moral and military decay that the U.S. bombing campaign may, in some ways, have deepened. When one of Lon Nol's associates urged him to act against corruption in the army, the president complacently replied, "The American B-52's are killing a thousand enemy every day, and the war will soon be over." Demoralized and dispirited, the army gave up position after position even behind the rain of American bombs. Its performance, admitted an official U.S. Defense Department appraisal, "was characterized by poor leadership, low morale, and the refusal of units to advance against enemy resistance." An American forward air controller reported an incident in which the Communists captured a 105MM howitzer from a government unit. The Communists used it until they ran out of shells and then let the government forces recapture it. As soon as the government unit had been resupplied with ammunition, the Communists captured the gun again. That cycle, the U.S. pilot told his superiors, was repeated several times. The officer corps was not only inept but also corrupt. Supply officers demanded bribes for delivering ammunition to front-line units, a U.S. Embassy officer reported, while commanders

pocketed the salaries of some 40,000 to 80,000 "phantoms"—imaginary men who existed only as names on military payrolls.

The real soldiers, meanwhile, regularly went unpaid for months—meaning they went hungry as well, since the Khmer army did not customarily issue rations but expected soldiers to buy food for themselves and their families in village markets. Numerous units refused to obey orders, usually because they had not been paid. On one occasion, hundreds of infantrymen who had no money and had not eaten for three days left the lines and marched into the heart of Phnom Penh to demand their pay. A sympathetic colonel met them with a jeep load of bread he had bought with his own money. The men seized the loaves and ravenously devoured them. A Cambodian lieutenant watched the scene, then turned to an onlooker. "You say there's a new government?" he said, referring to the new High Political Council the Americans hoped (vainly) would leave Lon Nol a figurehead while putting power in more capable hands. "I wish they were here now."

In March the U.S. defense attaché in Phnom Penh reported that the military situation "had approached the critical state," and by April Communist forces had ringed the city. In these desperate straits, the weight of U.S. bombing was shifted from the Freedom Deal zone to the Cambodian battlefronts in an effort to keep the ramshackle government army from collapsing altogether. But Communist units nonetheless succeeded in advancing to within rocket and even mortar range of the city and its airport—so close that on one occasion in late April, U.S. helicopters in Thailand were alerted in the middle of the night to evacuate the American embassy staff. The evacuation was called off at the last minute, after U.S. warplanes spent the entire night bombing Communist positions just beyond the city's edge to prevent a possible assault.

That scare passed, but during May, June, and July—while the U.S. Congress battled with President Nixon and finally set an August 15 deadline for the raids to stop—the government of the Khmer Republic continued to deteriorate. As the weeks passed the sound of air strikes outside the capital was nearly ceaseless. A permanent haze of dust and smoke hung over the horizon in the furnacelike dry-season heat.

Nine days before the bombing ended, the worst known accident of the war seemed to validate a feeling of doom. B-52s on missions over Cambodia were directed by ground-based radar beacons. In order to strike the correct target coordinates, however, a crewman on the bomber had to throw a switch from "direct mode" to "offset mode." If the switch were left on direct mode, the plane would automatically drop its bombs on the beacon itself. For fear of just such a mistake, a beacon that had been placed on the roof of the U.S. Embassy in Phnom Penh was removed. ("Although the precautions taken by the aircrews made such an occurrence unlikely," commented one classified air force document, the "repercussions" of accidentally bombing the American embassy "made the risk unacceptable.") But no one moved the beacon that was smack in the middle of Neak Luong, a garrison town and ferry port on the east bank of the Mekong River sixty kilometers downstream from Phnom Penh. Before dawn on the morning of August 6, a B-52 crewman neglected to throw the offset switch, and the huge plane dropped at least thirty bombs in a string through the center of the town. The central market and part of the local hospital were smashed, as were acres of soldiers' huts; 137 people were killed, most of them government soldiers or members of their families. Another 268 were wounded.

During the final weeks of the bombing, with the August 15 Congressional deadline already set, the Khmer Rouge inexplicably did not dig in but pressed toward Phnom Penh, despite heavy casualties. Why they did so, instead of delaying their offensive until the raids stopped, remains a matter of speculation; American commanders believed their leaders wanted to capture the capital before the bombing halt in order to inflict a propaganda defeat on the United States. Whether that was the reason, or if it was a matter of pure fanaticism, it was a decision that may have cost the Khmer Rouge a chance to end the war in 1973. A few days after the bombing ended, General John W. Vogt, the U.S. 7th Air Force commander, told air force historians that the

offensive "may have been the biggest strategic mistake the enemy made during the war. There is no doubt in my mind," Vogt added, "that had the enemy held off on this big push until after the U.S. bombing halted, the offensive would have succeeded."

Even then, until almost the last hours, many Americans thought it would succeed. During July the government army was losing the equivalent of a full-strength 500-man battalion in casualties every week. On July 19 Brigadier General John Cleland, the senior U.S. military representative in Phnom Penh, reported to his superiors that "as the situation now stands, neither the FANK [government army] nor the government will last long after the 15 August bombing halt if the enemy offensive continues." But with only days to go—on August 9, according to General Vogt—the offensive faltered. By the time the last American bombers left Cambodian skies at eleven o'clock on the morning of the fifteenth ("It was quiet enough around Phnom Penh today to hear an artillery shell drop," wrote the *New York Times*'s Sydney Schanberg),

the Khmer Rouge was falling back and government troops, for the first time in months, were advancing.

"The enemy offensive to seize Phnom Penh was turned off, and it was turned off by U.S. airpower!" General Vogt declared. The suicidal fanaticism of the Khmer Rouge also played a part, of course, and there was still no promise of negotiations or a settlement. If the Khmer Republic was saved in the summer of 1973 it was not for any brighter future; its remaining twenty months, like those before, would be full only of despair, devastation, death, and defeat.

Arnold Isaacs served as a war correspondent in Indochina for the Baltimore Sun from 1972–1975. He is the author of Without Honor, *an account of America's role in Indochina from 1972–1975, and is currently a free-lance writer living in Maryland.*

Among the 425 casualties of the accidental B-52 bombing of Neak Luong in Cambodia were this mother and child.

adopted the view of the South Vietnamese command that, in effect, defined ARVN cease-fire violations out of existence. The ARVN leaders argued that they had a right to operate anywhere in the country since they represented the sole legitimate government. Thus, according to the DAO's chief intelligence officer, Colonel William Le Gro, "RVNAF ground operations resulting in combat were not reported as South Vietnamese cease-fire violations."

Informal sources, such as journalists, were not able to offer much assistance either. Their numbers drastically reduced with the withdrawal of American troops, lacking the logistical cooperation that MACV had formerly provided to transport them around the country, and faced with President Thieu's deep suspicions and animosity, the international press corps drastically curtailed its visits to battlefields for firsthand reports of the fighting. Journalists became dependent on official South Vietnamese briefings. Nor was the report from Hanoi on the first anniversary of the cease-fire that "the Saigon administration [had] committed 301,097 violations" of much use to the serious observer.

The best evidence, in fact, comes from snippets and inadvertent phrases used in the secret DAO reports sent to Washington every three months. In its reports following the June 12 communiqué the DAO made the following comments:

On the PRG:	"Since the announcement of the 'new' ceasefire on 15 June the enemy has been reemphasizing the political struggle."
On Saigon:	"Current activity ... is the result of RVNAF attempts to eliminate Communist influence in the coastal lowlands."
On the PRG:	"The Communists, though reacting sharply to government attacks, were carrying out very few attacks of their own."
On Saigon:	"Aggressive ARVN operations against communist strongholds have continued following ceasefire II."
On the PRG:	"Generally speaking, enemy actions in the past month have been defensive."

The enemy was not entirely silent. Following cease-fire II the Communists maintained a siege of the Tong Le Chan Ranger outpost in MR 3, first attacked in late March. The NVA continued to fire artillery and rocket shells into the camp in the hopes of driving out the South Vietnamese forces. The Rangers received support from the South Vietnamese air force, depending upon airlift for all resupply efforts. The battle continued in stalemate throughout the summer months.

President Thieu and high-ranking officers inspect a cache of enemy weapons captured during ARVN offensive operations in Binh Dinh Province.

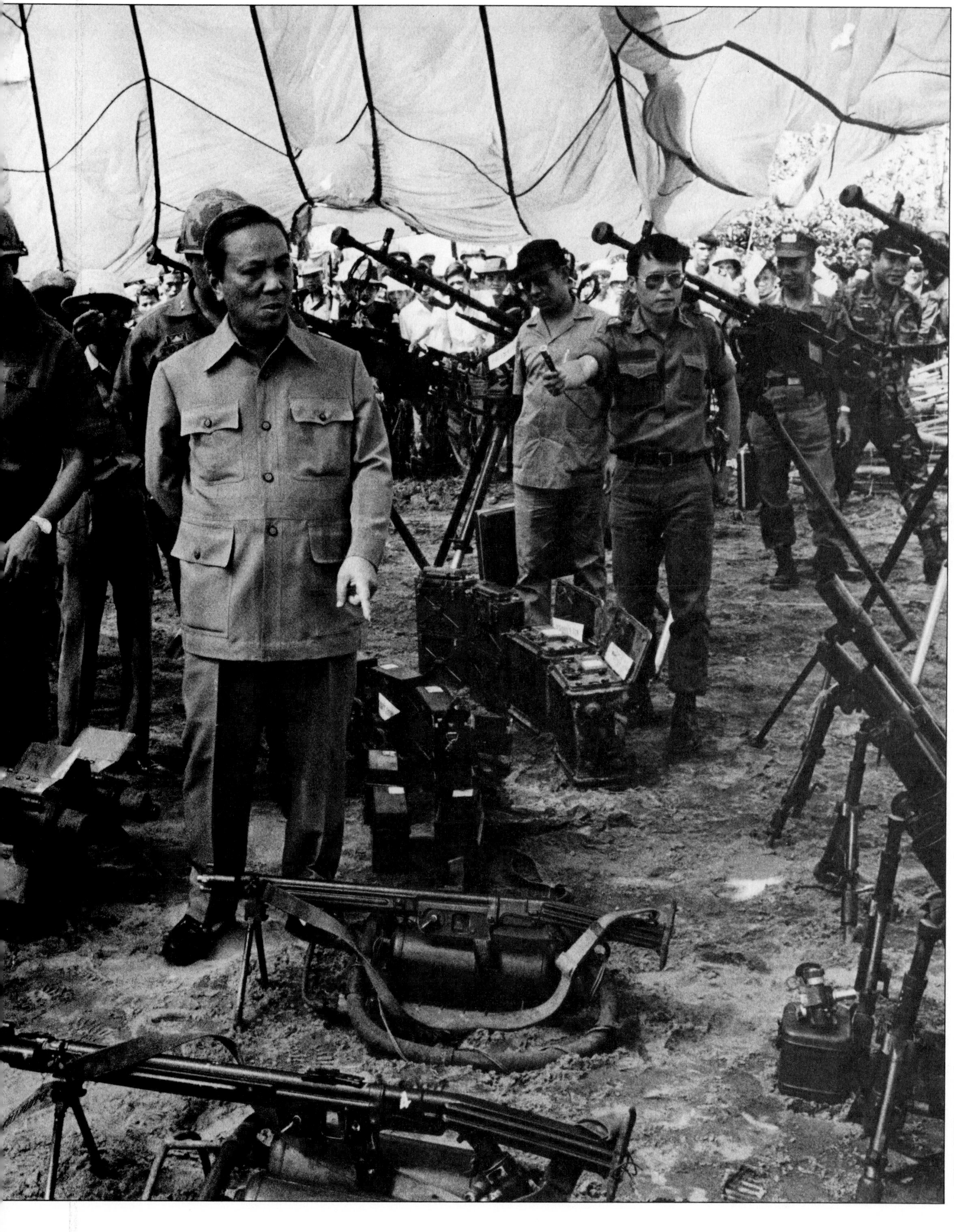

The Communists also attacked the district capital of Hong Ngu in northern Kien Phong Province, along the Cambodian border. This was part of a broader NVA effort to eliminate South Vietnamese pockets of control along the boundary between the two countries. Most of the area was already held by the PRG.

South Vietnamese efforts, however, were far more ambitious and centered on the country's two most populous regions, the coastal lowlands and the environs of Saigon, including the Mekong Delta. President Thieu had been kept carefully informed, sometimes on a daily basis, of the improvement in Communist logistics. He wanted to strike and consolidate his military position before the North Vietnamese were able to respond. Most ARVN operations, therefore, were part of a pacification drive designed to bring more hamlets and people under government control. This "pacification" effort, however, seldom went beyond a purely military "clearing and holding" operation. The Da Nang-Hue area received a high priority from ARVN commanders. In the wake of the 1972 Communist offensive, the refugee population in the region had risen to over 600,000. The South Vietnamese hoped to resettle more than half of them in their native villages by wresting those areas from Communist control. According to a DAO summary of the operations, "While the ARVN 3rd Division concentrated south and west of Danang, the ARVN 2nd Division had the formidable task of securing the coastal piedmont and plains from the Binh Dinh boundary north to Tam Ky in Quang Tin province, a distance of 135 kilometers." Confronted by only a few weak VC units, the 2nd Division achieved "substantial success . . . continuing the pressure on local VC units until they withdrew into the foothills." Reinforced by a South Vietnamese Ranger battalion, the 2nd Division continued its advance and "pushed into the foothills."

Farther south, ARVN's success was more uneven, and, as always, depended on the quality of the units and their commanders. In Chuong Thien Province ARVN initiated what the DAO called "aggressive . . . operations." There, as elsewhere in the delta, the prize of war was not only control of the population but the rice harvest as well. Chuong Thien was known as the "bottom of the rice bowl" and the "hub of the delta." Unfortunately the ARVN offensive was carried out by the ARVN 21st Division. The Defense Attaché Office rated it as one of the poorest divisions in South Vietnam:

Morale is low and the Division suffers from unimaginative and indecisive leadership. Individual misdeeds, coupled with the misuse of firepower, especially artillery, has made this Division's presence a pacification liability.

The division engaged in few aggressive actions and let the more poorly trained Territorial Forces take the brunt of enemy pressure. As a result, the Communists were able to maintain their dominance of the province and with it access to the valuable rice.

Rice was also the object of a more successful ARVN operation in the Seven Mountains region of MR 3's Chau Doc Province, long an enemy stronghold. The Seven Mountains served as a southern terminus of the Ho Chi Minh Trail as it crossed from Cambodia into South Vietnam. The 1st NVA Division, located there, was dependent for resupply on the lucrative illegal commerce, especially in rice, that crossed over from Cambodia into its region. In early July

ARVN's 7th Ranger Group and 4th Armor Group initiated a "slow and costly campaign to destroy the remaining elements of the NVA's 1st Division" and thereby close the route of this illicit commerce.

There were frequent firefights all during July and August as the South Vietnamese attempted to dislodge the NVA from their mountain bunkers. Just as it appeared in late August that the two sides were locked in an unbreakable stalemate, a Tong Le Chan in reverse, the NVA withdrew from the region to reassemble across the border in Cambodia. Records of the 101st Regiment, captured after the battle, revealed that 900 soldiers had died due to a combination of disease and ARVN firepower. On October 2 ARVN learned that the 1st NVA Division had been deactivated.

ARVN victories mounted up through the year. Few were on the scale of the Seven Mountains campaign; most were undramatic successes taking control of isolated villages from the enemy. But cumulatively they took their toll. By the end of 1973 South Vietnam had brought an additional 1 million people under its control, roughly half of those who had lived under Communist rule at the time of the cease-fire. In addition, they had reduced Communist-controlled territory by 15 to 20 percent. With both sides routinely violating the Paris treaty it was somewhat remarkable that the Pentagon could announce at the end of the year, "The South Vietnamese, by comparison with the North Vietnamese, have been exemplary in adhering to the ceasefire agreement."

Communists fighting in South Vietnam naturally thought otherwise. In their view, the cautious policy adopted by the Politburo had permitted South Vietnam to turn the strategic table on them. With their forces largely in a "defensive posture," the RVNAF could attack at the time and place of its own choosing. The insurgents had forfeited the advantages of surprise and mobility that had been their main assets throughout the conflict. With the mounting casualties and loss of territory, resentment of and opposition to the strategy ordered in Hanoi began to surface. Only the Politburo could alter that policy and, in the meantime, the southern forces would have to bide their time.

It was not a situation that the Communists could long endure without forfeiting their hard-won position in the South. Noting the impasse in the political negotiations, American and South Vietnamese intelligence analysts became increasingly concerned about the possibility of a change in Hanoi's strategy. While they were trying to determine whether and how the enemy would react, the NVA struck.

On September 22, 1973, a tank-supported regiment of the NVA's 320th Division suddenly attacked the Le Minh Ranger border camp, an outpost also known as Plei Djereng, just forty kilometers west of Pleiku City. It was the first time since the cease-fire that the enemy had mounted an attack of such size. For the South Vietnamese defenders, whose cease-fire military superiority was rapidly ebbing, it was a dangerous portent of the future.

Communist guerrillas display a captured government soldier before the residents of a Vietcong-held village in 1973.

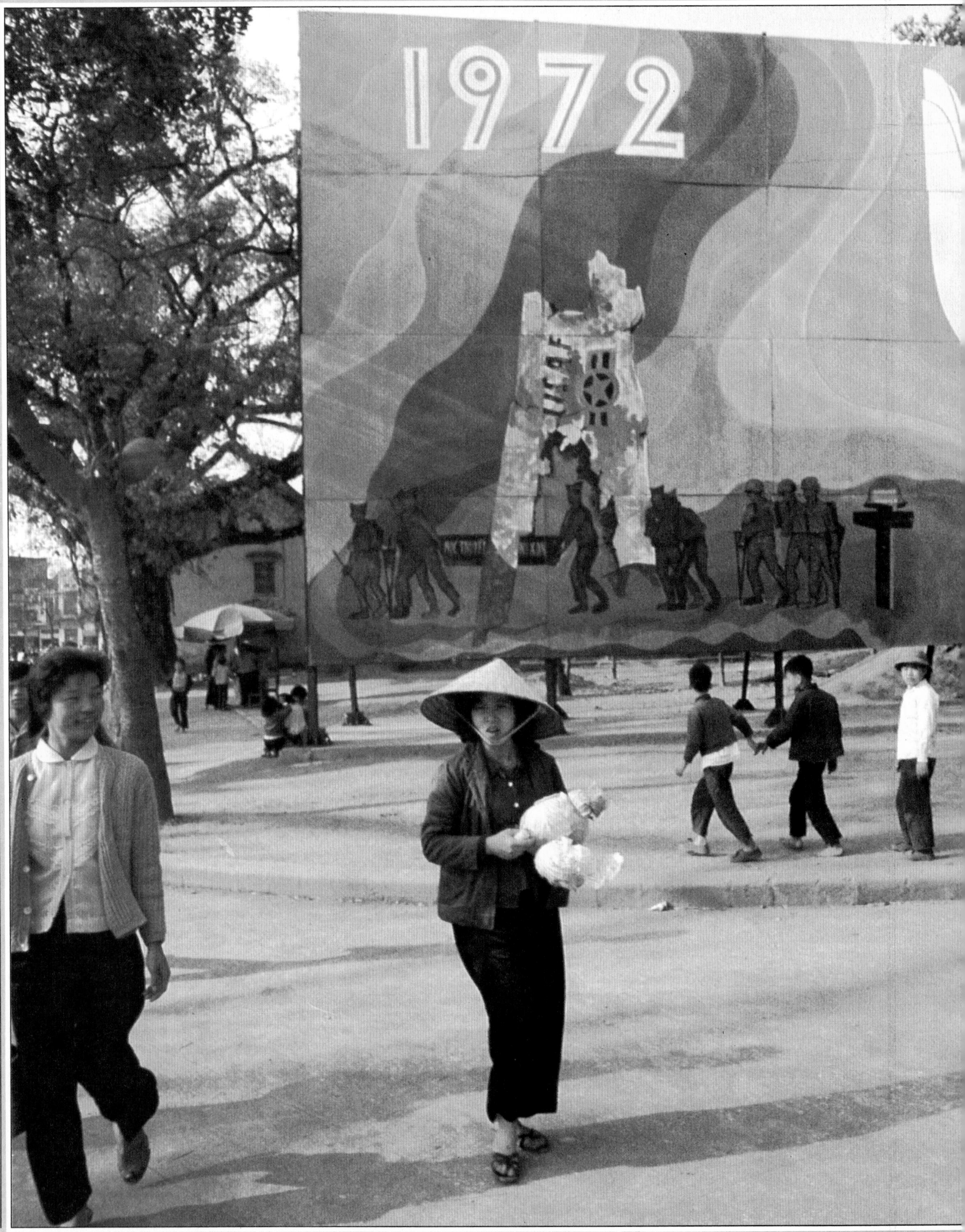
1972

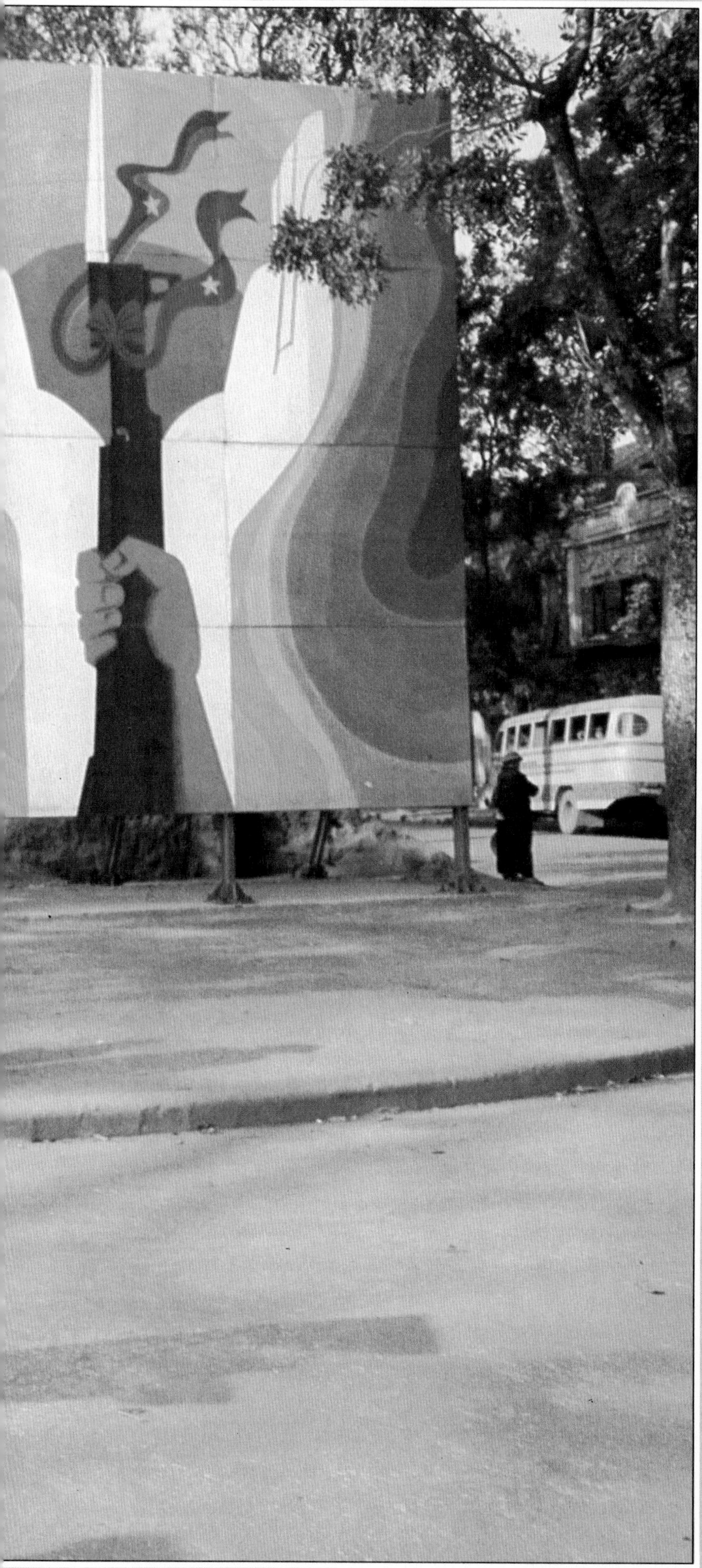

The Word War

The Vietnam War was waged not only with weaponry and tactics but also with propaganda. The governments of both North and South Vietnam used every means at their disposal to rouse support from the population. Slogans and symbolic messages were shaped to depict the savagery of the enemy and to celebrate the strength, righteousness, and perseverance of their own side.

The North Vietnamese favored posters and murals as forms of propaganda. For example, to commemorate a U.S. bombing operation, political posters were often erected at or near the area of destruction.

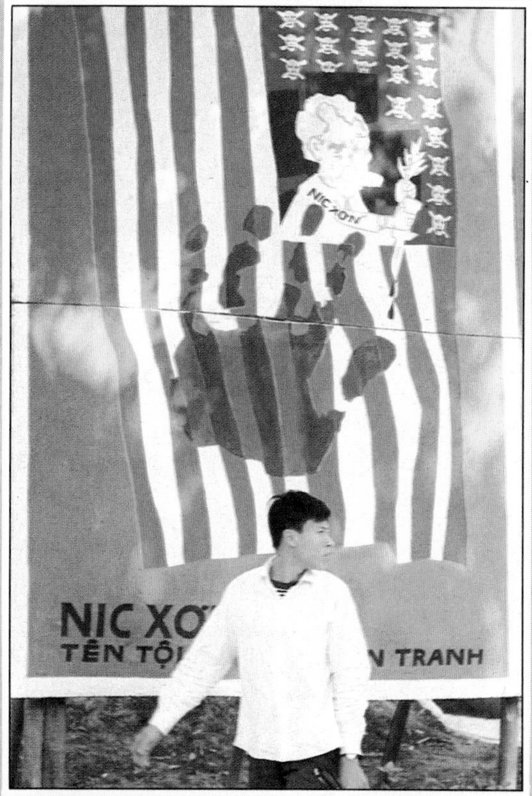
NICXON
NIC XO
TÊN TỘI
N TRANH

Hanoi recalls the 1972 Christmas bombings. Left. A park mural. Underneath the damaged aircraft wing "The Nixon Doctrine" appears on a coffin. Above. "Nixon the War Criminal" proclaims a poster.

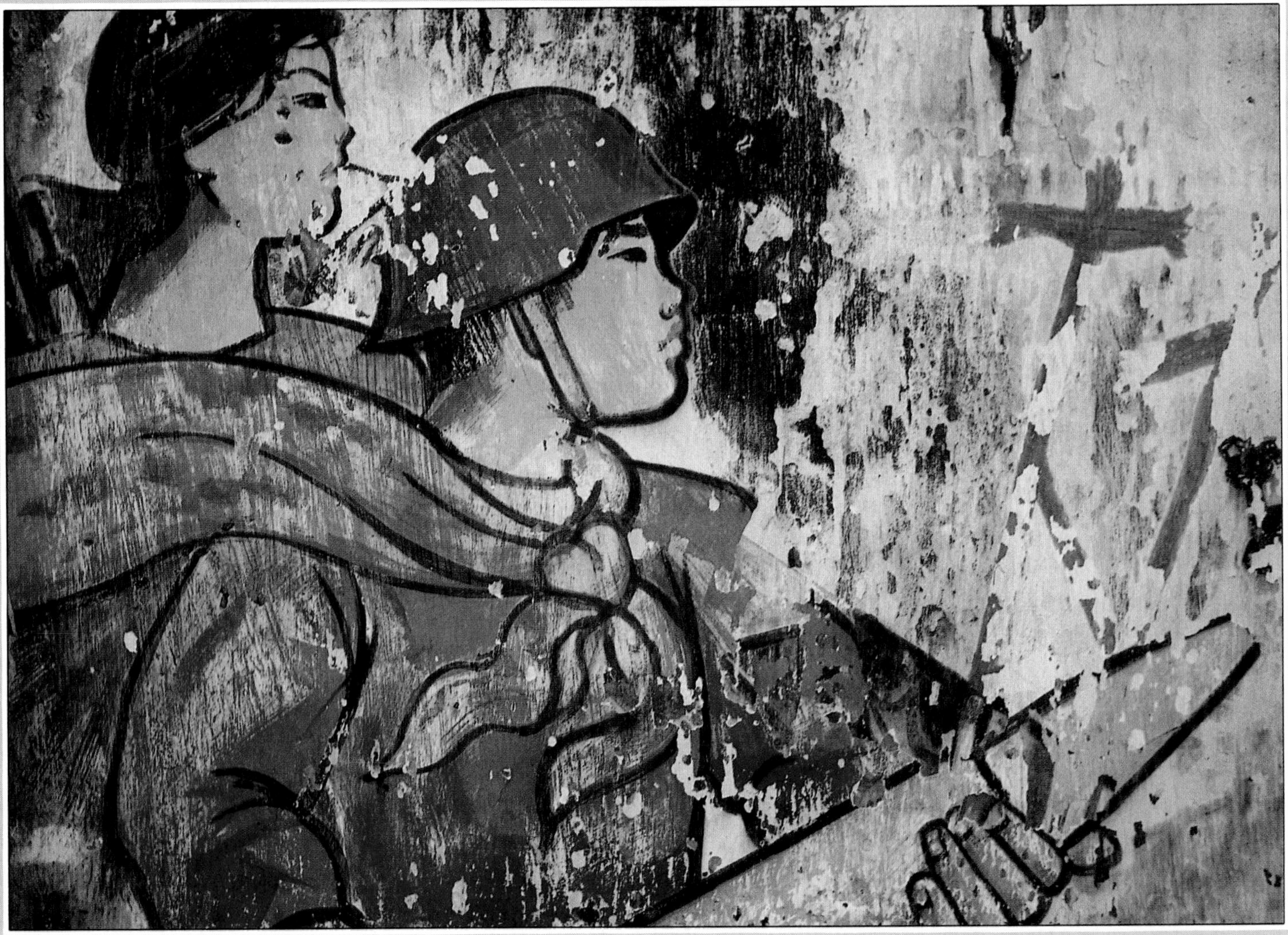

Northern Murals

In addition to propagandistic goals, the murals painted by the North Vietnamese served two other purposes: to decorate the villages and to repair bombed-out buildings inexpensively. Frequently, after a strike, damaged buildings were first whitewashed and then painted over with a decorative and "informational" mural. Cheaper to produce than posters, murals painted by trained artists were displayed throughout the North. Hanoi would send art students to the villages to paint them, often as part of their military service.

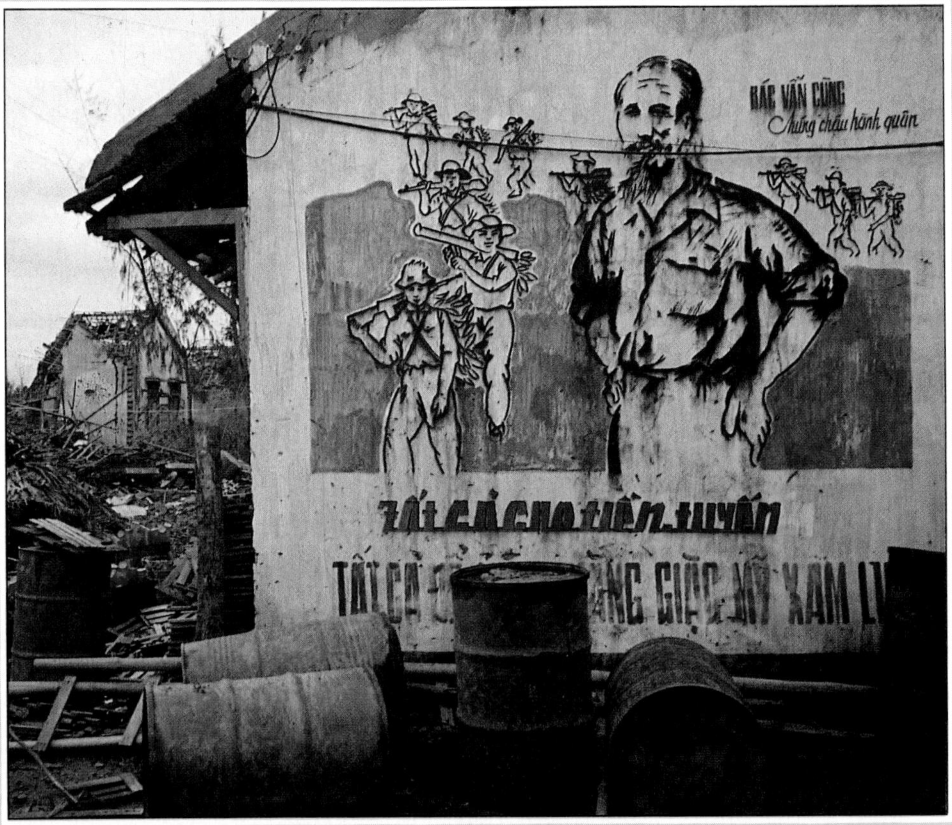
BÁC VẪN CÙNG
Chúng cháu hành quân
TẤT CẢ CHO TIỀN TUYẾN

Above. A mural in Phat Diem shows male and female militia members on the wall of a bombed-out Catholic cathedral. *Right.* Near Vinh, a mural declares that "Uncle Ho is still marching with us." *Opposite.* A mural near Thanh Hoa encourages agricultural production.

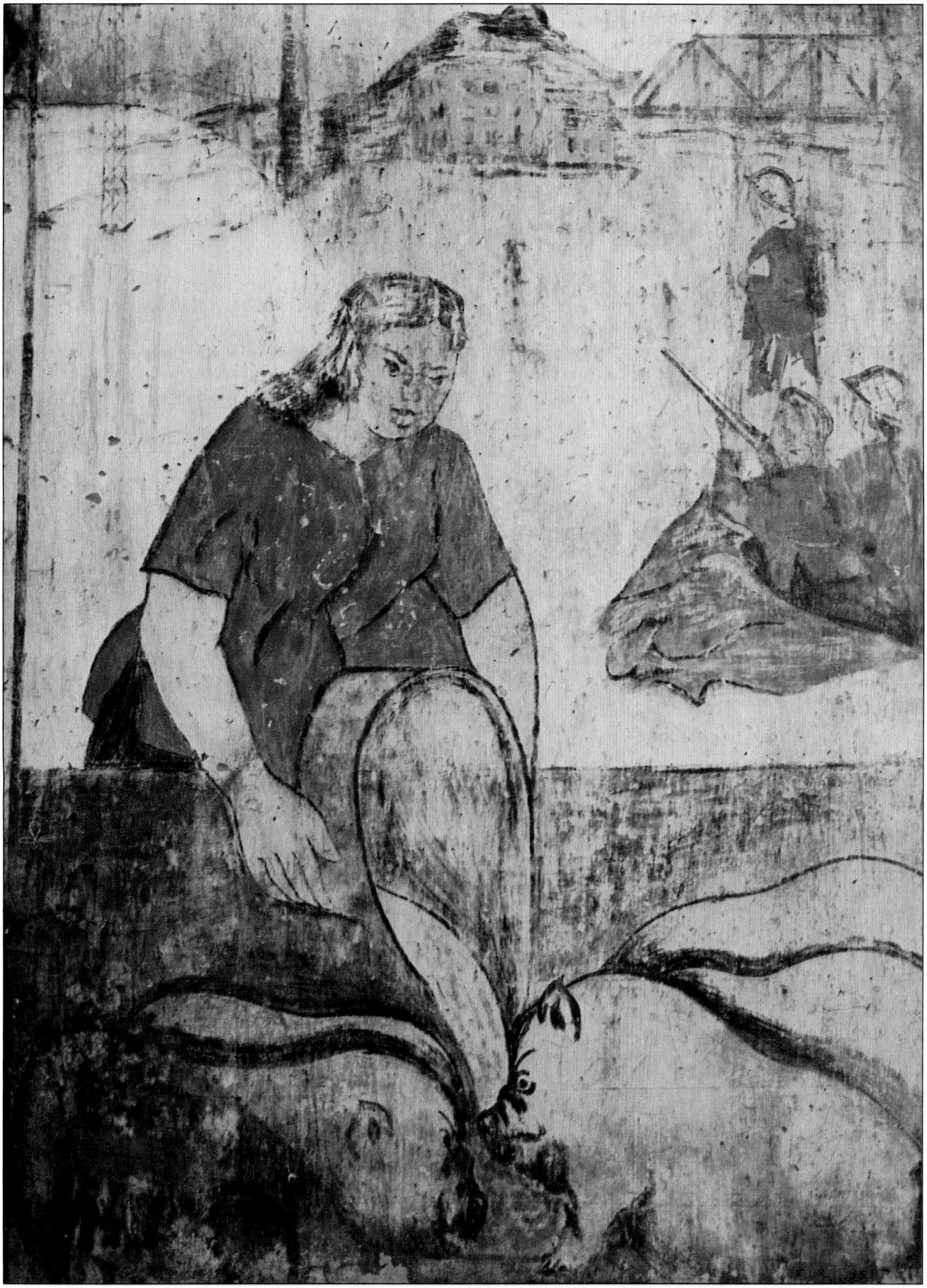

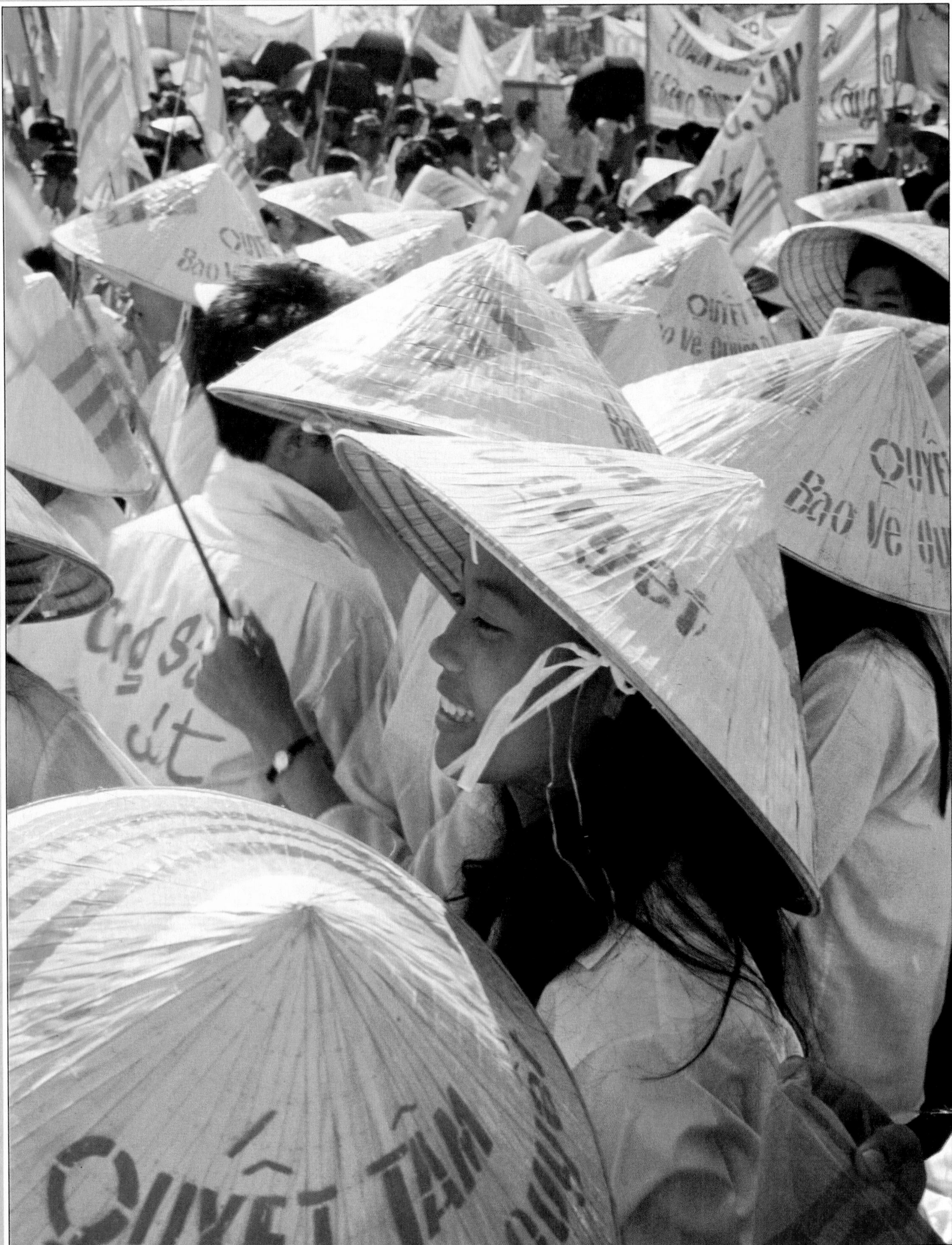

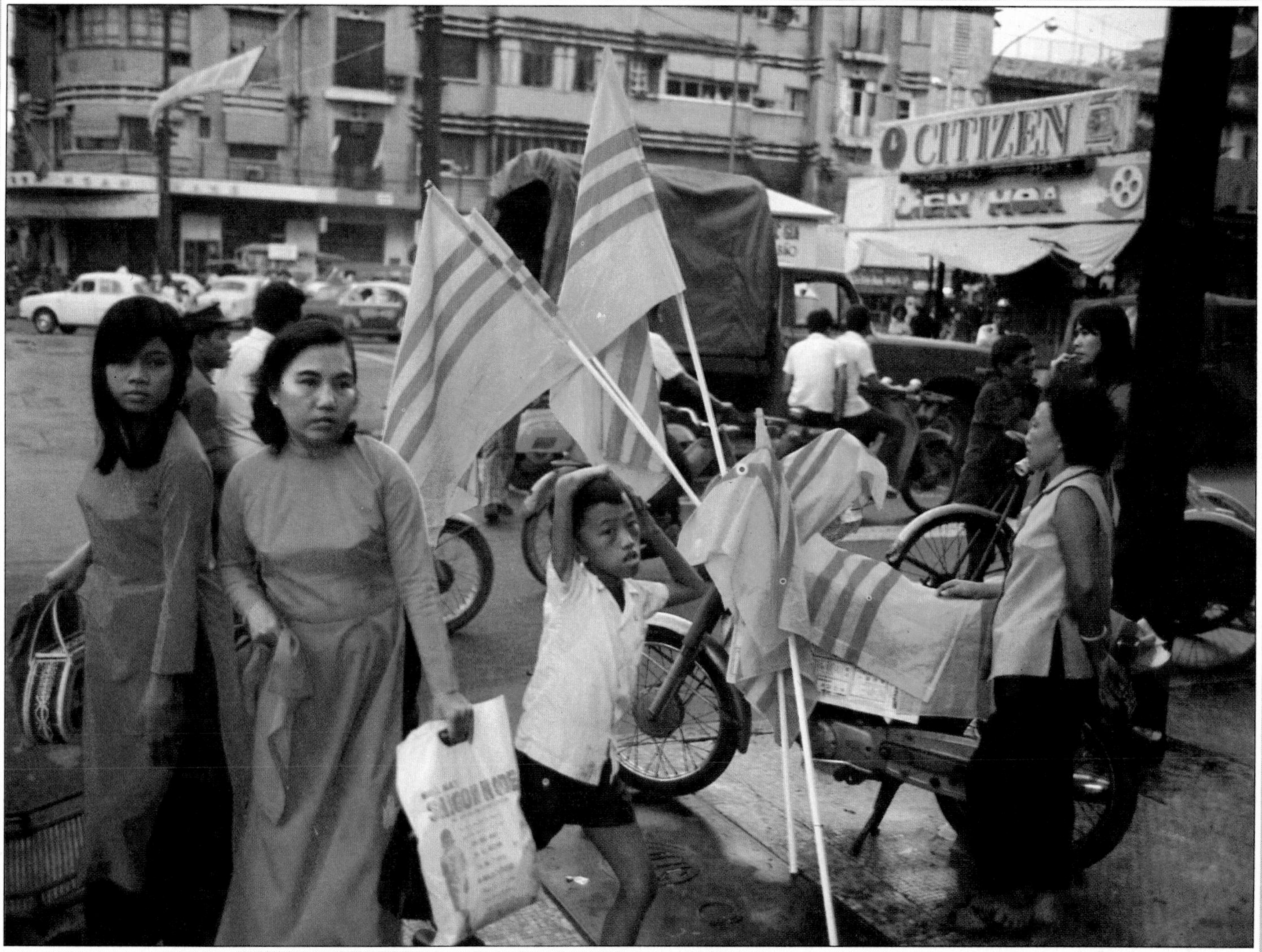
CITIZEN

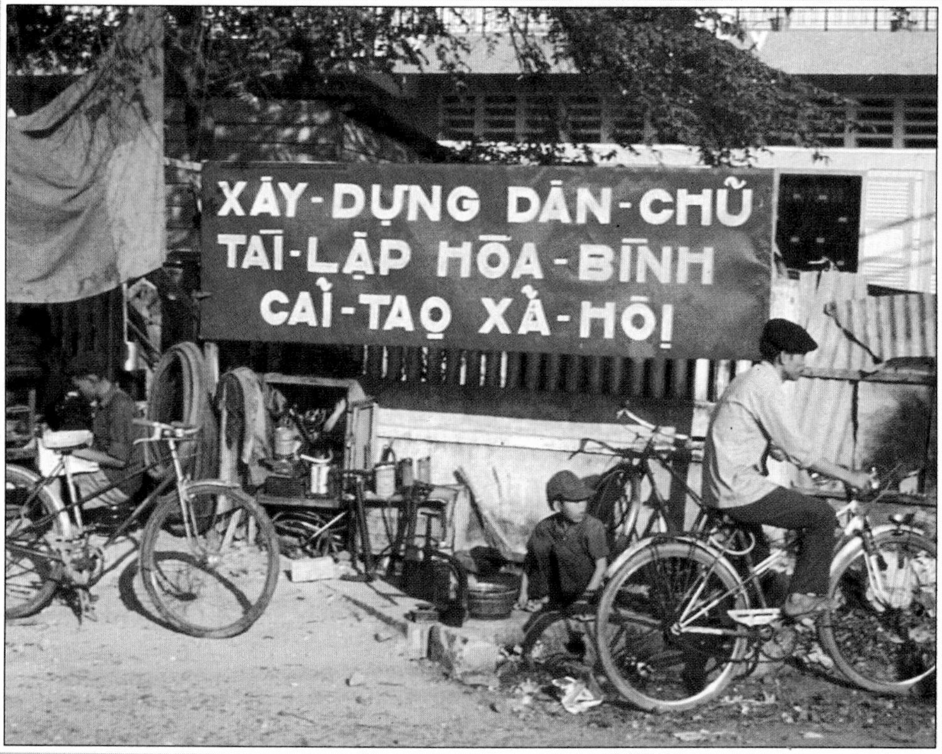
XÂY-DỰNG DÂN-CHỦ
TÁI-LẬP HÒA-BÌNH
CẢI-TẠO XÃ-HỘI

GVN Flag-Waving

The South Vietnamese government employed more conventional and, generally, less artistic approaches to propaganda. In addition to using billboards and paintings, the GVN focused its propaganda drives on the red and yellow flag of the Republic of Vietnam to arouse nationalistic sentiments among the population. Just prior to the cease-fire, Saigon ordered everyone to fly the flag and thereby announce their loyalty to the GVN.

Opposite. *South Vietnamese show their opposition to a coalition government in November 1972. Their hats declare, "We are determined to protect our self-determination."* Above. *Saigon street vendors sell the South Vietnamese flag.* Left. *"Build democracy, re-establish peace, reform society," reads a sign in Quang Ngi.*

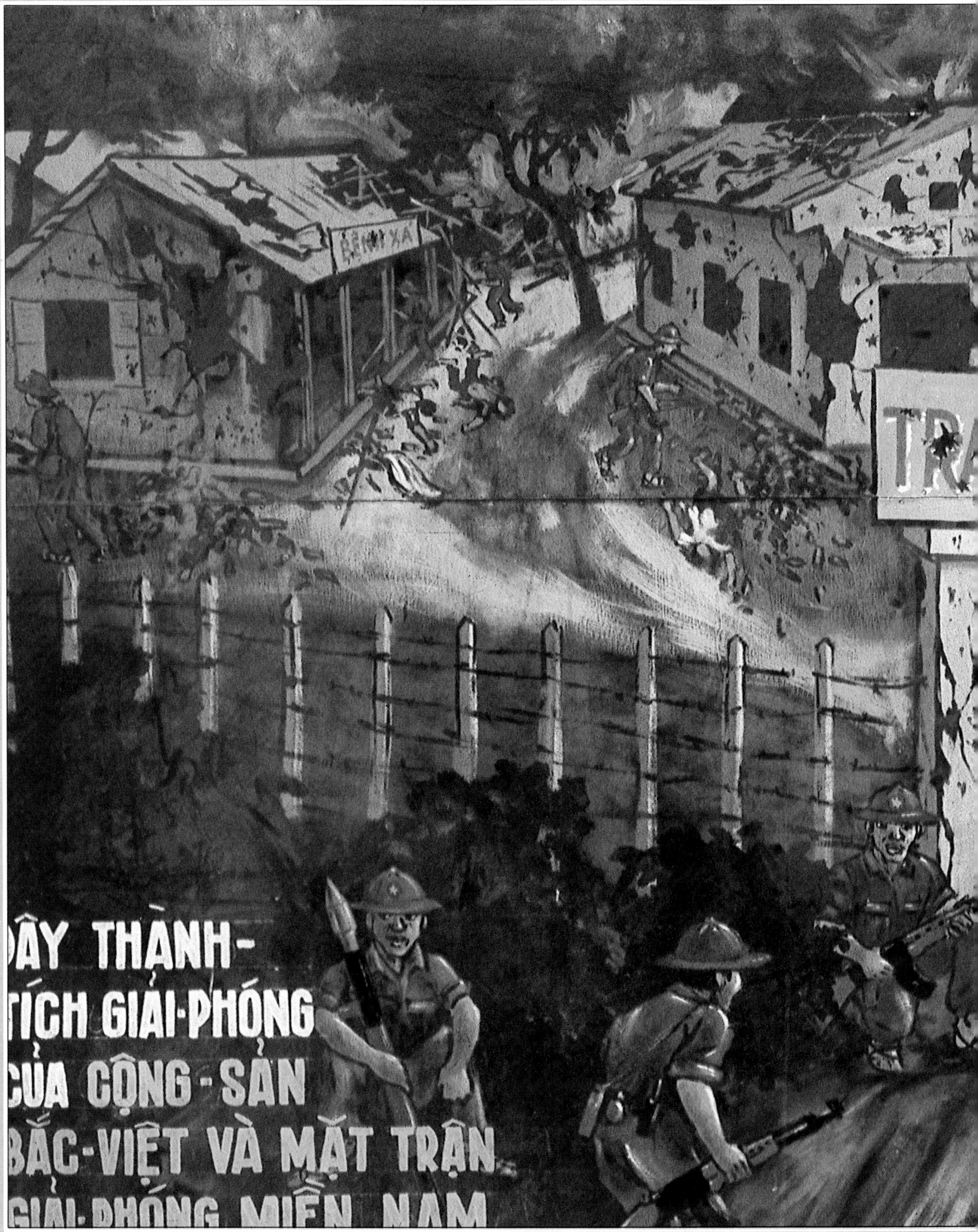
ĐÂY THÀNH-
TÍCH GIẢI-PHÓNG
CỦA CỘNG-SẢN
BẮC-VIỆT VÀ MẶT TRẬN
GIẢI-PHÓNG MIỀN NAM

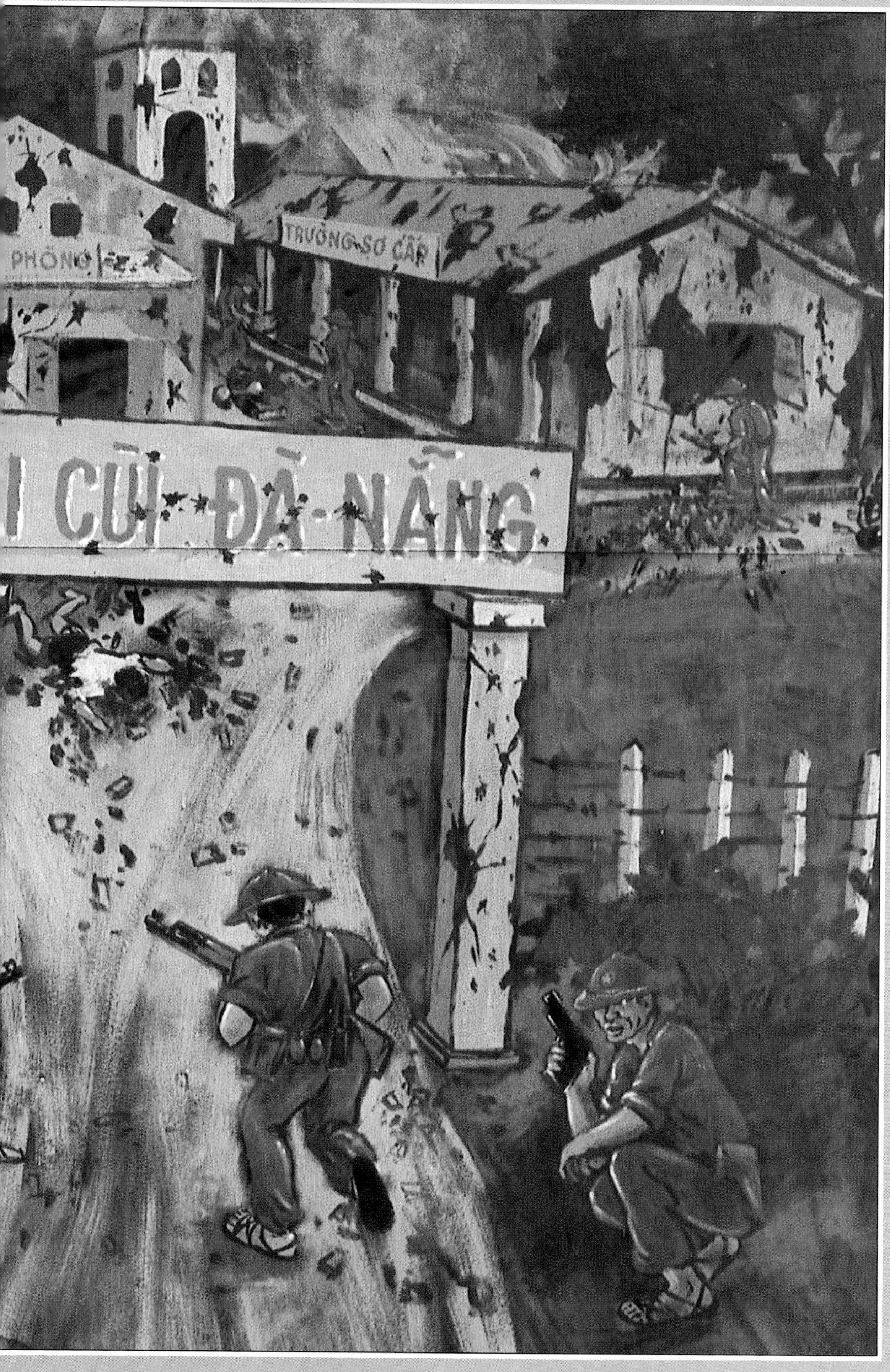
PHÒNG
TRƯỜNG SƠ CẤP
I CŨI ĐÃ-NẴNG

Propaganda, South Vietnamese style. This painting depicts a guerrilla attack on a leper sanatorium in Da Nang. The building at left is the medical building, at center is the administrative building, and at right is the grade school. The slogan below translates, "This is how the NLF liberates."

America at Peace

It was 10:12 in the morning on March 21, 1973, White House logs show, when the president's personal attorney, White House Counsel John Dean, entered the Oval Office. The boyish-looking young lawyer did not display his usual assurance. His voice quivered. With H. R. Haldeman—the president's closest assistant—and the revolving reels of a hidden tape recorder as his only witnesses, he told Richard Nixon, "I have, uh, uh, I have the impression that you don't know everything I know." On the essential point he was eloquent and obviously well prepared: "Mr. President, we have a cancer close to the Presidency, that's growing. It's growing daily. It's compounding." The political scandal known as Watergate no longer threatened only the president's most trusted advisers. It threatened to engulf Richard Nixon himself.

It was one of Richard Nixon's most ironic moments in the White House. Only two months had passed since his inauguration for a second term

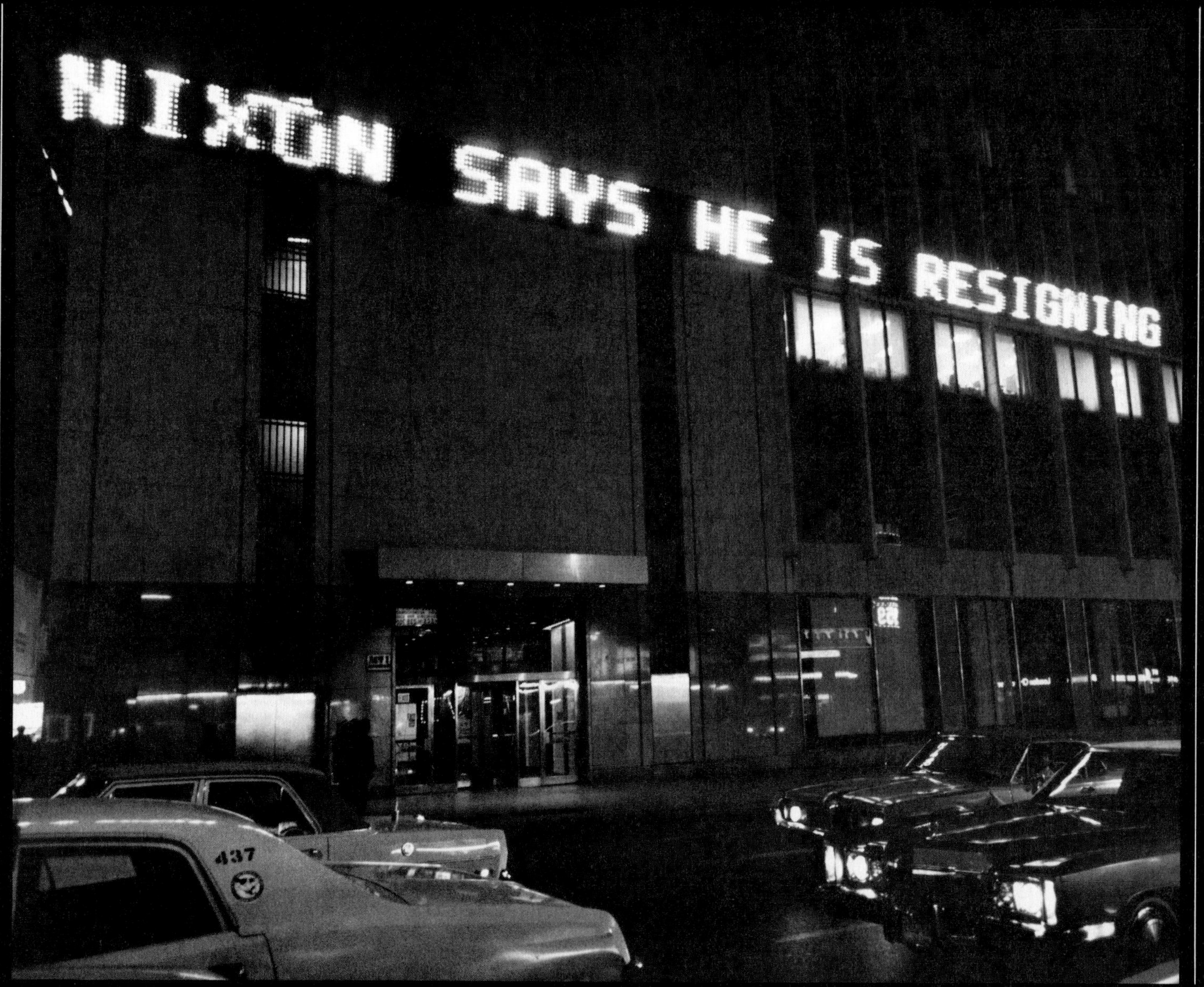
NIXON SAYS HE IS RESIGNING
437

after winning the approval of an unprecedented number of American voters. In public opinion polls his popularity hovered near the 70 percent mark. Now it was all slipping away, strangling in the quicksand of lies and deceit provoked by a clumsy burglary of the headquarters of the opposition party. Adding to the irony of the president's confrontation with his young assistant was the knowledge that his most emotional achievement in foreign diplomacy was only one week away: The last contingent of American troops and prisoners of war as well would be returning from Indochina. America's Vietnam era was giving way, imperceptibly, to the era of Watergate.

Coming home

The United States Army history of the Four-Party Joint Military Commission would later describe the repatriation of 653 prisoners of war held by the Communists—civilian and military personnel—and the withdrawal of the final 24,000 American troops in Vietnam as the "major accomplishment" of its work. That paragraph (a) of Article 8 alone among the provisions of the Paris agreement should be the single unequivocal success of Henry Kissinger's diplomacy was not accidental. He had appended to the agreement a protocol that explained how the POWs were to be released. All would be freed within sixty days of the signing of the agreement, in four increments fifteen days apart. Most important, the remaining American troops on active duty in Vietnam would depart simultaneously. If there were a delay in the release of POWs, the United States would delay the withdrawal of its troops. If Hanoi threatened not to repatriate the prisoners, American troops would remain in Vietnam indefinitely. It was a recipe that guaranteed success but not without some tense moments caused by Hanoi's intransigence and the strong sense of discipline of the American POWs.

The first release was scheduled for February 12, with 115 men listed by Hanoi and an additional 27 listed by the Vietcong. When American officials arrived in Hanoi on February 12 they learned that the North Vietnamese had added an additional prisoner to the list, navy Lieutenant Commander Brian Woods, whose mother was critically ill. It was, said the Communists, a sign of "good will." At Hanoi's Gia Lam airport an imaginary line served as a boundary between the United States and North Vietnam. On one side of the line a North Vietnamese officer ordered: "American captured military personnel, listen to your name called and step out." As each name was called, the prisoner strode across the line to safety and freedom.

The first release proceeded without a hitch. Future smoothness seemed assured when only a few days later North Vietnam announced that it would release an additional twenty prisoners ahead of schedule in honor of Henry Kissinger's visit to Hanoi. The release was set for February 18. When American officials arrived in Hanoi on that date they received a shocking message. The POWs announced that they would "refuse repatriation" unless directly ordered by a senior American officer.

As mandated by the Paris agreement, each prisoner had received a copy of the protocol on the release of prisoners. The protocol required that prisoners be freed in strict order of their capture. Hanoi's "good will" list of twenty prisoners had violated that rule and the POWs refused to leave. Only after an American officer explained the nature of the special release did the senior American POW grant permission for his men to depart.

During the second regularly scheduled release, it was Hanoi's turn to disturb the repatriation process. On February 26, the date established for the second scheduled release, Hanoi announced that it would not comply unless a variety of demands were met, including the establishment of regularly scheduled liaison flights between Saigon and Hanoi. Brigadier General John A. Wickham, Jr., deputy commander of the U.S. delegation, told the North Vietnamese that while such flights were required by the Paris agreement, they were not linked to the release of POWs. Wickham immediately informed the White House, and President Nixon ordered that withdrawal of American troops from South Vietnam be halted. Hanoi relented, and the second release took place on March 4.

Problems and delays affected the third and fourth increments of the process as well, but with the withdrawal of U.S. troops as leverage, the Americans on the Four-Party JMC were able to overcome all obstacles. The last of the prisoners were freed from Hanoi on March 28 and 29, only twenty-four hours behind schedule.

Each group of prisoners made its trip home according to a procedure the Pentagon called Operation Homecoming. Flown initially to Clark Air Force Base in the Philippines, each former POW was met by an "escort officer." The escort was carefully chosen, sometimes from among the friends of the POW or from active duty personnel with similar age, rank, family status, and interests. According to his orders, the escort was to be a "sort of combination valet-confidant-public relations man." His job was to smooth the prisoner's transition to freedom and to shield him from the press. At Clark Air Force Base each former prisoner was examined by medical personnel and brought up-to-date on personal family news, his accrued salary, promotions, and decorations. As doctors declared each one physically fit for travel, he was transferred to the

---

Preceding page. *The news flashes in New York City's Times Square on August 8, 1974: President Richard M. Nixon will resign his office.*

Right. *At Hanoi's Gia Lam Airport on February 12, 1973, an American air force officer greets the first group of U.S. pilots freed from North Vietnamese prisons.*

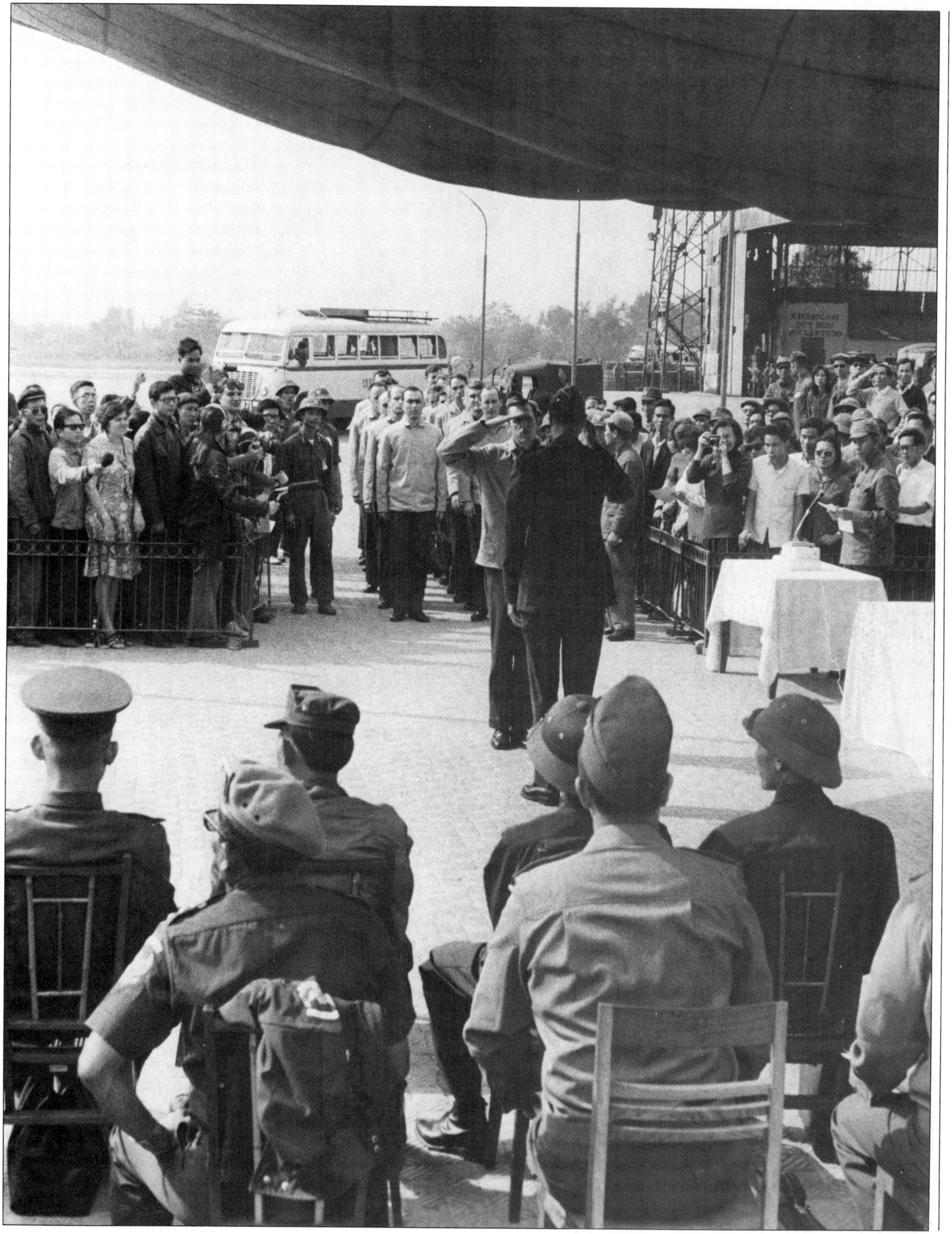

Communist Homecoming

American POWs were not the only ones whose freedom was secured by the Paris peace accords. South Vietnam released more than 25,000 enemy soldiers to the Four-Party JMC for return to the Communist side. Some Communist prisoners refused repatriation and, despite protests by the North Vietnamese, were sent to South Vietnamese Chieu Hoi centers. Those who did choose to rejoin their comrades shed the prison clothing provided by their South Vietnamese captors and returned in their skivvies. Most of the ex-captives soon found themselves again in regular army units.

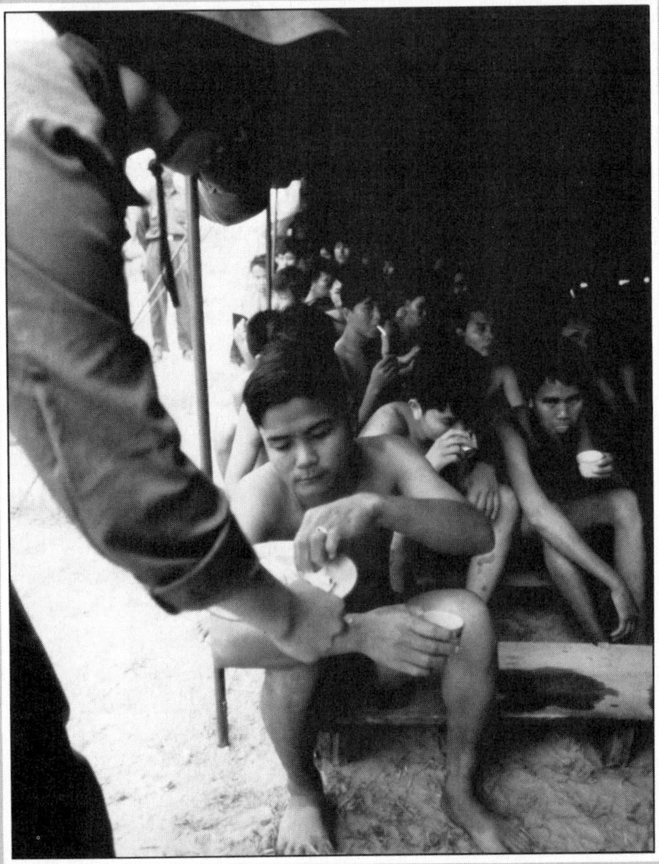

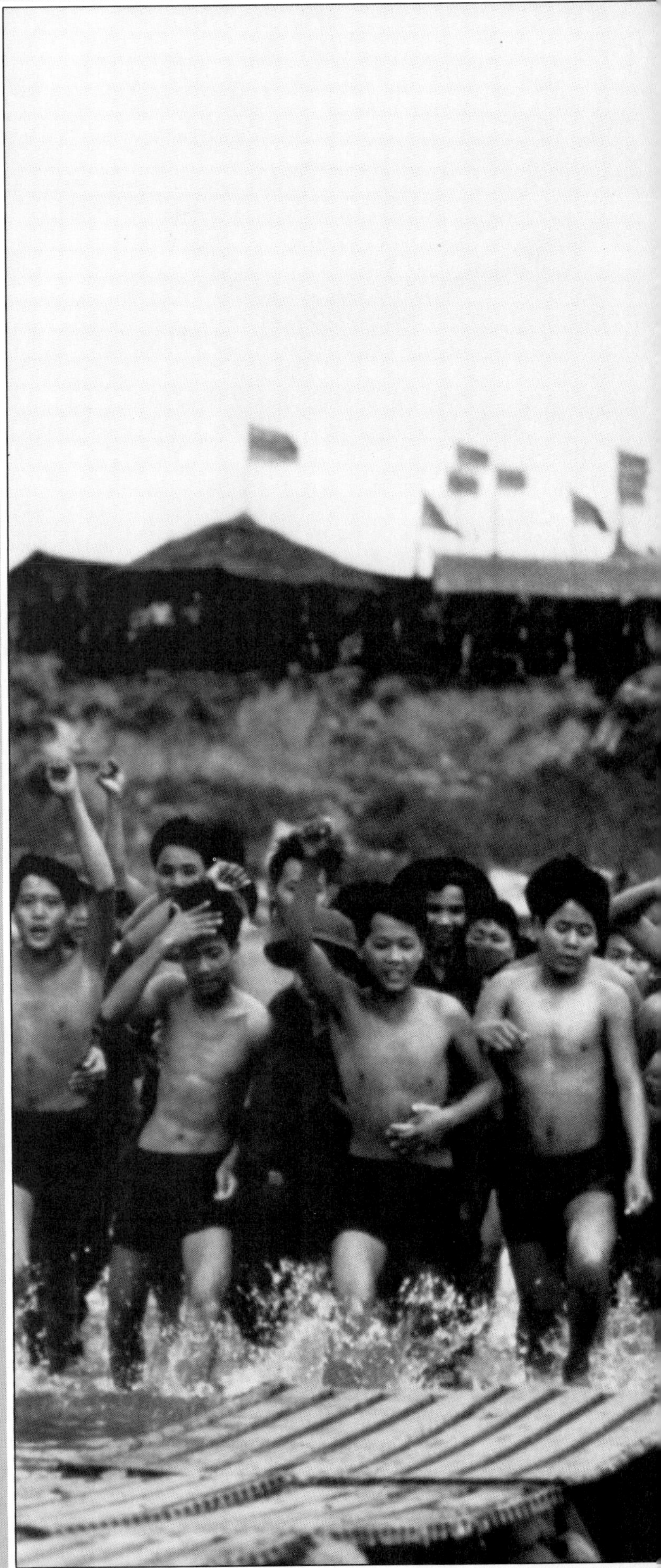

Right. *With a gate and South Vietnamese flags marking the two Vietnams' border, former prisoners of the GVN, escorted by Communist members of the JMC, wade across the Thach Han River to rejoin their comrades on North Vietnamese soil.* Above. *Once ashore, they are greeted with hot tea and cigarettes.*

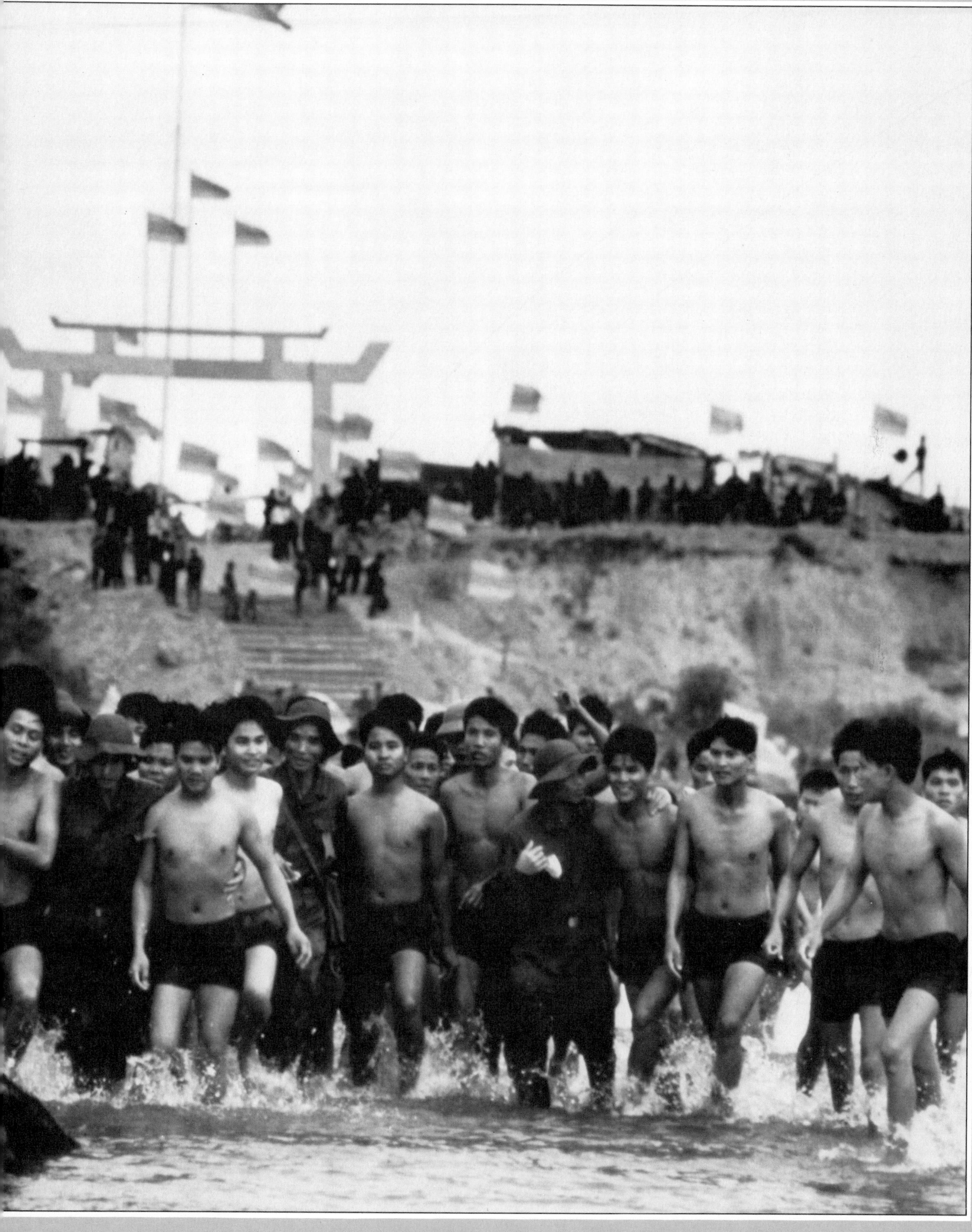

military hospital closest to his home. It was there that he would at last be reunited with his family.

The operation at Clark ran smoothly until it ran afoul of the freed men's appetites. Hoping to avoid a mistake made following World War II and Korea, doctors placed the former POWs on bland diets. The men would have nothing to do with it. "We've been thinking of ice cream for years," said one of the POWs as he and his mates wolfed down banana splits. No known casualties resulted from the breach of procedure.

For all their trying, the organizers of Operation Homecoming could not protect the men from the inquisitiveness of the press. According to the Defense Department, "It is neither dishonorable nor heroic to be taken prisoner. In the sense that the victim does not covet it, but finds himself unable to avoid it, capture is an accident." This rational assessment, however, gave way to the greater need of the American people to identify heroes from Vietnam. While the POWs may not have fit the classic description of war heroes, their survival in North Vietnamese prisons was heroic by any definition. By withstanding the longest captivity of any POWs in American history with determination and loyalty, they gave the public a sense of pride that had for the most part not marked the Vietnam experience. And the media were more than willing to give the American people what they wanted.

While much of the reporting was tasteful, some bordered on the grotesque. When air force Colonel Robert Purcell placed his first phone call to his wife after more than seven years in North Vietnamese prison camps, American television crews were on hand at the Purcell home to bring the intimate event live to the American public. Mrs. Purcell said, "The people of the news media have helped me all the way and have publicized the cause of the POWs."

Hundreds of small towns across America welcomed their own personal hero home. Thirty thousand people lined the streets of Burley, Idaho, to welcome back air force Captain Larry Chesley. "Cheers, Tears, Welcome Captain Chesley Home," ran the headline of the *South Idaho Press.* A parade was followed by a program in the high-school gymnasium where the people of Burley gave him a special Christmas party, with tree, carol singing, and a Santa Claus, to make up for the seven Christmases he had missed as a POW. Capt. Chesley's response: "I had dreamed in prison about my homecoming, but Burley's welcome outdistanced any possible imaginings by a million miles."

There was, of course, a less happy side to the homecoming. For over 1,300 families of men missing in action, it was an empty event. The release of the final POWs was yet another blow to their dim hopes of ever seeing their

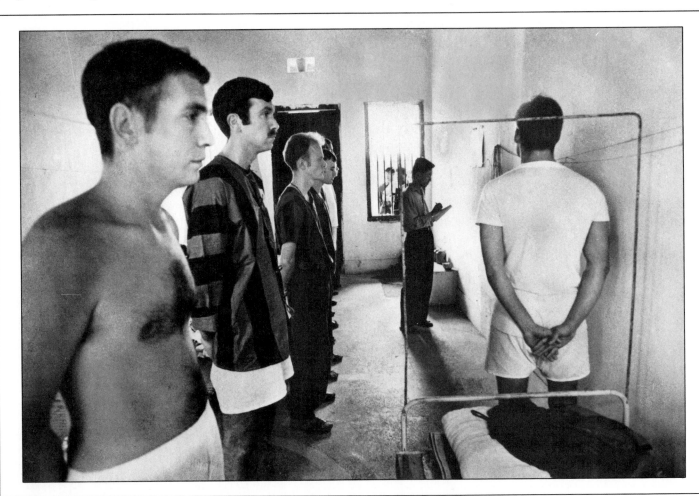

loved ones again alive. Yet few of these families would give up their struggle, if not to find their sons and husbands living at least to provide their remains with a decent resting place (see sidebar, page 78).

Those who did return home had their own darker secrets as well. Journalists watching the former prisoners arrive in the Philippines marveled at their physical condition, especially when compared with returning POWs from previous wars. Many assumed from this that the conditions of their imprisonment had been relatively benign, but soon the contrary became apparent. Under orders from the Pentagon the men would not discuss their treatment in Hanoi's jails. Only in April, when the last POWs had been returned, was the "Secret Agony of the POWs," as *Newsweek* headlined the story, told to the American people.

The treatment the POWs suffered in Hanoi "read like an index to the Marquis de Sade," wrote *Newsweek*. Commander Richard A. Stratton described having his wrists secured with manacles that were slowly tightened with a wrench, leaving him with scars he called his "Hanoi bracelet." His interrogator stuffed Stratton's mouth with sand soaked in urine and burned his body with cigarettes. "You better believe I talked," Stratton admitted. But his resistance still flickering in spite of the torture, Stratton posed for a picture showing him in an exaggerated bow

to his captors, a photograph he hoped the world would recognize as coerced.

Colonel Fred V. Cherry, the senior black POW, was tortured for ninety-two consecutive days after his captors failed to crack his stubborn loyalty by appealing to his "blackness." Cherry spit in their eyes and told them he was an *American*. For his courage he suffered a broken rib and punctured lung. Major Robert Jeffrey refused to answer his interrogators and was taken before a firing squad and given his "last chance." Shots rang out—into the air. Navy Lieutenant Commander Rodney Knutsen was beaten unconscious. After suffering a broken nose and cracked front teeth he was turned on his stomach and was "beaten until my buttocks were hamburger," he related. "There was blood spattering against the wall each time the club fell."

Many other factors also conspired to make the early days of freedom difficult. One was simply the passage of time, poignantly expressed by seven-year-old Michael Woods, whose father had been captured five years earlier. "Which one is daddy," he innocently asked when Commander Brian Woods landed in San Diego. Lieutenant Colonel Kenneth North admitted, "It's hard understanding a seventeen-year-old high school senior when you last knew her as a grade school child."

They also faced the enormous cultural changes that

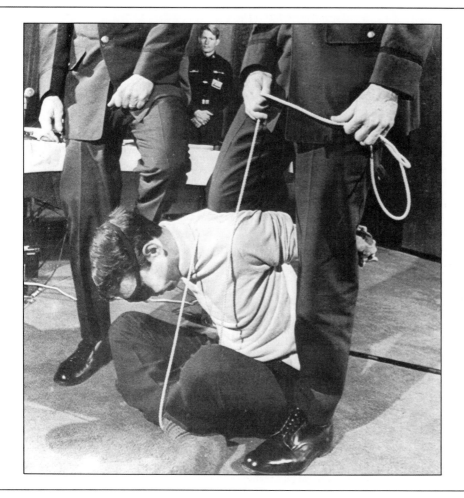

Deceiving Appearances

As viewed from a distance by journalists, the newly freed POWs seemed to be in remarkably fit condition. The American public had to wait to learn of the real conditions in the North Vietnamese camps. So as not to jeopardize their comrades' safety, the first repatriated POWs waited until all had been released before they revealed the full extent of their physical and psychological torture. *Opposite.* Before news came out of the harsh conditions they endured, apparently unharmed POWs 1st Lt. Robert M. Hudson, Capt. Richard T. Simpson, Capt. Robert G. Certain, and Capt. David I. Drummond line up in a North Vietnamese prison dubbed the "Zoo" for their final inspection, witnessed by news reporters, on the day of their release, March 29, 1973. *Left.* Former POWs Lt. Lewis Shattuck (squatting), Col. Laird Guttersen, and Maj. Charles Tyler demonstrate at an April 5, 1973, news conference a torture device called the "rope trick" by POWs and commonly used in Hanoi's jails.

Missing in Action

MIA parents, Mr. and Mrs. Henry Worrell, hold up a picture of their son Paul, whose navy jet was shot down over North Vietnam in 1966.

With a brief barrage of telephone calls from the Pentagon in the first week of February 1973, years of anguish and uncertainty for 562 families came to an abrupt end. Casualty officers assigned in advance to these families brought joyful tidings: The names of their loved ones appeared on the official North Vietnamese list of American POWs who would be released in the aftermath of the Paris peace agreement. These were the fortunate few. For some 1,300 families whose sons and husbands were not on this list, calls from the Pentagon marked the beginning of another bitter siege and seemingly endless waiting. In Georgia, the mother of Captain Larron Murphy, missing since 1970, was one of the unlucky majority. "I'm still expecting my son's name to come up. . . . I'm not going to give up hope," she bravely told reporters.

The task of resolving the problems of the missing in action was charged by the peace accords to the Four-Party Joint Military Team (JMT), comprised of the United States, the Republic of Vietnam (South), and the two Communist delega-

tions, the Democratic Republic of Vietnam (North) and the Provisional Revolutionary Government (Vietcong). Initially, the fourteen military and five civilian American representatives were sanguine about the Communists' intentions to obey the letter of the treaty. Their North Vietnamese counterparts assured them that they would meet their obligations "scrupulously"; information about downed American pilots was already being collected, they said assuringly. In this atmosphere of "friendly cooperation," duly noted in the official record of the JMT negotiations, there was every reason to believe that information about MIAs would be exchanged promptly, that the graves of the unaccounted for would be exhumed, and their remains repatriated. The Americans even anticipated that their mission would be concluded within a matter of weeks. One year later, the remains of only twenty-three Americans had been handed over. The early optimism of the American delegation had long since vanished and been replaced with what negotiation staff officer Captain Stuart Herrington recalls as "the sober realization that the Communists could be as implacable in peace as they had been on the battlefield."

★ ★ ★

A lazy fan futilely attempted to battle the late September heat in an old barracks at Camp Davis in the center of Saigon's Tan Son Nhut Air Base. Facing the Communist negotiator across a small coffee table, Dottie Fitton, a graying, bespectacled mother from Connecticut, pleaded for information about her son who had been missing for six years. Following the advice of her American escort officers, she worded her appeal carefully. "I'm not a political person, Colonel. I'm just a mother who has lost her son. ... I can't pass judgment on the rightness or wrongness of the war, but I can understand how you must feel about what has happened to your country. But my son Crosley is a good boy who was only performing his duties as a military man when he was shot down. Here is his picture. Could you please check with your government and tell me what has become of him?" The North Vietnamese colonel, who had earlier lectured Mrs. Fitton on American war crimes, listened impassively but promised to relay the message and photo to Hanoi. Eventually, Dottie Fitton's painful quest paid off; her son's remains were among the few Hanoi repatriated in December 1975, as a postwar gesture of good will toward Washington.

A "veteran" of the MIA negotiations, Mrs. Fitton shrewdly approached this volatile issue with a courteous, apolitical appeal. Other Americans did not maintain such stoic composure. When a group of six U.S. Congressional delegates met face to face with the JMT North Vietnamese representatives in February 1975, chaos ensued. Attempting to bring the MIA question immediately to the forefront of the discussions, Senator Dewey Bartlett of Oklahoma passed an MIA bracelet bearing the name of a pilot lost over North

Vietnam to the Communist negotiators and insisted on knowing his whereabouts. "Excuse me," he interrupted as the chairman of the North Vietnamese delegation, Lieutenant Colonel Bao, assailed United States "illegal intervention" in Vietnamese affairs, "but your remarks have nothing to do with our specific questions. What about Captain Fieszel? What do I tell his wife? Do I tell her that you have refused to answer?" A half-hour later, the Congressional representatives met with the PRG delegates. Once again the Communist spokesman's diatribe was halted midway. "I'm sorry but I don't want to hear this. I want to know where the forty-one bodies are," demanded Georgia Congressman John Flynt, referring to Americans who died in Communist prison camps. "Where are the forty-one bodies?"

In vain the JMT American delegates pressed the Communists to reveal the fate of other missing servicemen, weathering the inevitable verbose, strident replies that condemned the United States's continued involvement in the war. Meeting twice a week, the two adversaries frequently talked past each other for the entire three hours without even agreeing to an agenda for the day. It was, wrote Arnold Isaacs, like "a match between two different boxers in different rings, each sparring furiously with the air."

To the American negotiators who viewed the exchange of MIAs as an unconditional moral obligation, the impasse appeared unresolvable. Off the record, the Communists freely admitted that information had been obtained on the MIAs and that bodies had been located. Still, they remained intransigent, refusing to cash in such valuable bargaining chips until progress was made on unrelated issues. Before they would continue the MIA search, Hanoi insisted that Washington withdraw its support for the "Thieu clique," force its ally to maintain the cease-fire, and fulfill its promise to con-

tribute money to "heal the wounds of war." This last demand referred to President Nixon's commitment to provide some $3.25 billion in economic aid. The Communists considered that a written agreement to this effect was an essential part of the Paris peace agreement. When Washington refused this aid in reaction to the continued fighting in Cambodia and supported renewed Saigonese militancy, Hanoi stalled the MIA talks. The Communists hoped that the stalemate would generate another round of American domestic pressure on the Nixon administration to abandon once and for all the Thieu government.

Within these tumultuous politics born of the false peace, hope for progress in the MIA talks quickly faded. During the first year of the cease-fire, the American team by-passed the stillborn JMT by conducting its own investigations in GVN-held territory. For eight months the men labored, discovering the remains of nine Americans. On a fateful day in December 1973, three unarmed helicopters bearing orange-striped markings of the Joint Military Commission came under Communist fire in the town of Binh Chanh, sixteen kilometers southwest of Saigon. A Vietnamese pilot and an American officer, Captain Richard M. Rees, were killed. Protesting the deaths as murder "in cold blood," the embittered team canceled all future searches.

In Saigon, the four parties to the Joint Military Team continued to meet until June 1974, when the two Communist delegations decided to boycott all future sessions. With this decision all hope of progress on the MIA issue during the final year of the long Vietnam struggle disappeared. The American military and some 2,500 families of American servicemen whose bodies had not been repatriated could only hope that the Communist peace would end their long agony.

had taken place in America in their absence. They returned to a society that was in their eyes promiscuous, unrestrained, and divided. Then there was the rise of the feminist movement. The POWs had learned in fragments of some of these developments in prison camps as newly captured prisoners arrived, but it was something else to confront them in one's own home. Commander Jack Fellows admitted, "I came home no less bullheaded and ready to take charge than when I'd left. But now I had a wife who'd been in charge and done rather well at it, too."

The Department of Defense offered former POWs, their wives, and children follow-up counseling for a five-year period. But for some families it was already too late. By June, fifty POWs and their wives were already in divorce proceedings. During that same month one of the repatriated prisoners, after surviving seven years as a POW, slipped a plastic bag over his head and took his own life.

The former POWs also presented the Pentagon with a dilemma. Most of them believed their survival was the result of a disciplined sub-rosa organization they had created in prison called the 4th Allied POW Wing. (Similar POW wings—the 1st, 2d, and 3d—had been organized in WWI, WWII, and the Korean War.) The men adapted the prisoner's Code of Conduct to the "conditions at hand." Upon returning home they wanted to press charges against those prisoners who had violated their code. They feared that if such behavior went unpunished it would endanger the ability of future POWs to create the same environment of discipline.

The first to press charges was air force Colonel Theodore Guy, who accused eight fellow POWs of accepting favors from the North Vietnamese in return for making antiwar statements. Some eyebrows were raised when Guy, who had already stated his intention to continue his career in the air force, accused only enlisted men and none from the air force. Several weeks later, a twenty-four-year-old marine, one of the accused, became the second POW to commit suicide. Within days the departments of the army and the navy dismissed all charges for "lack of evidence."

More serious were the charges made by navy Rear Admiral James B. Stockdale, 4th Allied POW Wing director of operations, against two other former POWs, both under the jurisdiction of his own Navy Department. Both men were officers, one in the navy and the other a marine. Navy Secretary John W. Warner found that Stockdale's

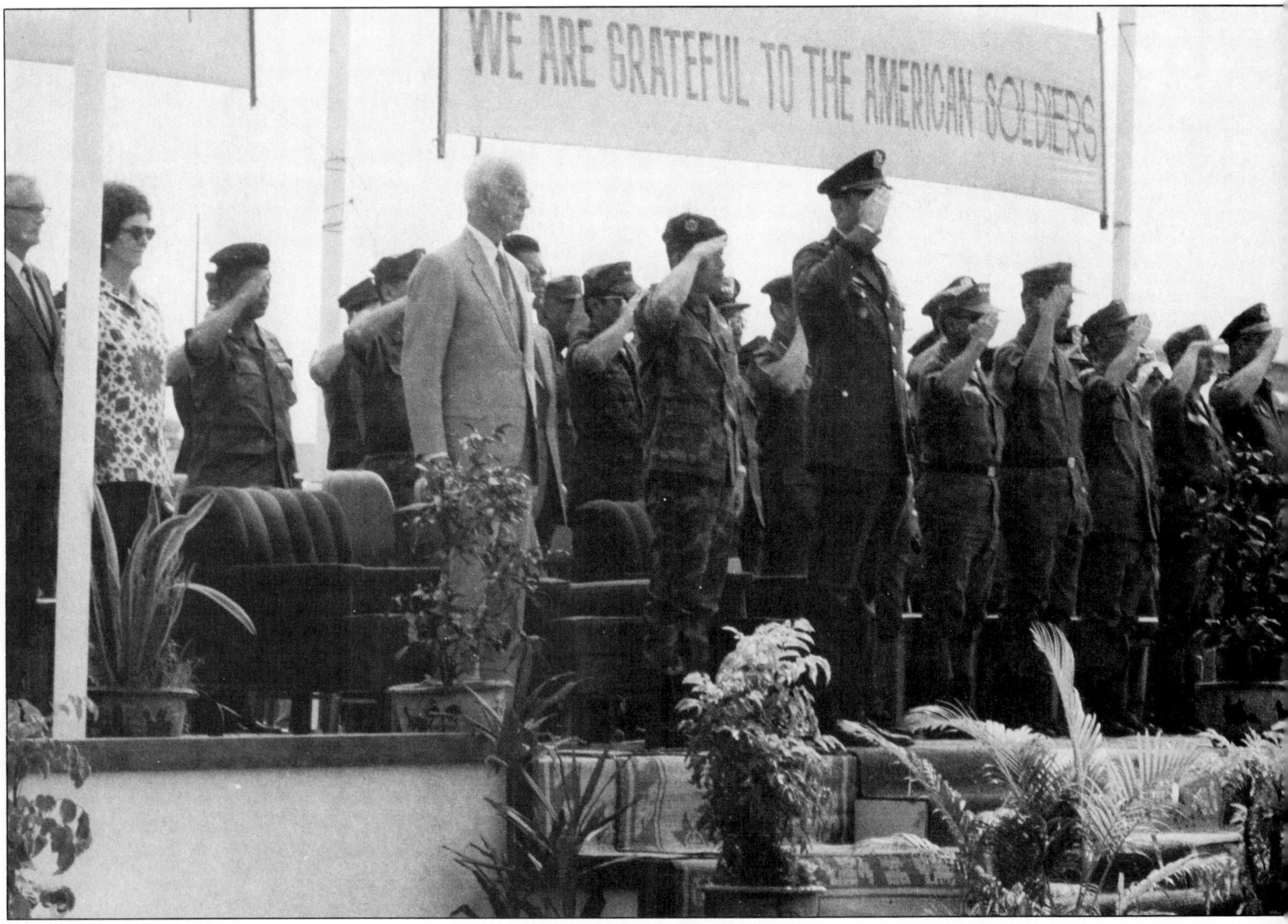
WE ARE GRATEFUL TO THE AMERICAN SOLDIERS

accusations "had merit" but decided to dismiss the charges rather than further disrupt the lives of POWs who would have to testify against them.

The Defense Department was clearly concerned that the release of the POWs not generate another round in the national debate over Vietnam. In that department officials could achieve only a partial success; for as much as America wanted to believe that the Vietnam War was over, the fighting in Indochina continued. And America would continue to play a role, even while it celebrated the false peace.

A handful of Americans

The release of the last American POWs from Hanoi on March 29 was linked to another milestone in the U.S. involvement in South Vietnam. Near the end of March the remaining 5,200 American servicemen stationed in Vietnam, most of them serving as advisers or support personnel, assembled at Tan Son Nhut Air Base's Camp Alpha. At midafternoon on the twenty-ninth, some 50 of them gathered for the stand-down of MACV. As the group stood at attention the final general order was read:

"Headquarters Military Assistance Command Vietnam is inactivated this date and its mission and functions reassigned." An honor guard lowered the MACV flag for a last time and handed it to MACV chief General Frederick C. Weyand for return to the U.S. A few hours later Weyand attended a ceremony with leading South Vietnamese officers to announce, "Our mission has been accomplished." The facilities at Camp Alpha were then officially turned over to the South Vietnamese.

American personnel had worked past midnight to transfer the facilities in immaculate condition for the use of the ICCS. Now those few who still remained cursed as Vietnamese civilians and off-duty soldiers rampaged through Camp Alpha carrying off tables, chairs, and crates of food. The looters ripped fans and electrical fixtures from the walls and ceilings. Within minutes the camp was in shambles. As one observer thought, it was "a tiny but telling metaphor . . . for the country we had thought to

Left. *The residual American force assembles at Tan Son Nhut Air Base for the MACV stand-down ceremony on March 29, 1973.* Below. *New U.S. Ambassador Graham Martin (left) arrives in South Vietnam on July 17, 1973.*

save with American technology and wealth but had never fully understood."

With the deactivation of MACV and the Four-Party JMC, only 209 uniformed American military personnel remained in Vietnam. Marine embassy guards accounted for 159 of them; the remainder were the 50 members of the Defense Attaché Office permitted by the Paris agreement. The military presence that had once dominated the United States Embassy and its civilian agencies would have to find its place in a radically reorganized U.S. Mission.

The top men in the new U.S. Embassy team were thus a product of the Paris treaty. They also reflected the personality of the new American ambassador to South Vietnam, Graham A. Martin. On June 24, 1973, Martin replaced Ambassador Ellsworth Bunker, who had served in Vietnam for over six years. Ambassador Martin was not new to the Far East. In 1963 he had become ambassador to Thailand. Two accomplishments in that post paved the way for his appointment to Saigon. Martin earned the gratitude of the State Department in countering the trend in neighboring Indochina countries by advising the Thais in their fight against a local Communist insurgency without an increase in U.S. military personnel. He seemed a perfect choice for the man to run the embassy in Saigon after the American military role was phased out. It also did not hurt that in 1966 a private American citizen traveled through Thailand and Ambassador Martin gave him the VIP treatment. The man was Richard Nixon, and in 1969 the newly elected president appointed Martin ambassador to Italy.

Martin and his wife were planning to retire near Rome when in 1973 Nixon asked him to accept the post to South Vietnam. Martin reluctantly agreed. South Vietnam held bitter memories for him. His son Glenn was shot down and killed in 1966 while serving as a helicopter pilot. Martin later recalled that when first asked to travel to Saigon he thought, "Hell no, I won't go!" But after thinking it over he accepted. "When the highest officials of your country say, 'I thought the Foreign Service took the tough posts as well as the nice ones,' you respond, 'Yes, we do,'" he later recounted.

Martin's appearance deceived. Frail-looking and stoop-shouldered, with iron-gray hair and gracious dignified "old Southern manners," only Martin's "stone gray eyes," as one associate described them, revealed his intimidating presence. According to one of his aides, Kissinger viewed Martin "as the meanest son-of-a-bitch around," a tough, dominating man who could manipulate domestic opinion and also serve as a "lightning rod for criticism that might otherwise be directed" at the White House.

Despite his strength of character, Martin brought a personality to his mission that was bound to be troublesome. He was a reclusive man. One of his friends admitted, "Graham was never people-oriented and he tended

merely to treat the Vietnamese like pawns to be moved about on a board." It was not only the South Vietnamese who received this treatment but also the American officials who headed the new Defense Attaché Office and the CIA.

The DAO was led by Major General John E. Murray, the last MACV chief of logistics. His background was ideal for the first commander of the DAO. The Paris agreement prohibited the defense attaché from acting in any advisory capacity to the South Vietnamese armed forces. Murray's logistics experience suggested that he would limit himself to the "nuts and bolts" task of providing military assistance. But temperamentally he and Martin were ill-suited for each other. Murray was, according to one of his subordinates, "not a patient man . . . . [He was] considerate of others, thoroughly professional, perceptive, and highly skilled in the use of colorful language, but not patient." Murray remained loyal to Martin. He scrupulously obeyed the ambassador's prerogative to restrict his contacts with the press, until the steady decline of U.S. aid to South Vietnam became more than he could bear. Shortly before his retirement he unloosed the vinegary tongue that Martin had tied and blasted Pentagon "fiscal whores" who forced the South Vietnamese to substitute "bodies, bones and blood" for bullets.

The CIA also received a new leader in Saigon as Thomas Polgar accepted the post of CIA chief of station. Born to Jewish parents in rural southern Hungary, Polgar fled his native land in the 1930s in the shadow of Nazi persecution. He served in the wartime OSS and joined the newly formed CIA after World War II, slowly rising through the ranks until he was offered one of the CIA's most prestigious positions, the post in Saigon, without any prior Asian experience.

Socially, Polgar and Martin were at the opposite ends of the spectrum. According to one of his associates, Polgar "could turn a cocktail party cold with an innocent off-color joke" and did not mix well with Ambassador Martin, the southern patrician.

After the Paris agreement, some new figures also appeared in Washington to conduct America's Vietnam policy—as well as one well-known figure who changed to a different hat. William Rogers had resigned as secretary of state, so Richard Nixon chose his national security adviser, Henry Kissinger, to fill the role. Now undisputed master of U.S. foreign policy, Kissinger would remain the leading architect of policy toward Vietnam. To replace outgoing Secretary of Defense Melvin Laird, Nixon chose a wide-roving cabinet member, Elliot Richardson, a Bostonian with a liberal reputation. Having provided Kissinger with liaison to the State Department while serving as undersecretary of state from 1969 to 1970, Richardson was unlikely to question Kissinger's leadership. But when the Watergate scandal forced Nixon to send Richardson to the Justice Department in August 1973, his replacement, James Schlesinger, proved to be a more formidable challenger to

Kissinger. In the course of the next twelve months, the rivalry between the two men heated up, until, according to Kissinger, "our internal disputes were no longer geared to substance; they had become a struggle for preeminence." And Kissinger added that Schlesinger "gave as good as he received."

Schlesinger, Martin, Murray; in comparison with names like McNamara, Bunker, and Westmoreland, they barely conjured up the far-off lands of Indochina in the public mind. It was perhaps inevitable that this should be their fate, but it also was the result of a clear policy conducted by the executive branch and echoed in the collective sigh of relief of the American people.

A nation distracted

"The war is over," President Nixon told the American people in a "message of thanksgiving" after the Paris agreement had been signed. "Vietnam no longer distracts our attention from the fundamental issues of global diplomacy," he reported to Congress on May 3 in his third "State of the World" report. The strategy of the president and his advisers was clear: to reunite America after the divisiveness and debate of Vietnam in order to pursue other foreign policy goals. The method was to encourage the nation in forgetting events in the country the U.S. had spent a decade trying to save.

To ensure that outcome Nixon drew the nation's thoughts as far away from Vietnam as possible. In his "State of the World" address he proclaimed 1973 to be the "Year of Europe." Fresh from his triumph in Paris, Kissinger, too, turned to new problems as an outlet for his talents. Because his Jewish background might give the appearance of favoritism toward Israel, Nixon had kept Kissinger in the background in the formulation of Middle East policy during his first term. But with Rogers's resignation Kissinger was free to turn his energy toward that part of the world. When war broke out between the Arabs and Israel in October 1973, Kissinger became increasingly preoccupied. Over the next twelve months of crucial debate on Vietnam in Congress, Kissinger could frequently be found shuttling between Middle Eastern capitals.

The extent of Kissinger's distraction is portrayed nowhere more vividly than in his memoirs. In the first volume, covering the years 1969–72, nine out of thirty-four chapters discuss Vietnam exclusively. In his second volume of twenty-five chapters, ending in 1974, Kissinger devotes only two chapters to Vietnam. He discusses no events in Indochina after June 1973, and the name Graham Martin does not appear even once in the book.

The American public was only too eager to follow in the path of its leaders. In March 1973 only 7 percent of 1,500 adults polled by the Gallup organization named Vietnam as the country's first or second most important problem. Only a few months earlier 35 percent had chosen Vietnam as the single most important problem. The March 1973 poll marked the first time since 1965 that Vietnam was not listed among the nation's most pressing problems. If Kissinger was more preoccupied with the Middle East, middle America was more concerned with the price of groceries. The high cost of living was named by more than half of all those polled as the country's gravest problem.

The major news media played their role in the new silence about Vietnam. With American troops no longer engaged in combat, the Saigon bureaus of countless smaller newspapers closed. Only the country's major periodicals maintained full-time, although reduced, staffs in Saigon. In 1965 when American combat troops first deployed to Vietnam, the two major news weeklies, *Time* and *Newsweek*, each established separate "Vietnam" sections in

Women in New York City demonstrate against the high price of meat on April 8, 1973, as inflation took the place of Vietnam as the number-one concern of Americans.

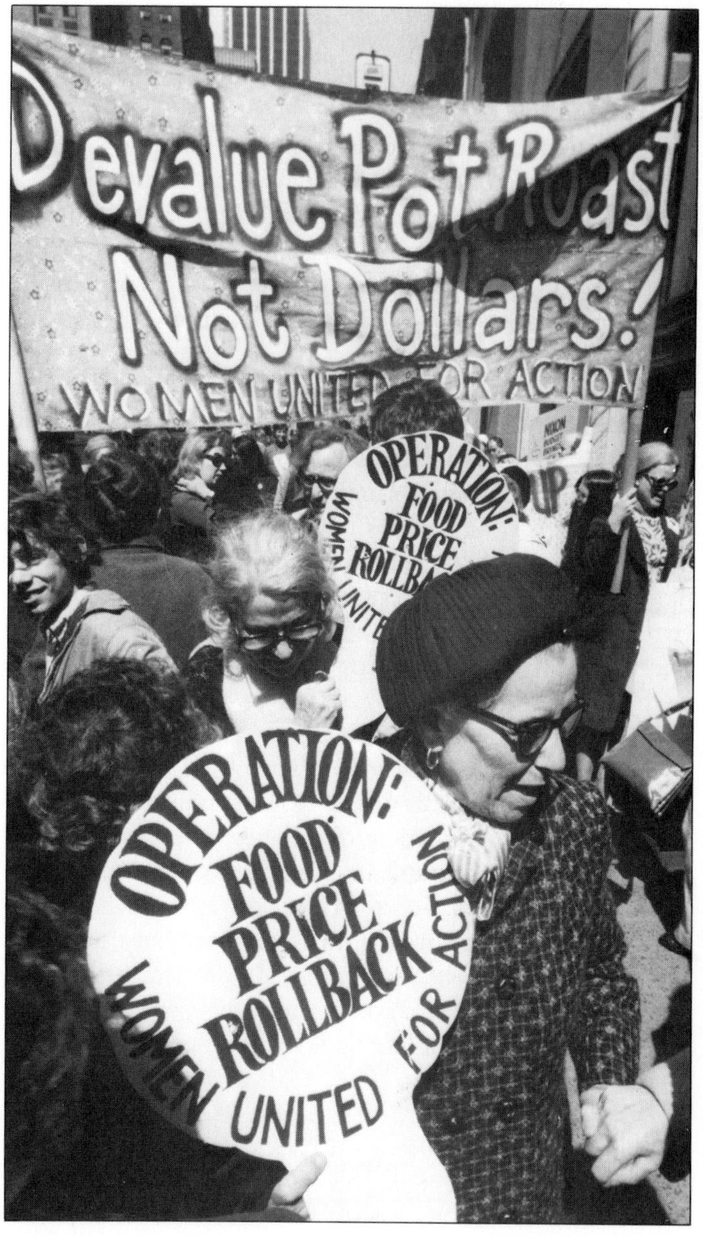
Devalue Pot Roast
Not Dollars!
WOMEN UNITED FOR ACTION
OPERATION: FOOD PRICE ROLLBACK
OPERATION: FOOD PRICE ROLLBACK
WOMEN UNITED FOR ACTION

their magazines. With the signing of the Paris agreement, those sections disappeared and the infrequent dispatches published from Vietnam simply became another item in "international" reporting. The total space devoted to Vietnam from June 1973 to the end of 1974 was less than that expended in some single issues during the height of the war. It was difficult for the American people to become concerned about events in Indochina when they were told so little about what was transpiring there.

A new story came to dominate the public's appetite for news. At the end of 1972 *Time* magazine had chosen Richard Nixon and Henry Kissinger to share its prestigious cover as "Man of the Year." The issue sold 214,000 copies on newsstands. One year later the editors chose an obscure Washington judge, John Sirica. His face on the cover sold 291,000 issues. Just two weeks later *Time*'s newsstand sales for a single issue reached an all-time high, passing the 325,000 mark. The cover featured the craggy face of a Texas lawyer, Leon Jaworski. The demise of Richard Nixon, it turned out, made for greater circulation than his greatest triumph.

The principal subject of this story, Richard Nixon, was not even in Washington during the early morning hours of Sunday, June 17, 1972, when five men were arrested for burglarizing the offices of the Democratic National Headquarters in the Watergate office building. Returning to the capital from a Caribbean vacation on Monday evening, the president was first briefed on the break-in on June 20. The substance of that crucial conversation between the president and his senior assistant, H. R. Haldeman, was lost to history when the White House erased eighteen minutes from the recording of the discussion. Details of a later discussion, held on June 23, in which Richard Nixon ordered Haldeman to halt the FBI investigation of the crime, did become known.

What the president learned on June 23 was that his close friend and former attorney general, John Mitchell, and Mitchell's assistant at the Committee to Re-elect the President, Jeb Stuart Magruder, had clearly been aware of the planned burglary and probably had authorized it. Nixon and Haldeman thus embarked on a cover-up of the break-in designed to serve two purposes. The president wanted the scandal contained at least until after the November election, and he further hoped to protect Mitchell from criminal prosecution. Henry Kissinger later suggested that Nixon was probably unaware of the illegality of his order and that the president believed that he was no more guilty of wrongdoing than had he attempted to fix a D.C. speeding ticket for his chauffeur. Kissinger also argued that Nixon frequently gave orders that he had no desire for his lieutenants to carry out. Kissinger blamed Haldeman for not realizing that the June 23 order to intercede at the FBI was one of these.

There is some evidence to support Kissinger's theory. Throughout the fall the president seemed oblivious to any

personal danger arising out of the Watergate controversy. When, during his confirmation hearings before the Senate in February 1973, L. Patrick Gray, acting director of the FBI, repeatedly implicated White House Counsel John Dean in the cover-up, the Senate requested that Dean testify. Nixon refused, invoking "executive privilege," but his goal seemed not self-protection but to shield his key aides, H. R. Haldeman and White House Assistant for Domestic Affairs John Ehrlichman.

The entire situation changed on March 21 when Dean barged into the Oval Office with his diagnosis that "there is a cancer growing on the Presidency." With several of the masterminds of the break-in now willing to testify before the Senate and criminal grand juries, it became apparent to the president that he could no longer save his troika of close aides. Mitchell, Haldeman, and Ehrlichman would have to be sacrificed to protect the president. Knowing that he could count on the silence of these three men, Nixon was confronted with the problem of how to control Dean and Magruder.

On April 30 Nixon accepted the resignations of Haldeman and Ehrlichman. In what seemed to be the perfect public relations solution to his problem, he announced that he would permit no plea-bargaining by those charged in the break-in and cover-up. To the nation he was implying that all those implicated would have to face the full penalty for their actions. In reality he was trying to remove any incentive for Dean or Magruder to cooperate with the investigation. The two men, however, drew the opposite conclusion and decided that the White House was "feeding them to the wolves." Both decided that their only option was to turn state's evidence.

On June 25, 1973, Dean read a 245-page opening statement before the Senate Watergate Committee, chaired by North Carolina Senator Sam Ervin. In his testimony Dean argued that the order to halt the FBI's investigation of the Watergate crime had come directly from the president. In their testimony before the senators, Ehrlichman and Haldeman categorically denied Dean's testimony.

It was one man's word against another until July 16. On that day an obscure White House assistant, Alex Butterfield, matter-of-factly testified that there was a way to resolve the discrepancy in the testimony of the president's advisers. A secret taping system monitored every conversation in the president's offices. The Watergate affair immediately became a battle for possession of the tapes of those conversations.

In retrospect the dénouement became inevitable with Butterfield's testimony, but Nixon's actions ensured that the nation would be treated to a real-life soap opera. On October 16 a U.S. court of appeals ruled by a five-to-two vote that Nixon must turn over the tapes to Judge John Sirica for use by Special Prosecutor Archibald Cox, who had been appointed by the Justice Department to investigate the Watergate case. Nixon ordered Attorney General Elliot

Watergate

"Like a ripe plum dropping from a tree, Watergate split open in late January 1973," recalled H. R. Haldeman, Nixon's former chief of staff. The exposure of the Watergate break-in and other illegal White House activities created an atmosphere of insecurity in the Nixon administration. While the president futilely attempted to weather the storm of public opinion, all foreign policy issues, including Vietnam, were pushed far into the background of White House consciousness. Once a great leader in world affairs, a now paralyzed Richard Nixon was preoccupied with his own political survival.

Former White House aide John Dean III is sworn in by Senate Watergate Committee Chairman Sam Ervin on June 25, 1973.

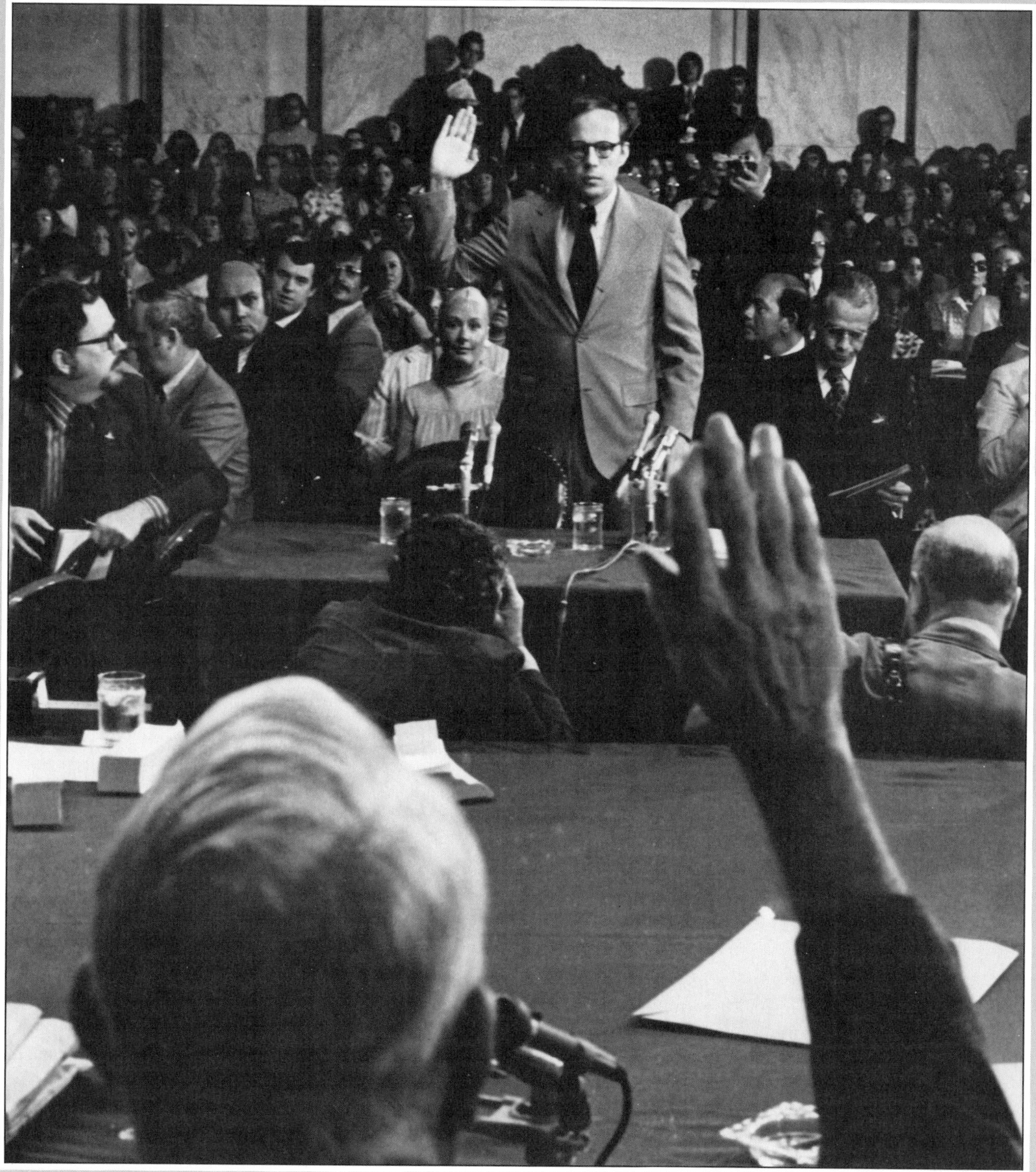

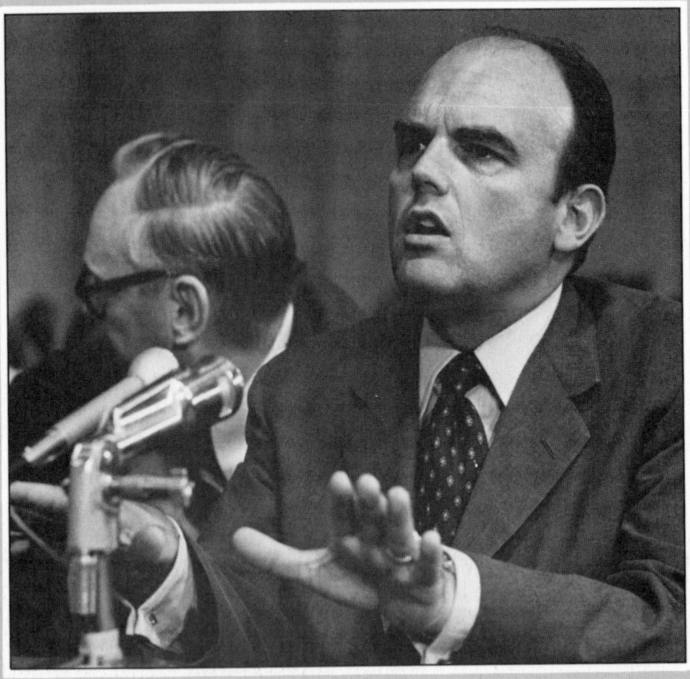

Above. *Former White House Assistant for Domestic Affairs John Ehrlichman testifies before the Senate Watergate Committee.*

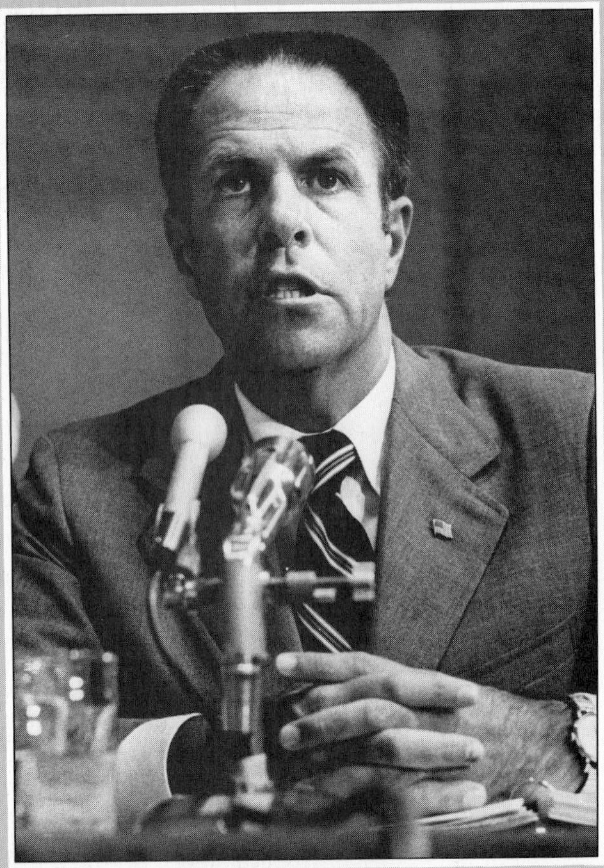

Above. *H. R. Haldeman speaks to the committee.* Right. *Senator Sam Ervin, chairman of the Senate panel, sits in the hearing room surrounded by other members of the Watergate committee.*

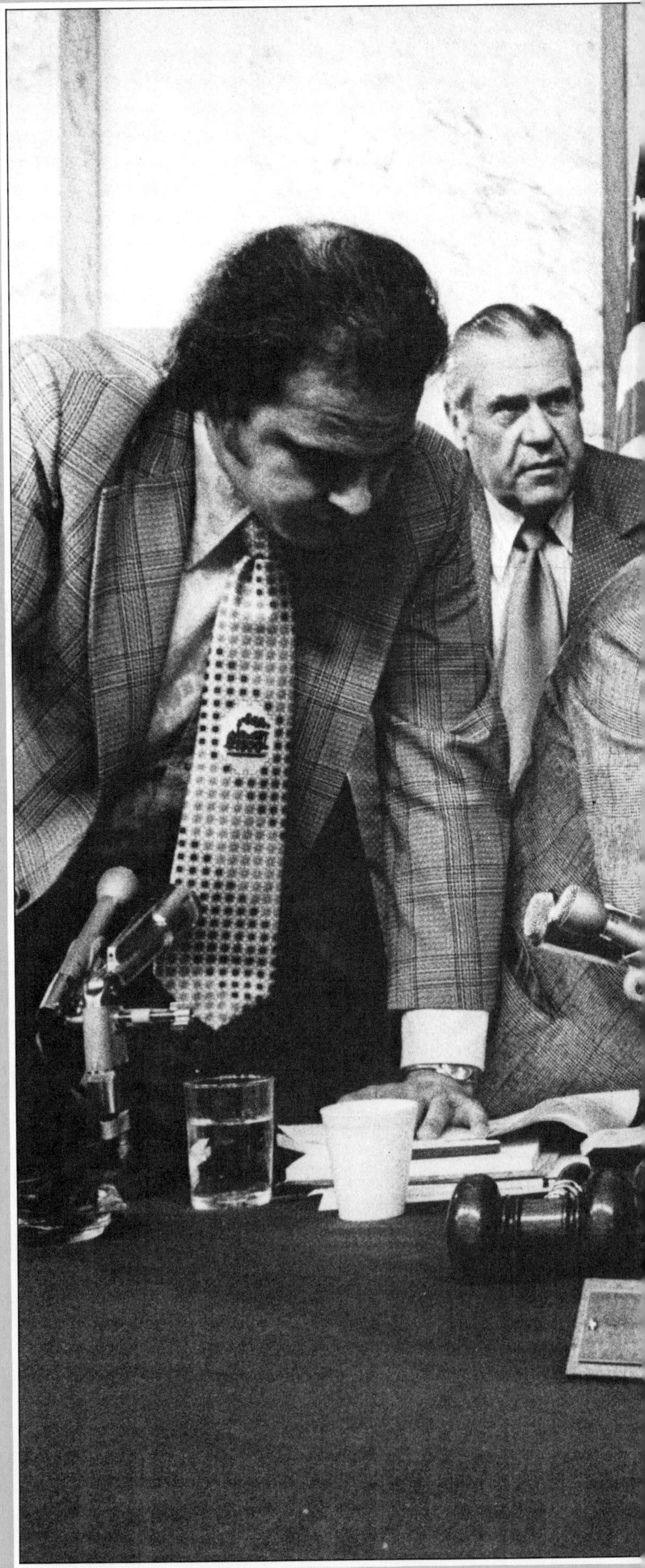

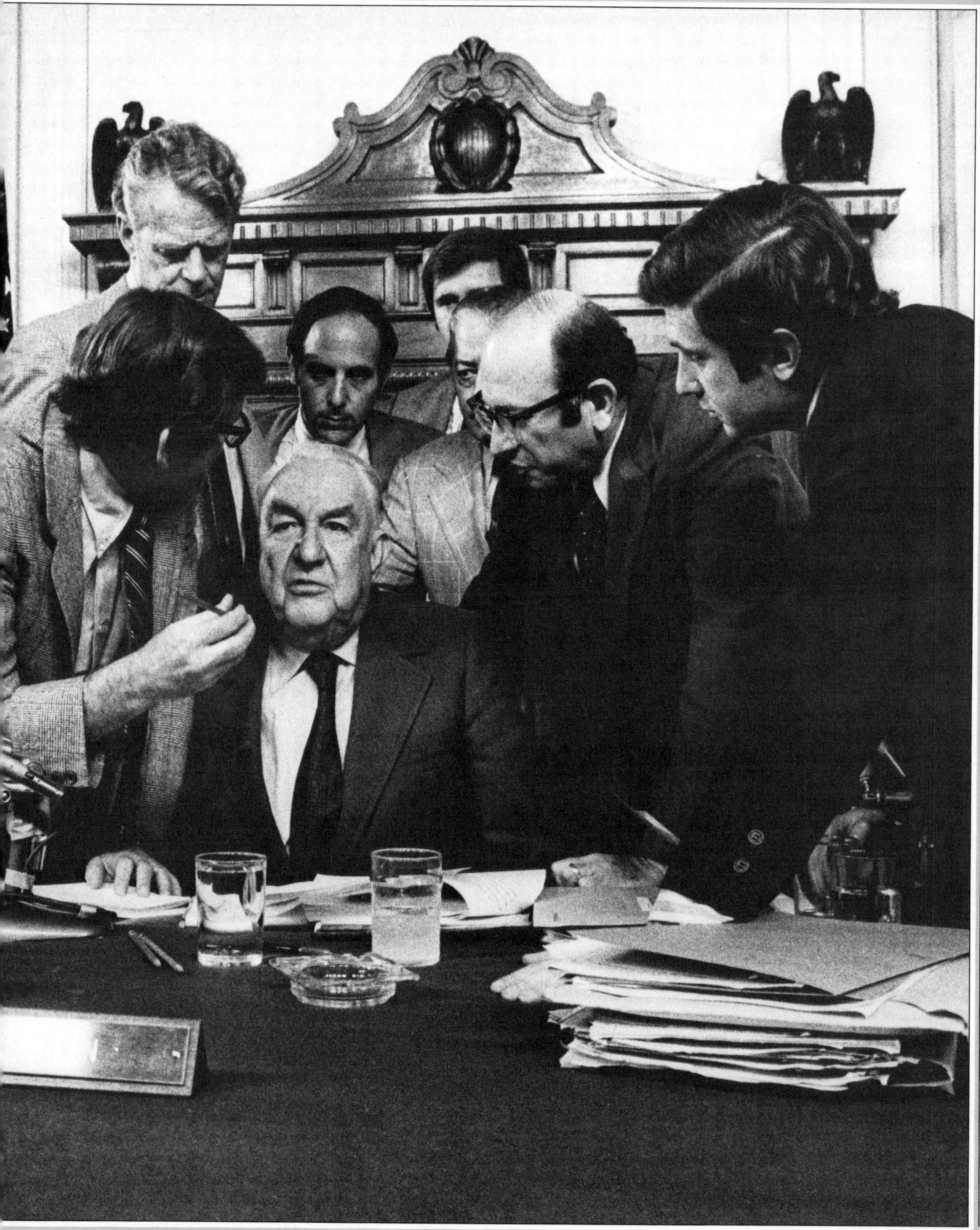

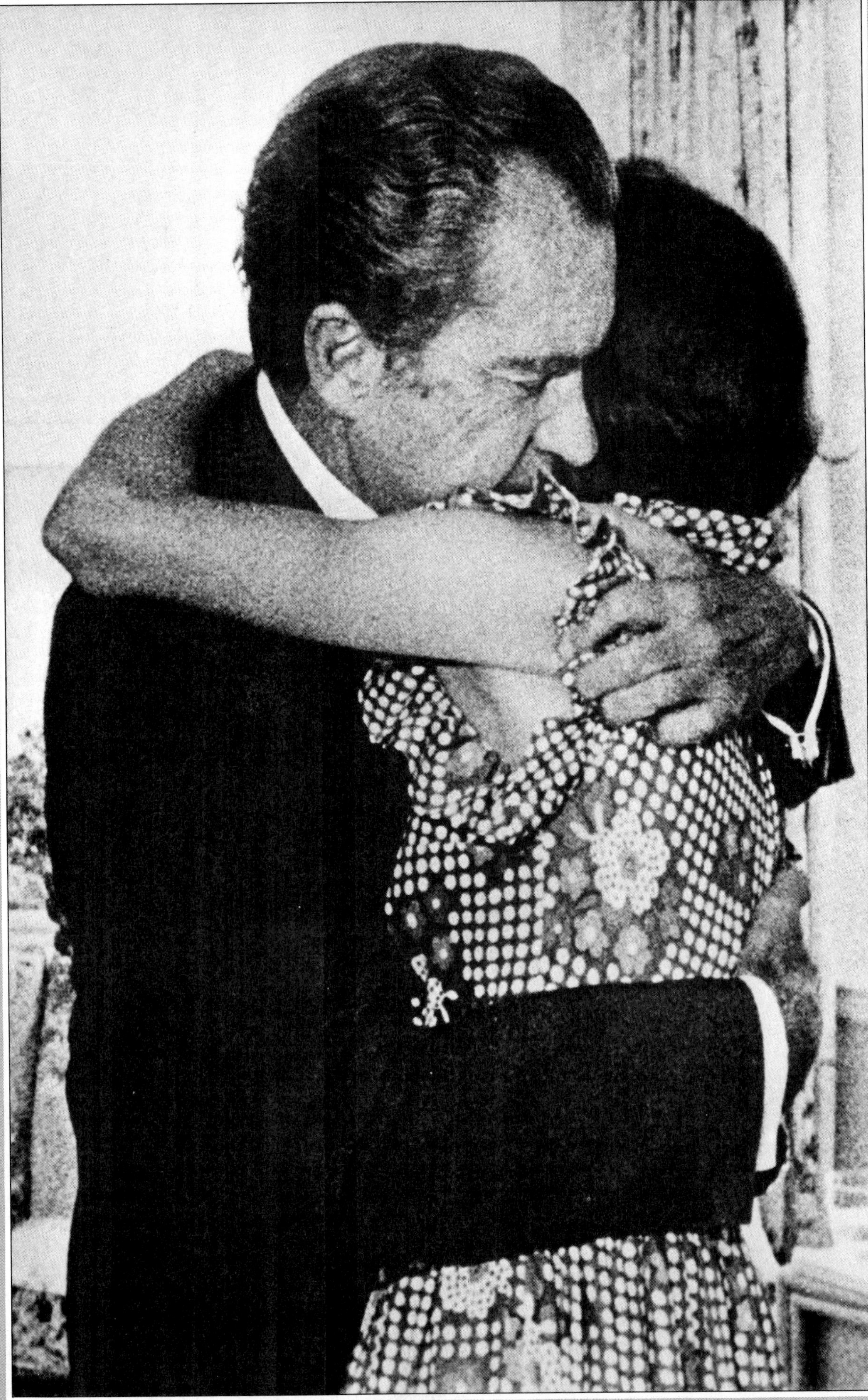

Richard Nixon is comforted by his daughter Julie Eisenhower on the night of August 7, 1974, after he had informed his family of the decision to resign the office of the presidency.

Richardson to order Cox to cease his efforts to secure the tapes. Richardson refused and resigned, as did his legal successor, William Ruckelshaus. The third in line at the Justice Department, Solicitor General Robert Bork, finally fired Cox, completing Nixon's "Saturday night massacre."

Realizing by now that the investigation was centered squarely upon himself, Nixon established a tripartite defense team at the White House. A Boston lawyer, James St. Clair, was brought in to handle his defense before Congress; Leonard Garment of the White House staff was given responsibility for arguing the president's case in federal court; and Alexander Haig, as White House chief of staff, handled the public relations efforts before the most important court of all, the American people. It was there that Richard Nixon's cause was suffering most. The president's approval rating plummeted from nearly 70 percent in February to 40 percent by July. By midsummer two-thirds of the American people believed him implicated in the Watergate scandal.

On July 24, 1974, the Supreme Court ended the national suspense. By an eight-to-zero vote it ruled that Nixon must turn over the tapes which contained evidence of his crime. On August 4, 1974, the House Judiciary Committee voted three articles of impeachment against the president. The contents of the conversation with Haldeman on June 23, 1973, were still unknown to the Judiciary Committee and to the president's own defenders. His supporters argued that circumstantial evidence was insufficient to impeach a president; a "smoking gun" was required.

On Monday, August 5, Leonard Garment read a transcript of the June 23 tape for the first time. He, like Haig and St. Clair, was devastated. There was little to do but prepare the president for the necessity of submitting his resignation. Then Garment had one last idea. Perhaps the president had not even remembered the orders he gave on June 23; perhaps he had not issued them seriously. (The coincidence between Garment's thinking and Kissinger's analysis is not surprising. Garment was the secretary of state's main source of information during the unfolding events.)

Garment sped to a vault containing the tapes. Ever since Butterfield had announced the existence of the tapes they had been held under guard by the Secret Service. By court order no one, including the president, could gain possession of the tapes without signing for them in the presence of a Secret Service agent. Garment checked the log. He was crushed. In mid-January 1974, Richard Nixon had checked out the June 23 tape. If not before that date, then at least for the remainder of 1974, Richard Nixon had been aware of what he had ordered and had continued in his efforts to suppress that evidence. No defense of the president was possible.

On August 8, 1974, Richard Nixon submitted his resignation from the presidency, effective at noon the following day. In doing so, he became the first president compelled by the threat of impeachment to leave office. By one of the quirks in the nation's constitutional system, the man who received Nixon's letter of resignation was his partner in his greatest triumphs, Secretary of State Henry Kissinger. Alone among Nixon's closest aides, he would not be indicted. The president's other assistants would see their lives shattered or at best changed dramatically. Kissinger's life would remain intact and his prestige and power in Washington would even increase, but still, much of his work, too, lay in wreckage. With the waning of Nixon's presidential powers, Kissinger would find it increasingly difficult to take the decisive action necessary to maintain his policy of détente.

Kissinger had paid a visit to the Oval Office on March 21, 1973, the afternoon after John Dean's fateful revelations. Kissinger's task was urgent. The president must decide, he told Nixon, how to respond to North Vietnamese violations of the cease-fire agreement. Kissinger presented Nixon with a series of options, including the one recommended by Kissinger—to renew the bombing of the Ho Chi Minh Trail. Nixon refused to make a decision, telling Kissinger that "the President, too, had a problem." By early April, still without any decision from the president, Kissinger gave up all plans for retaliation against North Vietnam. The rainy season in northern Indochina had made such an option ill-advised.

After the March 21 conversation with Dean, President Nixon's interest in foreign policy, the instrument of his greatest achievements as president, began to fade. In his memoirs, after that date, his discussion of foreign policy is scattered and brief. Instead, virtually every page is filled with "the incessant plotting," as journalist Seymour Hersh described it, about Watergate. Kissinger later noted, "Everything, including the Year of Europe and all foreign policy, was secondary to Nixon's 'revealing the whole truth.'" When former Defense Secretary Melvin Laird briefly inherited Haldeman's position as White House chief of staff he told reporters, "the government in some quarters is at a standstill." And Kissinger noted that Nixon, who in the past had "immersed" himself in foreign policy, no longer wrote comments in the margins of memoranda, and on one occasion even checked every box on an option paper, thus defeating its purpose.

The paralysis of the executive branch could not have come at a worse time. Not only did the enforcement of the Indochina peace agreement require constant vigilance but at home, in Washington, D.C., the presidency was faced with the sternest challenge to its control of foreign policy since the beginning of World War II.

The assertive 93d Congress

It did not require the Watergate revelations to move the 93d Congress to reassert what it considered to be Congressional prerogatives in determining the country's foreign policy and, in particular, in deciding under what conditions armed force could be used. Henry Kissinger had feared as much when he reviewed the results of the Congressional elections in November 1972, and these fears had played a major role in his negotiations, both with Saigon and Hanoi, during the remainder of the year.

When the new Congress convened in January it wasted little time in confirming Kissinger's fears. By overwhelming margins the caucuses of House and Senate Democrats each voted to cut off all funds for operations in Indochina once the safe return of American troops and POWs had been assured. The signed peace agreement cut short any effort on the part of the Democrats to translate this action into legislation, but the ire of Congress was raised again when the Pentagon announced in early February that bombing of Cambodia had been resumed.

Technically, the Cooper-Church amendment of January 1971, prohibited such military activity in Cambodia. The president had continued to bomb the country throughout the next two years in spite of the legislation, arguing that he was exercising rights inherent in his role as commander in chief to protect "American boys" fighting in Vietnam. With the American troops all now returned to the United States, Senate doves argued that the president had no justification for continuing the bombing. Senators Frank Church of Idaho and Clifford Case of New Jersey introduced a bill prohibiting any U.S. military action "in or over, or from off the shores of South Vietnam, Laos or Cambodia." The bill was joined to a Defense Department supplemental appropriations bill that reached the House floor in May.

On May 10 the hawkish House of Representatives passed its first antiwar measure, rejecting a DOD request to transfer defense funds for use in Cambodia. The House then passed, by a vote of 224 to 172, a version of the Church-Case amendment. This dramatic swing in Congressional opinion was made possible by the desertion of thirty-five Republicans and several conservative Democrats from the administration's camp, including House Speaker Carl Albert.

On May 15 the conservative Senate Appropriations Committee attached the Church-Case amendment to the same supplemental appropriations bill by a unanimous twenty-four-to-zero vote. Two factors seemed to be behind the decision of all committee Republicans to support the amendment. The first was simple war-weariness felt by liberals and conservatives alike. More important, conservatives joined liberals in fearing that the continued bombing of Cambodia might entice the country back into combat in Vietnam. As New Hampshire Senator Norris Cotton told reporters, "As far as I am concerned . . . I want to get the hell out of there just as quick as possible, and I don't want to fool around to the point that they might take more prisoners." On May 31 the entire Senate adopted the amendment by a vote of sixty-three to nineteen. Among

Senate Republicans, the White House lost the support of twenty members out of thirty-six voting. Waiting until Nixon returned from a summit meeting with Soviet leader Leonid Brezhnev, the House followed suit on June 25, passing the supplemental appropriations bill with the antiwar amendment attached.

When President Nixon responded by vetoing the bill on June 27, the two branches of government seemed headed for a stalemate. Senate Majority Leader Mike Mansfield vowed to attach the amendment to other bills, "again, again, and again until the will of the people prevails." Under this threat of a potential grid lock in Congress, Nixon agreed to a compromise, informing Congressional leaders that he would accept August 15 as the deadline for ending all bombing in Indochina.

On June 29, 1973, both houses of Congress adopted the compromise amendment, and the president signed it into law. In the end both Republican leaders in the Senate, Hugh Scott of Pennsylvania and Robert Griffin of Michigan, supported the antiwar position. Even Barry Goldwater reluctantly joined the majority. Representative David Dennis of Indiana spoke for many conservatives when, after reminding the House that he had consistently opposed such antiwar amendments, he explained his change of heart:

Because I think I can see reality. The American people are tired of bombing in Cambodia. I am tired of bombing in Cambodia. Everyone is tired of bombing in Cambodia.

Watergate may not have played a major role in the Congressional votes to cut off the bombing of Cambodia, but it almost certainly determined how the White House reacted. One option discussed by Kissinger with the president was to sign the bill into law and then ignore it. This would require Congress to test the legality of the prohibition in federal courts, where Nixon thought he could defend his power as commander in chief. But with assorted other actions of the Nixon administration already in court as a result of Watergate, the president felt it prudent to comply with Congress's intent. The law did not prohibit the nation from reintervening in Indochina, but it could only be done so with Congressional concurrence.

The intent of Congress in passing the "Indochina prohibition" was raised to the level of principle in November 1973, when both houses of Congress sustained the War Powers Act over the president's veto. Mustering two-thirds majorities, the House voted 284 to 135 and the Senate 75 to 18 to limit the president's right to engage in war without Congressional consent. The act specified that the president must report to Congress within forty-eight hours after ordering troops into action or "substantially [increasing] the number of foreign-based U.S. troops equipped for combat." Without positive Congressional approval, the president was required to halt military operations after ninety days. Congress, meanwhile, could rescind presidential orders at any moment by passing its own resolutions, not subject to executive vetoes.

The politics of the War Powers Act made for odd bedfellows. The hawkish chairman of the Senate Armed Services Committee, John Stennis, a Democrat, joined the outspoken dove, Jacob Javits, Republican of New York, in supporting the amendment, while the traditional hawk, House Republican Minority Leader Gerald Ford, opposed the measure in tandem with Democratic Senator Thomas Eagleton. Ford argued that the measure would weaken the president's "credibility" in handling foreign crises. What Stennis favored, and Eagleton feared, was that the measure also gave the president a right not explicit in the Constitution, to order American troops into combat without *prior* approval of Congress.

Despite this debate over the meaning of the War Powers Act, one that continued through the years after the war, there is little doubt that Congress was reasserting its constitutional control over the "Imperial Presidency" and once again wanted to take an active role in determining United States foreign policy. With American policy in Indochina in effect reduced to providing aid for South Vietnam, it was not difficult for this same 93d Congress to use its "power of the purse" to stamp its mark on U.S.–South Vietnamese relations. And the lawmakers wasted no time in doing so.

Blood, bullets, and dollars

In April 1973, President Nguyen Van Thieu paid his only official visit to the continental United States. President Nixon had promised Thieu the invitation in exchange for signing the peace agreement. Wanting to maintain the illusion that he was conducting foreign policy as usual, even in the face of the ominous developments in the Watergate scandal, Nixon kept his promise. But he cautiously decided to receive him at his San Clemente, California, compound rather than in Washington's more tumultuous atmosphere.

The major subject of discussion was future U.S. assistance to Thieu's government. So assured was he by President Nixon's promises that Thieu ordered a champagne celebration aboard his private jet as his plane took off from California. Henry Kissinger, who was not present at the talks, had a different impression, however:

It had a slightly unreal quality because the American participants knew that Congressional support even for economic devel-

Months before Watergate was to engulf him, Richard Nixon welcomes President Nguyen Van Thieu to the United States in April 1973 for discussions on continued U.S. assistance to South Vietnam.

opment assistance was eroding fast. The liberals were losing interest because they had little commitment to the survival of South Vietnam, and the conservatives believed that they had discharged their obligations by supporting the war to an honorable conclusion. Both reflected the war-weariness of the nation.

If the Nixon administration had some justification for misleading Thieu during the fall of 1972 concerning the peace negotiations, its continued refusal to be frank about assistance to his regime during 1973 was to become one of the fatal blows to South Vietnam's survival.

During the Enhance Plus program in November and December 1972, the Pentagon had extended to South Vietnam all the military assistance appropriated by Congress for fiscal year 1973, ending on June 30, 1973. Assistance extended after July 1, 1973, would come out of the FY 1974 budget. But as was so often the case, Congress was not close to completing action on the budget by that date. Aid to Vietnam was extended on the basis of a "continuing resolution," a permission granted by Congress to the executive to continue funding its programs at the level of the previous year.

General John Murray, defense attaché in Saigon, thus continued to manage a military assistance program during the second half of 1973 based on the administration's request for $1.6 billion in aid. As Congress continued to postpone action on the Defense Department budget, Murray showed no alarm until December 20, 1973. On that date he received a dire warning from the Pentagon. Congress had set a budgetary ceiling for aid to Vietnam at $1.126 billion. This ceiling, however, did not represent an actual appropriation but only a mark within which Congress would ultimately grant funds. And, the Pentagon told Murray, that actual spending authority was likely to be reduced to $900 million for Laos and Vietnam. South Vietnam's share would be $813 million.

Murray realized he had a full-fledged crisis on his hands. He had already authorized the spending of $723 million. This would leave South Vietnam with only an additional $90 million in aid for the next six months. After a quick inventory, Murray cabled the Pentagon with the bad news: "Unbudgeted critical shortages" for FY 1974 would surpass $200 million, of which $180 million was required for ammunition alone.

When Murray asked permission of Ambassador Graham Martin to brief South Vietnamese military leaders on the aid crisis, he was turned down. Martin thought he

Mr. Secretary

The president was floating on his back in the shallow end of the western White House swimming pool in San Clemente. Nearby, on the pool steps, sat the chief engineer of his foreign policy, National Security Adviser Henry Kissinger. Beneath the burning August sun of southern California, the two men coolly discussed answers to foreign policy questions reporters might ask the president at his news conference scheduled for the next day, August 22, 1973. Suddenly and matter-of-factly the president declared, "I shall open the press conference by announcing your appointment as the Secretary of State." This was the first time Nixon mentioned the topic to Kissinger, who one month later took the oath of office in the East Room of the White House.

Kissinger's appointment to the highest nonelected post in American government was not completely unexpected, at least to Washington insiders. The emerging Watergate scandal and the accompanying assault on the presidency catapulted him to the position of secretary of state.

Four and one-half years before, Nixon had assumed the presidency determined to concentrate control of foreign policy in the White House, working closely with his national security adviser. The State Department's traditional task of advising the president on the formulation of key policy and then executing his decisions was thus to a great extent usurped by the White House. Secretary of State William Rogers and the lumbering foreign service bureaucracy were left to implement policy that they had little opportunity to shape or influence and to tend to the inglorious tasks, details, and formalities of international relations. Meanwhile, Nixon and Kissinger concentrated on the preeminent issues of statecraft.

Conflict between Kissinger and Rogers was inevitable, for both had a defensible claim that his office should play the predominant role in the conduct of foreign policy. By November 1972, Nixon and his chief of staff, H. R. Haldeman, had decided to replace Secretary Rogers with someone who would yield quietly to White House control.

Kenneth Rush, the deputy secretary of state, was Nixon's choice. He was a loyal aide who had served capably in a variety of government posts and would not demand the customary State Department prerogatives that the White House had already claimed. Kissinger saw the appointment of Rush as a bureaucratic victory for Haldeman and was prepared to resign his post after a suitable interval and return to academe.

Had Rogers left at the end of Nixon's first term, Haldeman's plan would certainly have been implemented. By the time Rogers did submit his resignation, though, Watergate had drastically changed the political climate. The landslide victory in the November election was soon forgotten as the Nixon presidency came under fire from the press, the public, and the Congress.

It was thus Watergate that provided Henry Kissinger with his opportunity. What better way for the embattled president to restore his diminishing authority than to choose for the highly visible post of secretary of state someone who was respected, inspired confidence, and whose name was linked to some of the great successes of the first Nixon term? In these circumstances, Nixon chose a man whose prestige and fame he often felt had come at his own expense. It was a bizarre twist of affairs that Henry Kissinger fit the bill so well.

could handle the situation himself. Sending a cable directly to the president, Martin requested a supplemental appropriation of nearly $500 million, which would return the level of assistance to Saigon to $1.6 billion.

Murray continued to press the Pentagon for precise figures on what money had already been spent and what would be available. The Pentagon found $562 million in funds appropriated by Congress in prior years but never spent. The DOD informed Murray, however, that only $300 million of this could be expended because of Congress's $1.1 billion ceiling. Now thoroughly confused, Murray cabled, "Information appreciated but nothing conclusive or consistent enough to lock in on where we actually stand. No two messages cite same figures, and volume of information has created much concern, many questions, and virtually no answers."

No one else seemed to have any answers either. It was not until March that the Department of Defense finally realized the magnitude of the aid crisis in Vietnam. Early that month, Secretary of Defense James Schlesinger forwarded Martin's request that the aid ceiling be restored to $1.6 billion to Congress. One week later Congress was ready to act, initiating hearings on the administration's special request.

Deputy Secretary of Defense William Clements made the administration's case before the House and Senate Armed Services Committees. Clements argued, "The hard facts are that the level of combat in Vietnam has never subsided to the level we hoped for." Despite this failure of the peace agreement, Clements argued that a "rough if tenuous balance of forces in Vietnam" existed, one that had to be maintained to achieve "peace and stability."

In what the *New York Times* described as a "muted" replay of the debates that "raged when the United States was involved militarily in the Vietnam War," a coalition of seasoned Congressional doves and newly converted former supporters of administration policy opposed the Pentagon's request. They strove to keep assistance to Indochina at the level established in December, a budgetary ceiling of little more than $1.1 billion, with an actual appropriation of $900 million. Senator Edward Kennedy of Massachusetts led the fight against raising the budgetary ceiling, arguing that the administration's request was not "an issue of our national defense and hardly one of our national security." South Dakota Senator James Abourezk echoed the arguments made in favor of prohibiting the bombing of Cambodia: "Once again, it appears that the United States is bent on following the dangerous precedent of the late fifties and early sixties of increasing involvement . . . by increasing its military aid program."

Abourezk also played on the fears of many senators that U.S. aid to South Vietnam would never end, calculating that the nation would spend over $16 billion in the next fifteen years. Similarly, Senator Philip Hart of Michigan urged that the U.S. stop giving Thieu a "blank check." For many members of Congress who simply wanted to place Vietnam in the nation's history books, rather than in the daily newspapers, this argument may have been the most telling. California Senator Alan Cranston was blunt: "As things stand, Mr. Chairman, we are not getting any closer to peace in South Vietnam, and we might as well face it."

The fate of the administration's request was sealed when the most venerable Senate conservative, Barry Goldwater, echoed Cranston's lament. "For all intents and purposes," he frankly stated, "I think we can scratch South Vietnam."

On April 3 the Senate Armed Services Committee turned down the administration's request to raise the ceiling, but before the entire Senate could act, the House of Representatives settled the matter by voting 177 to 154 against the administration. Fifty House Republicans joined the battle against the new aid request.

The final vote may have been as much a result of Ambassador Graham Martin's intemperate remarks as of rational argument. On April 2 Senator Kennedy released to the press a copy of a cable sent by Martin to the State De-

U.S. Defense Attaché General John Murray, hosted by Lt. General Nguyen Van Minh (with three stars), examines a map at the Thu Duc Military Academy, November 1973.

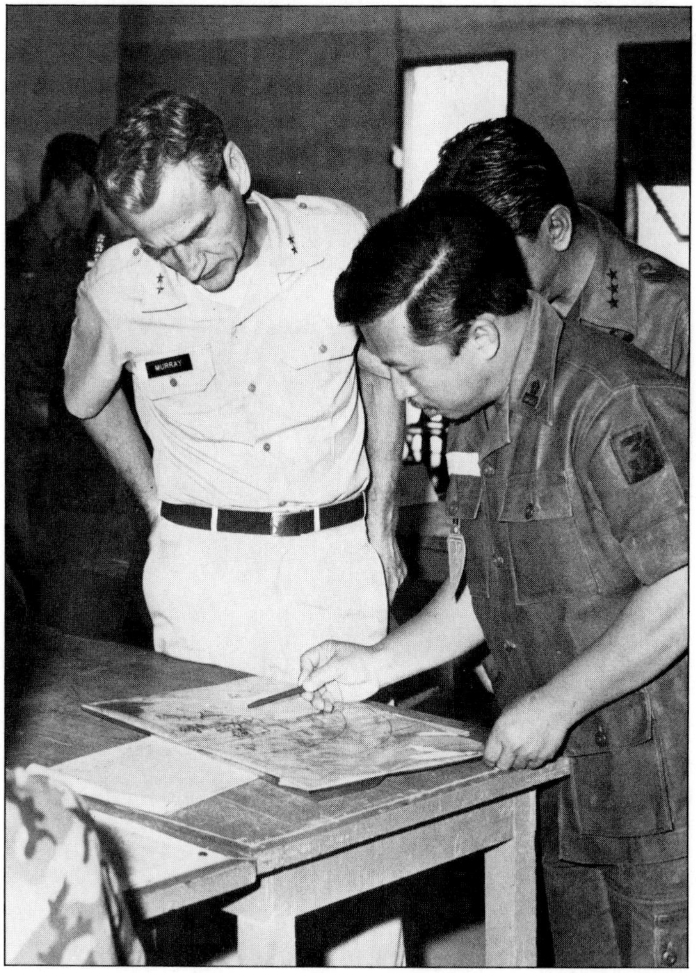
MURRAY

partment in response to the senator's request for information on U.S. policy in Southeast Asia. In his cable Martin linked Kennedy to a group "whose objective is to aid Hanoi." He then advised Kissinger, "It would be the height of folly to permit Kennedy the tactical advantage of an honest and detailed answer to the questions of substance raised in his letter." With the publication of Martin's letter and the unfavorable vote in the House, the administration withdrew its request in order to try a different approach.

The Pentagon's new proposal centered on the so-called prior year funds, monies allocated by Congress in previous years but never spent. Legally the Pentagon could spend any prior year funds that made up the difference between the $900 million appropriated by Congress and the $1.126 billion budgetary ceiling. The administration proposed that it be permitted to spend prior year funds beyond the $1.126 billion ceiling, an amount that would increase aid to South Vietnam by another $250 million.

Congress, however, was in no mood to assent to this "back door resort," as one congressman called it. Suspicious of the bookkeeping procedures adopted by the Pentagon to accumulate these prior year funds, conservative Representative John J. Flynt of Georgia told his colleagues, "It reminds one of the old story; figures don't lie but liars sometimes figure." Meanwhile, the General Accounting Office disputed the legality of the Pentagon's proposal. It argued that these funds would place the DOD over the $2.7 billion aid ceiling enacted for FY 1973.

Senator Kennedy again led the fight against this new effort to increase aid to South Vietnam. While not ignoring the GAO report, Kennedy placed the issue on a higher plane. Speaking to a Senate that had already asserted its

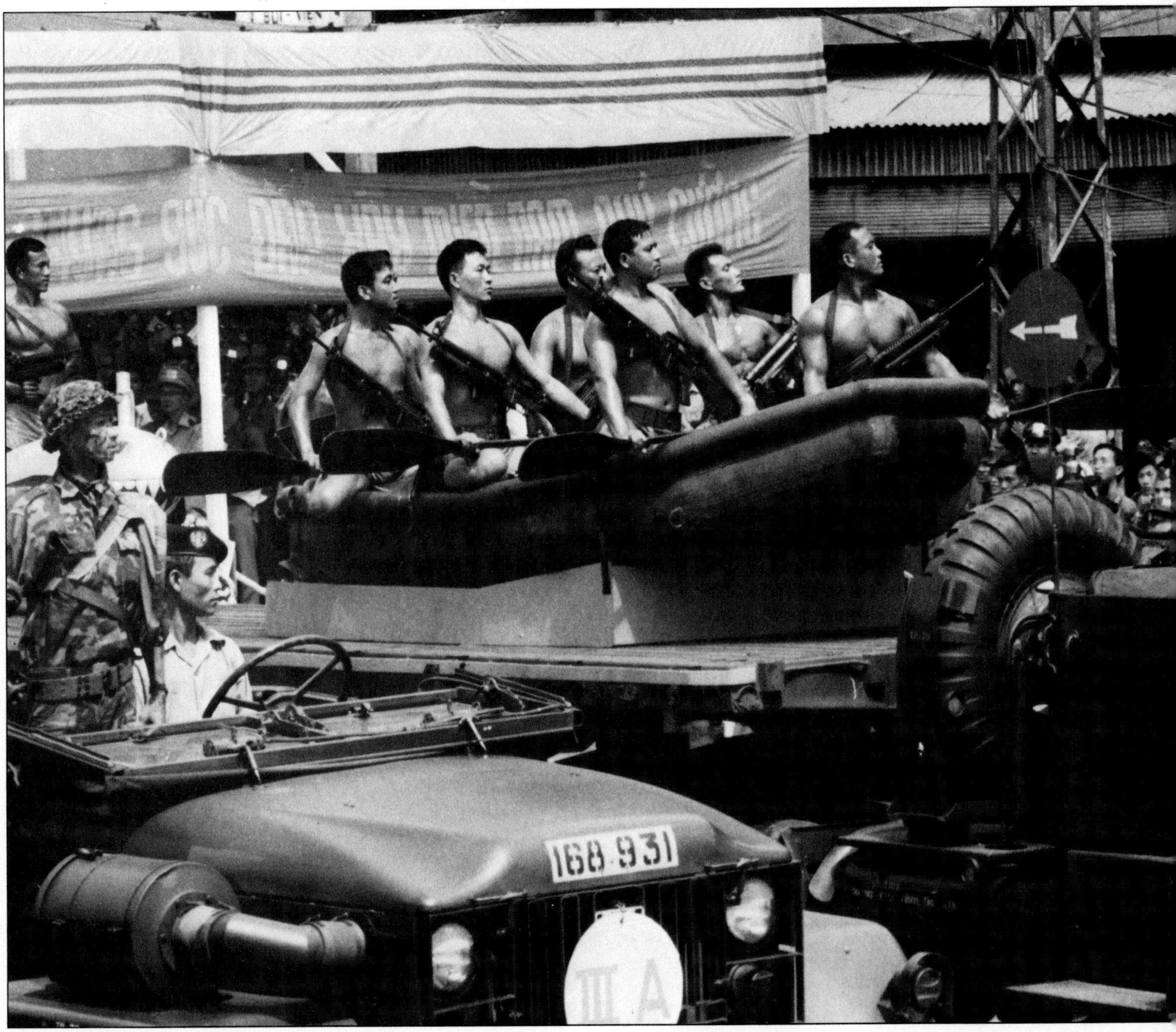

168-931

rights in the conduct of foreign policy, Kennedy asked whether such "creative bookkeeping" did not undo the intent of Congress:

The question is whether there is any real purpose in Congress setting a ceiling on spending for military aid to South Vietnam, if the Pentagon continues to spend as if the ceiling did not exist—assuming it will always get approval somehow, someway to spend more when it runs out.

On May 6 the Senate followed Kennedy's advice, voting forty-three to thirty-eight to accept an amendment that prohibited the accounting change. At the end of the month both houses of Congress passed the FY 1974 Defense Appropriations Bill, limiting aid to South Vietnam to the originally established ceiling of $1.126 billion. On June 8, in one of his last acts as president, Richard Nixon signed the bill into law. Three weeks later fiscal year 1974 ended, and

the entire merry-go-round began again as the Congress grappled with the FY 1975 military assistance budget.

The refusal of Congress to increase military assistance to South Vietnam could not have come as much of a surprise to administration officials. Kissinger had predicted such action since the fall of 1972. Although various administration spokesmen had loudly reiterated the nation's commitments to Saigon ever since the signing of the peace agreement, the executive bureaucracy was sending Congress a very different message. In January 1974 the *New York Times* reported that "key elements" in the Pentagon and State Department disagreed with the request to raise the aid ceiling. These unnamed sources feared that further aid "would sit around the docks in crates." Furthermore, they had other, higher priorities in the defense budget and believed that the administration's request would "create an unfavorable atmosphere" within Congress for the new defense budget as a whole.

President Nixon had asked the nation to "watch what we do, not what we say." The inactivity of his foreign policy bureaucracy thus spoke much louder than the empty phrases of commitments to Indochina. No administration official appeared before Congress to argue for more aid to Indochina until March, when the fiscal year was nearly three-quarters over.

The actions of the House and Senate were therefore not so much an assertion of Congressional prerogatives as a reflection of a new consensus in the country. This consensus, which Henry Kissinger described as the "new conventional wisdom," was stated by one of the administration's most steadfast supporters, *Newsweek* columnist Stewart Alsop. In a March 1973 column, Alsop asked:

Can the South Vietnamese not learn to defend their own turf within these many months? If not, why not? And if not, when?

According to Kissinger's paraphrase, Alsop's argument was that "if the South Vietnamese could not take care of themselves after a decade of assistance, they would never be able to do so."

This war-weariness was the cause of the new coalition in Congress between long-standing doves and conservatives, which proved fatal to the administration's requests for additional assistance. For better or for worse, the country was more united on its future policy toward Vietnam in 1974 than it had been in a decade.

Unfortunately for President Thieu and the Republic of Vietnam the "new conventional wisdom" could not have emerged at a worse time. Under Thieu's policies, South Vietnam had ruled out every option save eventual military victory. Now Thieu would be forced to play out his hand in the face of dwindling American assistance, with no assurance of future military aid, and against a foe that was growing stronger with each passing day.

Members of South Vietnam's elite frogmen unit ride past the reviewing stand during a June 1973 parade.

Home at Last

Few events in the Vietnam War stirred Americans as much as the return of the prisoners of war. By March 1973 the 653 POWs had made their way from North Vietnamese prisons and PRG camps in the South to Clark Air Force Base in the Philippines and, finally, to a reunion with their loved ones in the States. For these men, some of whom had endured nearly eight years of captivity, and even torture, arriving home meant rebirth—in a land of freedom and comfort.

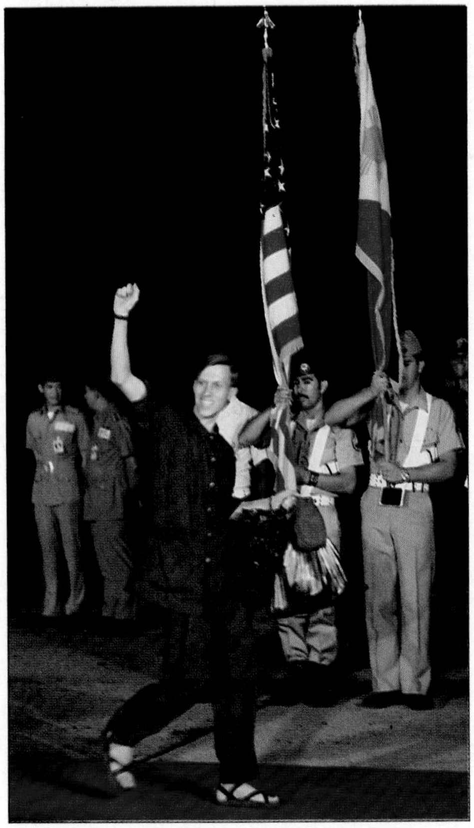

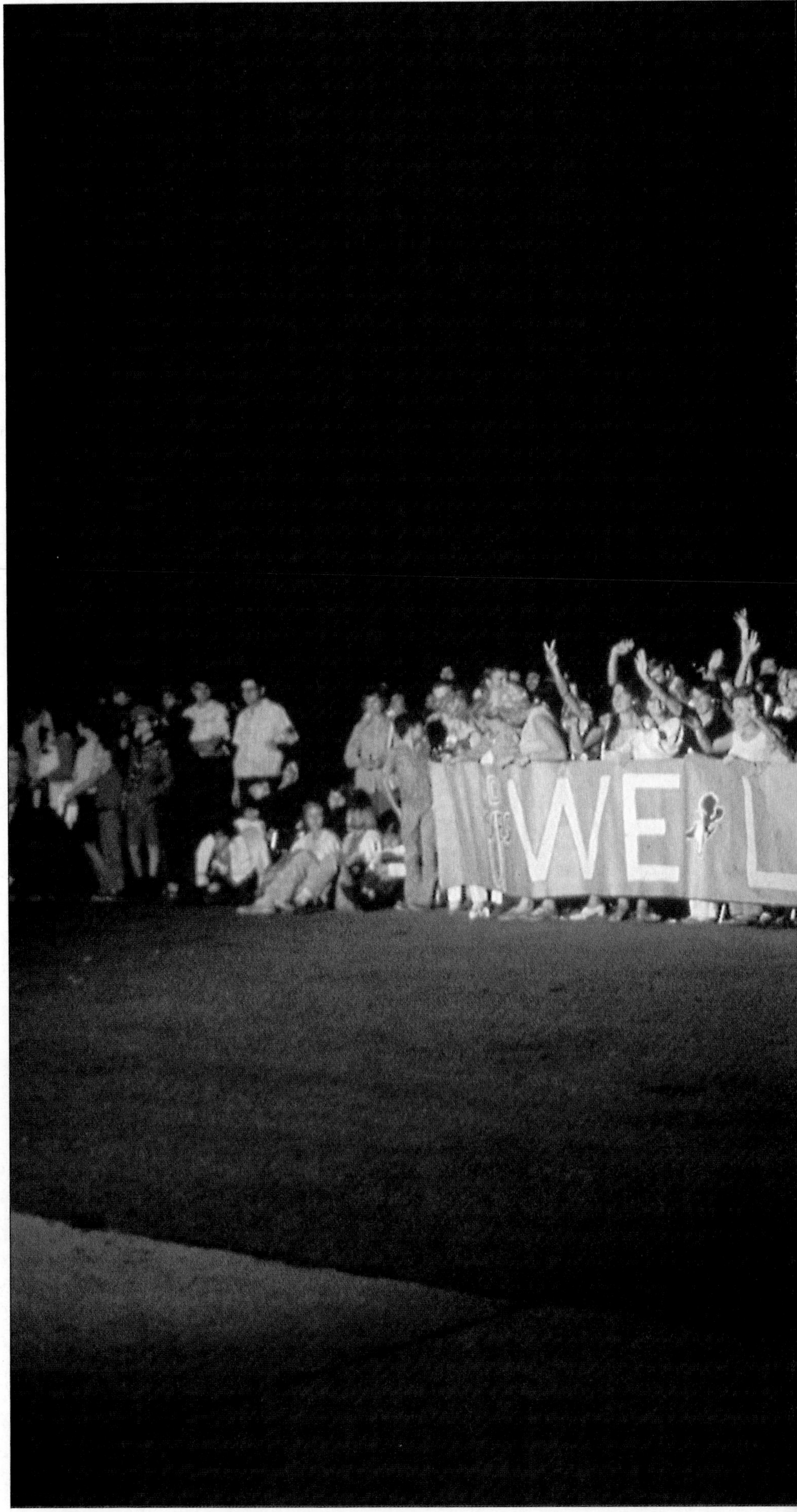

Above. *James Hestand, a captive of the PRG, arrives in Saigon on his way to the Philippines.* Right. *An adoring crowd greets the POWs at Clark Air Force Base.*

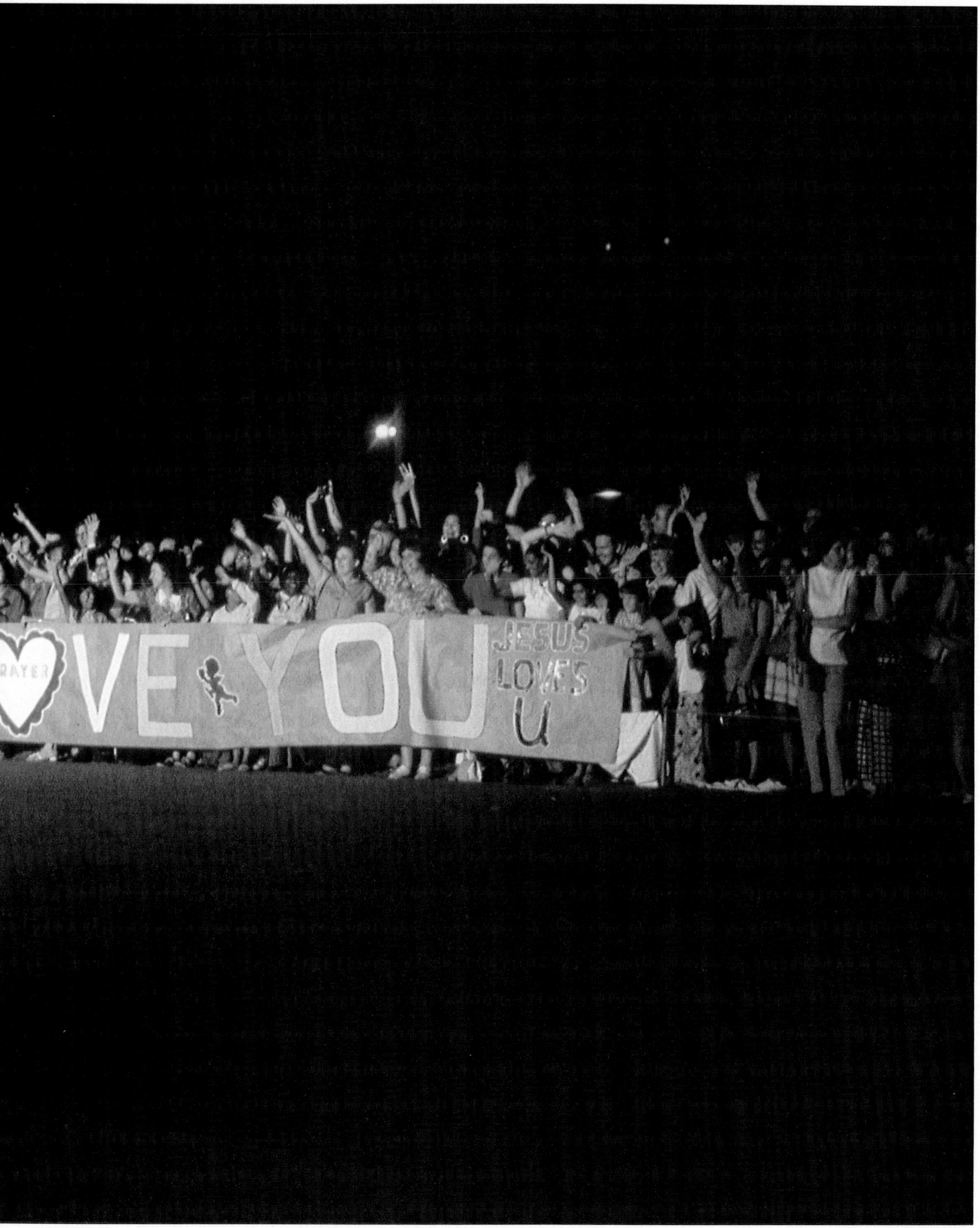
VE YOU
JESUS
LOVES
U

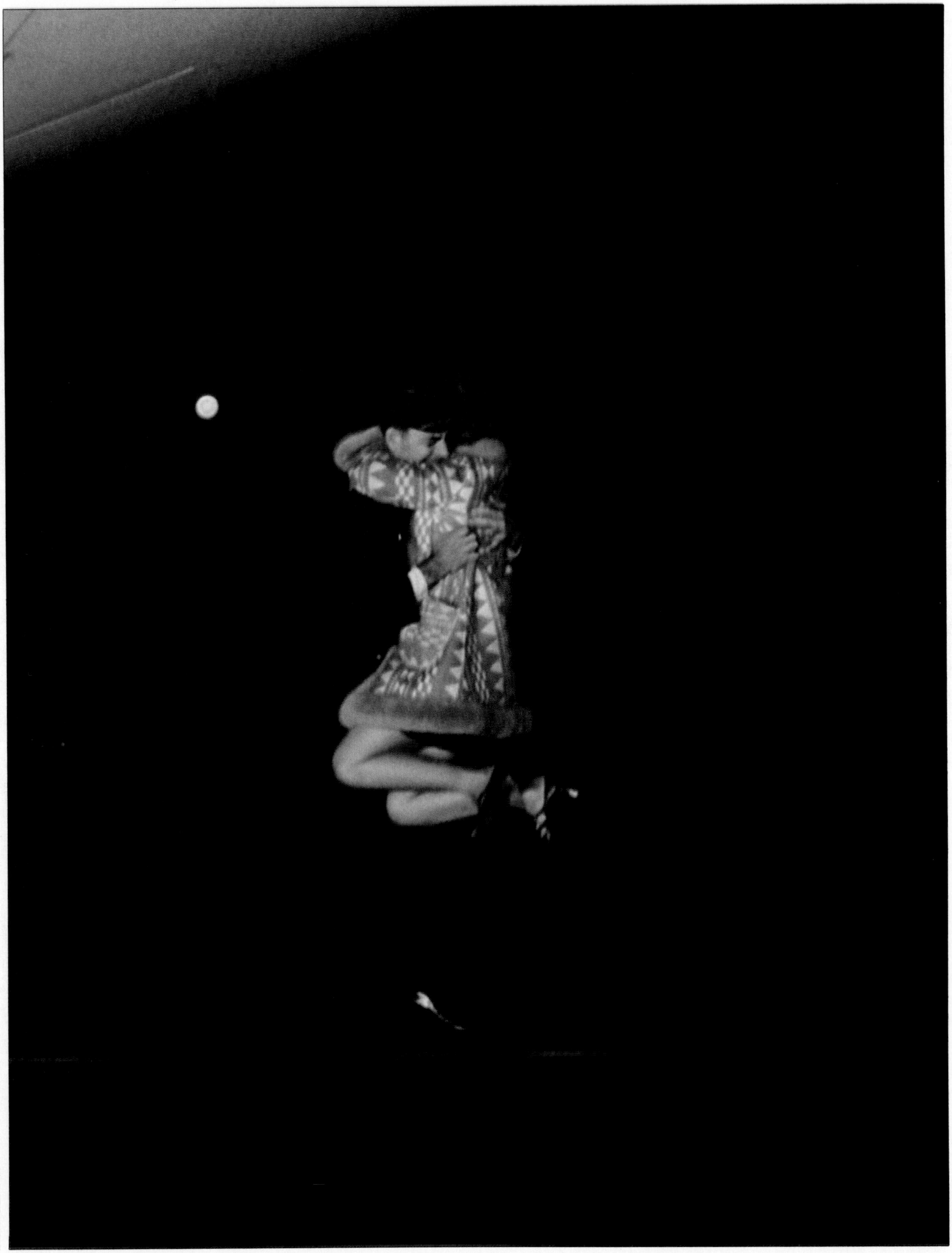

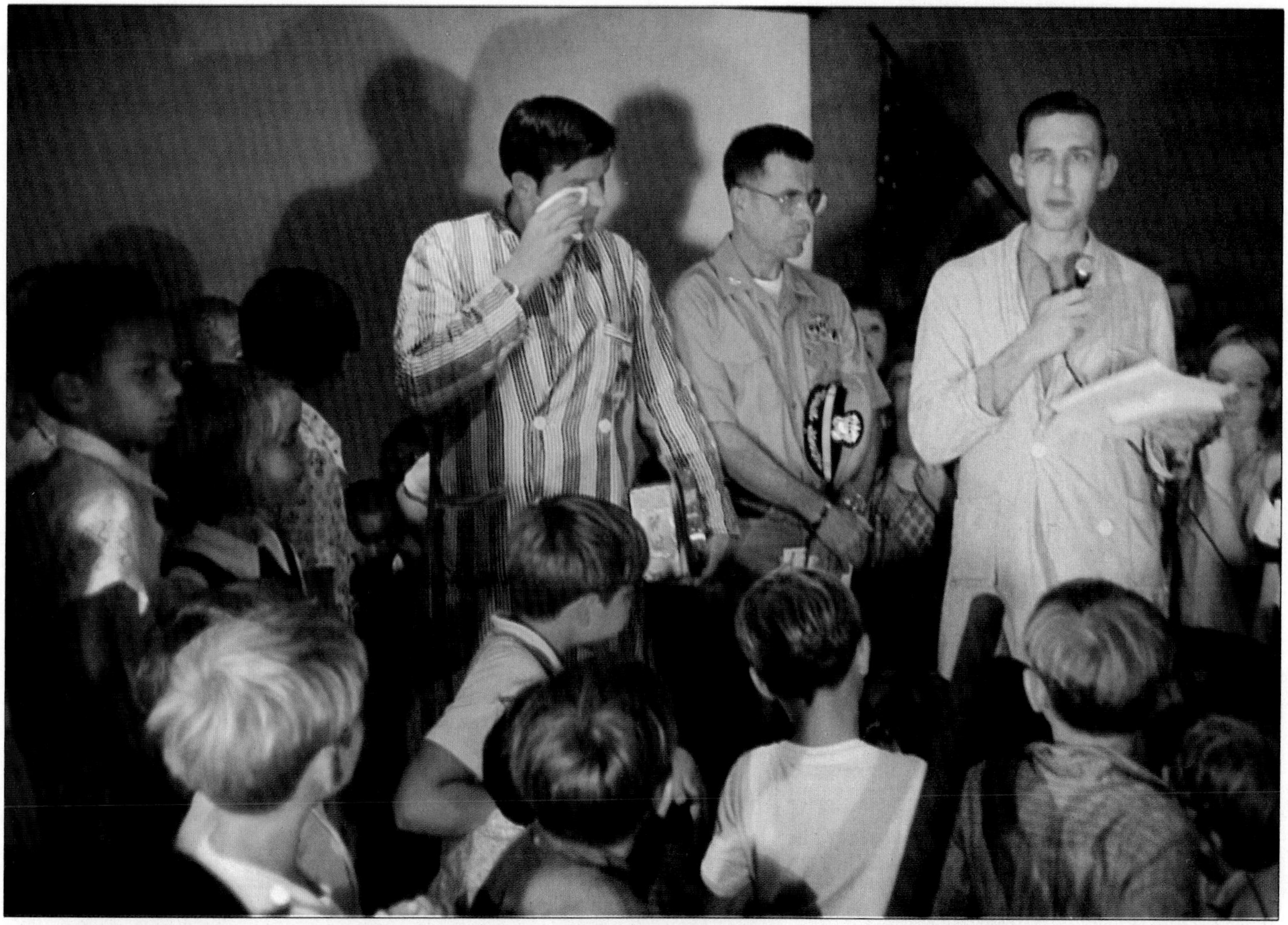

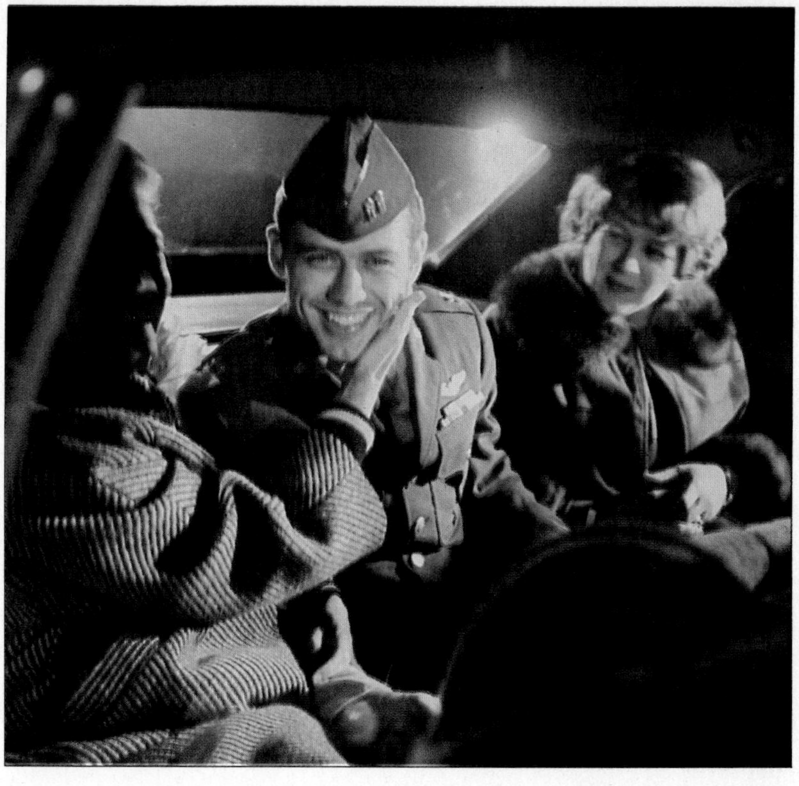

After many long years of bitter polarization, the American public united to give the returning POWs a heroes' welcome. Upon their arrival home, the POWs walked down a red carpet to be greeted by cheering crowds, parades, and telegrams. Americans showered them with gifts: clothing, taxi rides, cruises, and lifetime passes to baseball stadiums. Though comforted by these tokens, the POWs would long battle the physical and psychological scars of their imprisonment.

Opposite. *Maj. Arthur Burer, a POW for seven years, embraces his wife, Nancy, at Maryland's Andrews Air Force Base, February 1973.* Above. *Sgt. William Robinson (right) and navy Capt. Jeremiah Denton (center) receive gifts from schoolchildren at Clark Air Force Base.* Left. *Air force Capt. James E. Ray basks in the attention of his mother and sister at Lackland Air Force Base, Texas.*

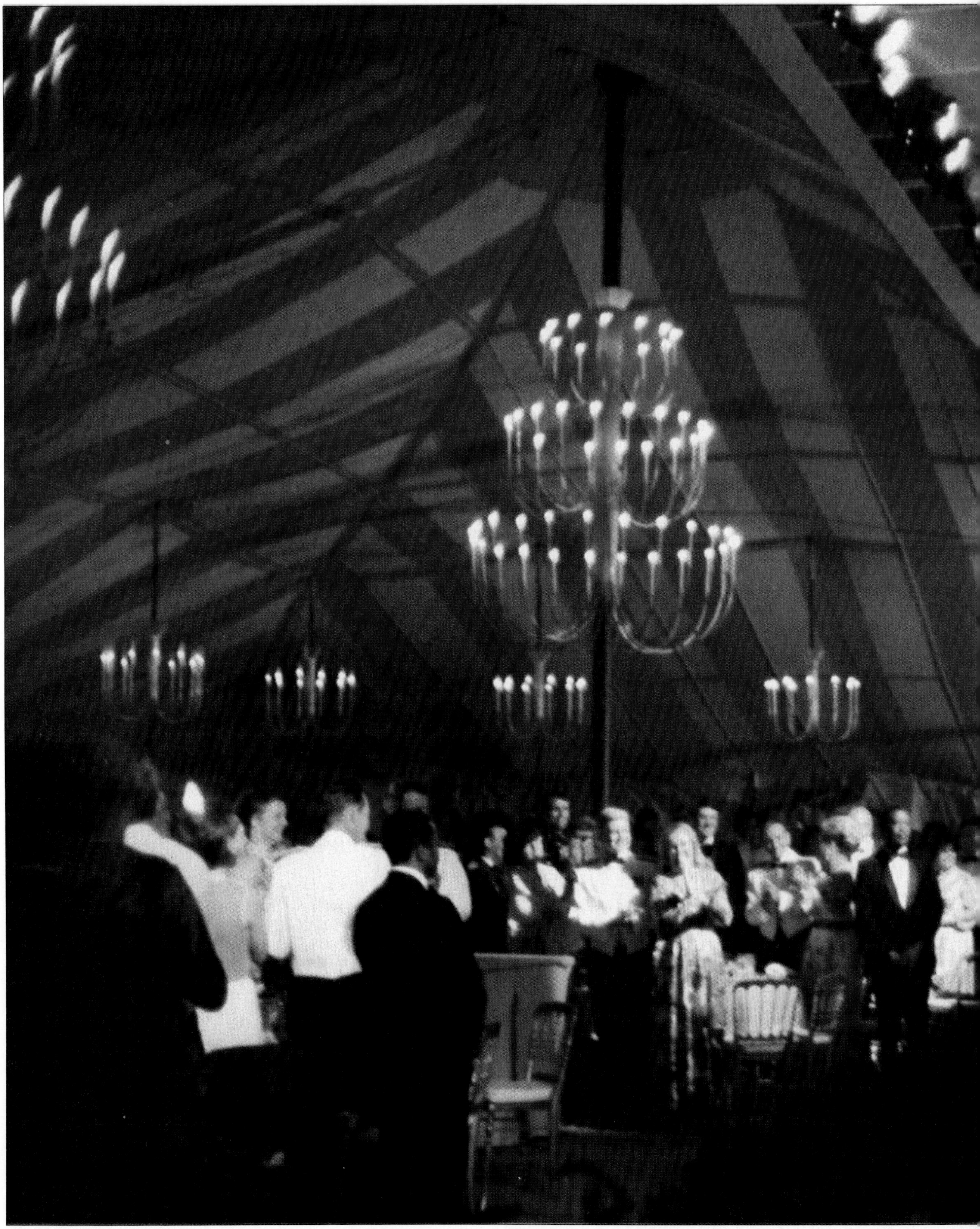

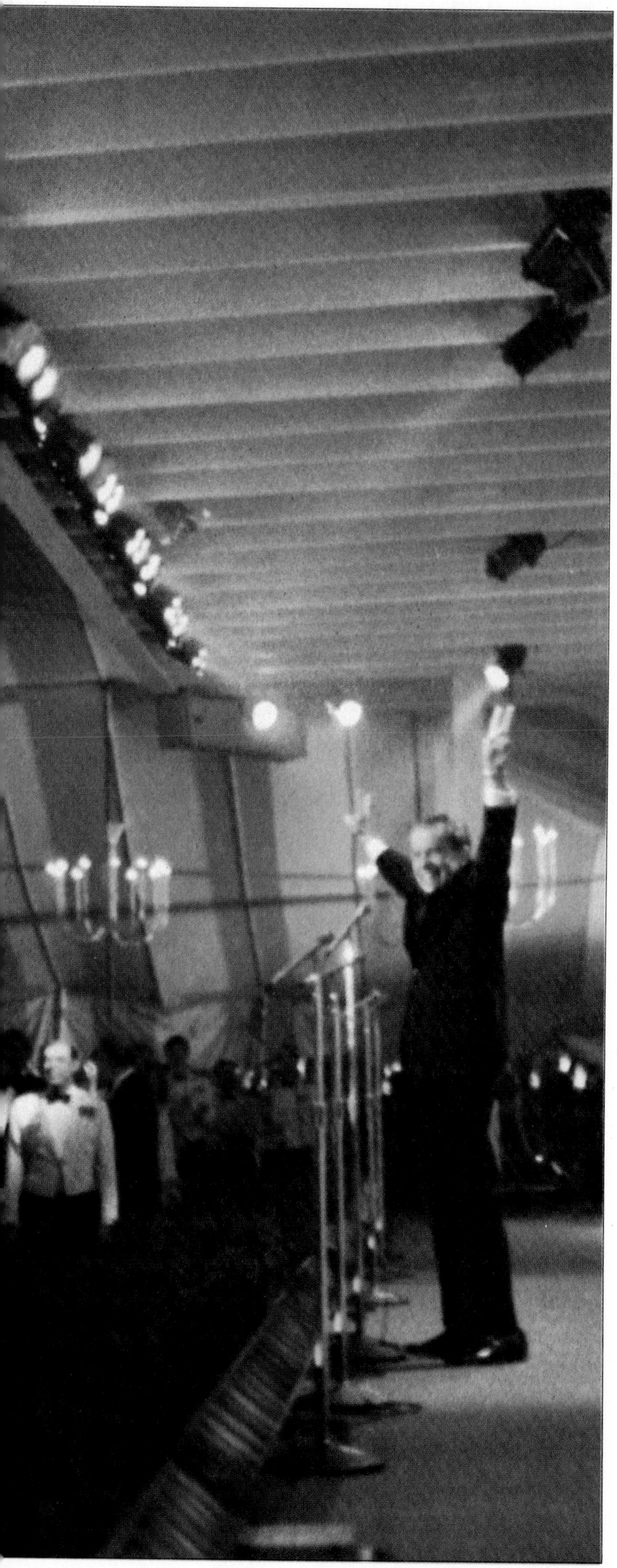

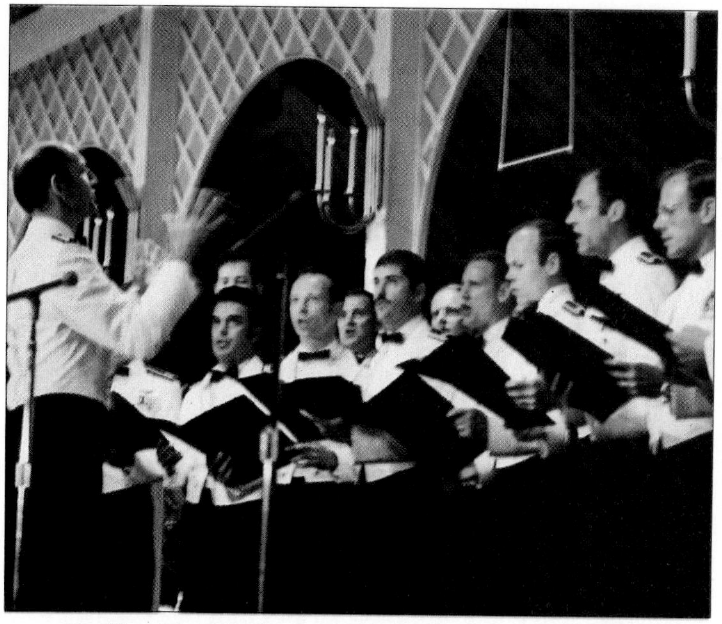

On May 24, 1973, President Nixon held a celebration at the White House for the returned prisoners of war. Here, during the event, a chorus of ex-prisoners sings a POW hymn composed by Lieutenant Colonel J. Quincy Collins while he was held in a North Vietnamese prison.

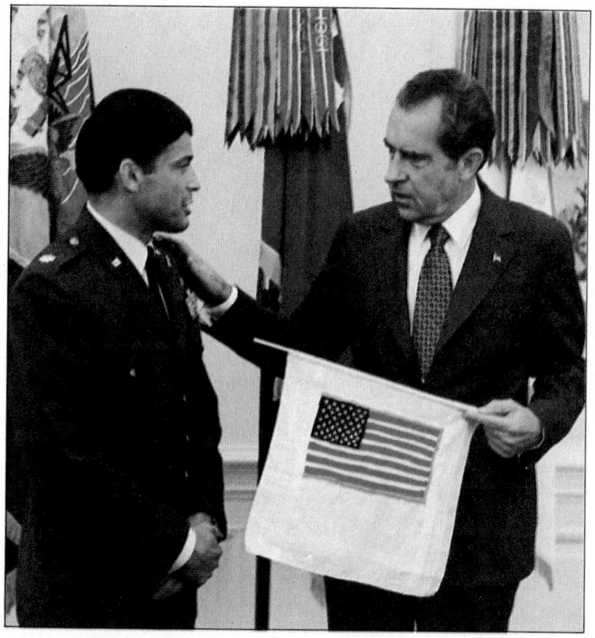

Above. *Air force Lieutenant Colonel John Dramese presents the president with a flag he fashioned from scraps of string and clothing he gathered during his imprisonment.*

Left. *At the dinner held that night on the South Lawn of the White House, President Nixon waves triumphantly toward his 1,260 guests, the former prisoners and their families.*

The Third Indochina War

Launched with bold hopes and high expectations, the 1972 Easter offensive left Communist forces in a state of utter exhaustion. At the end of the year their holdings in the South amounted by their own admission to little more than "rubber trees and bricks"—a thin strip of mountainous jungle along the western border and a handful of enclaves in the Mekong Delta. Devastated by American bombing, unanticipated ARVN resistance, and their own tactical blunders, the enemy had lost as many as 100,000 men in a futile attempt at headlong conquest. Communist Local Forces were decimated, their carefully constructed urban political networks in disarray. Initial infiltration could not make up the staggering human losses, while continuing B-52 raids in the North prevented the replacement of millions of dollars' worth of shattered tanks and abandoned armored personnel carriers. Laboring under a critical shortage of ammunition, many major units were capable at best of defensive action,

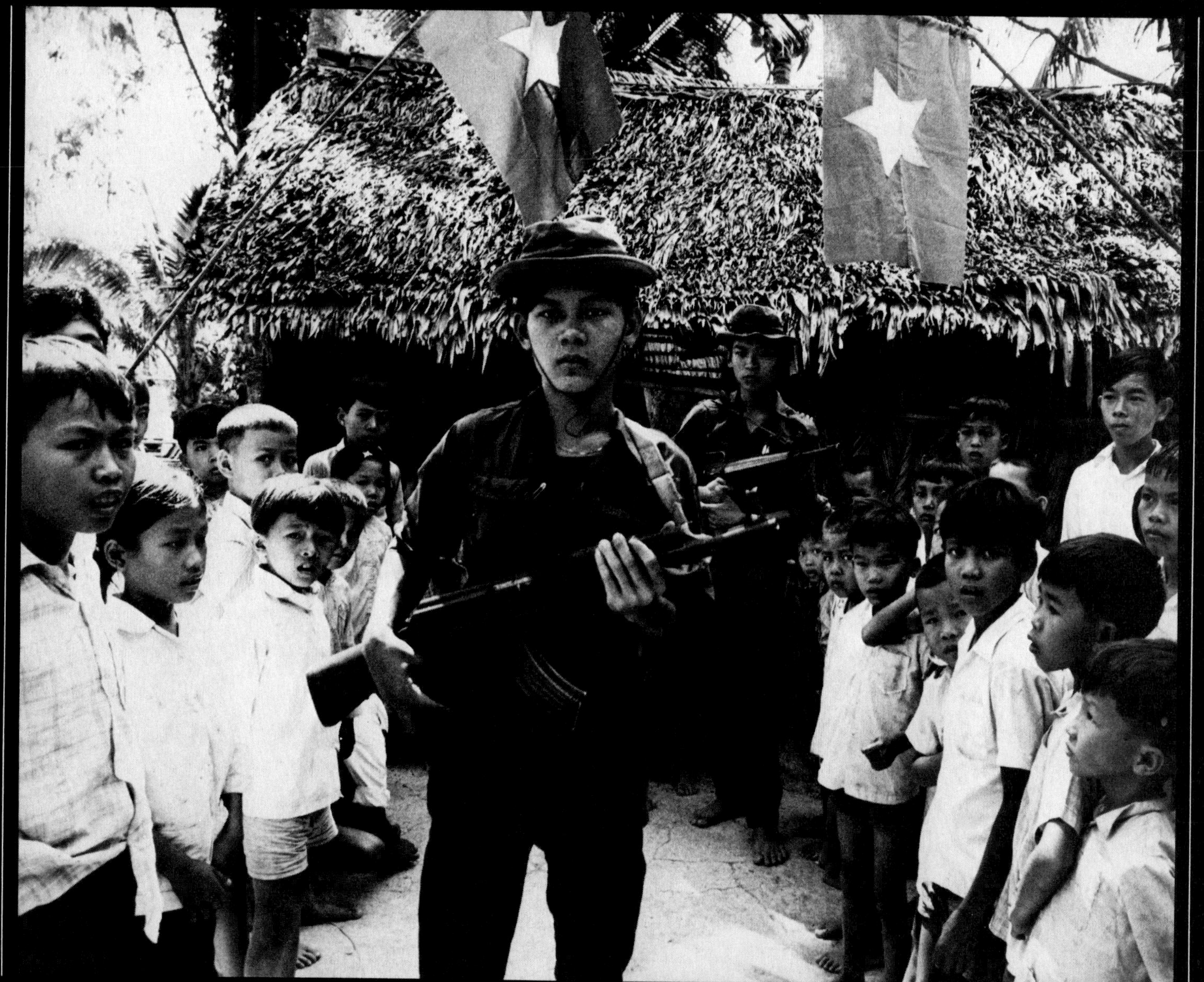

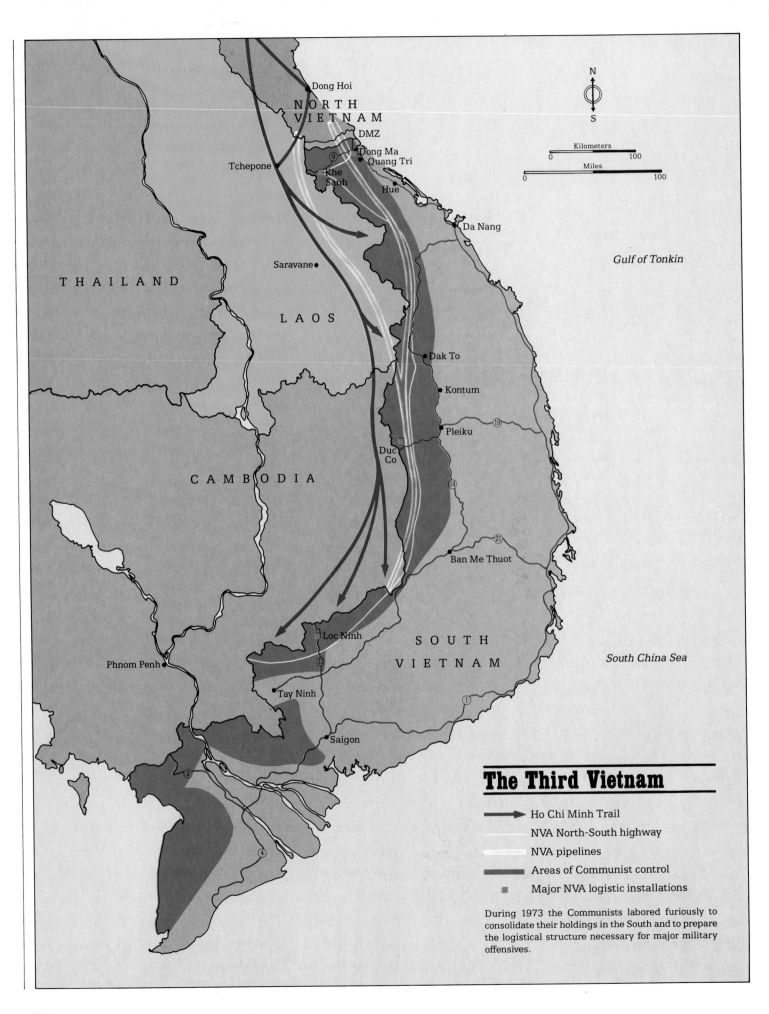

The Third Vietnam

→ Ho Chi Minh Trail

—— NVA North-South highway

—— NVA pipelines

▬ Areas of Communist control

▪ Major NVA logistic installations

During 1973 the Communists labored furiously to consolidate their holdings in the South and to prepare the logistical structure necessary for major military offensives.

North
Vietnam

Dong Hoi

DMZ

Dong Ma
Quang Tri

Tchepone

Khe
Sanh

Hue

Da Nang

Gulf of Tonkin

THAILAND

LAOS

Saravane

Dak To

Kontum

Pleiku

Duc
Co

CAMBODIA

Ban Me Thuot

SOUTH
VIETNAM

South China Sea

Phnom Penh

Loc Ninh

Tay Ninh

Saigon

intent no longer on victory but on their own survival.

Yet barely a year later U.S. analysts reported that the NVA was in "the strongest military position in the history of the war." During those twelve months the Communists constructed a new logistical corridor into the central highlands, refitted Main and Local Force units, stockpiled tons of military supplies in the South, created a seven-division strategic reserve, began the reorganization of their field commands, and built new training facilities from which poured a steady stream of replacements for the southern battlefields. This transformation reflected in part Hanoi's need to reequip its battered army after the losses of the previous year. But the build-up of 1973 had other, more powerful causes as well: the absence of American military might, the stalemate of negotiations with Saigon, and the growing pressure of ARVN operations into Communist-held territory. The result was the abandonment of a strategy emphasizing a political solution to the conflict and a fateful decision that would plunge Vietnam once more into a bloody and unrestrained contest of arms.

The "Third Vietnam"

In the wake of the Paris agreement one of the primary tasks before Hanoi was the consolidation of the territory under its control in the South. Stretching from the DMZ through the center of Quang Tri Province, down a narrow corridor along the border with Laos and Cambodia, across the watery flats northwest of Saigon into the Mekong Delta and the U Minh Forest, this newest piece in the geopolitical jigsaw puzzle of Indochina was the key to North Vietnam's post-cease-fire strategy: to forge a military base secure from ARVN encroachment and to institutionalize Communist political presence in South Vietnam. "It may be the last thing the world needs," observed a U.S. official in Saigon, "but the Communists are in the process of building a 'Third Vietnam.' "

Even before the final agreements were signed, Hanoi had begun to establish an administrative apparatus in its southern territories, bringing in as many as 5,000 political cadres, schoolteachers, and health officials. By January 1973, northern Quang Tri Province boasted local offices of the Departments of Communications and Transportation, Culture, Education, Finance, and Public Health. In the Phu My District of Binh Dinh Province the Communists created Village Administrative Committees with some positions filled by demobilized VC military cadres, constructed village offices, and confiscated South Vietnamese ID cards and replaced them with their own identification documents. If someone wanted to travel into government-controlled areas, he could obtain his South Vietnamese papers at the village office. When he returned, he would exchange the government documents for his Communist card. To further enforce their discipline, the Communists fortified the villages and told the peasants they were prepared to defend them in the event of South Vietnamese government interference.

The urgent need for economic development of the underpopulated region prompted the importation of thousands of civilians to build new farms and villages and to grow rice for North Vietnamese soldiers. Some peasants were led down Laotian trails into primitive areas of the central highlands. Farther south, refugees who had fled their homes for the comparative safety of Cambodia were resettled in Tay Ninh and Binh Long Provinces. They were joined by students from Hanoi and by young women brought from rural areas of North Vietnam to labor on agricultural and construction projects and to live among NVA troops.

To demonstrate the legitimacy and strength of the "Third Vietnam," and to combat the government's extensive refugee resettlement programs, the Communists opened the "liberated" area to people from surrounding provinces. Visitors were invited to tour farm cooperatives and new settlements. Military units organized shows and displayed their growing arsenal of modern weapons. More practically, the PRG set up a fund for peasants who were willing to change sides, offering attractive credit terms for the purchase of water buffaloes with repayment in produce instead of cash.

The most glittering jewel of the new Communist possessions was Dong Ha, which had fallen to the NVA during the first month of the Easter offensive. An undistinguished former district town on the Cua Viet River in northern Quang Tri Province, Dong Ha was transformed into a modern city complete with electricity, running water, and a public transportation system consisting of thirty brand-new buses. Equally remarkable for the economically straitened North Vietnamese were the plentiful Chinese consumer goods conspicuously displayed in the city's marketplace.

Dong Ha was more than a showcase of modern socialist life, however. Its proximity to North Vietnam and its access to the sea made the city's rebuilt port facilities the major economic conduit for goods destined for areas farther south. Some of the ships docking at Dong Ha carried agricultural supplies and construction equipment. But the bulk of the material that flowed through the city was of a different nature entirely. Whatever other functions it served for Hanoi, Dong Ha was first and foremost a vast military depot. Through it in a growing volume during the summer of 1973 came weapons and supplies to refurbish Communist forces and prepare for a new round of war. For although Hanoi sought what advantage it could through political agitation and negotiation, there were those in the Politburo who remained convinced that in the

Preceding page. *Communist militiamen, armed with AK47s and flanked by the yellow-starred flag of the NLF, occupy a South Vietnamese village in January 1973.*

end the only solution to Vietnam's problems would be a military conquest of the South.

Preparing the military option

In his account of the final North Vietnamese offensive in 1975, Chief of Staff General Van Tien Dung wrote of the need to "organize the field of battle" to fully exploit the NVA's military assets. "[We] needed enough communications routes and motorized transport to bring sufficient food, ammunition, and weapons to the front. A key problem was to develop a system of roads for good mobility."

For nearly twenty years the Communists had made do with a maze of paths, trails, and dirt and paved roads snaking through Laos and Cambodia and known collectively as the Ho Chi Minh Trail. The steadily expanding network had served the North well, funneling a regular supply of men and arms south despite repeated American and South Vietnamese efforts at interdiction. The very primitiveness of the system had worked to the Communists' advantage, making detection difficult and repairs relatively simple. What had once supported a combination guerrilla and conventional infantry force, however, could no longer adequately sustain the modern mechanized army Hanoi now had at its disposal. By the summer of 1973 construction of a new all-weather hard-surfaced road system was well under way.

Some 30,000 soldiers, Vanguard Youth, and impressed montagnard workers hacked, bulldozed, and blasted their way south from Quang Tri Province through thick jungle and rugged mountains to Dak To where the new road joined Highway 14. Radiating from this central artery secondary roads stretched west to the Ho Chi Minh Trail and east toward the coastal lowlands. "Almost every day," recalled ARVN 3d Division commander Major General Nguyen Duy Hinh, "our observation planes discovered a new stretch of road being built, its red clay color shining through the dark green jungle canopy."

Dirt roads and makeshift pontoon river crossings soon gave way to paved highway and concrete bridges. Large rear-service areas appeared along the infiltration corridor: warehouses, storage depots, and major logistical bases at Khe Sanh and the A Shau Valley. Paralleling the new route ran an eight-inch fuel pipeline complete with pumping stations and fuel-storage areas capable of supplying the thousands of gallons of petroleum necessary to run the tanks, trucks, and armored vehicles on which the NVA had come to depend.

As the new road system pushed steadily ahead, men and materiel began pouring into South Vietnam in direct violation of the Paris agreement. During the first year of the cease-fire between 70,000 and 85,000 new troops crossed into PRG-held territory. This was a sizable number, but far less than the infiltration during the previous year of all-out offensive. Nor did it represent more than a

partial net gain for the Communist order of battle as other NVA soldiers were deployed to the North, returned home for rest and relaxation, or died in battle. More significant than the rate of infiltration during 1973 was the new method of travel. What was once an arduous journey on foot taking up to three months to complete now could be accomplished by truck in little more than three weeks.

Convoys of unprecedented size—sometimes as great as 200 to 300 trucks—brought with them not only men but a vast quantity of food, boots, uniforms, weapons, and ammunition. DAO analysts estimated that in September alone over 16,000 tons of materiel entered South Vietnam. The amount of supplies was so great that much of it had to be left in the open until enough warehouses could be built to store it. Such cavalier treatment of precious military commodities would have been unthinkable during the days of American bombing, but now without the B-52s to contend with, hundreds of tanks, rockets, armored personnel carriers, assault guns, and artillery pieces rolled south unimpeded.

Although they had on paper the fourth largest air force in the world, the South Vietnamese were unable to halt or even seriously disrupt this growing stream of men and supplies. The reasons were numerous, but the chief cause was not far to seek. One of the most notable aspects of the military build-up in the South was the increasing size and sophistication of Communist air defenses. By the end of 1973 the NVA had twenty-two antiaircraft regiments in South Vietnam, twice the number they had at the time of the cease-fire. These units were equipped with 12.7MM and 14.5MM antiaircraft machine guns, automatic cannon, including the 57MM radar-controlled model, a new version of the hand-held, heat-seeking SA-7 Strela missile accurate to 15,000 feet, as well as the formidable SA-2 surface-to-air missiles with a range in distance and altitude of nineteen nautical miles and 85,000 feet. Lacking the electronic countermeasures employed by the U.S. Air Force, South Vietnamese pilots were forced to operate far above effective reconnaissance or attack altitudes. Making penetration of Communist airspace even more difficult was an expanding radar network that eventually covered all of MR 1 and large parts of MR 2 and 3.

The influx of new soldiers and the modernization of weapons and equipment placed a high priority on enhanced training. New training centers were created on either side of the DMZ capable of accommodating up to eighteen recruit battalions at a time. Simultaneously, Local Force VC units in the South received new instruction and weapons, including AK47 rifles, B40 and B41 grenade launchers, and heavy machine guns.

If the resurgence of Hanoi's forces in the South was of mounting concern to GVN and American officials as the year went on, equally troubling was the speed with which the Communists reconstituted a strategic reserve. Shortly after the cease-fire, the 308th and 312th NVA Divisions redeployed from Quang Tri Province to an area just north of the DMZ. Over the next months they were joined by the rebuilt 341st Division and from Laos the 320B and 316th Divisions. When added to the 308B Division garrisoned near Hanoi, and the 968th Division located in southern Laos, North Vietnam had seven reserve divisions totaling 51,000 men. With their proximity to the southern battlefields, and the new rapidity with which they could be deployed, these units hung like a dark and menacing cloud over the horizon of South Vietnam.

A critical situation

The Communist build-up in South Vietnam did not proceed at a steady rate. While substantial amounts of supplies, artillery, and armor were brought south during the first six months of 1973, the number of Communist combat personnel dropped by approximately 25 percent. Whether this represented a desire to reduce the level of fighting, a willingness to give the political process time to work, or simply the normal decline in infiltration during the southern rainy season is difficult to determine. Sometime between July and September this trend was reversed, and by December VC/NVA combat forces in South Vietnam would be larger than they had been at the beginning of the year. But for the first nine months of 1973 the mounting materiel and expanding logistical system were not matched by a corresponding increase in offensive military operations.

Throughout the summer and early fall of 1973 COSVN directives and party resolutions circulated among the southern cadres continued to emphasize political struggle, propaganda, and proselytizing activity rather than military action. Communist attacks were primarily designed to protect their burgeoning logistical system and screen the build-up of their military infrastructure. For that reason they were most intense in the mountainous highlands of MR 1 and MR 2 and in the region northwest of Saigon.

What most attracted Communist attention during these months were isolated ARVN outposts that stood in the way of their advancing north-south highway or threatened

Contributing to the expanding Communist logistical network in South Vietnam, North Vietnamese volunteers construct a new all-weather hard-surfaced road in Quang Tri Province in the summer of 1973.

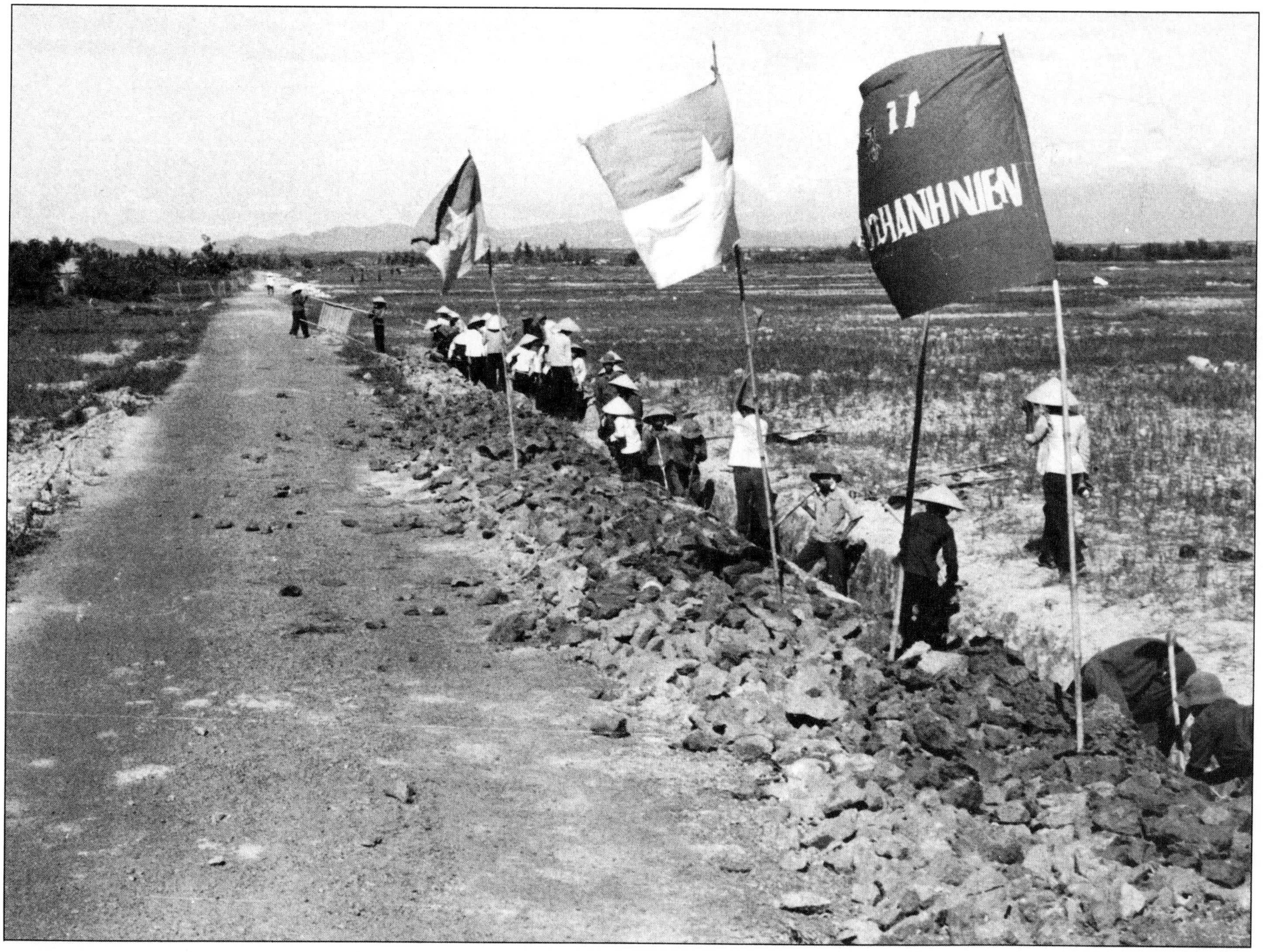

CHANH NIEN

communication lines with the coast. Heavy fighting broke out in June at the village of Trung Nghia, ten kilometers west of Kontum City. After a bloody campaign lasting nearly three months the 23d ARVN Division succeeded in driving elements of the F-10 NVA Division from the village, both sides suffering heavy casualties. The euphoria produced at II Corps headquarters by the success of the operation was short-lived, however. On September 22 NVA soldiers supported with heavy artillery and tanks overwhelmed the Le Minh Ranger Camp at Plei Djereng seventy-two kilometers west of Pleiku. Two weeks later another ARVN outpost at Bach Ma Mountain near Da Nang was also overrun.

Farther south the 92d ARVN Ranger Battalion continued to hold out at Tong Le Chan under increasing NVA pressure. Elsewhere in Tay Ninh Province the Communists pummeled GVN outposts at Soui Day and Nui Ba Den Mountain with artillery and mortar fire, using SA-7 rockets against VNAF helicopters attempting to resupply the beleaguered garrisons. NVA strategy in MR 3 was designed to prevent GVN encroachment into Communist base areas and supply corridors by putting pressure on vulnerable ARVN units, while at the same time undermining the tenuous hold the government maintained on vital communications links to the north and northwest. Attacks against an outpost at Don Luan and the Song Be airport in Phuoc Long Province were followed by sharp fighting south of Phu Giao where the 7th NVA Division attempted to block Route 1A between Saigon and Song Be. Meanwhile, a line of ARVN outposts ringing the Ho Bo Woods and Iron Triangle regions along the Saigon-Tay Ninh corridor was subjected to constant harassment.

The need to protect base areas and lines of supply also led to fierce encounters in the delta. The focal point of the fighting was the Tri Phap, a wasteland of swamp and brush honeycombed with permanent fortifications and hidden storage areas that had served as an insurgent base since the war with the French. As Communist units began moving into the Tri Phap in greater numbers during the early summer, a surge of battalion-sized attacks erupted against government outposts and firebases in the western half of Dinh Tuong Province. ARVN forces under IV Corps commander Major General Nguyen Vinh Nghi responded vigorously, causing heavy casualties the Communists were forced to accept because of the importance of infiltration corridors from Cambodia running through the Tri Phap and because of the need to secure as much as possible of the delta's most precious commodity, rice.

The demand for rice and the importance of retaining their political leverage in the countryside provoked a wave of sapper attacks and assassinations in the delta during the fall. The same motives marked an upsurge of guerrilla activity in MR 1 among the coastal hamlets of Quang Nam Province. In Quang Ngai refugees, not rice, were the main target. Attempting to destroy the GVN refugee program with its threat of increased government presence in contested territory, VC units launched a campaign of harassment and destruction against resettlement villages. As the frequency and scope of the attacks increased, the Communists resorted to mortar fire, demolitions, and antipersonnel mines planted along hamlet footpaths, resulting in a mounting toll of civilian casualties. In the early morning hours of September 6 the VC staged their most spectacular raid of the campaign, attacking An Tinh Hamlet with B40 rockets and incendiary grenades. Fanned by high winds, over 300 thatched houses were burned to the ground in a demonstration of Communist strength visible for miles around.

Yet for all they had achieved in consolidating the "Third Vietnam," expanding their logistical capabilities, and rebuilding the army in the South, by October 1973 the Communists faced, in Dung's words, a "critical situation."

Adopting a strategy of "half war, half peace," the DRV leadership had wagered that a combination of political pressure and military strength would compel Thieu to negotiate. Within two months of the cease-fire, however, it became clear that political action was proving far less successful than Hanoi had hoped. By May provincial-level cadres were already discussing the necessity of armed violence on a large scale, talking openly of "strategic raids" against Hue and Da Nang. Party commissars from MR 2 concluded at a meeting held in July that if the GVN refused to establish a coalition government the Communists had the capability to launch a "general offensive and general uprising." As the summer drew to a close it became more and more difficult for southern commanders to restrain local cadres from abandoning the post-cease-fire strategy.

The restlessness of their troops reflected mounting casualties produced by South Vietnamese military pressure. Although occasional forays had been made into GVN territory, VC/NVA attacks during this period were primarily designed to protect their own zones of control. President Thieu, however, was determined to take advantage of the government's initial military superiority. After throwing Communist forces out of villages and hamlets seized during the landgrab campaign, the ARVN had gone on the offensive, eliminating PRG "ink spots" in the delta, conducting successful pacification operations in the coastal lowlands of MR 1, imposing an economic blockade on the southern border zones, destroying scattered Communist base areas, spearheading the resettlement of 750,000 refugees into contested territory, and staging major operations that extended government control into remote areas dominated by the Communists for many years. The penetration of the Seven Mountains region and the destruction of the 1st NVA Division was only the most striking example. Although their overall strategic position continued to improve, the Communists found themselves absorbing a growing number of tactical setbacks.

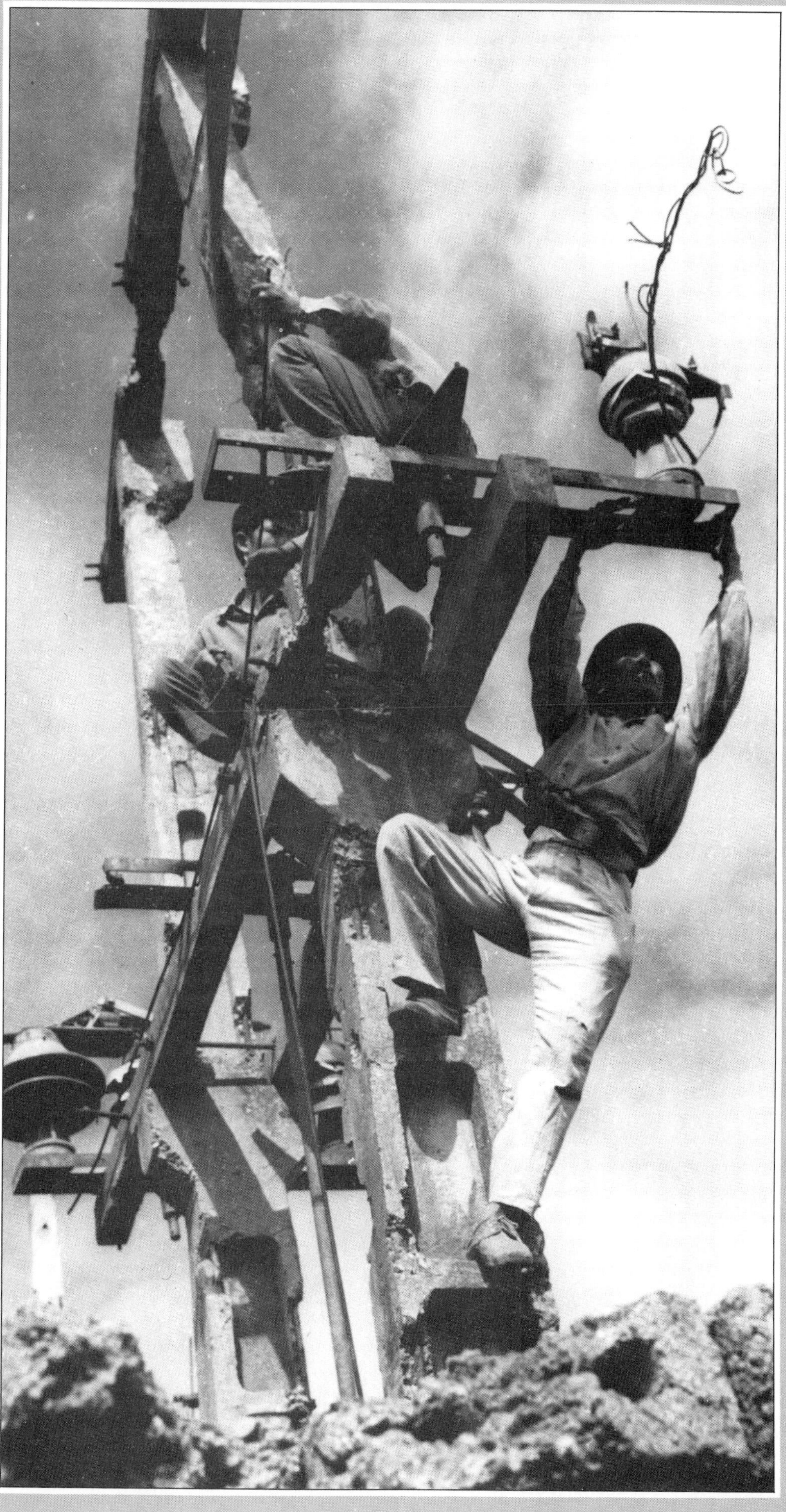

Northern Renewal

In 1973, with its skies empty of the deadly U.S. aerial arsenal, North Vietnam could again turn to rebuilding—its industry, its agriculture, its villages and roads. The rebuilding program of the late 1960s following Lyndon Johnson's bombing halt had been undone when President Nixon once more sent American bombers over the North, especially in 1972. This time, there would be a difference: Although the North Vietnamese were not to be sure of it until nearly the end of their final offensive of 1975, American aircraft would never again besiege the people of the North.

American bombs had taken their toll on the North's economy. Yet, in part because of North Vietnam's small industrial sector and in part because of the Communists' diligence in moving plants underground and in other ways protecting their factories, the bombing did not bring the North's economy to its knees. With the bombing halt, the people of the North could return their plants to more normal conditions and begin to beef up what had been a limited industrial capacity.

A linesman from the "Hero unit" repairs a severed power line in Thanh Hoa Province south of Hanoi.

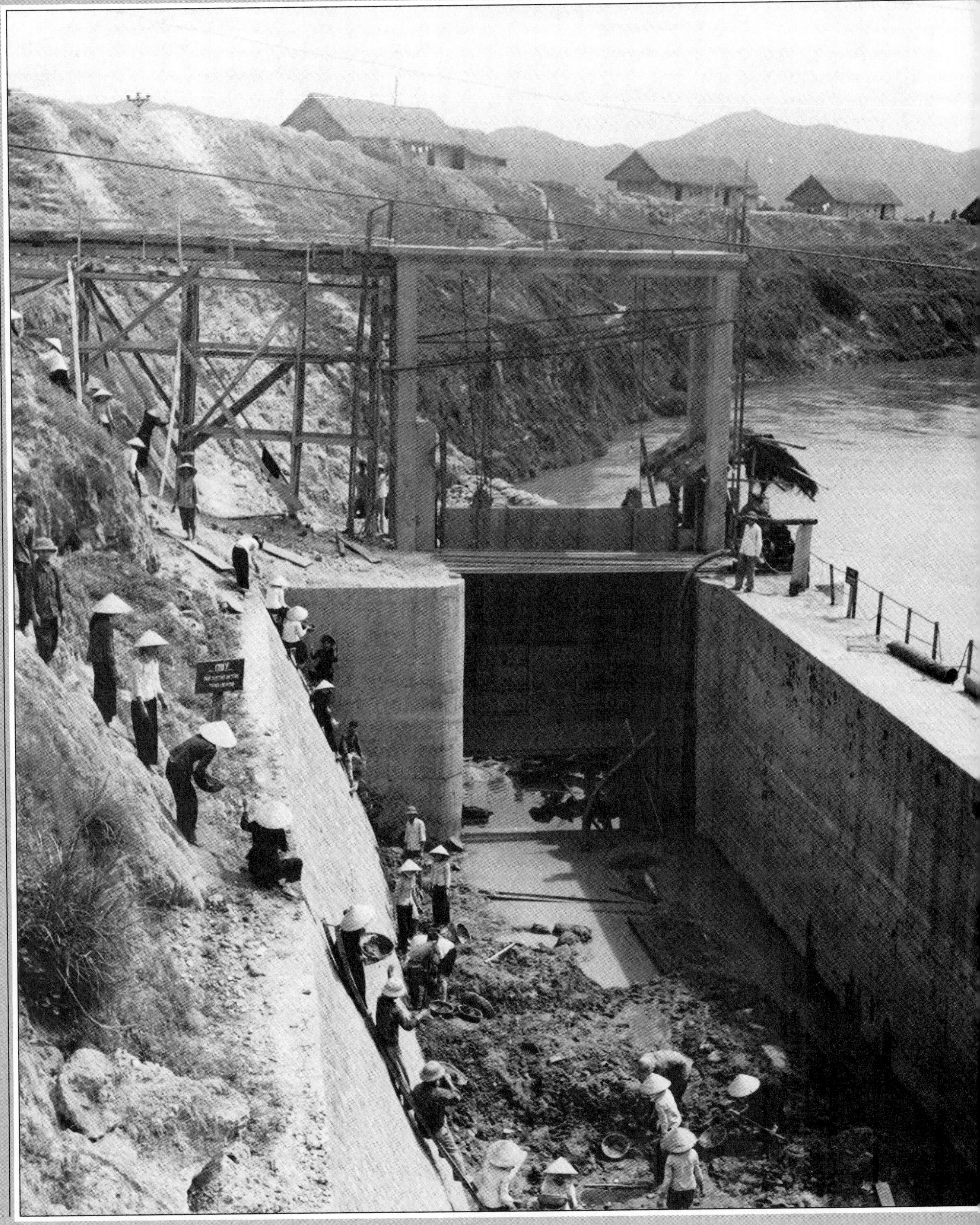

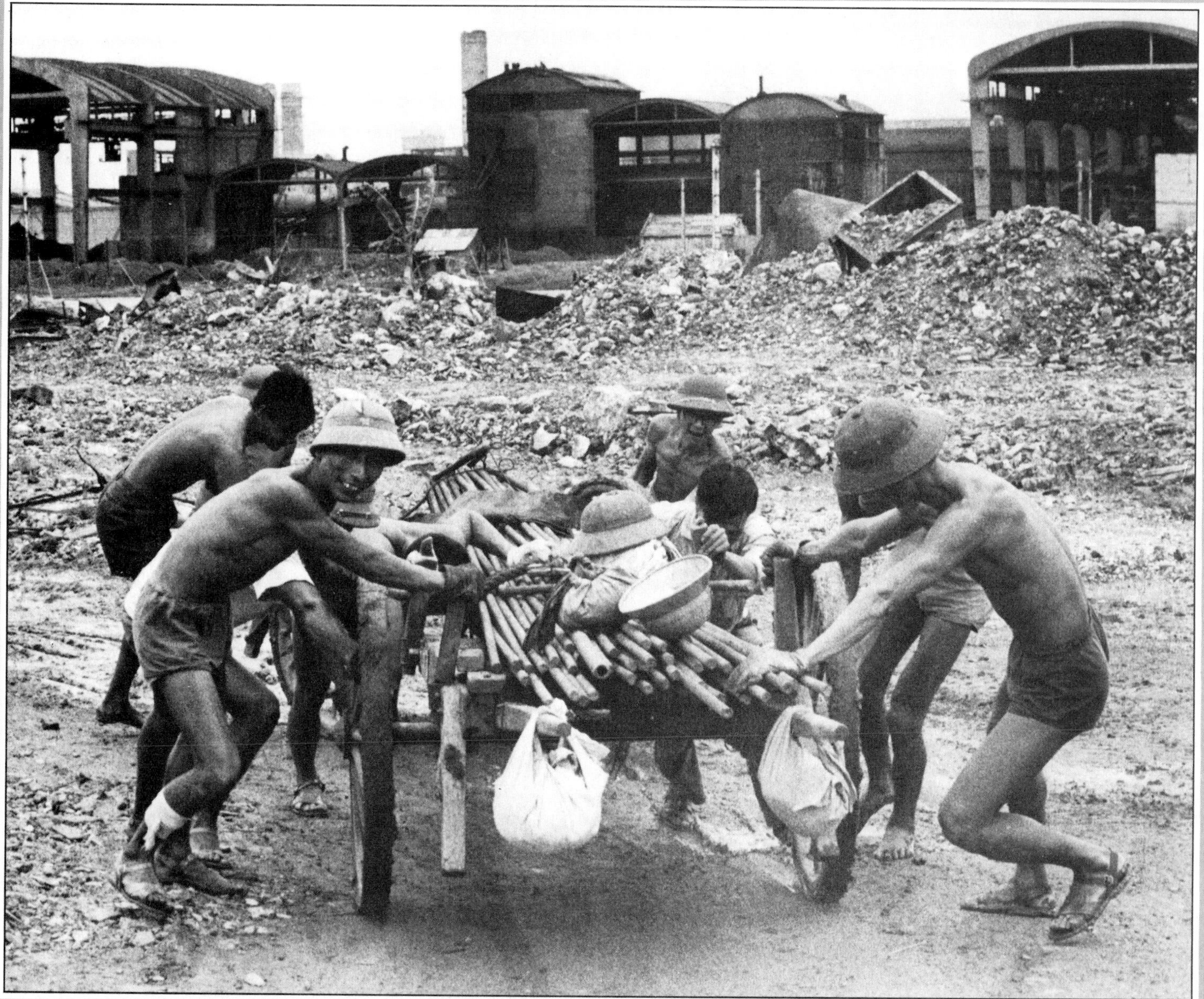

Above. *In Haiphong, workers clear the rubble from American-bombed factories.*

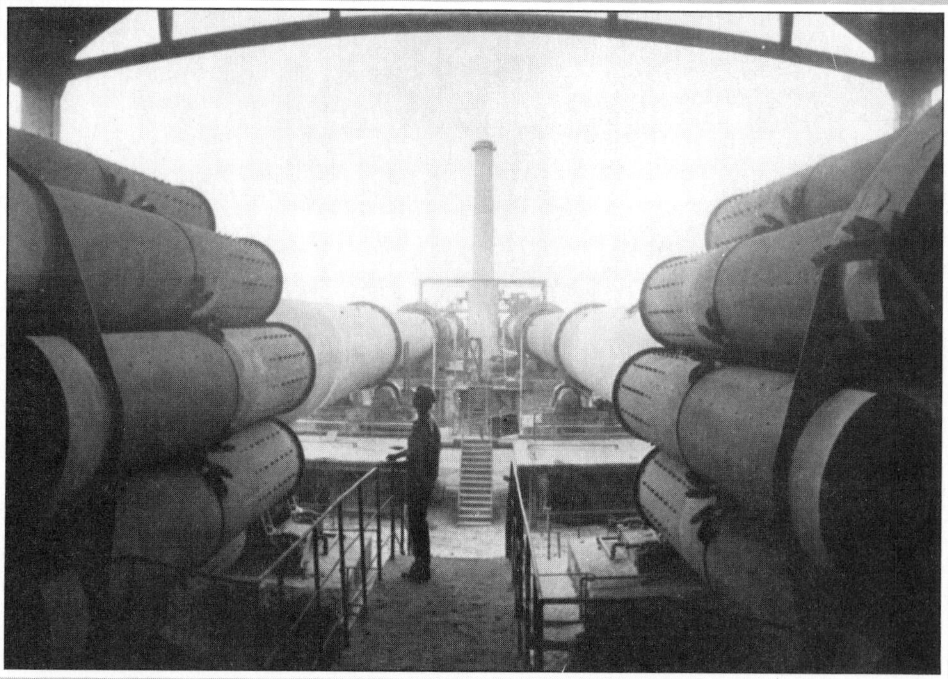

Left. *Peasants rebuild the Song Kha dam near Vinh in early 1974.*

Right. *The Haiphong cement works in November 1973. A year earlier, the works had been nearly destroyed by American bombs.*

At the same time, the vital task of rebuilding the Vietcong infrastructure in the South had met with little success. COSVN directives continued to reflect marked dissatisfaction with the performance of the VCI, citing failure to recruit new party cadres at local levels, lack of confidence in the revolution, and neglect of propaganda and troop proselytizing missions. Even more disturbing to the southern command was the growing isolation of the cadres from the local population of the countryside. Some U.S. officials believed that the Vietcong had so deteriorated that their position was untenable without North Vietnamese Main Force support.

The leaders of the DRV also had to contend with urgent problems much closer to home. With the end of American bombing it was imperative to begin the reconstruction of North Vietnam's war-shattered economy. Much of the nation's nascent industrial plant and large sections of its road system had been severely damaged. Whole sections of the North Vietnamese panhandle from Vinh southward were virtually destroyed. But the economic situation proved even more desperate than had been imagined. Shortages of food and consumer goods had already sent prices sharply higher, creating a lively black market, when flooding nearly wiped out the fall rice harvest. A property survey uncovered empty warehouses, missing farm machinery, and a startling level of waste, inefficiency, mismanagement, and petty corruption. Even more shocking, the first census in fifteen years disclosed a population increase of nearly 50 percent, far greater than government economic planners had anticipated.

Fortunately for the North Vietnamese, their allies in Moscow and Peking extended record amounts of economic aid during the two years following the cease-fire: $670 million in 1973, an increase of 45 percent over the previous year, and nearly $1.3 billion in 1974. At the same time, however, military aid from the two Communist superpowers dropped precipitously from $750 million in 1972 to $330 million in 1973, recovering only slightly to $400 million in 1974. The military build-up in the South during 1973 consisted largely of equipment and fuel the North Vietnamese already possessed, for they were getting little in the way of new supplies.

The unwillingness of the Soviets and Chinese to maintain high levels of military aid reflected the waning importance they placed on North Vietnamese conquest of the South. For Moscow the possibility of détente with the United States, and with it the prospect of arms limitation and liberalized trade, placed Hanoi's needs in a less compelling light. For Peking, which now looked upon the Soviet Union as its chief enemy, the preservation of American influence in Southeast Asia as a counterweight to the growing Russian military presence on China's northern border was more vital than Vietnamese liberation.

In addition, each had reason for coolness in their dealings with the DRV. The Soviets had been placed in an embarrassing dilemma during the Easter offensive of 1972 when they had to choose between calling off a summit meeting with Richard Nixon or welcoming the American president while bombs still fell on Soviet ships in Haiphong Harbor. For its part, Hanoi regarded Moscow's negotiations with Washington as an act of betrayal, giving way only grudgingly to Soviet pressure to reduce its military presence in Laos and Cambodia. The North Vietnamese were even more enraged with the Chinese for treating with their enemy "behind our back," as they later complained. Nixon's promise to reduce the U.S. military presence on Taiwan, coupled with urgings by the Chinese leadership that Hanoi abandon for a time its attempt to unify Vietnam, evoked bitter memories of China's "perfidy" at Geneva in 1954 when Peking accepted the division of their country and so condemned the North Vietnamese to twenty years of continued struggle. Whatever the truth of these suspicions, the cold shoulder they received from their patrons during visits to Moscow and Peking in June and October convinced the DRV leaders that their military life line was no longer secure.

Only slightly less problematic were the intentions of Hanoi's enemy in Washington. The damage caused by the Christmas bombings, while not as severe as initial reports indicated, had been serious enough to warrant extreme caution, a concern made more plausible by the continued

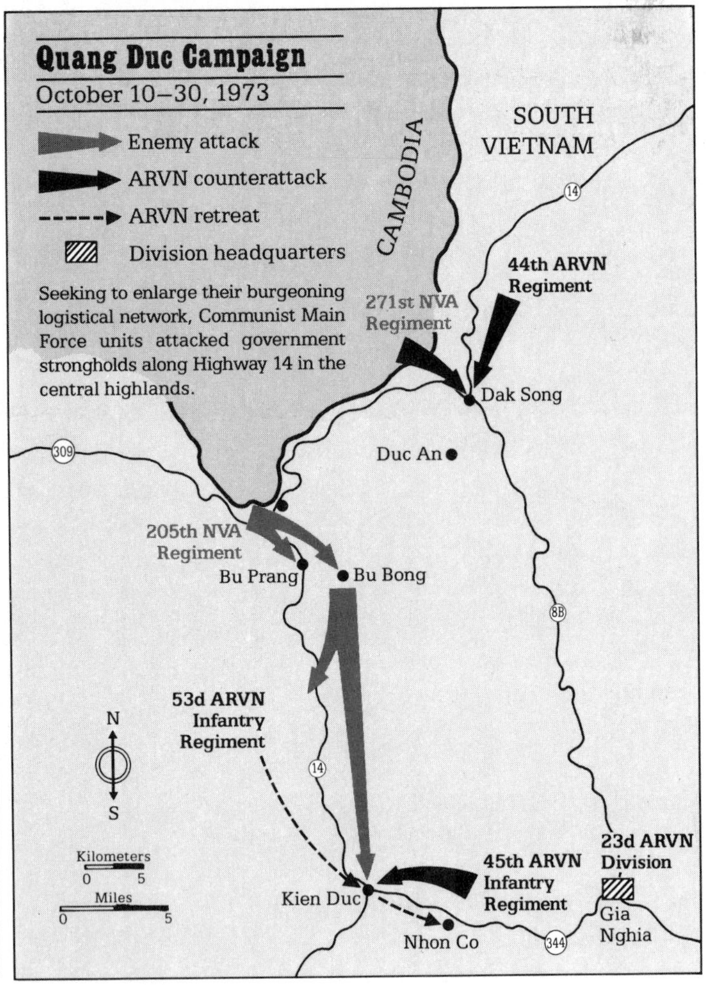
Quang Duc Campaign
October 10–30, 1973
Enemy attack
ARVN counterattack
ARVN retreat
Division headquarters
Seeking to enlarge their burgeoning logistical network, Communist Main Force units attacked government strongholds along Highway 14 in the central highlands.
CAMBODIA
SOUTH VIETNAM
14
44th ARVN Regiment
271st NVA Regiment
Dak Song
309
Duc An
205th NVA Regiment
Bu Prang
Bu Bong
8B
53d ARVN Infantry Regiment
N
S
Kilometers
0 5
Miles
0 5
Kien Duc
45th ARVN Infantry Regiment
23d ARVN Division
Gia Nghia
Nhon Co
344

presence of B–52s in Thailand only an hour and a half from Hanoi. Moreover, the massive Enhance Plus shipments to the South preceding the cease–fire, plus the liberalness with which South Vietnamese commanders continued to expend American–supplied ammunition, suggested that Washington remained committed to the survival of the Saigon regime. How the Americans would respond in the face of North Vietnamese advances remained an open question. Although Congressional restrictions and the growing paralysis of the presidency might preclude retaliation, Richard Nixon remained a dangerous and unpredictable opponent.

Return to revolutionary violence

All of these considerations played their part in the policy debate that divided the North Vietnamese Politburo during the fall of 1973. Out of that debate emerged the resolutions of the 21st Party Plenum and a decisive shift in Communist strategy.

On July 19, 1973, ARVN soldiers take cover behind their APC during a firefight just north of Saigon near Song Be, where GVN forces attempted to reopen Route 1A.

The issue was joined in early October when the Communist party Central Committee convened to assess the progress of the revolution in the South. Warning that the morale and discipline of the army could not be allowed to deteriorate further through excessive passivity, and arguing that the preparations of the previous nine months made Chinese and Soviet support less vital, General Dung and Minister of Defense Vo Nguyen Giap pushed strongly for a resumption of aggressive military operations. To the civilian leadership of the Politburo, however, men like Premier Pham Van Dong and party First Secretary Le Duan, stepped–up fighting meant draining resources from the urgent tasks of reconstruction in the North. Many units in the South remained understrength, and there was no assurance that the fuel, ammunition, and equipment necessary to sustain a renewed offensive

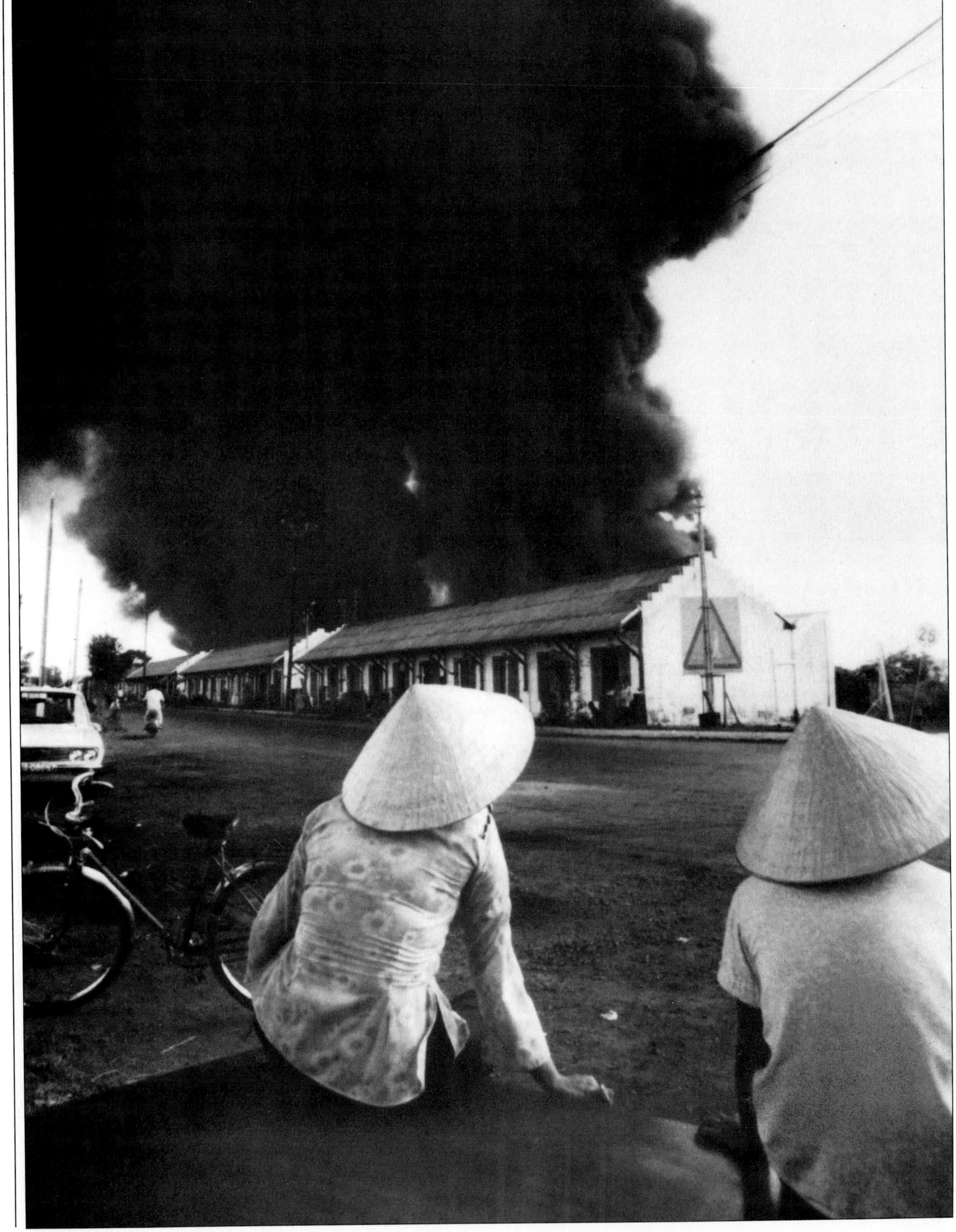
25

could be readily replaced. Moreover, to undertake major military activity without the backing of Moscow and Peking would be to invite American reprisals.

The result was the compromise Resolution 21, made public in a general order to Communist units on October 15 and in a radio broadcast from Hanoi the same day. Reestablishing the preeminence of military action, the committee declared that the "road for the South is the road of revolutionary violence." The resolution directed the armed forces to "strike back" at the GVN whenever possible, to "firmly seize the opportune moment," and to launch a "strategic offensive" that would regain territory and population lost to Saigon. The objectives of the new offensive, however, were less all-encompassing than the rhetoric that surrounded them: not an all-out assault, but an escalating series of "strategic raids" to bleed enemy units, eliminate obstacles to further expansion of base areas and supply corridors, capture strategic ground, and further disrupt the already shaky South Vietnamese economy. Military activities would be consistent with a policy of flexibility, advancing as the situation warranted, and coordinated with diplomatic efforts. Although war would resume in earnest, the resolution cautioned, victory could not be expected for many years. The struggle would be "protracted and complex," General Giap acknowledged, a contest between "anti-nibbling forces and the nibblers."

The first blow of the strategic-raids campaign fell on Highway 14 in Quang Duc Province. On November 4 elements of a division-sized task force attacked and overran ARVN outposts at Bu Prang and Bu Bong. Two days later another NVA regiment routed ARVN troops at Dak Song, cutting off the province capital of Gia Nghia and severing the only remaining land access to Phuoc Long Province. As II Corps commander Major General Nguyen Van Toan rushed reinforcements into Quang Duc, the 205th NVA Regiment swept south from Bu Bong toward Kien Duc District Town, encountering stiff resistance along the way but reaching the outskirts of the city on November 21. With a regiment of the ARVN 23d Division digging in at Kien Duc, General Toan sent the 44th Infantry into Dak Song, retaking the vital road junction on November 28. Meanwhile, Communist forces continued to gather outside Kien Duc. On December 4 the 205th NVA Regiment, now bolstered by a sapper regiment and tanks, blasted through ARVN lines and drove the defenders from the town. It proved to be a short-lived occupation. A few days later the 45th ARVN Infantry recaptured Kien Duc, forcing the 205th to withdraw with heavy casualties. The route from Ban Me Thuot through Gia Nghia to Phuoc Long was open once more. But sizable Communist forces remained in control of Bu Bong and Bu Prang.

Even as the fighting raged in Quang Duc, Saigon felt the effects of the Communists' new resolve. On November 6 NVA rockets slammed into Bien Hoa Air Base north of the city, destroying three F-5A fighters. Sapper teams attacked South Vietnamese navy docks east of the city and on December 2 blew up the giant Nha Be petroleum tank farm on the Saigon River, igniting over 9 million gallons of fuel and sending a towering pillar of black smoke boiling into the sky over the capital. Two weeks later, the Communists attacked a U.S. Joint Casualty Resolution Center team only sixteen kilometers southwest of Saigon. Killed was American army Captain Richard M. Rees, the first U.S. serviceman to die since the cease-fire. Rees's death effectively ended all American MIA searches into any but the most securely held government territory.

As Communist troops launched their attack on Quang Duc in early November, the first operation of that size since March, the Politburo watched anxiously to see what response the United States would make. Not only did the B-52s fail to materialize, but on November 7, one day after Dak Song fell, Congress overrode a presidential veto and passed the War Powers Act. The hawks immediately renewed their demands for an escalation of the fighting. Only with difficulty were the moderates in Hanoi able to persuade their colleagues that the necessity of economic recovery and the fragility of relations with Moscow and Peking precluded a more adventurous military policy for the time being. To cement their victory, they convened in mid-December the party's 22d Plenum which formalized the priority of reconstruction.

Nonetheless, an important watershed had been crossed, a crucial change of emphasis reflected in COSVN Resolution 12 issued in late December 1973 or early January 1974. Communist forces, asserted the southern command, were in a stronger military position than at any time since 1954. The strategy for the coming year would be one of "war in peace," attacking "point by point, grasping partial victories and advancing toward final victory." Military operations, employing combined-arms tactics, would be larger in scale, directed not only against isolated outposts but also against more important targets such as district towns, subsector headquarters, ARVN rear bases and division headquarters. Whatever the difficulties that remained, whatever the constraints with which they still had to deal, the North Vietnamese and their southern allies were intent upon regaining the military initiative they had lost during the previous twelve months.

That they had the capacity to do so there was little doubt. By the end of 1973 the Cua Viet Estuary and the port of Dong Ha had become a major logistics complex handling more than 6,000 tons of supplies a month, while truck traffic across the DMZ had reached levels greater than anything seen in the years before the cease-fire. An estimated 3,000 buildings had been erected in northern Quang Tri Province to handle the surge of goods, with a

Black smoke clouds the sky over the Saigon River after Communist sappers set petroleum storage tanks on fire at Nha Be in December 1973.

capacity of more than 400,000 tons of supplies. The logistics corridor now extended from Dong Hoi in North Vietnam through Dong Ha and along Route 9 to Khe Sanh, then south along Highway 14 to the northern border of Quang Duc Province, with new supply areas at Dak To, Tan Canh, and Loc Ninh. A 480-kilometer, two-lane macadam highway through southern Laos had been completed, as well as a new road linking logistics sites in Kontum and Quang Ngai Provinces. Communist engineers had pushed the fuel-oil pipeline south of the A Shau Valley and constructed a telecommunications system centered at Loc Ninh that enabled COSVN to communicate directly with Hanoi and with units in the field. The new forward supply areas and vastly expanded lines of communication made logistics, in the words of a DAO report, "no longer a limiting factor in North Vietnamese planning."

During the course of the year, the North Vietnamese had renovated twelve former American airfields within their zone of control and studded their logistical corridors with antiaircraft emplacements. More than 500 tanks had been deployed to the South during 1973, many of them destined for the central highlands and the region around Saigon. The number of 122MM and 130MM guns had increased from less than 100 to more than 350. Thousands of tons of other military supplies had already accumulated in the South when a new "transportation offensive" got under way in December. By the first anniversary of the cease-fire, DAO analysts estimated that the NVA had sufficient fuel and ammunition to sustain an offensive comparable to that of 1972 for between thirteen and eighteen months. Manpower was also on the rise as the year drew to a close. Order of battle experts listed NVA combat strength at approximately 185,000 men, with an additional 30,000 indigenous guerrillas: between 20,000 and 30,000 more than at the time of the cease-fire. Although this still left Communist forces short of the number estimated necessary to launch a major offensive, infiltration rates at the end of December indicated that the most significant shortages would be made up by February.

Another development was taking place during the final months of 1973, less dramatic than the swelling arsenal of weapons and the growing strength of Main Force units but equally ominous. Starting in October the NVA high command had begun reshaping its army in the South. Independent regiments were consolidated into new divisions, and divisions collected into corps commands able to wage war on a scale beyond what the Communists had ever before attempted.

In his year-end assessment U.S. Defense Attaché General John Murray minced no words. "The dominant fact is the enemy's strength. Positioned better. Structured better. Unharassed by U.S. air. Supported with: better roads, longer pipelines, larger stockpiles, more guns and tanks and sophisticated equipment." If the "enviable logistic

simplicity of a bag of rice and a bandolier of bullets" was a thing of the past, Murray warned, the new road system meant that the enemy could "ride quickly, not walk slowly, wherever he opts to fight."

The North Vietnamese and their southern allies had in the space of a year effected a remarkable recovery. More important, they had begun to shift the balance of power in their direction. Frustrated in their hopes for a political conquest of the South, they had returned to the road of violence, still determined to wrest from their adversaries the prize for which they had fought so long. In the face of their resolve the United States found itself nearly helpless. No longer in a position to employ direct military sanctions, the Nixon administration sought other means to bring the deteriorating situation under some measure of control. It would prove a frustrating and largely futile quest.

The equilibrium of peace

The Paris agreement rested on the idea of a balance of power. Henry Kissinger, the architect of the accords, recognized that neither the provisions of the agreement nor the "understandings" reached with Hanoi and its allies could themselves assure its success. Peace depended instead on the maintenance of an equilibrium of political strength and military force within and among the states of Indochina. The United States hoped that continuing military support of its clients would produce a stalemate on the battlefield that, combined with diplomatic pressure from Washington, would ultimately lead to a de facto stabilization of the entire region.

But only in Laos did this policy bear fruit. There the relative balance of forces, an absence of the corrosive hatreds that afflicted the rest of Indochina, and the skill with which American diplomacy was applied enabled Washington to gain a political settlement that halted the fighting and extricated the United States from its commitment.

The fighting in Laos had never risen to the brutal intensity of the rest of the Indochina war, and with the conclusion of American bombing in April it rapidly died down. Reported military incidents dropped precipitously even as political discussions between the government of Prince Souvanna Phouma and the Pathet Lao dragged on with no conclusion for nearly seven months. The desultory talks might have gone on longer still if dissident rightist elements had not brought the issue to a head.

In the early morning hours of August 20 a small band of exiled military officers led by General Thao Ma, the former chief of the Laotian air force, slipped across the Mekong River from Thailand and took control of the Vientiane airport. Joined by some sixty sympathizers, they began

Laotian General Thao Ma is carried away from the wreckage of his plane after a failed attempt to overthrow the government of Prince Souvanna Phouma, August 20, 1973.

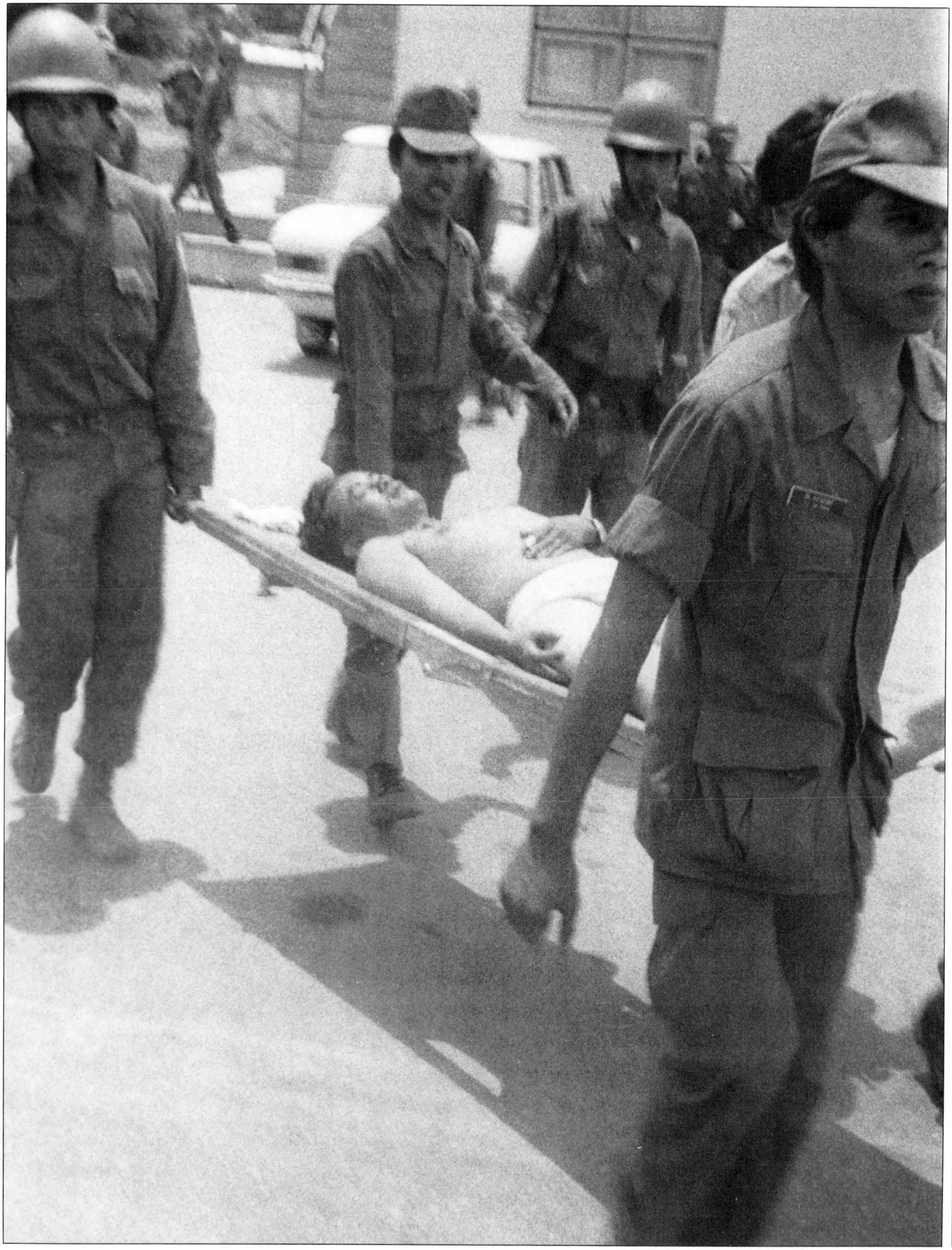

distributing blue-and-white ascots to anyone willing to join their nascent rebel army. At first everything went like clockwork. With little hesitation airport police, mechanics, even local employees of the CIA-run Air America donned the revolutionary scarves. By dawn the exiles had seized the national bank and the government radio station. Meanwhile, Ma and three other pilots commandeered two T-28 fighters and flew off to attack the army's Chainimo garrison just outside the city.

Ma and his compatriots hoped to gain the support of right-wing military officers and conservative politicians unhappy with the emerging shape of the agreement that Souvanna, under intense American pressure, was expected to sign. Instead of rallying to the rebels, however, the generals hesitated, giving U.S. Chargé d'Affaires John Gunther Dean the opportunity to exploit the situation to his own ends. After seeing that Souvanna was safely hidden, Dean spent the morning racing about the city assuring Communist delegates at the Pathet Lao compound that the U.S. had nothing to do with the plot and warning senior government military officers that under no circumstances would the United States withdraw its support from Prince Souvanna. Unwilling to jeopardize their only source of arms and equipment, the generals rallied to the prince and the coup collapsed almost as quickly as it had begun. When government troops advanced on the airport the erstwhile revolutionaries turned their guns on Ma's returning plane, shooting it down short of the runway. The leader of the coup, pulled from the wreckage alive, was executed on the way to the hospital. By noon the rest of the rebels had all either been killed or escaped back into Thailand.

The abortive uprising removed the last obstacle to an accord. Three weeks later negotiators initialed a protocol that was signed on September 12. The agreement established a coalition Consultative Council, arranged for the demarcation of a new cease-fire line, outlined procedures for the exchange of prisoners and the return of refugees to their native villages, arranged for the neutralization of Vientiane and Luang Prabang, provided for the withdrawal of foreign troops from Laotian soil, and divided cabinet ministries among the two parties. With the provisional agreement in place, Communist troops established a garrison in Vientiane and negotiations on implementation resumed at a languid pace. It was not until April 1974 that the new coalition government was finally established.

As one American journalist pointed out, the United States had not so much resolved the conflict in Laos as "left it to find its own level—an outcome that could only favor the Communist side." If the Laotian settlement served Washington's interests more than those of its client, however, if it cast some doubt on the integrity of American protestations of support for the Souvanna government, it at least reflected the military and political realities with which all parties to the conflict had to deal.

Tigers and running dogs

The same could not be said for Cambodia. American policy toward the Khmer Republic had been fashioned almost solely in terms of South Vietnam's strategic needs, consisting of little more than a determination to prevent a Communist takeover, whatever the cost to Cambodia and however incompetent the existing government. Thus, in the wake of the August bombing halt Washington persisted in assuring Lon Nol of military support, a promise it was not likely to be able to keep for long, and in calling for negotiations between Phnom Penh and the Khmer Rouge, a step neither Cambodian side was willing to take. At an emotional farewell press conference on September 6, 1973, outgoing U.S. Ambassador Emory Swank observed bitterly that the war was "losing more and more of its point and has less and less meaning for any of the parties concerned."

Secretary of State Kissinger was also pessimistic about the immediate prospects for peace in Cambodia but for different reasons. Convinced that the cessation of bombing meant he could no longer negotiate from strength, he left the embassy in the hands of Deputy Chief of Mission Thomas Enders with orders to keep the Lon Nol regime alive until, somehow, the military situation improved.

While Kissinger turned his attention to Europe and the growing crisis in the Middle East, tons of American ammunition and new equipment—artillery pieces, armored personnel carriers, heavy river craft, mortars, grenade launchers, M16 and recoilless rifles—arrived in Phnom Penh to bolster the government's sagging military fortunes. Along with the new arms came headquarters and combat support equipment for four infantry divisions that General John Cleland, the chief of the U.S. Military Equipment Delivery Team, hoped to create. Although officially prohibited from advising the Cambodian army, U.S. personnel extended their influence over the Khmer National Armed Forces (FANK) in a variety of ways, supervising the army's financial arrangements, refusing to allow an increase in the military payroll beyond 235,000 men, and attempting unsuccessfully to prevent the creation of an entire division whose sole purpose was to serve as the president's palace guard. The Americans were even more involved in the management of the Cambodian economy. Enders and other U.S. officials set Cambodian exchange rates, regulated utility prices, and did what they could to moderate declining production. Unfortunately, noted one embassy economist, such measures were like "picking fleas off a dog that has cancer."

After three years of American bombing and civil war, the Cambodian economy barely functioned. The nation's small rail system had been utterly destroyed, along with 40 percent of its roads. Four-fifths of the rice mills, 75 percent of the sawmills, and the only oil refinery in the country had ceased operation. Production of timber and rubber, Cambodia's only significant commercial exports, had declined by 80 percent. The 1972–73 rice harvest was less than a quarter of what it had been in the last prewar year, and with major areas of the country in Communist hands the nation's freshwater fish supply, a major source of protein, had been sharply reduced. Shortages of every kind drove prices upward at a rate of 250 percent a year. The cost of food was nearly twenty times greater than it was at the beginning of the war. Unemployment could not even be measured, but it was clear to those in Phnom Penh that the vast majority of refugees who by the end of 1973 had swollen the population of the capital from 600,000 to nearly 2 million had no means of livelihood. They also had almost nothing in the way of food, shelter, or medical care.

The military situation was only slightly less critical. Most foreign observers were convinced that without the B-52s there would be nothing to stop the Khmer Rouge offensive, a belief apparently confirmed when in late August 5,000 insurgents laid siege to Kompong Cham, a pivotal transportation junction eighty kilometers north of Phnom Penh. Smashing through government positions behind a barrage from captured American 105MM howitzers, the Khmer Rouge drove toward the center of the city, rounding up some 15,000 civilians and leading them away into the countryside. But less than ninety meters from the governor's mansion, the Communist advance ground to a halt. In their first serious test without U.S. air support, government troops held their ground. After two weeks of bloody house-to-house fighting, the Khmer Rouge ran out of ammunition and withdrew.

Ignoble Nobel

BULLETIN • PEACE PRIZE

OSLO, NORWAY, (AP)—U.S. SECRETARY OF STATE HENRY KISSINGER AND NORTH VIETNAMESE POLITBURO MEMBER LE DUC THO WERE AWARDED THE 1973 NOBEL PEACE PRIZE TODAY FOR THEIR EFFORTS TO OFFICIALLY END THE VIETNAM WAR. CB1050PED OCT 16

In a war replete with ironies this was, perhaps, the strangest episode of all. While rival Vietnamese armies continued to pound away at each other, the White House praised the announcement as "deserved recognition to the art of negotiations itself in the process of ending a war and laying a groundwork for peace." Declared the secretary of state: "Nothing that has happened to me in public life has moved me more than this Award."

Some of Kissinger's colleagues were less enthusiastic. "The Norwegians must have a sense of humor," remarked former Undersecretary of State George Ball. Another senior Democratic official called Kissinger to congratulate him, observing that he must be particularly happy that the IRS would not be taxing the $65,000 cash prize that accompanied the award. "Why not," asked Kissinger. "Because it's unearned income," laughed his caller. The secretary was not amused.

Neither were his critics both in America and abroad. The worldwide astonishment that first met the announcement from Oslo soon turned to outrage. Regardless of which side was held responsible, it was clear to all that the war in Vietnam raged on at a barely slackened pace for the same reasons it had always been fought. The prize had been given to two men who had negotiated a peace that did not in fact exist.

The *New York Times* dubbed the award the "Nobel War Prize." The *Hartford Times* wondered, "Honor Without Peace?" and the *Richmond Times-Dispatch* declared it an "Ignoble Nobel." The French newspaper *Le Monde* pointed out that Kissinger had played a major role in some of America's most "unpeaceful policies," while Tho's life had been devoted to violent wars of liberation. "The fighting in Indochina will go on," said former Ambassador Edwin O. Reichauer. "Theirs was not a great achievement."

Kissinger himself was "ill at ease" with recognition for his "precarious achievement," but he welcomed the award as an opportunity for reconciliation. Unmoved by such sentiments, Le Duc Tho informed the Nobel Committee that he could not accept the prize so long as the Paris agreements continued to be violated.

In the end, Kissinger also absented himself from the awards ceremony in December, fearing his presence would provoke disruptive demonstrations. It was a prudent, if not a bold, choice. His replacement, U.S. Ambassador to Norway Thomas Byrne, had to slip into the auditorium at the University of Oslo in order to avoid a salvo of anti-American snowballs.

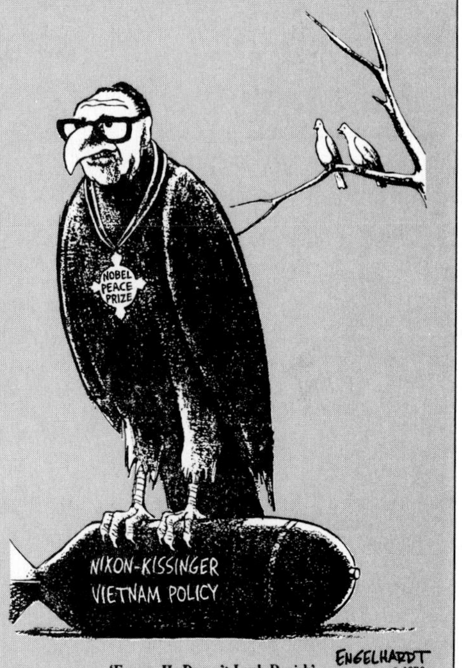
NOBEL PEACE PRIZE
NIXON-KISSINGER VIETNAM POLICY
ENGELHARDT © 1973
'Funny, He Doesn't Look Dovish'

The secretary of state donated all financial proceeds from the award to the establishment of a scholarship fund to help children of American soldiers killed or missing in Indochina. After the fall of Saigon in 1975 he offered to return the prize and the money, but the members of the Nobel Committee declined to accept them. Their "appreciation of Mr. Kissinger's sincere efforts to get a cease-fire agreement put into force in 1973," they declared, remained undiminished by subsequent events.

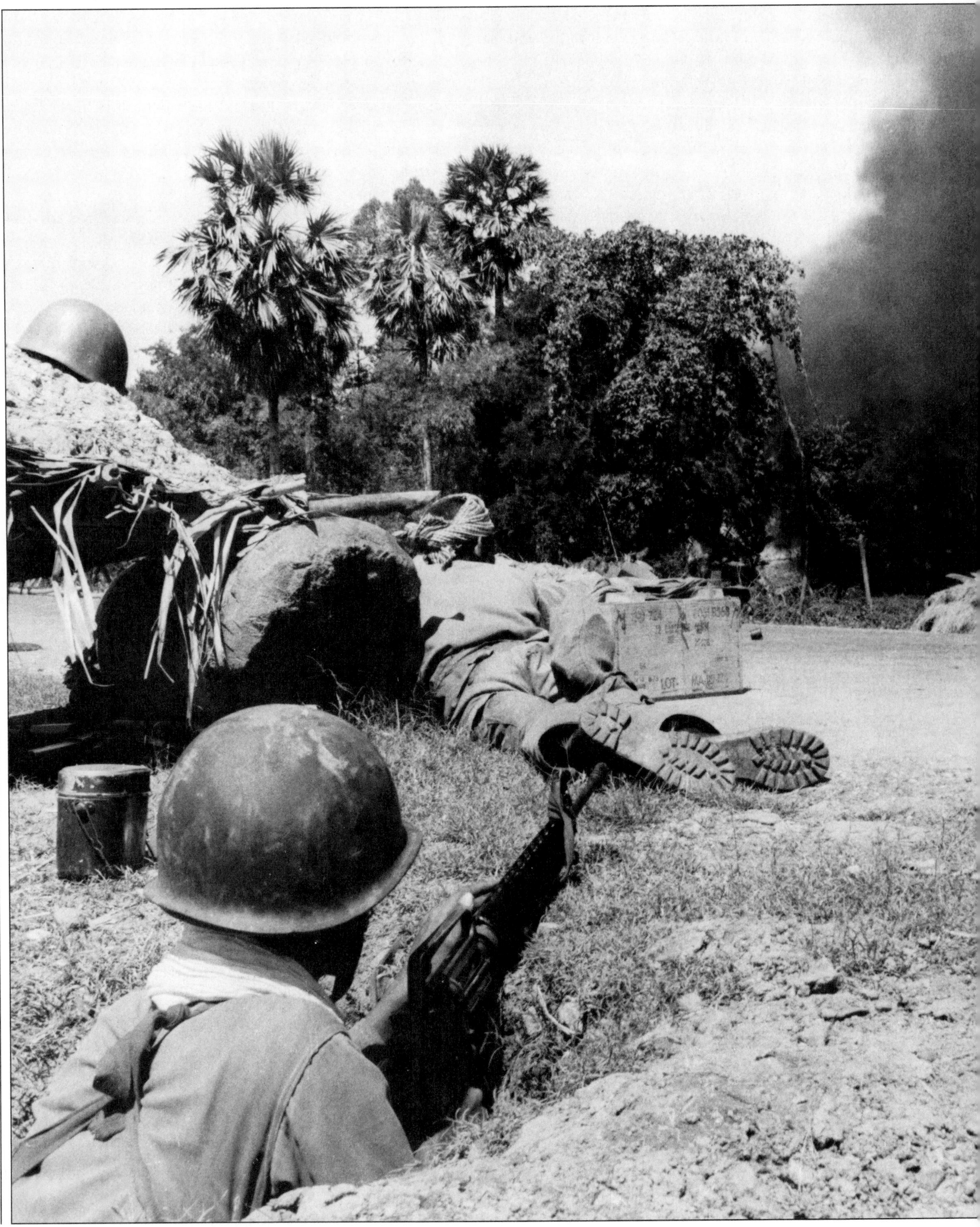

Its success at Kompong Cham, however, could not hide the fact that the army was in desperate condition. The problems began at the top. Lon Nol refused to establish a rational command structure, routinely by-passing his general staff and relegating to himself alone the authority to pass on all military decisions. The battlefield tactics employed by his officers were a prescription for failure. "The normal attack pattern of the Khmer Republic's army," reported Cleland's successor, General William Palmer, "was characterized by a dull plodding, belated advance, devoid of surprise, coordination or motivation. When the enemy chose to resist, friendly casualties were high and objectives rarely attained." Much of the American-supplied equipment never made it into battle at all. Skilled technicians were rare, maintenance almost nonexistent.

Equally serious was the wretched treatment of enlisted men and the irresponsibility of the officer corps. Ill-trained, ill-paid, and ill-led, ordinary soldiers regularly abandoned their positions to return to their families or forage for food. The desperate economic circumstances in which they found themselves at least made such practices understandable. What was harder to justify was the corruption of their officers, who falsified payroll lists, stole wages and rice from their troops, diverted military equipment to the black market, and sold ammunition and weapons to the enemy. So widespread were desertions and phony unit rosters that no one really knew how many men the government had to defend itself. Those soldiers who did remain in the field experienced horrendous casualties and crumbling morale.

The political deterioration of the Cambodian government marched in step with military decay and economic collapse. Aloof and impenetrable, Lon Nol had lost the respect of most of his countrymen, some of whom openly blamed the government's disabilities on the president's "mental illness." American pressure for reform brought few results. Corruption continued unabated, and a new High Political Council that Washington hoped would neutralize Lon Nol's influence and allow the government to function effectively soon lapsed into quarreling impotence.

As a result, the initiative remained with the Khmer Rouge. Within two weeks of their withdrawal from Kompong Cham, Communist rockets destroyed one of Phnom Penh's two working electrical generators, and by the end of the year government troops were battling insurgent forces sixteen kilometers from the capital. Khmer Rouge rockets soon gave way to artillery bombardments that ravaged the city's densely packed refugee area. With some seventy-four battalions ringing Phnom Penh, and every highway leading into the city in Communist hands, the insurgents adamantly rejected American pleas for ne-

As the Communists begin to close in on the capital, Cambodian government troops battle Khmer Rouge insurgents twenty kilometers north of Phnom Penh in October 1973.

gotiations between the two sides. "It is like putting a tiger and a dog in the same cage," explained Prince Norodom Sihanouk. "Things will be settled only when one animal eats the other. And that is how it will be in Cambodia. We are the tiger, and Lon Nol and his people are the running dogs."

Maintaining the status quo

If American policy in Cambodia continued to founder on the incapacities of its client, Washington remained hopeful of success in Vietnam where the government's military gains during the spring and summer were a major source of encouragement. Reports from the battlefield convinced Secretary of State Kissinger that the time was ripe to renew pressure on the North Vietnamese to abandon their aggressive designs on the South. The result was a secret meeting between Kissinger and Le Duc Tho in Paris on December 20, with Ambassador Graham Martin in attendance.

Kissinger attempted to convince his old adversary that the fundamental reality in South Vietnam was military stalemate. With the ARVN stronger than it had ever been, Communist prospects for victory anytime in the near future were nil. The only sensible course for the DRV was to reach a modus vivendi with Thieu that would preserve what territory and political leverage it still had in the South. The secretary suggested that this could be accomplished if Hanoi would agree to cease military activity in the delta and around Saigon. In return, Kissinger held out the possibility of a demarcation of zones of control in the two northern military regions and the establishment of the National Council of National Reconciliation and Concord that Thieu had so far refused to implement.

Tho was unconvinced. In fact, Kissinger's proposals came at least two months too late. The Politburo had concluded in October that for the time being at least there was no realistic prospect of a political settlement. From Hanoi's point of view there was nothing to be gained from negotiations until the military balance in the South had been clearly reversed, a process that was already well under way.

Ambassador Martin was only slightly more successful with Thieu when he broached the subject of concessions to the South Vietnamese president on his return from Paris. At the ambassador's urgings Thieu grudgingly agreed to release some of the Communist cadres being held in South Vietnamese prisons. But on more fundamental issues relating to the Paris agreement he remained adamant. Both the creation of the national council and a delineation of territory would give the Communists a legitimacy in the South Thieu was totally unwilling to grant. The idea of demarcation did gain support from General Cao Van Vien, the chairman of South Vietnam's Joint General Staff, and Prime Minister Tran Thien Khiem, who by February 1974 had come to the conclusion that South Vietnam "could continue to fight and suffer defeat or it could negotiate and cede part of its territory to the Communists to gain time." But for Thieu's cousin and close adviser Hoang Duc Nha, any concessions to Hanoi were anathema. Once begin down that road, he warned, and there was no telling where it might end.

Nor did Graham Martin push Thieu in such a direction. The American ambassador had been "bitterly opposed" to the Kissinger-Le Duc Tho meeting. Anxious to "lessen our long range investment" in Indochina, Martin opposed direct U.S. negotiations with the North Vietnamese. Convinced that the Paris agreements were in many ways "clearly illogical," and unwilling to "take the knife and guide it to our ally's throat," he would not pressure the Saigon government to embrace the cease-fire accords. "I don't believe that it is incumbent upon the United States to come up with all the answers for other people's problems," Martin commented after the war. "We had to get out of the business of being big brother and monitoring this or pushing that or doing it ourselves. It was basically their baby."

A distinct departure from the role adopted by previous U.S. envoys to Saigon, Martin's strategy sought to overcome a common criticism of American overinvolvement in South Vietnamese affairs. At the same time, it left U.S. policy a hostage to events, even as Hanoi and Saigon inched steadily closer to all-out war. Investigators from the Senate Foreign Relations Committee reported in early 1974 that they could detect no evidence that American policy-

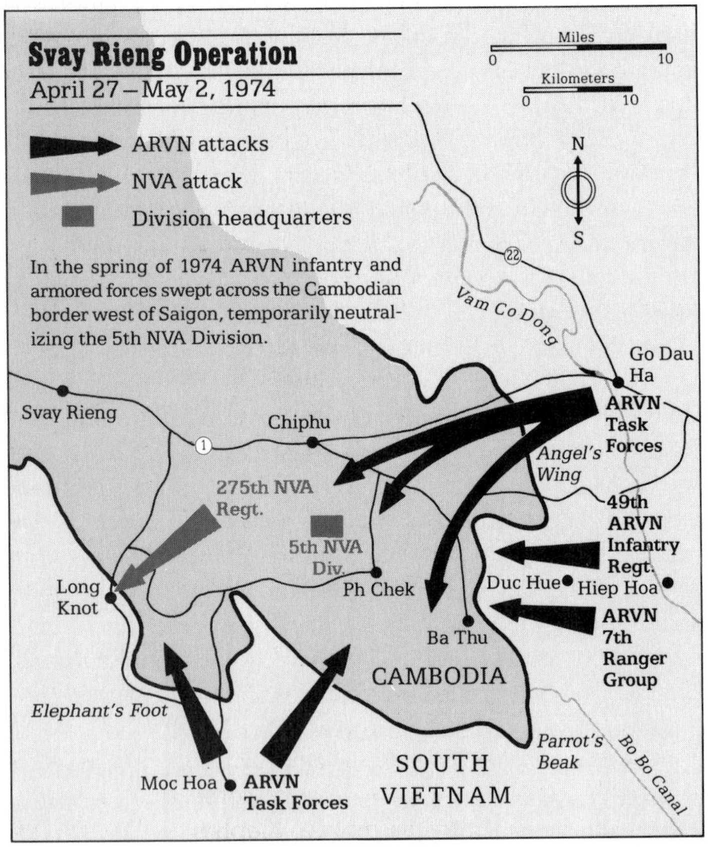
Svay Rieng Operation
April 27–May 2, 1974
Miles
0
10
Kilometers
0
10
ARVN attacks
NVA attack
Division headquarters
In the spring of 1974 ARVN infantry and armored forces swept across the Cambodian border west of Saigon, temporarily neutralizing the 5th NVA Division.
N
S
22
Vam Co Dong
Go Dau Ha
ARVN Task Forces
Svay Rieng
Chiphu
1
Angel's Wing
275th NVA Regt.
49th ARVN Infantry Regt.
5th NVA Div.
Long Knot
Ph Chek
Duc Hue
Hiep Hoa
ARVN 7th Ranger Group
Ba Thu
CAMBODIA
Elephant's Foot
Parrot's Beak
Bo Bo Canal
SOUTH VIETNAM
Moc Hoa
ARVN Task Forces

makers were prepared to force Thieu to modify his "Four No's." "What we saw and heard, including conversations with senior officials, suggested to us that our present policy toward Vietnam is directed to the maintenance of the status quo at a time when Washington's attention is directed elsewhere."

Nonetheless, Thieu could not afford to rely indefinitely on American good will. Should the demand for concessions become more insistent, he decided, it would be wise to strengthen his hand.

The Third Indochina War

Hailing the beginning of what he called the "Third Indochina War," the South Vietnamese president abandoned all pretense of restraint. "We will not allow the Communists to enjoy stable security in their staging areas from which they will harass us," he told officers of the delta command in early January. "Appropriate punitive actions" would be taken "not only right in our zones of control, but also right in the areas in which the North Vietnamese Communist troops are still stationed." What is more, the ARVN would not simply react to NVA operations. "These appropriate punitive actions must be taken beforehand," Thieu declared, "because otherwise, the lives of the compatriots and the troops and their families will be unjustly lost."

A rationale for military action so elastic as to justify whatever offensive operations the government wished to undertake, it bore a striking resemblance to Communist plans for a new "strategic offensive." By the first anniversary of the cease-fire there was no apparent difference between the announced policies of both sides and an unqualified state of war.

The two major thrusts of the new ARVN offensive were both directed against the veteran 5th NVA Division, which during January began moving from Tay Ninh toward Dinh Tuong Province. Time was of the essence, for if the 5th was able to occupy the Communists' Tri Phap base it would be extremely difficult to root out. Moreover, its presence in Dinh Tuong would place Route 4, Saigon's vital link to the delta, in grave jeopardy.

During the second week of February elements of the 7th and 9th ARVN Divisions attacked the Tri Phap from the south and east. Taken by surprise, the Communists fell back with heavy losses in men, ammunition, and supplies. For the rest of February and through the entire month of March, fighting spread across Dinh Tuong and Kien Tuong Provinces, but the focus of the campaign remained in the Tri Phap where government forces continued to score heavily. Hoping to divert ARVN's attention while reinforcements were deployed to the battle area, COSVN staged widespread attacks on isolated positions and stepped up its terror campaign in the delta. Twenty-three children died in a mortar attack on a school in Cai Lay.

Nine more people were killed and sixteen wounded when terrorists hurled grenades into a religious gathering in Bac Lieu.

Such outrages failed to deflect the government's assault on the Tri Phap. After six weeks of fighting the operation had netted more than 1,000 enemy killed, 5,000 tons of food, over 600 weapons, eight tons of ammunition, and a large quantity of other military equipment. Looking to consolidate their victory, ARVN engineers began construction of fortified positions that were soon occupied by Regional Force battalions. At the end of April the NVA overran two of the RF outposts but were quickly driven back by regular government troops. By the first week of May the army of South Vietnam was in firm control of the Tri Phap. Communist forces in the area had been badly mauled, and the soldiers of the 5th NVA Division had been denied the crucial base area.

The division itself, however, now located in the Parrot's Beak salient along the Cambodian border west of Saigon, remained a serious threat to the Tay Ninh–Saigon corridor. That threat had materialized on March 27 when units of the 5th Division attacked and invested the ARVN base at Duc Hue. As April wore on, and Communist forays out of Svay Rieng Province in Cambodia increased, II Corps commander Lieutenant General Pham Quoc Thuan collected twenty South Vietnamese maneuver battalions around the Parrot's Beak, determined to neutralize the North Vietnamese before the onset of the heavy rains of the summer monsoon.

On April 27 General Thuan sent the 49th Infantry Regiment and the 7th Ranger Group through the swamplands around Duc Hue toward the Cambodian border as South Vietnamese warplanes attacked known and suspected base areas of the 5th Division. Simultaneously, two RF battalions pushed north from Moc Hoa, establishing blocking positions on the southwestern edge of the 5th Division's logistical base and assembly area. On April 28, with eleven ARVN battalions already in the field mounting a variety of operations preliminary to the major assault Thuan had readied for the following day, the 275th NVA Regiment and 25th Sapper Battalion launched a furious assault on Long Khot District Town just inside the border of Kien Tuong Province. Whether planned in advance or a reaction to the initial ARVN maneuvers, the attack on Long Khot did nothing to change Thuan's plans. On the morning of April 29 three South Vietnamese armored columns plunged across the Cambodian frontier west of Go Dau Hau, driving straight toward the Communist 5th Division headquarters.

The threat to the division's base had become so critical that the NVA was compelled to retrieve units fighting at Long Khot to defend Communist forces and logistical installations in the path of the ARVN advance. Meanwhile, South Vietnamese infantry and armored cavalry units based at Moc Hoa crossed into the Elephant's Foot, threatening to isolate the retreating 275th Regiment. As the armored columns continued to drive forward, penetrating as much as sixteen kilometers into Cambodian territory before wheeling south toward Hau Nghia Province, and government helicopters ferried troops into surprise attacks on enemy positions, other ARVN units conducted sweep operations between Duc Hue and Go Dau Hau. By May 10, when the last ARVN units turned for home, Communist communications and logistics in the area had been severely disrupted. The NVA had suffered more than 1,200 men killed, 65 captured, and hundreds of weapons lost. On the other hand, the speed, secrecy, and coordination of the multifaceted operation had limited ARVN KIA to fewer than 100.

Yet for all its apparent success, the new offensive could not arrest the steady deterioration of South Vietnam's position. Whoever was impressed by Thieu's unofficial declaration of war it was not the U.S. Congress, which in early April voted against the administration's request for supplemental aid. Desperate to persuade the Americans of the seriousness of the threat facing his country, and perhaps to forestall the renewed pressure for a political settlement the Congressional action seemed to herald, Thieu seized upon the loss of the ARVN outpost at Tong Le Chan on April 15 to suspend bilateral talks with the PRG in Paris and withdraw the "privileges and immunities" of the PRG delegation to the Joint Military Commission in Saigon. After a month of growing harassment—telephone lines to their compound at Tan Son Nhut cut off, press conferences with foreign journalists canceled, the weekly liaison flights to PRG headquarters at Loc Ninh suspended—the Communists walked out. By late spring all of the instruments designed to implement and enforce the Paris agreement, including the moribund ICCS, had ceased to function.

Thieu could live without peace talks as long as his generals continued to maintain the upper hand over the NVA. But the military progress of the preceding months was largely an illusion. The Svay Rieng campaign would be the last major offensive mounted by South Vietnamese forces. From this point on Communist military initiatives, declining U.S. aid, economic prostration, and political turmoil would keep Saigon on the defensive. Although few Americans recognized it at the time, the unraveling of South Vietnam was already well under way.

The bodies of slain Vietcong and North Vietnamese soldiers litter the ground after a battle near the Cambodian border forty kilometers northwest of Saigon, April 24, 1974. ARVN troops claimed more than 100 enemy KIAs during the battle in which the Communists had tried to close Route 1.

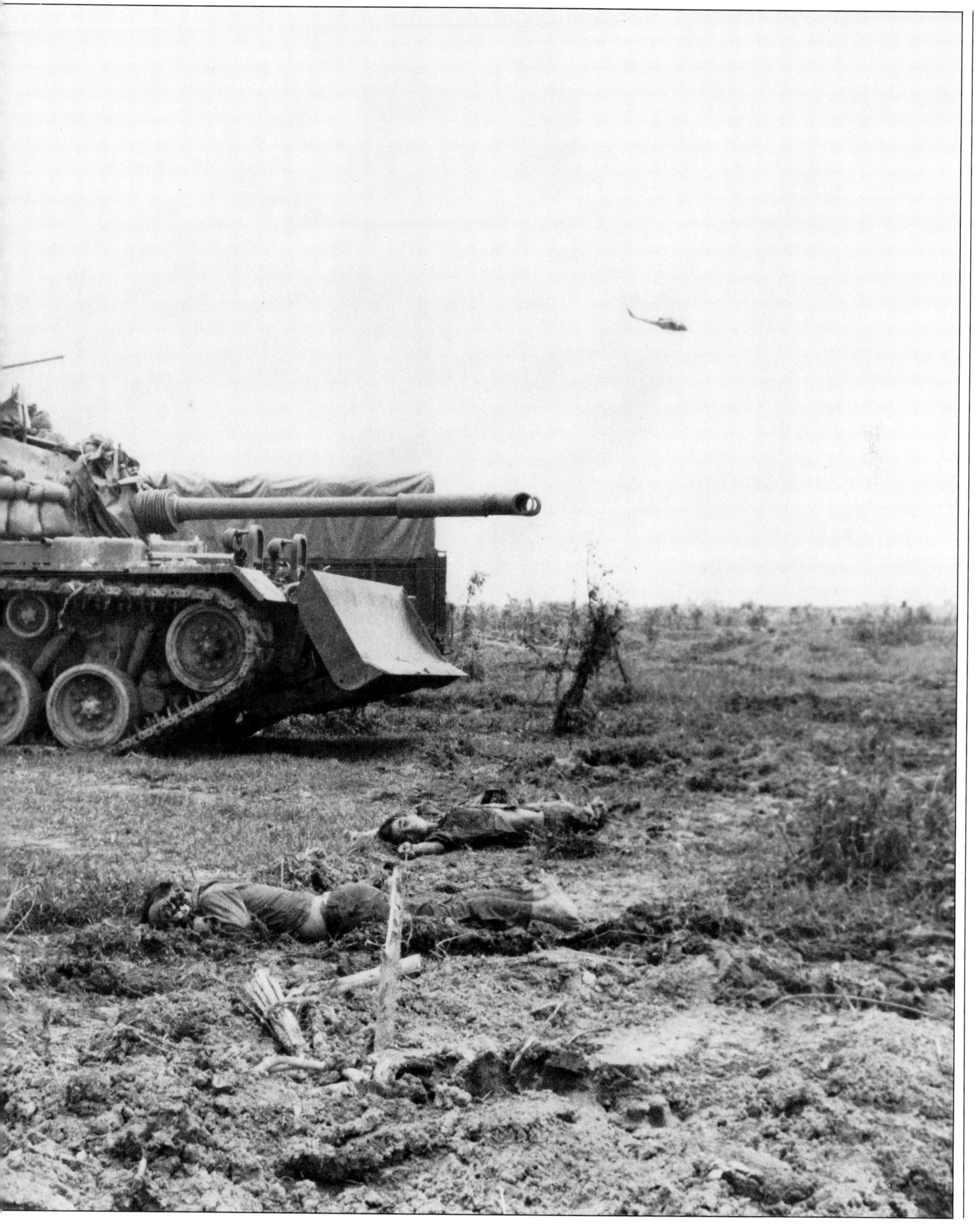

Eye of the Storm

The Paris agreement brought Cambodia not even the illusion of peace. Instead, for more than two years after the declaration of a cease-fire in South Vietnam, the Cambodian people witnessed an accelerating spiral of terror and brutality. In late 1973, the Khmer Rouge resumed their offensive, which had been temporarily brought to a halt by the American bombing campaign earlier that year. The insurgents battered government forces throughout central Cambodia and, by the beginning of 1974, had virtually besieged Phnom Penh. In the months that followed, the capital city endured a hurricane of death and devastation.

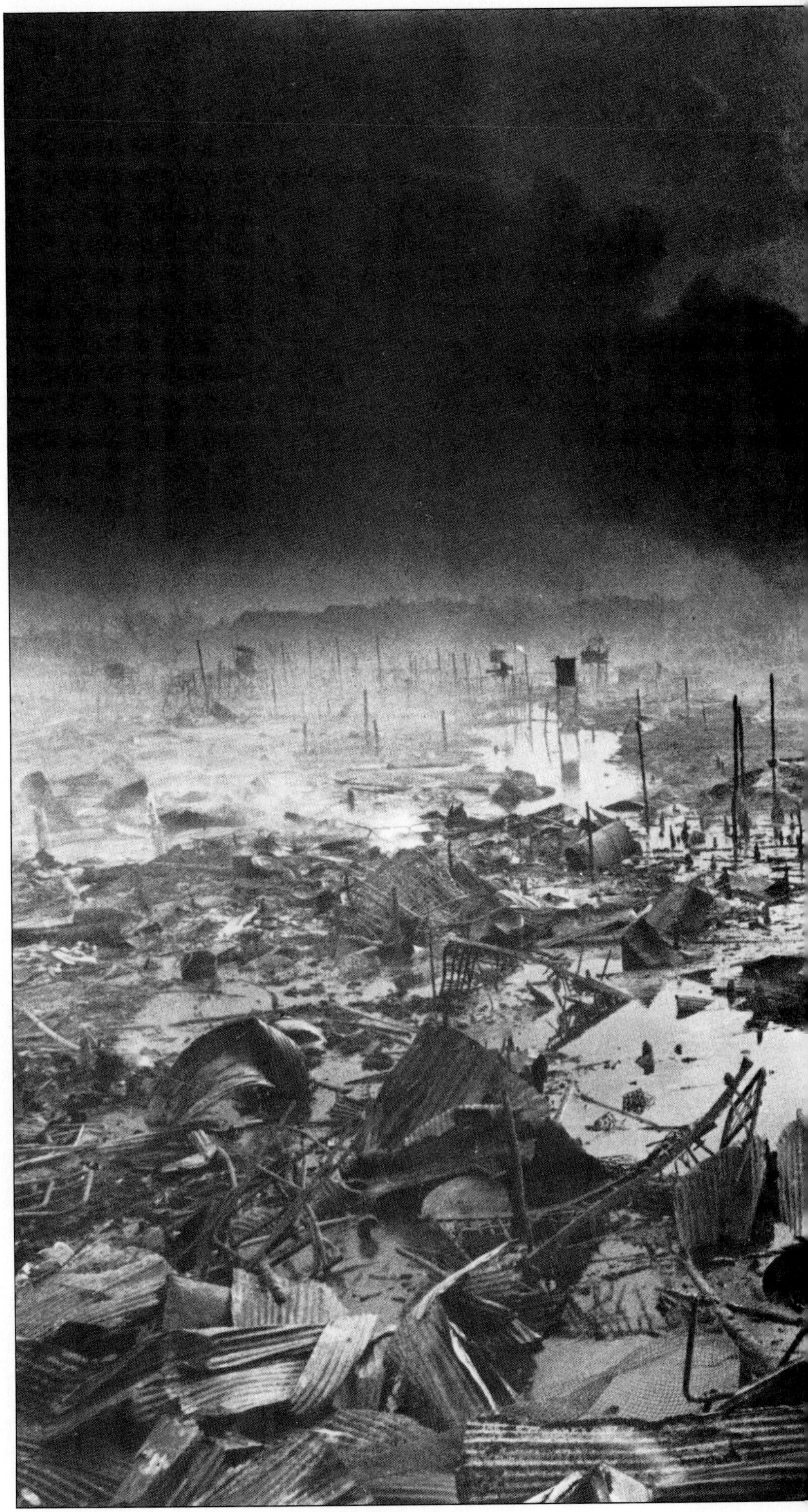

On February 11, 1974, a section of Phnom Penh shows the devastation wrought by the worst attack against the city since the beginning of the war. Communist shelling killed 140 people, wounded 200 more, and left 10,000 people homeless.

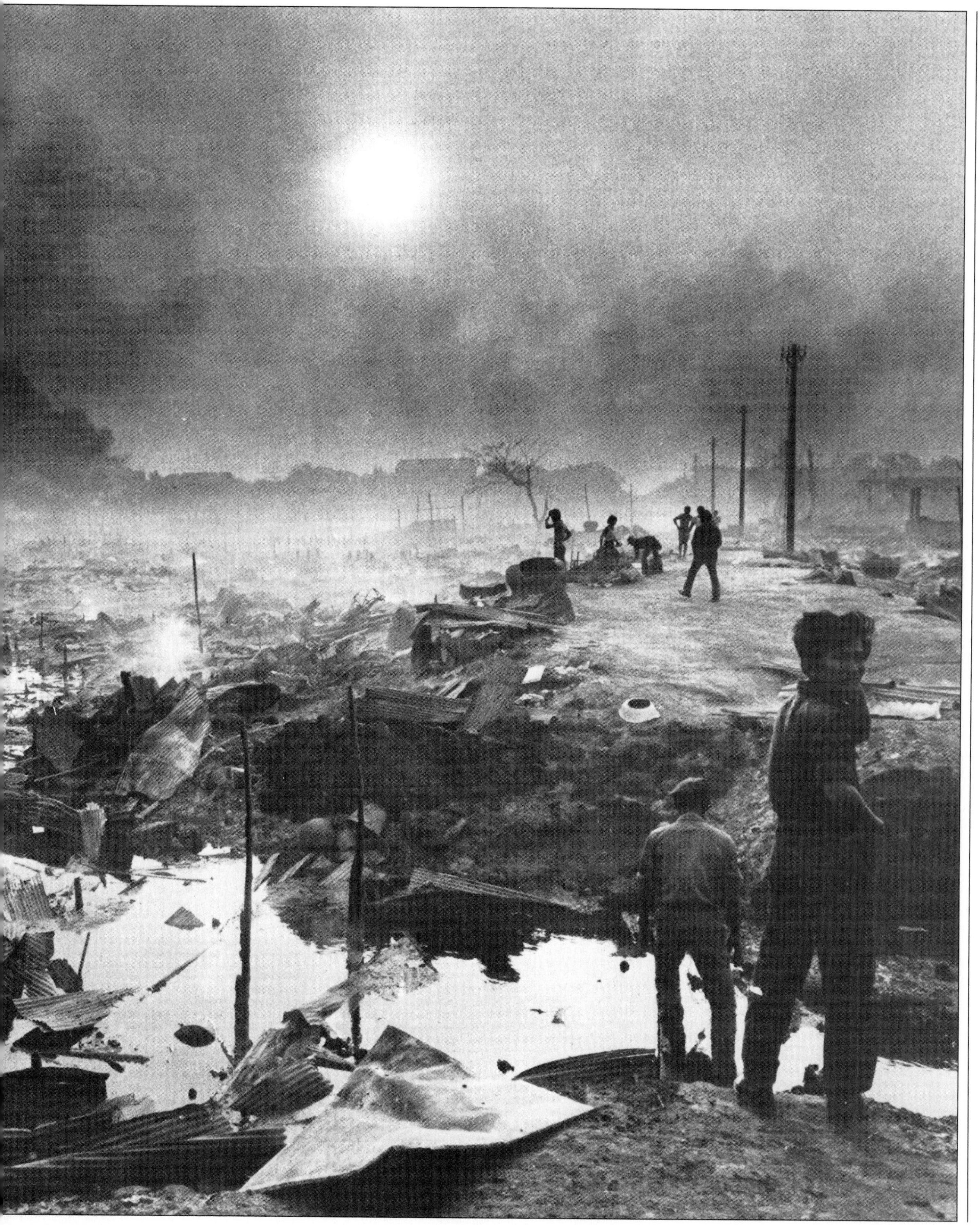

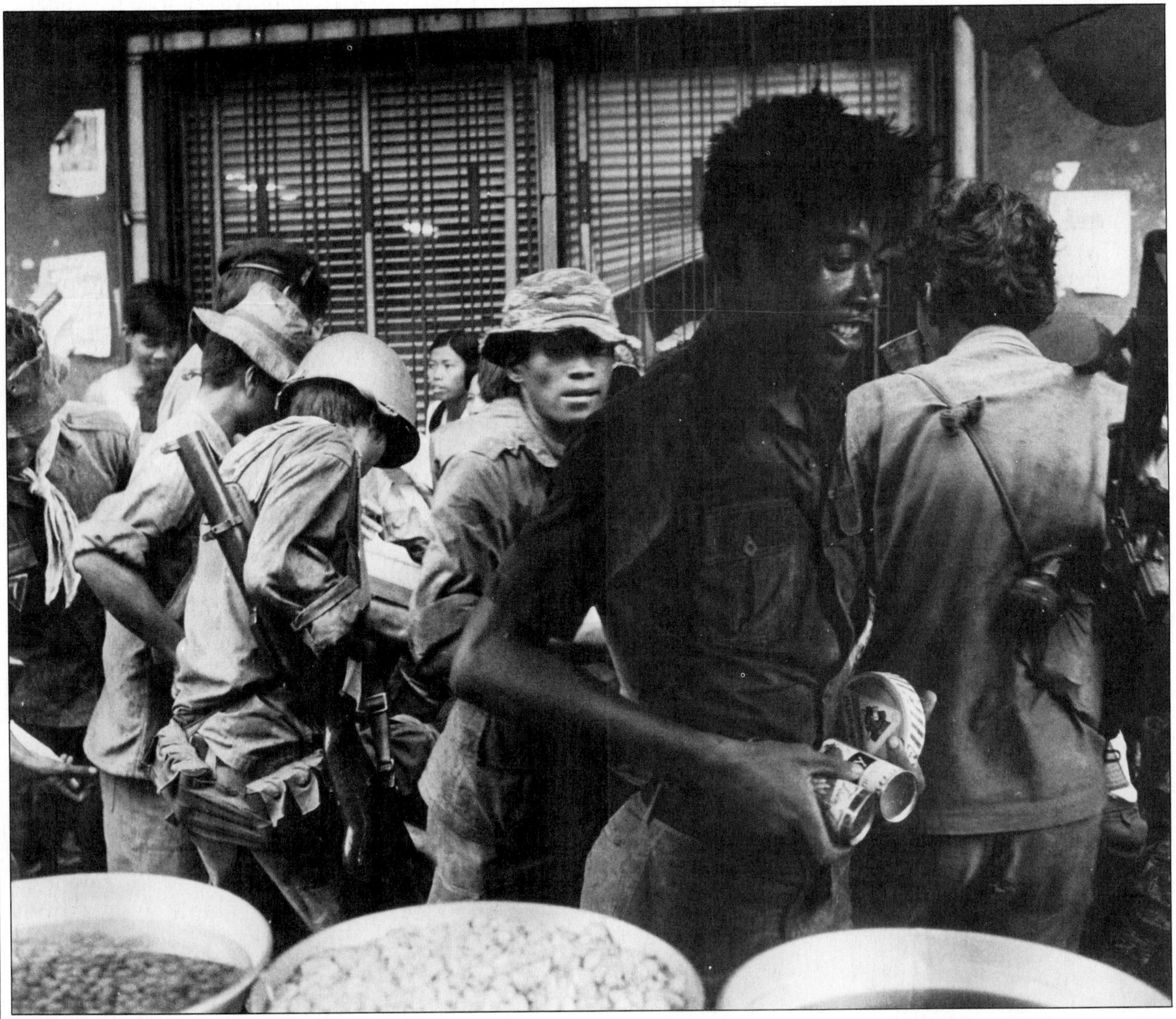

While ordinary Cambodians cowered beneath the storm of violence, the military forces of the government disintegrated. Soldiers abandoned their positions to steal food and livestock; artillery officers refused to work more than forty hours a week; air force pilots demanded bribes from ground units before providing air support; battalion commanders lounged in Phnom Penh villas purchased from the salaries of "phantom" troops.

Above. *Government soldiers, who had not been paid for three months, plunder food shops in Phnom Penh in May 1973.*

Right. *By 1974 the government's military manpower deficits had grown so severe that even boys were drafted into the ranks. Here, one young recruit guards a Khmer Rouge prisoner.*

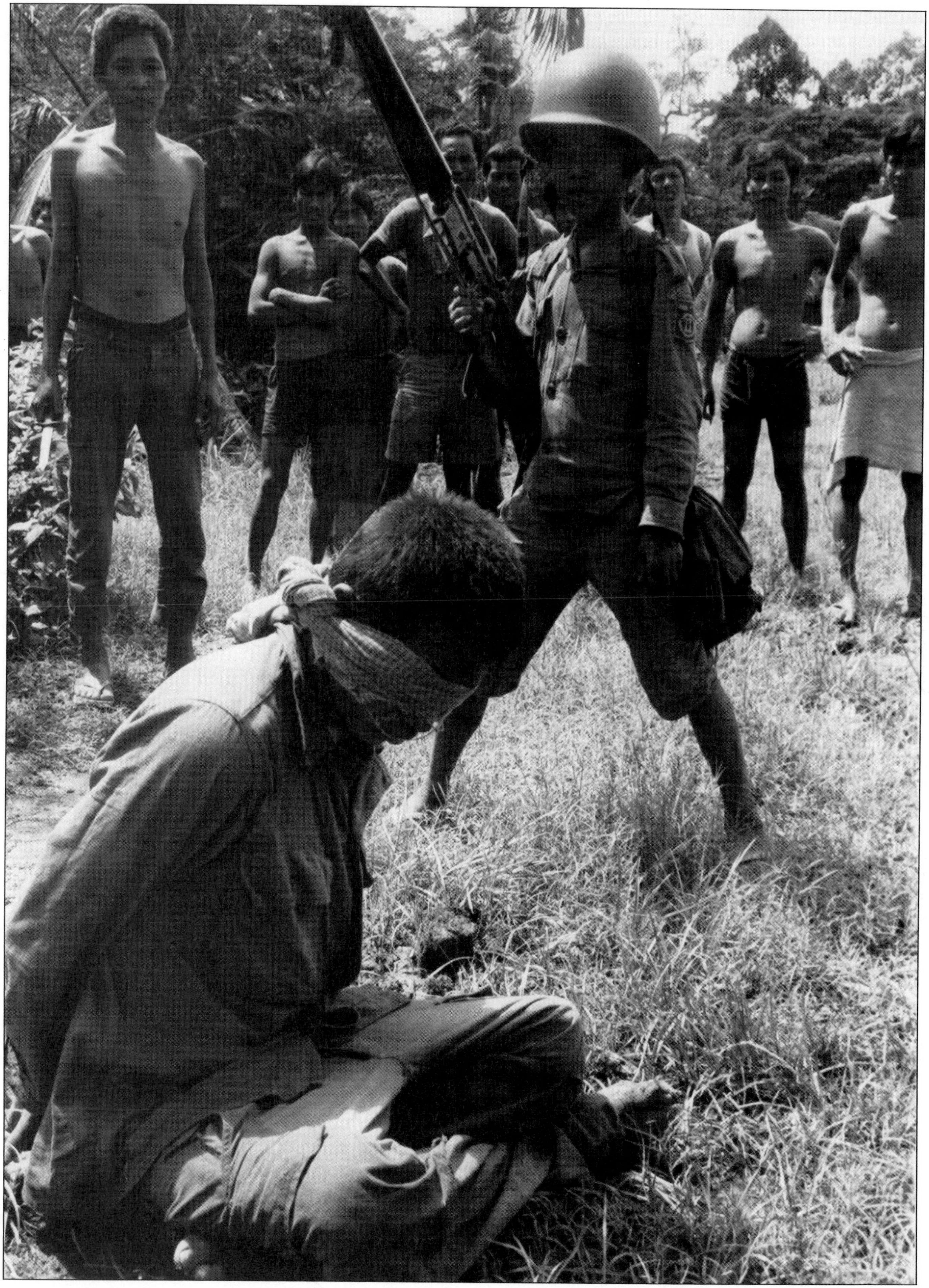

The government was completely unprepared for the swarm of refugees that descended on the capital during the last two years of the war. Here, dozens of families crowd the once-grand lobby of Phnom Penh's most luxurious hotel, the Cambodiana.

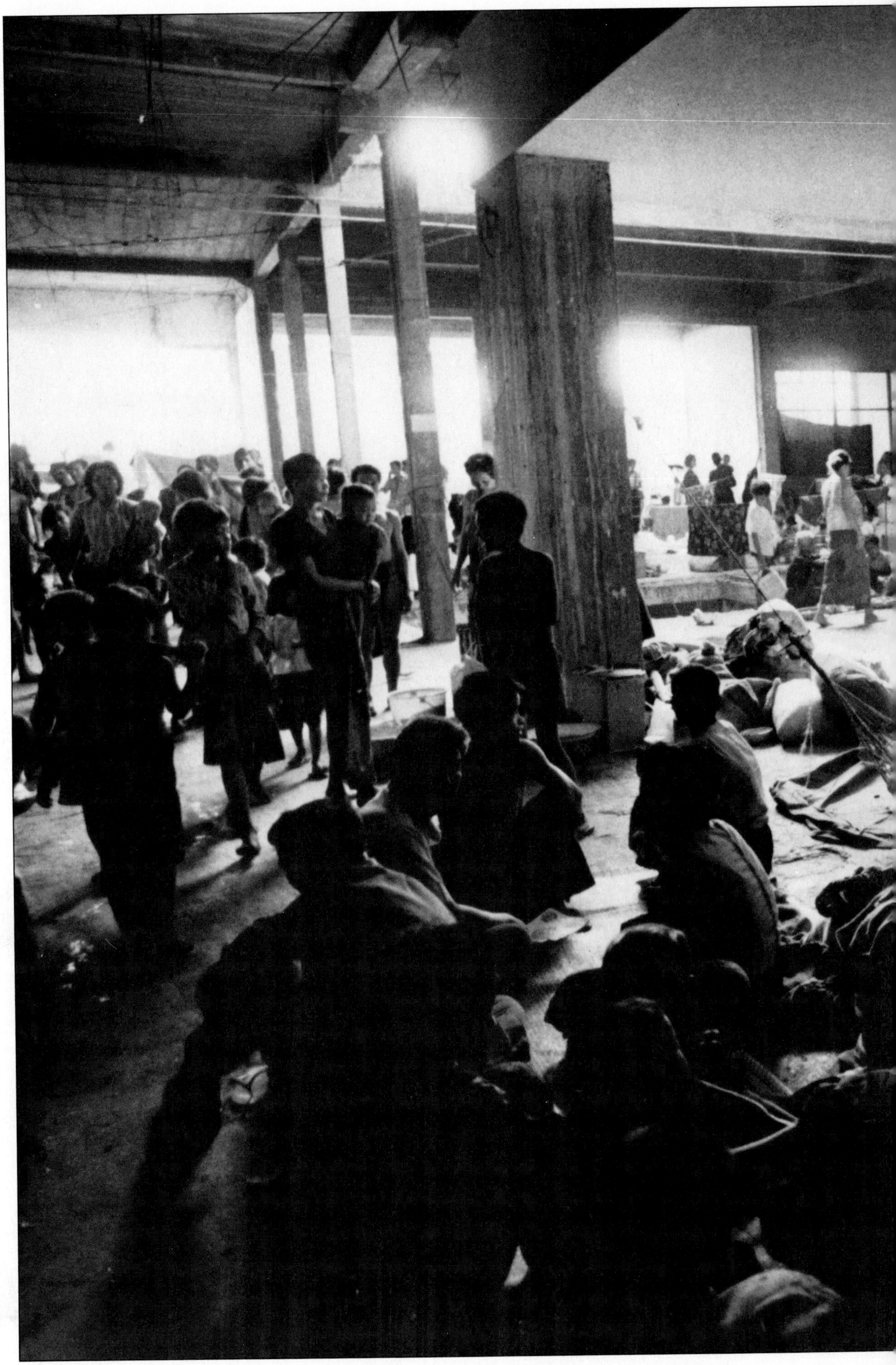

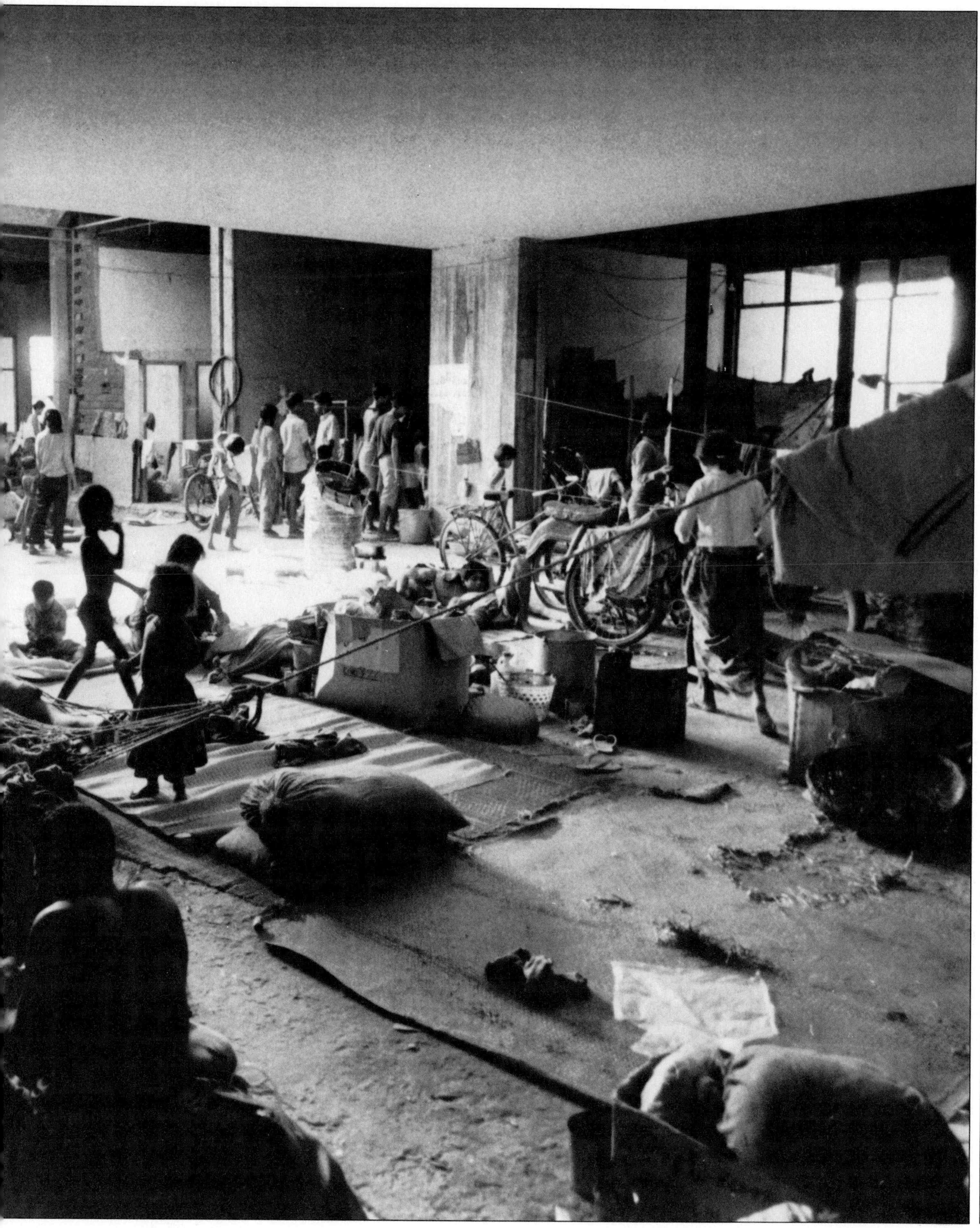

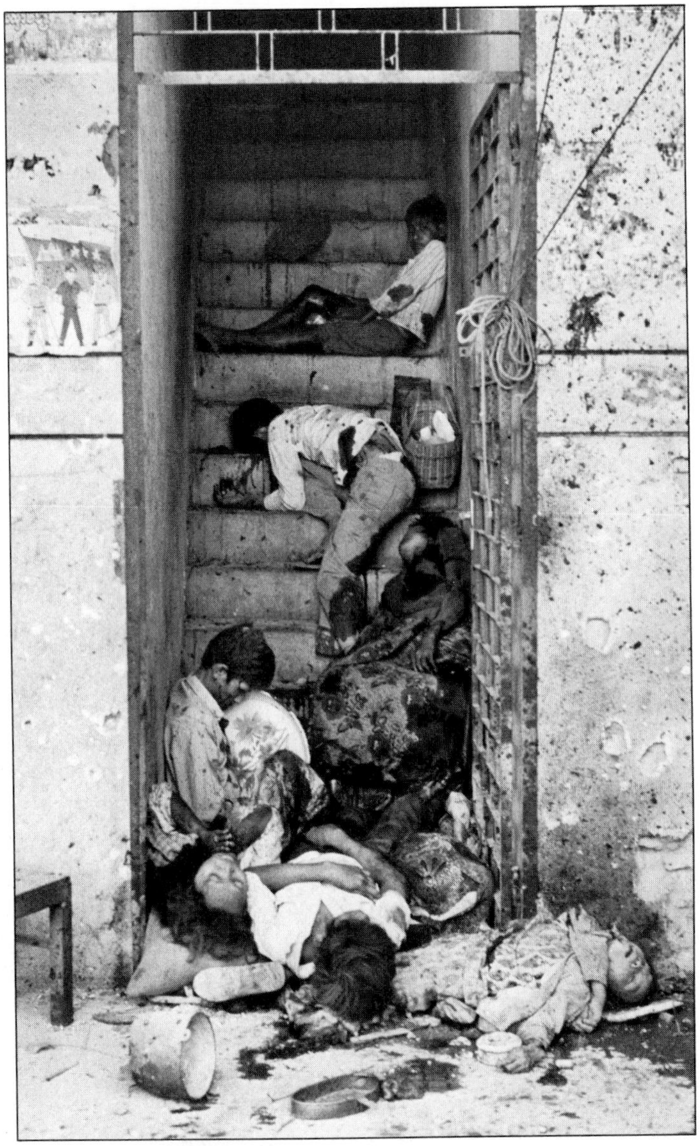

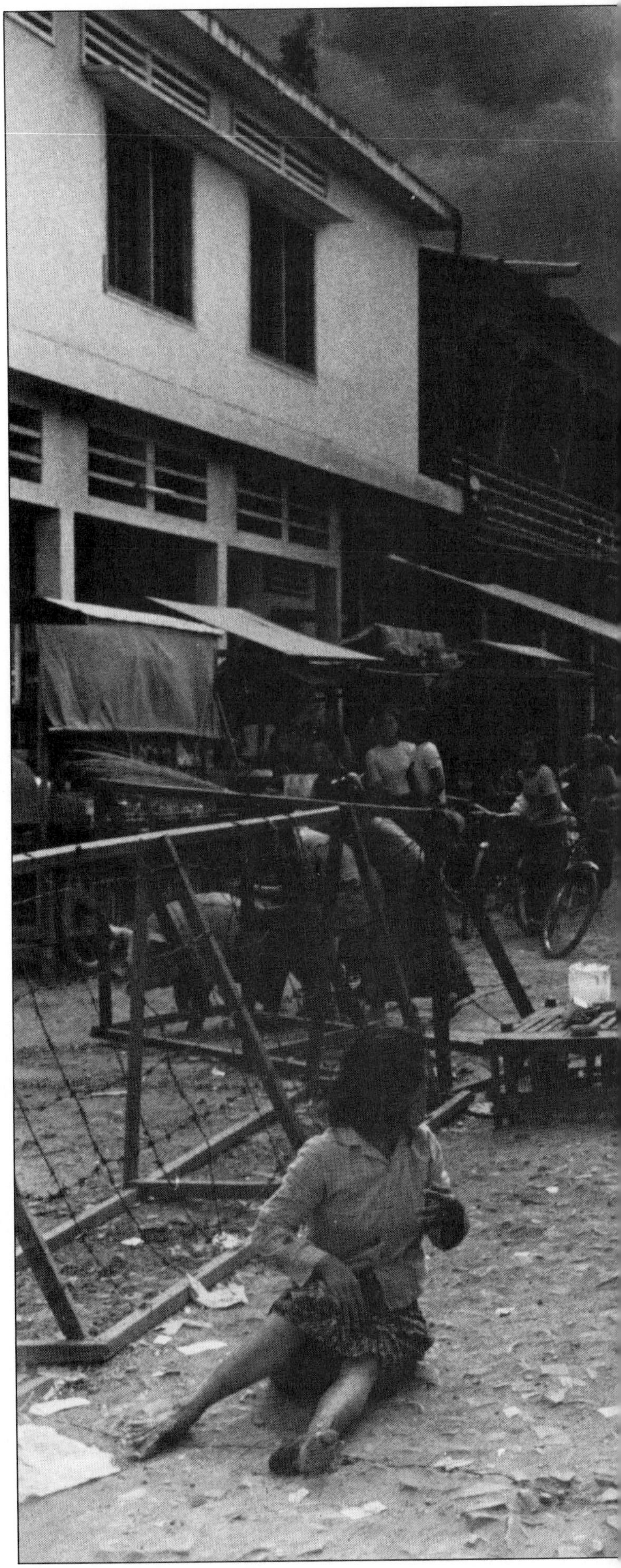

So savage were the bombardments that ravaged the capital, so desperate were the shortages of food and medicine, that many of the inhabitants of Phnom Penh only wanted the fighting to stop. "We keep praying every day for the war to end," said one woman. "But whichever side wins, we don't care. We just want to live in peace."

Above. *A lone survivor peers fearfully from a shattered doorway after a rocket attack killed his family, February 1974.*

Right. *In January 1974 civilians flee in terror down a Phnom Penh street as Communist artillery pounds the capital's central district.*

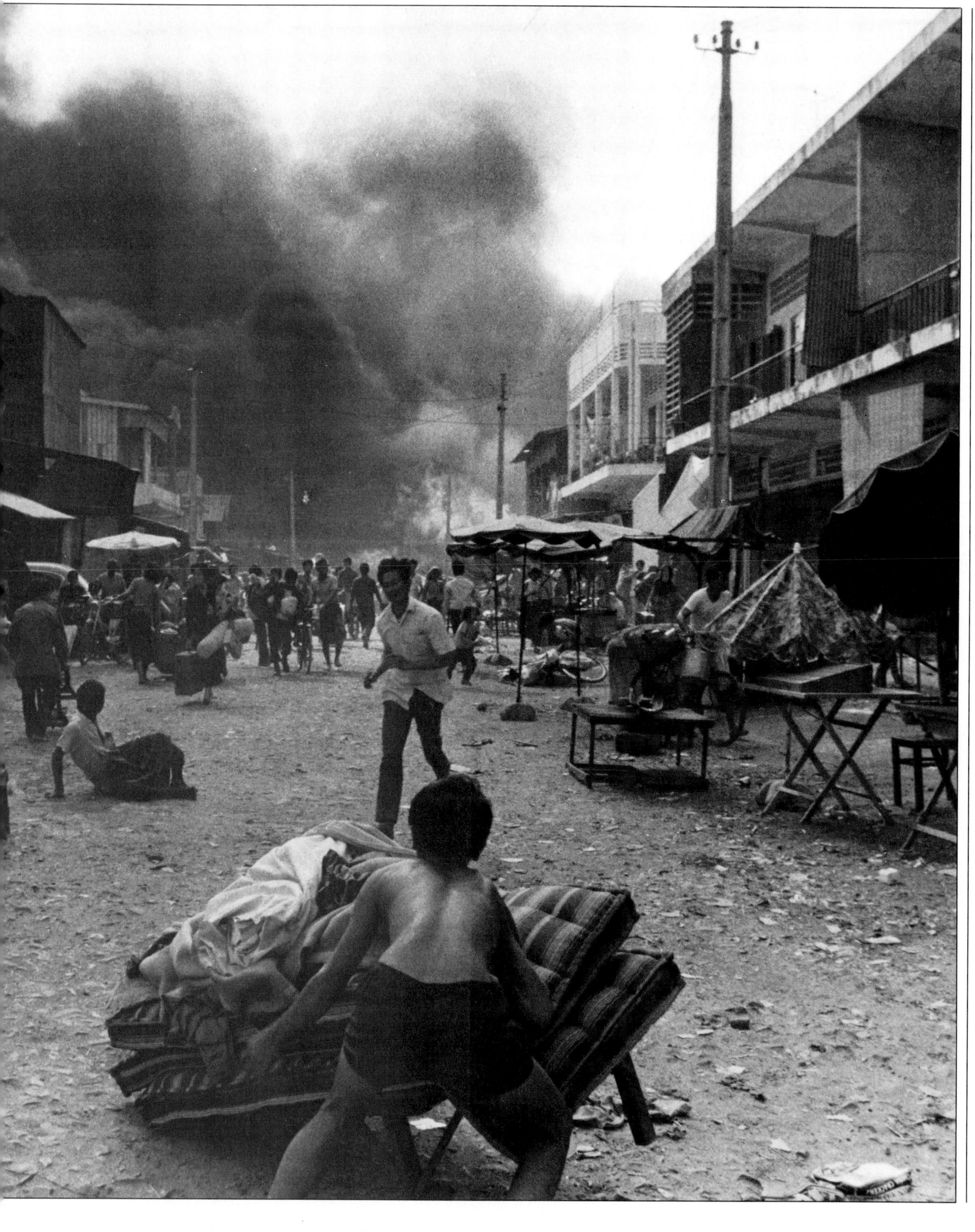

Portents of Disaster

Unlike its adversary, South Vietnam began 1973 in relatively good shape. During the previous year the armed forces of the Republic had thrown back the most massive Communist offensive of the war. Although portions of Quang Tri Province remained in enemy hands, most of the rest of the country, including the vast majority of the population, was under government control. The confidence of the army was at an all-time high, losses of equipment had been more than made up by arms shipments from the United States, and the imminent cease-fire promised at least a halt, if not an end, to the fighting. Taking advantage of the emergency powers granted him during 1972, President Thieu had achieved a measure of political control unmatched since the days of Ngo Dinh Diem. Planning for major economic development programs was well under way, while the first of hundreds of thousands of refugees had begun returning to their homes. If many viewed the Paris agreements with skepticism, if

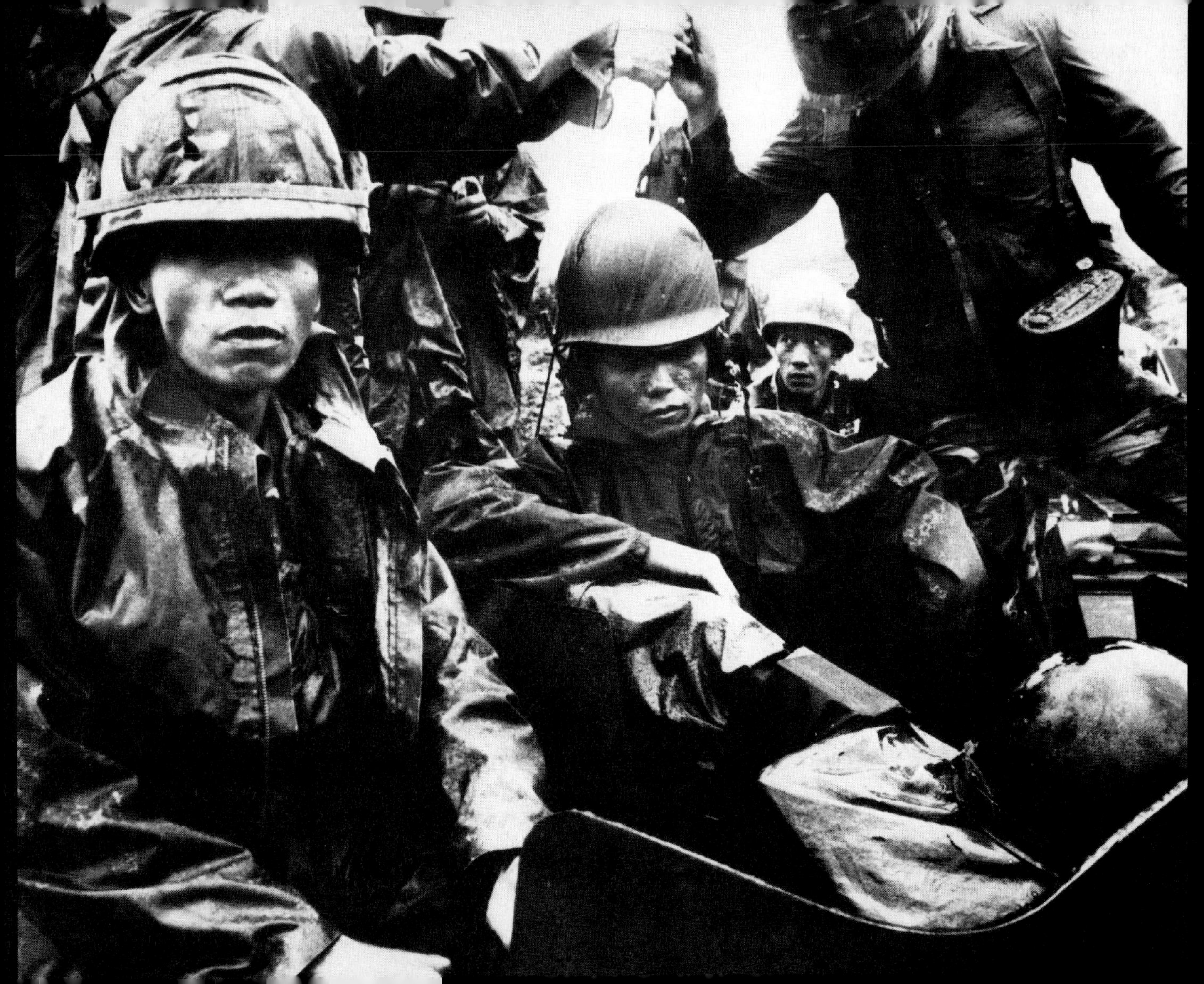

few believed the Communists would willingly honor their end of the bargain, the South Vietnamese people could not repress the hope that peace was truly at hand.

But there would be no peace. Over the next eighteen months the promise of prosperity would collapse in devastating economic hardship. The appearance of military strength would disappear under the weight of declining resources and internal disabilities. And the political leadership of the nation, preoccupied with the perpetuations of its own power, would lose the confidence of the people. With its destiny now largely in its own hands, South Vietnam succumbed to a progressive disease whose sources were manifold but whose chief symptom was a virulent corruption that steadily weakened the nation's capacity for resistance.

The "new" corruption

Like so many human societies Vietnam was no stranger to corruption. Under the rule of the emperors, mandarin officials frequently used their position to exact bribes from those seeking favorable judicial decisions, a practice enlarged upon in a hundred ways by Vietnamese "middlemen" and French bureaucrats during the colonial era. Until the arrival of the Americans in the mid-1960s, however, the scope of corruption was limited by the modest resources of a poor, almost wholly agricultural country. The sudden influx of millions of dollars in aid and a veritable flood of consumer goods created temptations for venality on an unprecedented scale. The relatively meager salaries of public officials, a steadily increasing rate of inflation, and a tradition of personal favoritism and nepotism exacerbated the problem, encouraging price manipulation, theft, office-buying, and petty graft of every conceivable kind.

Yet the "new" corruption of the post-cease-fire years displayed characteristics absent even in the period of greatest American largesse. It was, to begin with, pervasive. What had once been the preserve of a relatively limited number of officials now existed at every level of the government and military bureaucracies. Moreover, it had come to involve virtually all figures of substantial authority. In interviews conducted by the Rand Corporation in 1976 with twenty-seven former senior officers and civilian officials, the respondents accused every single high-ranking member of the Saigon government of participation in corrupt activities. According to Colonel Nguyen Huy Loi, a former adviser to the South Vietnamese delegation to the Paris peace talks, "to benefit from corruption was actually the principal motivation" of the military and civilian leadership. Under the later Thieu regime, contended opposition leader and former General Tran Van Don, "virtually everyone who was able took advantage of his position and engaged in profiteering." As corruption spread throughout the highest echelons of South Vietnamese society, its effects were felt more and more sharply by shopkeepers and civil servants, peasants and soldiers. With the American withdrawal there was "less fat around to live off," explained a member of the National Assembly. "So corrupt officials these days have to turn for money to ordinary Vietnamese." The mounting anger they felt at the unbridled greed and indifference of their leaders assumed a political momentum that eventually threatened to topple the Thieu government from power.

The source of their anger lay everywhere about them. Smuggling operations masterminded by high officials poured untaxed whiskey, soap, and other goods into the country. This illegal traffic deprived the government of desperately needed revenue and in some cases cost Vietnamese jobs by flooding the black market with items like matches and cigarettes, the manufacture of which were government monopolies. Profiteering in vital commodities like rice, sugar, and fertilizer reached epidemic proportions, provoking scandals that implicated wealthy merchants, government officers, even Buddhist and Catholic priests in hoarding and price manipulation schemes.

During 1973 and 1974 South Vietnamese newspapers made repeated accusations of official malfeasance: that high-ranking generals and officials in the prime minister's office had attempted to smuggle 16,000 tons of scrap metal worth $17.3 million out of the country; that three delta province chiefs had taken bribes to allow rice and other goods to be sold to the Vietcong; that II Corps commander General Nguyen Van Toan was raking in $20,000 a month in illegal "taxes" on lumber trucks in Pleiku Province; that the Quang Ngai Province chief had sold tons of scarce supplies to the Communists in exchange for cinnamon later exported at a profit of several hundred thousand dollars.

The refugee aid and resettlement program was a particular source of official misconduct. In 1973 a province chief, district chief, and several officials from the Ministry of Social Welfare were found guilty of "misappropriating" millions of piasters in rice and relief money intended for Da Nang refugees, a scandal that many observers regarded as no more than the tip of the iceberg. Citing testimony before the South Vietnamese National Assembly, one Vietnamese periodical charged that Dr. Phan Quang Dan—chairman of an interministerial committee for refugee resettlement and commissioner of the Develop Virgin Land and Construct Hamlets program—was "stealing funds earmarked for refugees and using the spoils in all kinds of shady undertakings." His alleged crimes included the parceling out of resettlement land to influential friends, the sale of monopoly rights to timber in Long Khanh Prov-

Preceding page. *ARVN soldiers on the offensive near Tay Ninh Province, January 1973. By the following year the deterioration of the army had become part of a national crisis threatening South Vietnam's survival.*

ince, and the diversion of 70 million piasters in refugee relief aid to furnish his Saigon office and those of a dozen associates.

Another source of growing discontent was the highly regarded "Land-to-the-Tiller" program the Thieu government had instituted in 1971. After successfully dissolving large landholdings and distributing them to poor tenant farmers, the program started slipping backwards as local officials aided former landlords in reclaiming their property. A favorite device was to designate such land for industrial and housing projects under the so-called urbanization program, withdraw the titles given to the peasant farmers, and restore them to the landlords, who either charged the farmers rent or threw them off the land. The practice was particularly prevalent in Long Khanh and Gia Dinh Provinces near Saigon and in Tuyen Duc, where landlords and officials evicted sixty families of disabled veterans and widows from their land, threatening them with murder if they attempted to get it back.

For most South Vietnamese, however, the rising tide of corruption affected their lives in dozens of smaller ways. Petty bribery and official extortion were rapidly becoming a way of life: $4 for a ride home with the police after curfew; $25 for a graduation certificate needed to get a job; $100 for a desk job in Saigon to keep a son out of the army. Police in Saigon began arbitrarily arresting people and demanding money for their release. One woman had to pay bribes to the local police station three times in eighteen months before getting her son out of jail. Government bureaucrats required payment for such services as supplying identification cards. An American Friends Service Committee worker in Quang Ngai recounted in 1974 that the cost of an authentic ID card had risen to 20,000 piasters. To get phony identification, useful for avoiding military service, officials were demanding twice as much. Even those for whom the army had no use could be turned to profit. The American journalist Fox Butterfield reported in September 1973 that the family of one mentally retarded young man, who also suffered from epilepsy, had to go into debt to raise the million piasters required by government officials to certify him unfit.

If petty bureaucrats could make life miserable for ordinary citizens, the most egregious practices were those of senior military officers, province chiefs, and the wives of

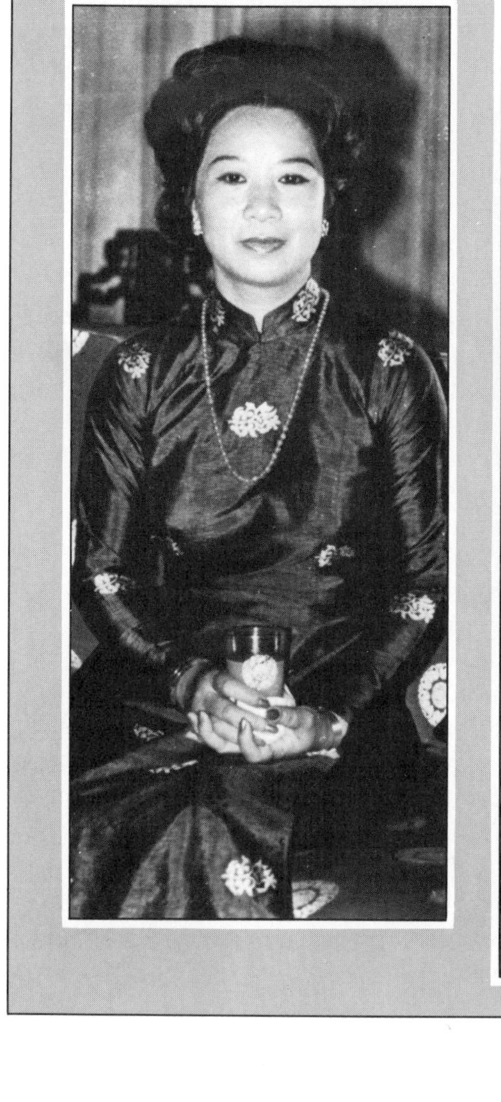

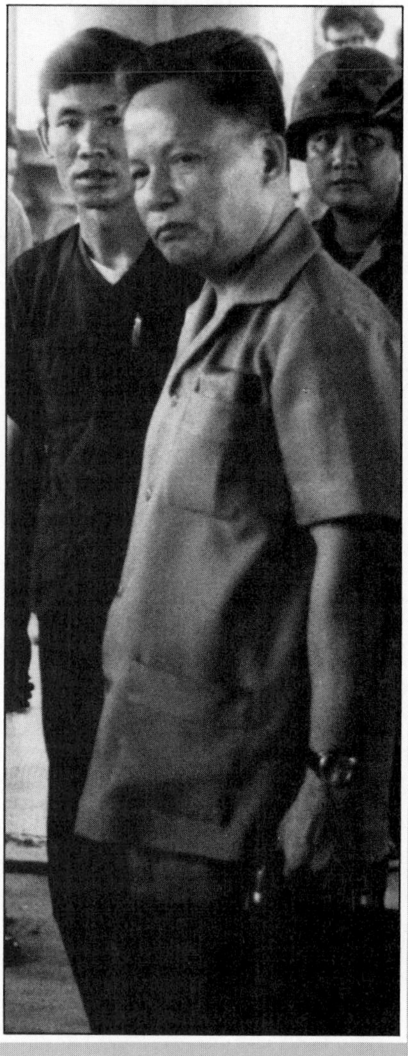

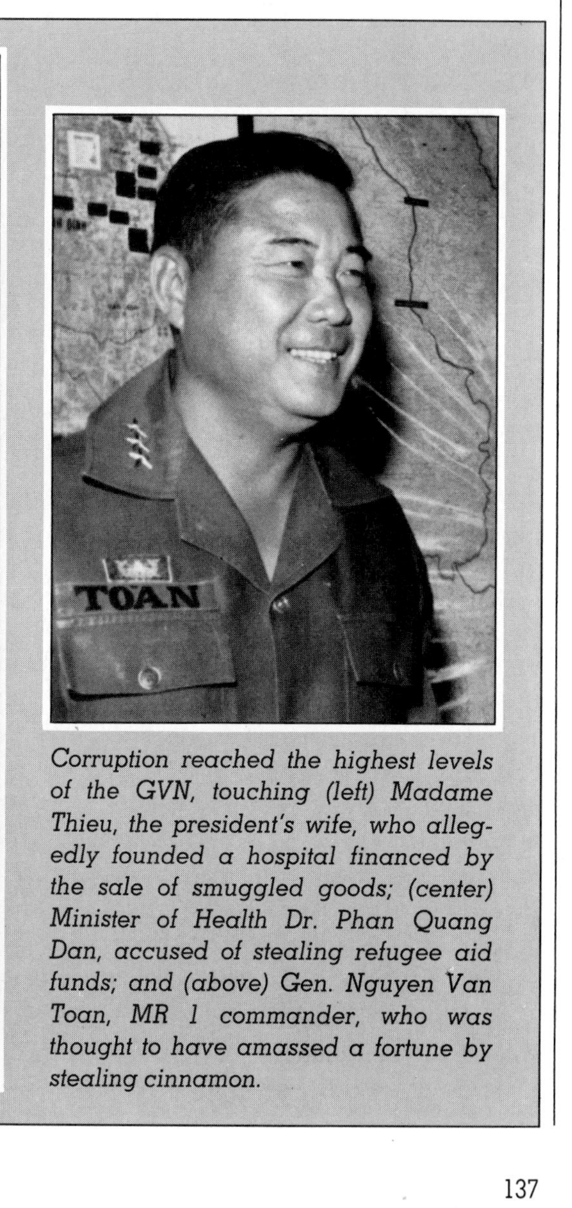
TOAN

Corruption reached the highest levels of the GVN, touching (left) Madame Thieu, the president's wife, who allegedly founded a hospital financed by the sale of smuggled goods; (center) Minister of Health Dr. Phan Quang Dan, accused of stealing refugee aid funds; and (above) Gen. Nguyen Van Toan, MR 1 commander, who was thought to have amassed a fortune by stealing cinnamon.

high-placed officials. It seemed that few senior commanders were able to resist the potentially huge payoffs that came with their positions. A 1974 study conducted by Nguyen Van Ngan, one of President Thieu's closest aides, revealed that out of sixty ARVN generals and full colonels less than one-third were not involved in some form of illegal activity. Only one of the four corps commanders, Lieutenant General Ngo Quang Truong, was untainted by rumors of corruption.

The reputation of province chiefs was, if possible, even worse. The job frequently went to the highest bidder, who turned over as much as 80 percent of the "monthly take" to his patron—the regional commander or a ministerial official in Saigon—a sum that could reach as much as $1 million a year. Part of that money came from the sale of other lucrative government and military positions, part from such practices as rice profiteering, trading with the enemy, and a host of unofficial exactions on the local populace. When it came to using political influence for illegal gain, however, few could compare with the wives of prominent generals and government officials. According to one survey, these "generals of internal affairs," including the wives of the prime minister, the JGS chief of staff, and the president himself, had amassed as much as $500 million in the period from 1954 to 1975 thanks to rigged land deals, black market transactions, smuggling operations, and the sale of official positions.

The efforts of the Saigon government to come to grips with the scourge of corruption ranged from the ineffectual to the pathetic. Officially there existed three anticorruption units. The first, the General Censorate, headed by Thieu's uncle Ngo Xuan Tich, failed to conclude 90 percent of its investigations. The second, an army inspectorate, was composed of officers considered unfit for regular command. The third unit, a special anticorruption committee headed by Vice President Tran Van Huong, was nothing more than a showcase. Those who tried to expose official corruption outside government channels ran terrible risks. During 1973 one publisher who had written articles on corruption in the army was assassinated by two men wearing paratrooper uniforms. Another critic of corruption was ambushed on one of the safest roads in the Mekong Delta.

Opposition editors Ngo Cong Duc (right) and Nhu An. Their daily newspaper Tin Sang *was censored ninety-eight times in one year alone.*

Some cases of illegal activity did reach the courts. In early 1974 the army caught two NCOs trying to sell twelve tons of steel plate intended for armored personnel carriers. Investigation of an ARVN payroll embezzlement scheme resulted in the sentencing of nineteen officers to prison terms of one to eight years. And in mid-1974 the Customs Service broke up a large smuggling ring dealing in cognac and cigarettes, two of the convictions resulting in death sentences. But by and large prosecution of corrupt officials was so rare that those few cases that did result in substantial punishment were cause for amazement. More typical was the case of an army training center commandant who was simply transferred to the Ministry of Defense after junior officers accused him of skimming $6,000 a month from funds meant to purchase food for draftees. In another instance a delta province chief charged with misappropriation of supplies and trading with the enemy was promoted to assistant army inspector.

Although the disposition of such cases scandalized many South Vietnamese and eroded support for his presidency, President Thieu was reluctant to take forceful action against corrupt officials. In the first place, he feared that any substantive move would create a backlash among those senior military commanders on whose support he depended. Thieu also worried that any major upheaval within his government would be unacceptable to the Americans. He claimed privately that he was prepared to remove Prime Minister Khiem, whose nepotism had exceeded even Thieu's patience, were it not for pressure from the U.S. Embassy, and even hinted at American collusion in some illegal activity. More to the point, a thorough house cleaning would threaten the president's closest associates.

Even had he been willing to brave these obstacles, Thieu faced what many believed was the impossibility of real reform. The cancer of corruption had spread to every organ of the state. To have excised it would have meant the decimation of both the officer corps and the administrative hierarchy. "The whole body is sick," lamented the former president of the South Vietnamese Senate, Nguyen Van Huyen.

Roman Catholic protesters prepare to burn an effigy denoting government corruption in front of a church in suburban Saigon in October 1974.

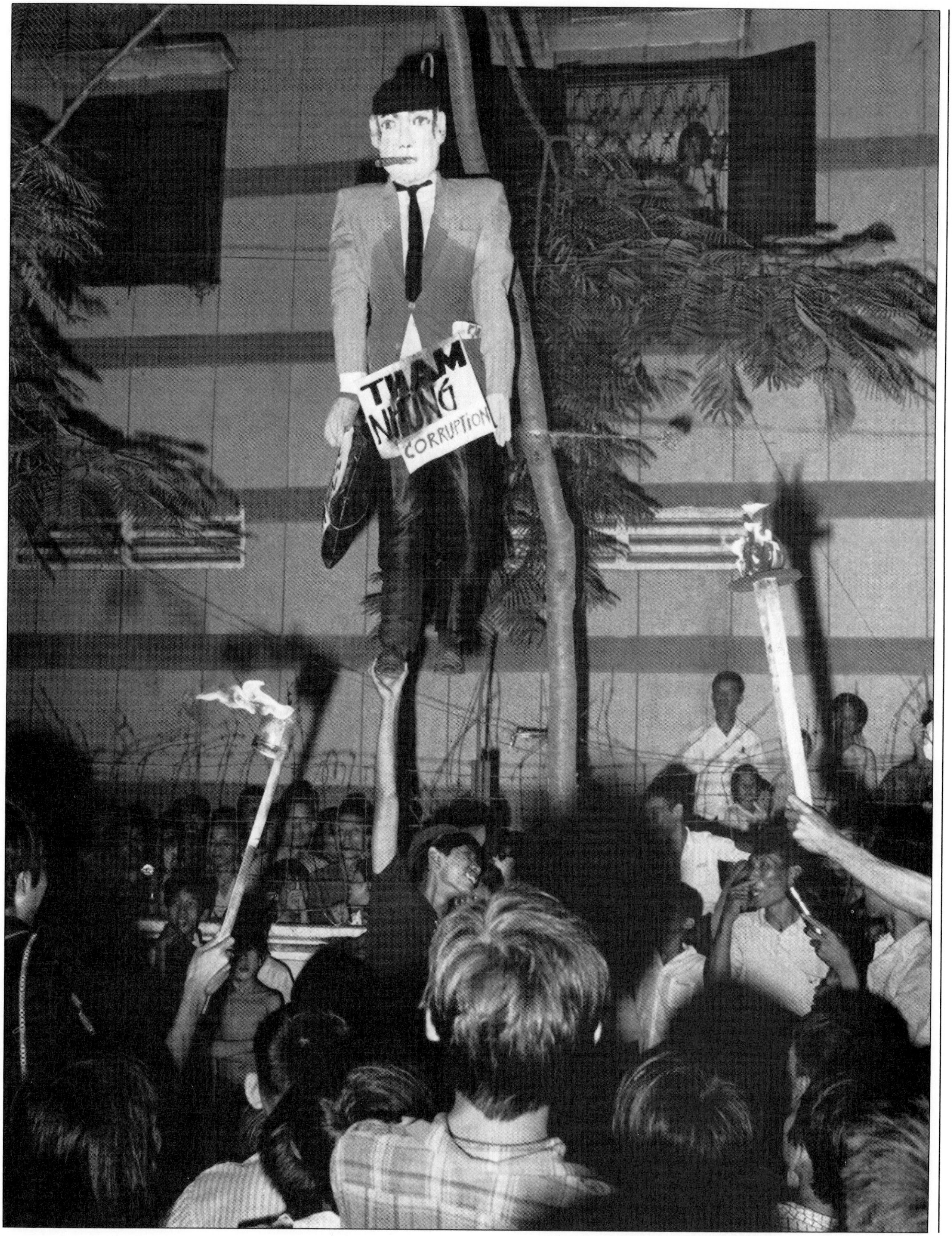
THAM
NHŨNG
CORRUPTION

> The whole system is involved in corruption . . . from top to bottom. All the chiefs of province, all the big civil servants, all the high-ranking members of the executive. How in this condition can we suppress the sickness?

Instead, Thieu covered the tracks of the guilty as best he could, promoting men like Lieutenant General Pham Quoc Thuan to the command of Military Region 3, despite widespread charges of profiteering and other crimes, and dismissing Nguyen Van Ngan after his investigations had reached members of Prime Minister Khiem's and even the president's own family.

In this he found a ready ally in Ambassador Graham Martin. Intent on portraying the Thieu regime as positively as possible, Martin made light of the situation, observing that "a little corruption over here oils the economic machinery." In a message to Washington during the summer of 1973, the ambassador asserted that "the level of corruption currently existing in South Vietnam corresponds roughly to that in the state of Massachusetts and the city of Boston during the first decades of the century. That problem was eliminated," said Martin, "and perhaps even more rapid progress may be made in Vietnam." American officials testifying before Congress parroted the embassy's rhetoric, contending that most of the reports of corruption were "malicious rumor and unsubstantiated slander" and that those charges that were "essentially true" had already been corrected.

Such complacency was not shared by the South Vietnamese. Tired of official extortion, scornful of repeated promises that something was being done, enraged by each day's quota of fantastic new stories of corruption, they directed their fury at the small number of senior military and government figures whom they held responsible for the "plague on society." If they understood the economic necessity that drove ill-paid civil servants and common soldiers to engage in petty graft, for those who grew rich on the backs of a steadily more impoverished people they had nothing but contempt. For what fueled their anger was more than corruption itself. As the South Vietnamese economy slid downward in an ever-accelerating spiral, what had been tolerated in better days could no longer be endured. "The house leaks from the roof down," said the Saigonese, and the water was rising.

Economic crisis

A year and a half after the signing of the Paris accords South Vietnam faced the prospect of total economic collapse. The figures alone were staggering. The cost of living, which had surged upward 65 percent in 1973, climbed an additional 27 percent during the first six months of 1974. The overall rise reflected even sharper increases in essential commodities; rice up 100 percent by the end of 1973; sugar, 107 percent; cooking oil, 139 percent; kerosene, 112 percent. At the same time, per capita income shrank by nearly half. Unemployment was estimated at nearly 1 million people, a full one-fifth of the civilian labor force. The piaster, devalued twelve times in eighteen months, had dropped by 25 percent against the dollar. A yawning annual trade deficit of approximately $750 million dwarfed the $100 million worth of exportable logs, rubber, scrap metal, and shrimp that South Vietnam could muster, and ate up three-fourths of the government's foreign exchange reserves.

Agricultural production could not meet the country's needs, many consumer goods had disappeared from urban markets, industries dependent on imported materials had ground to a halt, and thousands of refugees displaced by the war flooded into the cities to swell the army of the jobless. So severe was the economic crisis that gripped

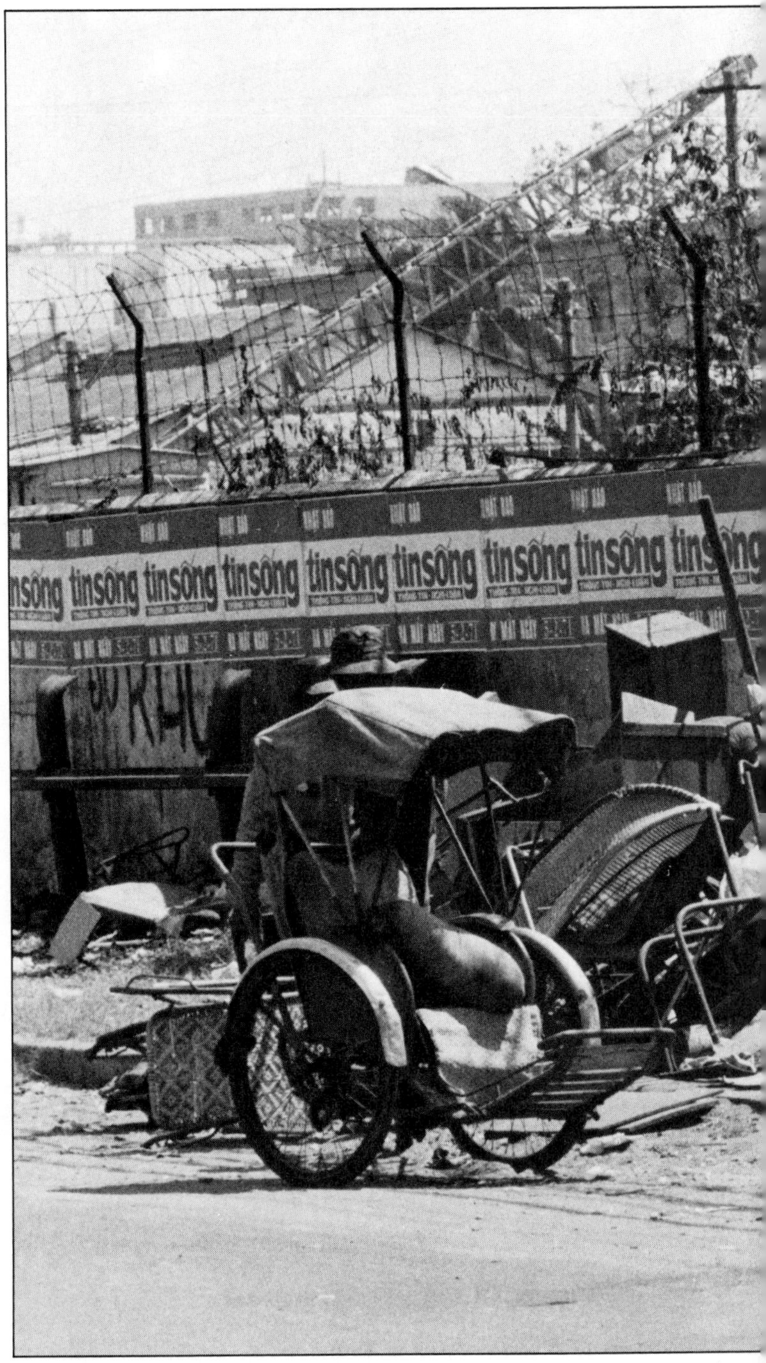
tinsông

South Vietnam it could be compared in American terms only to the Great Depression of the 1930s.

The distress was due in part to poor rice harvests throughout Southeast Asia in 1972 that drove up the price of Vietnam's staple food, in part to the 1973 Arab oil embargo which in the space of months quadrupled the price of oil. The impact was felt not only in the industrial sector but even more by millions of farmers and city dwellers whose consumption of petroleum products—kerosene for cooking stoves, gasoline for motorbikes and irrigation pumps, fertilizer necessary to cultivate hybrid strains of "miracle rice"—had increased fivefold over the previous ten years. The inflation caused by the oil embargo further diminished the real value of declining American aid. Now it was lower than at any time since 1965.

Equally devastating were the economic effects of the U.S. military withdrawal. The shutdown of American bases had eliminated as many as 300,000 Vietnamese jobs, as well as cutting off the flow of dollars spent by GIs and American contractors for food, taxis, servants, souvenirs, drinks, and prostitutes. In 1971 South Vietnam had taken $400 million from American pockets. Although two years later the sidewalks of Saigon's Nguyen Hue Boulevard were still jammed with street merchants hawking velvet paintings, brass ware made from discarded shell casings, souvenir nylon jackets and Confederate battle

As displaced peasants swarmed into Saigon during the final years of the war, squalid refugee quarters sprang up, transforming the "urban revolution" into an urban crisis.

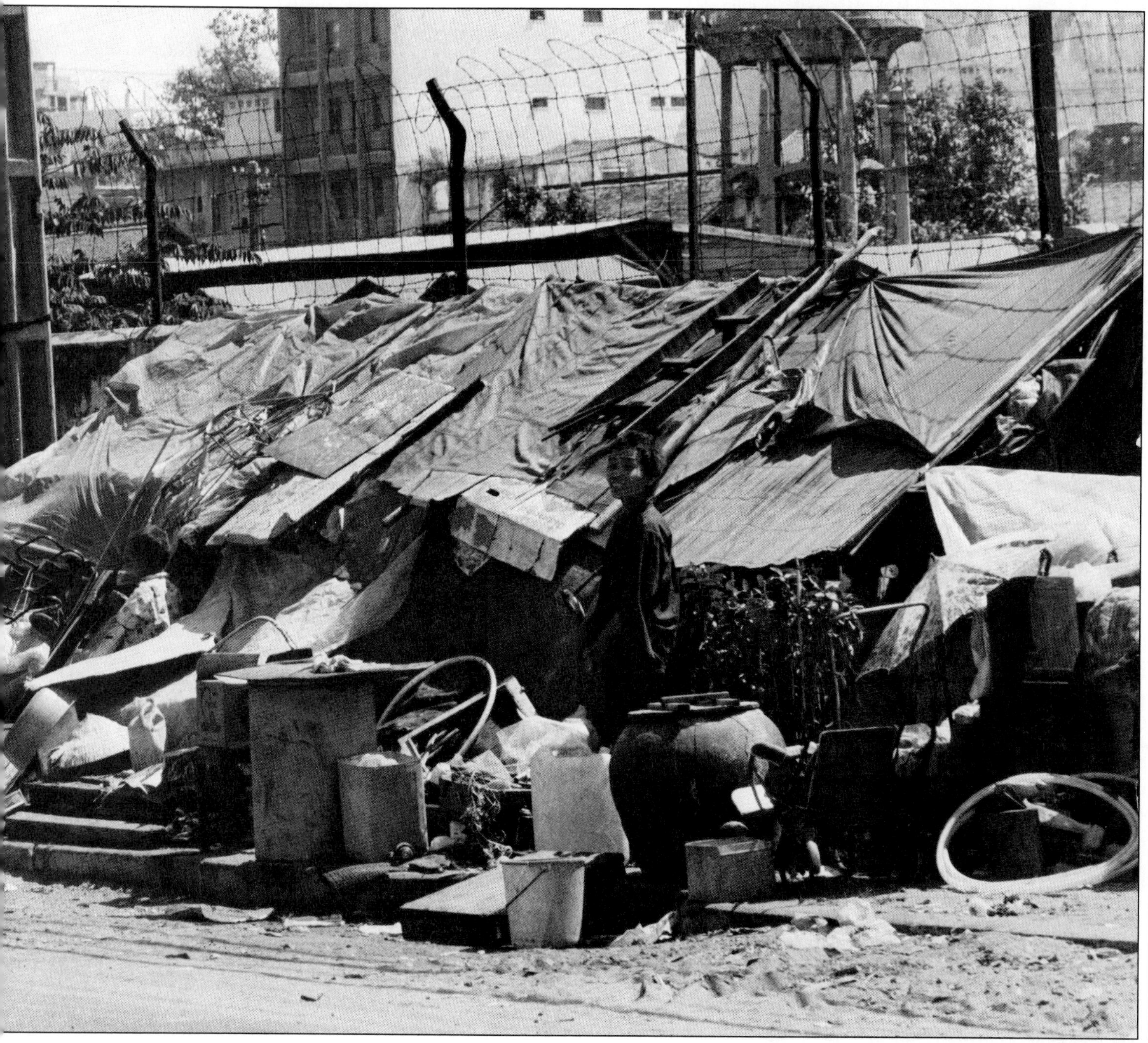

flags, they had few customers. By 1974 American spending had shrunk to less than $100 million.

Ironically, at the time of the cease-fire the GVN had been enthusiastic about the possibilities for rapid and sustained economic growth. Twenty years of American aid, training, and construction had left South Vietnam with modern ports like those at Saigon and Cam Ranh Bay equipped to handle sophisticated cargo operations, numerous airports, highways, and bridges linking all of the major cities, and a nucleus of trained personnel with some measure of technical and management expertise. The government moved swiftly to take advantage of these assets. On May 20, 1973, President Thieu initiated an Eight Year Reconstruction and Development Plan with the goal of increasing rice production, resettling refugees, and financing development projects. The centerpiece of the new plan was a series of measures designed to attract foreign capital and to encourage overseas collaboration with Vietnamese businessmen in joint investment ventures. The incentives provided were among the most liberal and attractive in Southeast Asia: 100 percent repatriation of capital, a five-year exemption from taxes, simplified procedures for obtaining export licenses, easy financing, and an unconditional guarantee against nationalization.

To further encourage foreign investment the government established export processing and industrial development zones, guaranteeing the security of the installations and assisting in construction and maintenance of plants. At the same time, Thieu sent high-ranking missions on shopping trips to Europe, the United States, and Japan in search of foreign aid. Most important of all in South Vietnamese eyes was the dazzling promise of oil in the continental shelf off the Mekong Delta. In early May concessions were sold to twenty-four international oil companies to begin exploratory drilling.

As the year progressed Thieu also took steps to arrest the momentum of economic decline. The government imposed a 10 percent value-added tax on all transactions and services and sliced 25 percent off planned spending for fiscal year 1974. Power use was controlled, gasoline for cars severely rationed, and government air conditioners (except for high officials and military commanders) were removed. To ensure that an adequate amount of food reached the capital, rice trading between provinces was banned. Province chiefs directed villagers to sell their crops only to officially licensed merchants who were ordered to truck large quotas of their supplies to Saigon. The skyrocketing cost of petroleum forced authorities to raise the official price of fertilizer, the increased agricultural production costs offset to some degree by a simultaneous increase in the official price of paddy rice. To restrain the money supply, the government boosted interest rates to 26 percent. To close the trade deficit, officials placed an import ban on items such as liquor, cosmetics, and other luxury goods.

All of this activity was not without result. During 1973 exports almost tripled from the year before. Tax collections doubled, with an increase in real terms of about 35 percent, and a substantial cutback in nonessential imports helped strengthen indigenous textile and bicycle industries. Government efforts to improve agricultural production were rewarded with the largest rice harvest on record. Credit to rural banks was expanded, and several hundred thousand refugees were resettled, many of them in previously unfarmed areas.

But the overall picture remained bleak. Industrial production continued to decline, with manufacturers reporting more layoffs and reduced sales. Despite record harvests the nation was still far short of self-sufficiency. Nearly 300,000 tons of rice had to be imported from the United States during the first six months of 1974 alone. Meanwhile, some of the government's remedies proved impossible to implement. Only six weeks after the introduction of austerity taxes Saigon yielded to public pressure and rescinded levies on all retail transactions. Pressures of a different kind halted a plan to curb inflation and attract foreign investment by divesting some twenty-odd government-owned businesses. After getting off to a good start, the program was abruptly abandoned amid allegations of conflict of interest and dishonest collusion when members of the government objected to the sale of the lucrative Vietnam Sugar Company.

Nor had other measures meant to lure foreign capital met with success. A Hong Kong businessman reflected the attitude of many in the region when he told of a letter he had received from a friend in Saigon saying that the smart money was getting into Vietnam. "I couldn't believe it," the businessman said. "I didn't even answer him. The guy must be going bananas. One minute the place is going up in rockets, the next minute peace is breaking out. Nobody knows what the hell's going on. You can't do business in a place like that." The search for "third country" foreign aid yielded no more than $50 million, and the euphoria surrounding confirmation of oil deposits off the South Vietnamese coast in early 1974 belied the tentative nature of the findings and the fact that at best it would be five more years before substantial returns could be expected.

A contagion of despair

In fact, neither official optimism nor grandiose programs could overcome fundamental disabilities of the government's own making. Despite constant American prodding, the GVN had never seriously undertaken long-term economic planning. Instead of encouraging production geared to development, construction and manufacturing had been directed toward short-term consumption by Americans and wealthy Vietnamese. Instead of exploiting Vietnam's own natural resources, equipment and raw materials had been purchased at considerable cost from overseas. Instead of creating employment in industry, tens of thousands of civilians had been allowed to drift into an artificial service economy that had no work for them once the Americans departed. Now on their own, the South Vietnamese reaped the harvest that many had warned would be the inevitable result of such policies.

Moreover, by its aggressive refusal to work within the terms of the Paris agreement the government squandered what opportunity it had to get its economic house in order. The continued high level of fighting, which during much of 1973 had been largely the result of Thieu's desire to gain the military upper hand, had disrupted agricultural production, severely hampered the commercial development of the country's forests, generated large numbers of new refugees, increased by a third the ranks of disabled veterans and families of deceased servicemen who depended on government assistance, frightened away desperately needed foreign investment, and perpetuated the enormous financial burden of the nation's defense. The Communists' "strategic raids" campaign only exacerbated the impossible demands the war was already making on the South Vietnamese economy. With 60 percent of the GVN budget going to maintain its million-man army, and another 20 percent devoted to refugees and veterans, the government had almost nothing left for the urgent tasks of economic reconstruction.

The result was a breadth of misery unparalleled in the nation's thirty-year history. Symptoms of economic depression were visible wherever one looked. The motorbikes that had given their name to the imported prosperity of the "Honda boom" began to give way to bicycles on Saigon streets. Unable to afford the cost of fuel, a few ingenious taxi drivers attempted to keep their ancient blue-and-white minicabs running on a mixture of peanut oil and paraffin, but more than half of the capital's crazy assortment of tattered jalopies sat quietly rusting away. In their place was a growing number of beggars and homeless children roving the streets or scavenging in the city's trash heaps for something to eat.

The margin of safety had disappeared even for those with steady jobs. Government workers, whose wage increases since 1972 offset less than one-fourth of the rise in the cost of living, no longer earned enough to meet the minimum necessities of life. One immaculately dressed

Their families unable to afford kerosene or charcoal, these Saigonese children peel bark from the city's trees to use as cooking fuel, April 1974.

senior civil servant told an American visitor that after years of service he could no longer afford to feed his family. Every Saturday he had to take a bus out into the country to get what food he could from his mother for the week ahead. For millions like him a frenzied search for extra income became a way of life. In a society that prized education highly, many parents were forced to take their children out of school—not only from lack of money to pay for fees and books, but also from the necessity that children find some means of casual employment to help their families survive. Between 1972 and 1974 Saigon's schools had recorded a 40 percent drop in attendance. "Moonlighting such as offering taxi service on motorcycles, tutoring or peddling, wives turning into bar girls, and daughters into prostitutes were a few ways of beating the high cost of living," recalled a former military officer. "It was therefore problematic whether to label as corrupt those lowly civil servants and policemen who asked small fees for their services in order to buy rice for their hungry families." Nonetheless, such exactions were becoming impossible for ordinary people to meet.

For those on fixed incomes, such as disabled veterans, or those with no income at all, like refugees, the suffering was even greater. Hunger and malnutrition were prevalent even in the Mekong Delta where a ready availability of food usually kept living standards much higher than in other parts of the country. In Da Nang, poor laborers and unemployed fishermen lived on watery gruel because they had no money for rice. In Quang Ngai, whole families attempted to survive on one meal of three sweet potatoes and a few land crabs a day.

All of Vietnam's despair could be seen in the fate of a Saigon cyclo driver named Vo Van Nam. A former enlisted man in the South Vietnamese army, Nam eked out a bare living with the help of the lottery tickets his wife sometimes managed to sell on street corners. As conditions grew worse he took to selling his blood for a few extra piasters at the Cong Hoa Hospital. One day after he left the hospital he discovered that his cyclo had been taken. "He wandered about town trying to find his cyclo, but he couldn't, and he complained that it was as if all the money from his blood had been, in a way, stolen," recalled his wife. "He was very sad." The next day Nam sold his wrist watch to a pawnbroker, then brought his five children to a movie, a treat they could rarely afford. After the movie he bought a plastic bag of gasoline and a box of matches. Standing by the side of a church he told the children he could no longer think of any way to get money for the family. "I'm giving up now," he said to them. "You stay with your mother and obey your mother and take anything she can bring back to give you." His eldest daughter, Tam, pleaded with her father not to leave them alone in the world. "I don't want to," he told her, "but I see no other way." Then he ran across the street into a park as the children screamed and begged for help. "I cried to passersby 'Stop my daddy, he wants to kill himself,'" remembered Tam, "but nobody cared, nobody paid attention." She ran after him, desperately trying to knock the matches from his hand as he poured the gasoline over his body. But he pushed her away, shouting, "You fool, do you want to die too?" Tam cried again for help, but it was too late. Nam struck a match. In an instant he was consumed by flames.

In the fall of 1972, in the wake of the Communist offensive and amid rumors of an agreement in Paris, the people of South Vietnam had begun to look hopefully to the future. Now in place of hope a deepening malaise eroded the nation's spirit. The death of Vo Van Nam was one index of social illness, the panic that reigned in Saigon after the destruction of the Nha Be refinery was another. For even as corruption strained the social bonds that held the nation together, and economic crisis betrayed the promise of prosperity, the military shield behind which the people sheltered had begun to decay.

The military morass

To all appearances, South Vietnam remained a formidable military power. The armed forces of the Republic numbered altogether more than a million men, including some 500,000 regular ARVN soldiers, an equal number of Territorial Forces, 65,000 airmen, 40,000 sailors, and nearly 15,000 Marines. Moreover, the $753 million worth of new airplanes, helicopters, tanks, artillery pieces, and other military supplies provided to South Vietnam under the Enhance and Enhance Plus programs of late 1972 left the RVNAF better equipped than ever before. "If we had given this aid to the North Vietnamese," observed one American general, "they could have fought us for the rest of the century."

As a gesture of American good will that substantially increased the official South Vietnamese military inventory against which replacements could be made after the cease-fire, the arms shipments had been a welcome addition to the RVNAF arsenal. But like many American gifts the new hardware proved a double-edged sword. Hastily conceived and hurriedly ordered, the Enhance Plus program encouraged among the GVN leadership a false sense of security, while simultaneously increasing South Vietnamese dependence on continuing American aid to purchase the spare parts, ammunition, and fuel necessary to operate the new equipment. The build-up also created management and maintenance requirements that the RVNAF simply could not meet. As a result, much of the new equipment remained in storage "sitting around rusting," as one U.S. official noted, right up until the final North Vietnamese offensive in 1975.

Rusting bodies of U.S.-supplied jeeps and other military vehicles at a storage lot in Nha Trang.

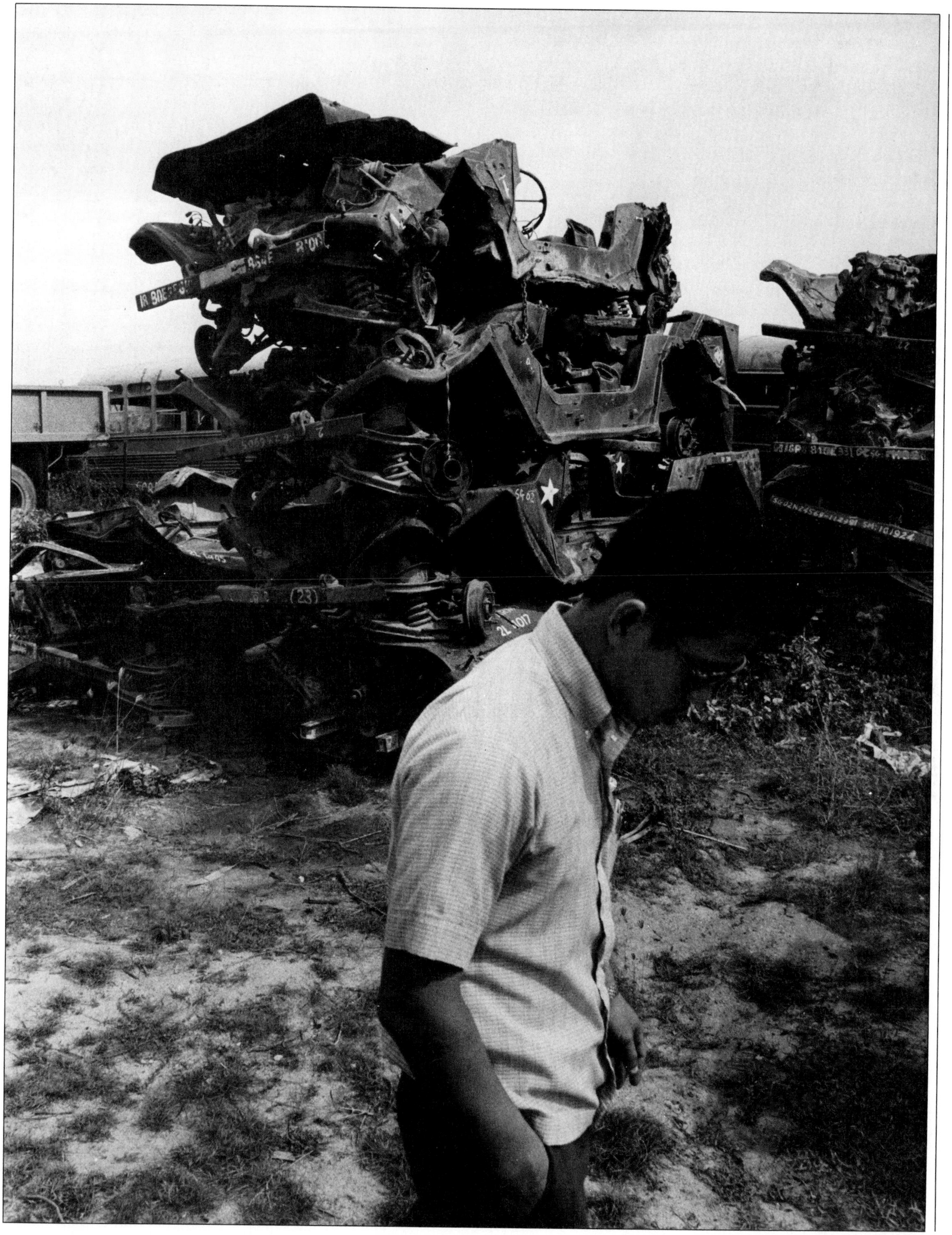

Meanwhile, by the spring of 1974 ARVN field commanders had begun to complain of growing shortages of more prosaic, but far more vital, supplies: ammunition, fuel, rations, bandages, ponchos, and radio sets. By the middle of the year both GVN and American officials were warning that the lack of adequate equipment and supplies had become so critical that it threatened South Vietnam's very survival.

Not everyone agreed. Debate raged between DAO analysts and senior GVN military officers, between Pentagon spokesmen and American reporters over the sources, extent, and seriousness of the reported shortages. Some held the United States responsible, citing sharp reductions in military aid. Others pointed to mismanagement by Saigon or placed the blame on the rising cost of ammunition and petroleum. For South Vietnamese soldiers in the field, who complained with increasing vehemence about inadequate supplies and reduced fire support, the matter seemed much more clear cut: there was not enough. Infantrymen accustomed to going into battle with six to ten hand grenades now made do with two. Artillery fire was limited to clearly identifiable targets. Harassment and interdiction fire was eliminated entirely. Ammunition and fuel allowances were cut to the minimum. The contraction of the fuel program permitted only 55 percent of RVNAF equipment—trucks, armored personnel carriers, river patrol craft, airplanes, etc.—to operate at greatly reduced levels. Testified III Corps commander General Pham Quoc Thuan:

In the last quarter of 1973 ... fuel and ammunition supply was cut 30% as compared to the first quarter, or 60%; if compared to the same period of the previous year. The supply was further reduced 30% in the first quarter of 1974, and another 20% in the next quarter. ... At the beginning of 1973, III Corps was allotted 200 tactical air sorties a day; by the end of 1973, only 80 sorties were made available, and during the first half year of 1974, the number of sorties allotted fluctuated between 30 and a maximum of 60. This huge reduction in air sorties stemmed not from a shortage of aircraft but from a shortage of fuel, bombs, and ammunition.

Medical services suffered as well. Helicopter evacuations were cut back while stocks of lifesaving supplies, such as blood collection bags, intravenous fluids, antibiotics, and surgical dressings, became seriously depleted.

Requisitioning of spare parts was also sharply curtailed, with immediate and dangerous results. One-fifth of the air force, 35 percent of medium tanks, and half of the RVNAF's armored personnel carriers ceased to function from lack of maintenance. "In fact the total supply picture was bleak," recalled DAO intelligence chief Colonel William Le Gro of the first half of 1974. "Roughly half of the items on stockage lists were not there, and shipments into the depots had fallen off dramatically: from about 24,000 metric tons received in March to less than 8,000 in May." The success of the South Vietnamese armed forces during 1973 had been made possible largely because of their ability to move quickly to attack suspected Communist concentrations or reinforce threatened positions. According to Le Gro this mobility "had all but vanished with the decline in funding for maintenance requirements and the skyrocketing cost of all supplies, particularly fuel." The effects of other forced economies were visible in the curtailment or cancellation of equipment modernization projects, the engine-rebuild program, the recruit training program, and a variety of planned communications improvements, including the replacement of worn-out AN/PRC-10 radio sets with newer models.

For individual units, shortages meant declining tactical effectiveness and mounting casualties. American observers reported that experienced infantrymen "responded with less confidence and aggressiveness in holding threatened positions. Defenders in beleaguered outposts, restricted to two or three mortar or artillery rounds, were not inclined to wait and watch enemy sappers break through the wire and drag their recoilless rifles into firing position after ARVN artillery had fired its meager allocation." Meanwhile, hospital admissions of wounded soldiers climbed from 8,750 a month during the first quarter of 1974 to over 10,000 a month by early summer.

There could be no doubt that the growing shortages sapped the strength of the RVNAF. But they were not the only, nor perhaps the most important source of South Vietnam's military weakness. The extension of government control in the countryside during the three years following the 1968 Tet offensive, and the vigorous defense mounted by South Vietnamese forces during the Communist offensive of 1972, had been hailed in Washington and Saigon as evidence that the RVNAF had met the test of Vietnamization. But that image of success was created while the ARVN still enjoyed the protection of American air power, superior artillery, and an efficient U.S.-run logistics system. Although the American withdrawal erased most of these advantages, Saigon's post–cease-fire strategy failed to reflect the new realities. Fearing that a political settlement would be forced upon him, Thieu insisted that the integrity of the South Vietnamese territory had to be defended at all costs. "Everywhere there was a Communist attack or infiltration, the South Vietnamese forces must respond immediately," commented one of the president's advisers. "So the flag of South Vietnam should be everywhere, even over the remotest outpost of the country." But the RVNAF lacked the means to carry out such a policy. However sound politically, from a military point of view the president's strategic imperative was a prescription for disaster.

The difficulty of carrying out Thieu's orders was only too apparent to the South Vietnamese military command, which doubted that their forces were prepared to assume the full burden of the nation's defense. "How could they—without a substantial increase in the number of major combat units—effectively replace seven divisions, four brigades, and innumerable support units of the U.S. forces committed in Vietnam in addition to other non-Communist forces?" asked JGS Chairman Vien. "No amount of training, equipment, or political exhortation could effectively fill the physical void. Our forces began to stretch and soon suffered the consequence." Although they outnumbered the enemy three to one, the demands of protecting a dispersed population and long lines of communication left the RVNAF without the flexibility of a single reserve division. Moreover, government troops had to contend with the traditional disadvantages of the defender. Explained Vien: "It was fairly easy for the enemy to concentrate a force five or six times greater than ours at any remote place and with abundant fire support overwhelm an outpost at will. To attempt to hold all remote outposts, therefore, amounted to sacrificing a substantial number of troops who could be employed elsewhere." Yet, Vien conceded, to abandon the outposts "would be tantamount to turning over to the enemy a sizable part of the national territory."

While his commanders wrestled with this insoluble dilemma, Thieu remained convinced that whatever the military limitations of his strategic design, the Americans would not permit South Vietnam to fall. His confidence rested in part on the assurances he had received from President Nixon. But equally important was the fact that after the cease-fire, contingency arrangements for the reintroduction of American air power in the event of a major Communist offensive remained in

Used to vast amounts of ammunition, the RVNAF was unprepared for cuts in U.S. aid.

place. Provisions of the plan, which called for RVNAF forces to hold their positions for seven to fifteen days in order to allow time for Congress to approve the air strikes, were disseminated to all four corps commanders as a basis for operational planning. Direct liaison was set up between I Corps and the U.S. Support Advisory Group in Thailand. Target lists continued to be compiled and regularly updated. A hot line was established between the JGS and the U.S. 7th Air Force at Nakhon Phanom, where senior Vietnamese officers periodically reviewed plans for American reintervention. With little understanding of American constitutional processes or the limits of presidential power, RVNAF commanders assumed that the

contingency plan accurately reflected American intentions. "Our leaders continued to believe in U.S. air intervention even after the U.S. Congress had expressly forbidden it," wrote one member of the Joint General Staff. "They deluded themselves into thinking that perhaps this simply meant that U.S. intervention would take a longer time to come because of the complex procedures involved." This fatal misconception, which would haunt the Vietnamese command in 1975, reinforced in the meantime the belief that ARVN units could be dispersed without serious risk.

Over-reliance on the United States not only encouraged strategic inertia, it also had serious tactical consequences. After nearly twenty years of American aid and advice, the RVNAF had "acquired the habits of a rich man's army," two of its generals would later write. As early as 1971, with the war at a low ebb and no hint of the inflationary pressures of the Arab oil embargo, Pentagon systems analysts estimated that unless Saigon modified its tactics South Vietnam would require a minimum of $3 billion a year in military and economic aid for the indefinite future. That same year the Rand Corporation's Brian Jenkins recommended the creation of a "people's army" trained to operate with a more austere level of equipment and supplies. Citing the likelihood that economic difficulties following the American withdrawal would produce "popular unrest, political agitation, and government instability, which ultimately would be reflected in weakness on the battlefield," Jenkins concluded that the South Vietnamese "have no choice but to try to develop a cheaper way to defend their country, and to do so before reductions in foreign aid immobilize the army they have now, and before the country collapses trying to support and man it." Instead, Washington substantially increased its military support of the RVNAF, a policy that climaxed in the massive Enhance shipments. "In those circumstances," wrote former ARVN 3d Division commander Major General Nguyen Duy Hinh, "the RVN could not possibly think of tightening its belt for the simple reason that military aid was forced into its hands and no one could foresee a day when this aid would be reduced. So when aid *was* suddenly reduced, the RVN was really in trouble."

The high command seemed incapable of waging war without fleets of helicopters, massive firepower, and mechanized transport. A committee appointed to write a field manual on tactics for a "poor man's war" got nowhere. "The Committee members had experience only as fighters of a rich man's war," explained Colonel Hoang Ngoc Lung, a senior Vietnamese staff officer. Even when new tactics were suggested, few commanders were willing to implement them, fearful they would signal to their troops a declining military posture and unsure the soldiers would accept them. As Lung saw it, "relinquishing the old ways of fighting would prove far from easy."

[F]ew soldiers would like the idea of medical evacuation by man-packed litter or truck, having gotten used to evacuation by helicopter. The same reaction would apply with respect to fire support provided by mortars versus that provided by air. Besides, it would require time for the troops to acquire the needed endurance and training. For example while formerly reconnaissance units would be brought to or removed from objective areas by helicopter, [and] supplied with adequate and nutritious canned rations, now they would have to go overland and be weighted down with heavier unprocessed foods and heavier equipment.

Everything would have to be revised from scratch, acknowledged Lung, "from the training conducted in school to the practice in the field."

Having failed to make changes while they still enjoyed the benefits of active U.S. support, the RVNAF leadership shrank from the formidable task of remaking the armed forces in the midst of escalating confrontation with the Communists. Their failure to adjust to new circumstances permeated the entire officer corps. On an inspection tour of outlying areas in early 1974, a GVN Security Service team discovered that many outposts were receiving no protective maintenance whatsoever because the U.S. had discontinued the supply of heavy equipment.

Instead of using limited available materials, these units take no action and their installations deteriorate. The clearing in a defense perimeter can be done with machetes by personnel of the unit. But these units request and wait for a dozer tractor and defoliation chemicals. In a situation where supplies are short, if these units still rely on such supplies, disaster to the units can be expected.

Despite the unavoidable facts of absent air support, declining aid, and serious logistic shortfalls, neither senior commanders nor their subordinates were able or willing to tailor their U.S.-trained forces to Vietnamese realities.

Meanwhile, the RVNAF labored under disabilities wholly of its own making. One example was Territorial Forces. A 1974 study conducted by the JGS focusing on casualty and weapons lost/captured statistics concluded that mobile operations by territorials were immensely more profitable than defense of fixed outposts. Yet the fear of surrendering contested villages to the Communists kept most RF and PF units tied down in isolated positions that invited attack. Those militia battalions that did aggressively seek out the enemy were frequently placed under the operational control of an ARVN division in another province. All too often the division commander, reluctant to risk his own men, would employ the battalion in a particularly dangerous role without adequate logistical or administrative support, generating heavy casualties and declining morale that swiftly reduced the best RF units to the level of the majority.

Another case was the RVN navy, whose performance in the delta suffered from lack of coordination with other services and within its own ranks. Although MR 4 commander General Nguyen Vinh Nghi had authority over all government military forces in the region, the same authority was not possessed by individual ARVN combat commanders, who received little cooperation from naval units in their areas of joint operations. According to the DAO, the naval commanders remained "independent and aloof, often unwilling even to attend sector planning and briefing sessions." For much the same reason the navy failed to restrict the flow of Communist supplies down the coast from Cambodia. The "blue-water" navy's boats were too large to intercept suspicious sampans in the shallow coastal waters, while the "brown-water" navy insisted that its responsibilities ended where the rivers emptied into the sea.

The strategic cul-de-sac in which the RVNAF found itself, the tactical inefficiencies and lack of leadership were all made worse by a serious and growing manpower shortage. In order to maintain South Vietnam's armed forces at their assigned strength of 1,100,000 men, between 240,000 and 250,000 new recruits had to be inducted each year to overcome attrition due to combat losses, noncombat deaths, desertions, and discharges from service. Yet the pool of men available for the draft never exceeded 150,000, resulting in a perennial deficit of between 90,000 and 100,000. Projected draft quotas went unfilled due to extensive draft dodging, a practice that provoked little public complaint. The American journalist Arnold Isaacs asked a Vietnamese friend if there were any disgrace in dodging the draft. "She looked at me in amazement. 'It's like eating,' she finally answered, 'it's something you do to stay alive, that's all.'"

Those who were inducted scarcely equaled the number of men who deserted. By 1974 the rate of desertion averaged 1.5 to 2 percent of total strength monthly, meaning that the RVNAF was losing up to 25 percent of its manpower each year. Because it was politically impossible for the government to deal with deserters more harshly than it treated Communist "Chieu Hoi" ralliers, and because the chronic need for manpower periodically resulted in amnesties during which men could return to their units without penalty, prospective deserters were not deterred by fear of punishment if they were caught. And, like draft dodgers, those who fled the army were frequently sheltered by family members, employers, even Buddhist priests, who made little effort to assist government officials attempting to recapture them.

Adding to the problem was a large but undetermined number of men who had paid off their commanders to keep them on unit rosters while they went about their private business and a soaring number of soldiers incapacitated or killed in the line of duty. During 1973, the first year of the "cease-fire," South Vietnamese combat deaths were two-thirds of what they had been in 1972, and higher than in any other year except for 1968. All of these factors contributed to the steady decline of actual unit strengths. The effective authorized strength of combat battalions fell from 800 to 500, and even this figure was often difficult to meet. One DAO study of Military Region 2 found that only 65 percent of authorized ARVN manpower was present for duty or otherwise excused. Among RF units in the delta the situation was much worse. Some battalions were down to assigned strengths of 300. In heavily contested Chong Thien Province, it was not unusual for an RF battalion to operate with 150 men, less than what a company would normally have fielded. Yet, soon after the cease-fire the government instituted a plan to reduce the overall size of the armed forces by 100,000 men in the expectation that a lower level of fighting would permit the transfer of some military manpower to agricultural production. By the time the program was canceled in the face of a deteriorating battlefield situation, the NVA was on the offensive with substantially increased forces of its own.

Crumbling morale

The RVNAF's manpower problems sprang more than anything else from the desperate economic situation in which enlisted men and officers alike found themselves. In 1974 the consumer price index was more than twenty-three times higher than it had been in 1963. During that same period military pay had increased by less than a quarter, and the gap continued to widen. A 1973 survey of soldiers in the 3d ARVN Division revealed that 90 percent of enlisted families had not eaten meat during the entire previous month and only 50 percent had eaten far less costly fish or shrimp. Later that summer the RVNAF substituted a cash allowance for the soldiers' regular monthly rice rations. Since inflation steadily reduced the buying power of the fixed allotment, the change amounted to a severe cut in pay.

Even officers had a difficult time making ends meet. A full colonel with twenty years' service earned less than 40,000 piasters a month, or about $80.00, with which he supported a family group of perhaps ten people. At prices current in the winter of 1973, half of his salary went to rice. An army captain made $47.00 a month, enough to pay for rent and rice for his four children but leaving nothing for vegetables, fish, meat, condensed milk, medicine, or gasoline for his motorcycle. Yet officer's pay was munificent

compared to the wages of enlisted men. A sergeant with fourteen years' service earned $25.00 a month, plus a maximum family allowance (for a wife and at least four children) of $9.50, while the cost of feeding one person averaged 400 piasters a day or $23.00 a month. Less senior NCOs made $20.00 a month, a private only $10.00, a sum capable of meeting at best one-third the cost of bare subsistence for an average family. DAO investigators reported in the summer of 1974 that more than 90 percent of enlisted men and junior officers were not receiving enough to sustain their families. Eighty percent complained that standard rations were inadequate, half of those surveyed had insufficient clothing, and 40 percent reported inadequate housing and medical care.

Although many turned to moonlighting for desperately needed extra income, in the process frequently neglecting their duty, others inevitably found illegal means to supplement their regular pay. "Judging by reports from reliable sources, corruption abounds," admitted the DAO. "Inflation appears to force leaders at all echelons to condone graft, and in fact, corruptive practices seem to be a prerequisite to survival." A secret government investigating team found that "command echelons, especially battalion and company commanders," were selling weapons, ammunition, and other military supplies to the enemy, embezzling public funds, extorting money from subordinates, and "devoting their attention to private business for personal gain." Some commanders made a tidy sum by pocketing the pay of "phantom" or "ghost soldiers" who existed only on unit payroll lists. Others made money from "ornament soldiers" who paid to be given safe assignments, such as office boy or interpreter, and "flower soldiers" who bribed their superiors to allow them to work elsewhere. Unscrupulous officers used their positions to exact "protection" money from villagers or demand payment for services such as land clearing, which should have been rendered for free. Air force pilots sold so much space on military aircraft to civilians—generally charging 50 percent of the commercial rate—that Air Viet Nam began publicly protesting its loss of revenue.

Sometimes RVNAF personnel became involved in even more flagrant, and lucrative, schemes. The navy, for instance, carried on a bustling illegal business in the delta selling much sought after diesel fuel to fishermen along the South China Sea. In September 1973 one of the boats engaged in the trade was sunk by gunfire with several casualties. The official cause was listed as a VC ambush. In fact, members of the 412th RF Battalion had decided to muscle their way into the racket, demanding 1,000 piasters per fifty-five-gallon drum sold. When the crew refused, explaining that all proceeds had to be sent to the chief of naval operations in Saigon, the RF troops turned their guns on the sailors. Eventually both sides arrived at a mutually agreeable arrangement, and the boats resumed their illicit traffic in stolen fuel.

A Shortage of Answers

"A coroner's certificate for South Vietnam might well read 'snubbed to death,' but that would be a cover up for political euthanasia," wrote former DAO chief General John Murray ten years after the fall of Saigon. "What actually happened in the intensive care ward was a withdrawal of life support systems. America pulled the plug."

From the beginning of 1974 Vietnamese military and political leaders, Congressional supporters of South Vietnam, and American officials in Saigon repeatedly linked declining U.S. financial support with the serious shortages of ammunition, equipment, and fuel that degraded RVNAF capabilities during the last two years of the war. The responsibility for those shortages, however, their extent, and even their importance remained the subjects of controversy and dispute long after the end of the war.

The Americans

For those who were assessing blame, the primary villain was the United States Congress. During fiscal year 1973 U.S. military aid to South Vietnam totaled $2.27 billion. In the fiscal year ending on July 1, 1974, that support had been cut by more than half to slightly over $1 billion. Meanwhile, worldwide inflation drove up the cost of arms, ammunition, and petroleum that had to be purchased from abroad, rendering the effective level of aid even lower.

But declining American assistance was only one reason why shortages began to develop. The DAO's unwarranted assumption that funding requests would be met in full meant that when a lower Congressional ceiling was established in early 1974, 75 percent of authorized aid had already been spent, leaving no flexibility for adjustment of priorities. Thus, even though South Vietnamese forces were using "about one-fifth of the ammunition and one-tenth the gasoline they had used when they had unlimited U.S. backup," according to the embassy's military liaison, General Charles J. Timmes, the demands of combat outstripped the flow of supplies.

At the same time, the Pentagon failed to use its political muscle in support of GVN requests for additional aid. Some Department of Defense officials argued that the South Vietnamese were unable to utilize the equipment they had. Many felt increased aid would only encourage the RVNAF in wasteful practices that needlessly jeopardized adequate reserves. Others were concerned that a major battle over funding for Vietnam would threaten more crucial national defense appropriations. DOD policy was to provide only the minimum necessary to sustain the RVNAF in relation to the scale of activity generated by NVA attacks. Since much of the fighting in 1973 had been at ARVN's initiative, equipment replacements were minimal.

The South Vietnamese

To fix responsibility for the shortages solely on the Americans, however, was to ignore the substantial South Vietnamese contribution to the problem. JGS Chairman General Cao Van Vien would later claim that "the Republic of Vietnam made every effort to enforce austerity and maintain and preserve invaluable military assets as soon as the ceasefire was in force." In fact, as one U.S. military officer in Kontum remarked, "The Viets [were] expensive to keep in ammo." The Pentagon regarded the pre-cease-fire level of RVNAF ammunition expenditures as "inordinate," and even though restraints were placed on replacement allowances to reach a "reasonable rate," excessive reliance on firepower and simple overconsumption continued to eat up precious ammunition stocks.

Moreover, according to a 1975 DAO report hundreds of millions of dollars worth of materiel had been lost or squandered during the two years following the cease-fire. In addition to a growing number of weapons abandoned to the enemy during military engagements, large amounts of equipment had been stolen or sold to the Communists, including $10 million worth of small arms that simply disappeared from supply depots.

When in early 1974 the JGS finally imposed strict quotas on the amount of ammunition and equipment supplied to troops in the field, the cure was worse than the disease. "So arbitrary were the restrictions, and so hastily applied," wrote CIA analyst Frank Snepp, "they finally did far more damage to the army's capabilities than was necessary." Instead of tailoring a rationing system to actual need, each of the country's four military regions received approximately the same amount of supplies regardless of the widely different combat requirements in various parts of the country.

Hoarding and mismanagement exacerbated the situation. In his study of the Vietnamese Air Force, former USAF General William W. Momyer cites "chronic problems" with depot operations once the bulk of American logistic personnel were withdrawn. For example, "the main problem in [one] depot was not inadequate spare parts, but accounting procedures to determine where the parts were." General Murray, who laid the blame for South Vietnam's logistical difficulties on lack of adequate training by the Americans, recounted a visit he made to an engineer depot with ARVN Chief of Staff Lieutenant General Dong Van Khuyen.

We found two of his countrymen sitting on the floor in the middle of an acre of spare parts, nuts, bolts, wires, diodes, light bulbs, floor tiles, hammers, filters, screw drivers, faucets, field manuals, rifle stocks, spark plugs, valves, back-up mirrors, shovels and blank two-year old calendar pads. It was wall-to-wall expiation of the helter-skelter shape of Vietnamese logistics.

A December 1973 DAO report revealed that even when supply parts could be identified, "the system which should ensure timely provision of required supplies and repair parts at the user level is unresponsive." Six months later U.S. officials were complaining that the "limited number of personnel capable of fully understanding U.S. technical manuals" continued to hinder depot operations, and that the RVNAF was "still plagued by in-country transport problems."

The full utilization of military equipment was also hampered by an inadequate number of trained personnel for operations and maintenance. The most glaring case was the Vietnamese Air Force. Thanks to Enhance and Enhance Plus the VNAF possessed 2,075 aircraft of twenty-five different types, many of which it could neither fly nor maintain. While a thousand pilots were recruited, and several thousand more underwent additional training, Saigon was forced to rely on American maintenance technicians at a cost of over $30 million a year. Although their stated mission was to train Vietnamese to perform services previously provided by U.S. military and civilian personnel, most of the contractors actually spent their time doing the maintenance work themselves. Not only did their presence violate the Paris agreements, it also retarded the process of South Vietnamese self-sufficiency.

Surveying the continuing U.S. role in the provision of maintenance, ammunition, weapons, trucks, fuel, and electronic parts, one Department of Defense official based in Saigon wryly observed that "we Vietnamized the fighting, but we never Vietnamized logistics."

Unanswered questions

Beyond the debate over the cause of the shortages were questions about how serious they really were. In some cases it was clear that artificial shortages had been created to exert pressure on Washington. In 1973, when requested diesel fuel failed to arrive promptly, the government restricted allocations in highly vis-

ible areas such as hospital power generators and vital communications networks. Moreover, emergency supplies of some critical items continued to remain in good shape. As late as December 1974, RVNAF contingency POL (petroleum, oil, and lubricants) storage depots were filled to the brim. Even ammunition stocks, according to the DAO, had slipped no more than 9 percent below established levels.

In no area was the confusion greater, however, than in this most elemental of all military supplies. Not everyone agreed on how much ammunition was actually needed. Apparently contradicting their

The lack of equipment after the cease-fire forced the ARVN to improvise. Here a makeshift stretcher replaces the standard medevac stretcher.

own public statements that RVNAF pre-cease-fire ammunition expenditure rates had been excessive, Pentagon officials continued to maintain that the necessary "intensive combat rate" was 54,000 tons a month, the amount consumed during the 1972 offensive. As a minimum "theater sustaining rate" they set a requirement of 18,000 tons a month—the amount actually being used in 1974. But that rate was almost identical to expenditures in the latter months of 1973 when, despite large offensive operations, there had been no talk of shortages.

How meaningful these figures were was open to question, for no one knew with certainty how much ammunition the RVNAF was actually using. "All is

plagued by spurious reporting," complained General Murray in late 1973. When the DAO chief asked the JGS a few months later to provide him with figures on existing ammunition stockpiles, they told him that expenditures had been much larger during the past year than previously reported. Claiming that the stockpiles had fallen well below "prudent levels," they asked for $221 million worth of additional ammunition to bring them back up to cease-fire levels. The possibility existed that RVNAF commanders were simply "storing up ammunition for a rainy day," admitted one U.S. officer.

The suspicion that Saigon was exaggerating consumption rates was heightened when Senate investigators reported in May 1974 that the "data being provided to the DAO by the South Vietnamese army [does] not substantiate the reported firings on which the ammunition requests were based." Compounding the confusion was the fact that no one seemed to know how much American money had been spent for ammunition or how much ammunition had actually been delivered.

Meanwhile, as field commanders despaired over a precipitous drop in fire support, figures compiled by the DAO showed no overall reduction. ARVN artillery expenditures between October 4 and December 31, 1974, after tight restrictions were put on harassment and interdiction fire, and after severe rationing had supposedly taken place, averaged 67,443 rounds per week, only 2 percent less than the 68,920-round weekly average for the same period a year earlier.

Shortages of equipment and supplies during the last half of 1974 clearly affected the ability of many RVNAF units to defend their positions or reverse the Communist advance. Whether those shortages were as serious as many later claimed, however, and whether they were due primarily to inadequate financial support or inefficient South Vietnamese utilization and management, are questions that may never be fully resolved.

The lure of profit even led some units to direct their ferocity at the enemy. At the town of Phuoc Tan near the Cambodian border, 100 ARVN soldiers fought off an enemy force five times their size in order to protect their cut in the profitable trade in such items as gasoline and medicine heading into the Communist zone. But venal officers usually found their fellow soldiers an easier prey. By 1974 selling artillery support—at the rate of one or two dollars a round—had become a common occurrence. The most notorious practice, however, was perpetuated by helicopter pilots who charged fees to evacuate wounded soldiers: eight dollars for an enlisted man, sixteen dollars for an NCO, twenty-five dollars and up for an officer. If money was not available, some pilots would settle for what they could get. One chopper reportedly hovered for an hour over a bleeding militiaman while the pilot bargained on a price with the local hamlet chief. They finally agreed on six ducks from the hamlet pond.

A Vietnamese boy carries his father, a disabled veteran, through the streets of Saigon to beg for handouts.

The terrible economic conditions among the soldiers and their families, and the dire need to keep combat units at fighting strength, led many officers to overlook temporary absences and, more serious, a growing incidence of criminal behavior among the enlisted ranks. The theft of military equipment, for instance, was widespread. According to a February 1974 DAO assessment: "Commanders in MR 1 freely admit that they cannot keep sufficient ponchos, entrenching tools, mechanic tool kits, etc., on hand, because soldiers, whose families are in desperate need, sell these items on the black market to buy food." Government troops increasingly left restaurants without paying, stole livestock from farmers, extorted rice from merchants, and took money and goods from travelers at gun point. One particularly bad area was Route 1 in central Vietnam. Truck drivers making the run from Saigon to Da Nang told of soldiers from the 2d and 22d Divisions stopping them with demands for money at least four or five times a trip. In the village of Hoai My in the central highlands, a middle-aged woman told *New York Times* reporter David Shipler that ARVN troops had torn the corrugated metal roof off her home to cover an outhouse. "When the government soldiers came they took the cows and buffaloes away or they killed them," the woman said. "They sold one cow for 20,000 piasters and one buffalo for 25,000, and we dare not say anything."

The fear shared by the woman and her neighbors reflected what one American observer called a "terrifying prevalence of casual violence." Claudia Krich, the codirector of an American Friends Service Committee hospital in Quang Ngai Province, wrote to Representative Paul McCloskey about a young woman who had recently been admitted with a bullet wound that paralyzed her legs.

Two soldiers were walking along the road a few feet from her and just shot her. This is more common than [you] imagine. One old woman patient of ours was told by ARVN soldiers to come out of her shelter. She came out feet first, and as she did, they shot her in the leg. Her leg had to be amputated. Had she come out head first, she said, the "children" as she calls them, would have shot her in the head.

Embittered and frustrated by years of compulsory service, seeing the war claiming more and more of their comrades, knowing that they might well die the next day, many South Vietnamese soldiers no longer seemed to fear the consequences of their actions.

As discipline deteriorated the incidence of alcoholism, heroin addiction, and suicide mounted. Officers found it increasingly difficult to manage their men. One lieutenant told an American reporter it was necessary "to use sweet talk" to convince a private to do something. "Never give an order," he warned. Reports of "fraggings" became more common. In some infantry units soldiers demanded and received leaves at the point of a gun. "Only the most submissive go AWOL," testified one trooper. "The others want authorized leaves—whenever they want." In Saigon a corporal sentenced to ten days in the stockade for having gone AWOL grabbed an M16, shot a captain, then killed himself. Nor were violent acts of desperation limited to enlisted men. The American journalist James Markham recounted the story of one army major who ran out of money. "The man burst into the office of his commanding general, and flashing a pistol, asked for a loan. The general complied."

Surveying the disintegrating state of the RVNAF, Colonel William Le Gro expressed admiration for the "many honest, devoted officers who managed through strength of character and with the help of friends and families, not only to survive but also to take care of their less fortunate subordinates." Those dedicated commanders still struggling to do their duty, however, could not arrest the crumbling morale all around them. By the end of 1973 even highly respected units like the Airborne and 1st Infantry Divisions exhibited the corrosive effects of mounting casualties, uninspired leadership, and debilitating poverty. The manifold ills of the armed forces, concluded a prophetic DAO report, had caused "a deterioration of performance which cannot be permitted to continue if the South Vietnamese military is to be considered a viable force." But the one man, above all, who might still provide inspiration and purpose to his nation's beleaguered forces had little to offer. President Nguyen Van Thieu had too many problems of his own.

Cracks in the surface

It was a testament to his skill as a politician that even those who disliked him recognized his capacity. "Mr. Thieu had leadership qualities," admitted two of his generals critical of the president's performance. "He was cautious, cunning, persevering, intelligent; he was also a courageous man." But his regime was constantly undermined by the antinationalist history of many of those in high positions, by its lack of a coherent ideology, its class bias, its

Army dependents in Dinh Tuong, 1973. Inadequate housing for their families was a major source of discontent among RVNAF enlisted men and junior officers.

authoritarianism, its corruption and inefficiency, and most of all by Thieu's inability to win the hearts and minds of his people to a common national cause. Over the years these disabilities had seriously compromised the government in its contest with the North. After the cease-fire, when the need for decisive action to meet the Communist threat was greater than it had ever been, Thieu remained preoccupied with political infighting and the consolidation of power.

Toward that end much had already been accomplished. The elimination of hamlet elections, the passage of the Press and Political Parties laws, and the formation of his own New Democratic party made Thieu the undisputed master of the South Vietnamese political landscape even before the conclusion of the Paris negotiations. His passionate resistance to the peace terms imposed by Washington won him new respect from many of his countrymen, while the obvious determination of the Americans to keep Thieu in power left his most important constituency—the generals—nowhere else to turn.

Yet Thieu remained insecure. Partly as a result of his own megalomania, in part because the Americans had for so long assured him it was so, he had become convinced that South Vietnam's destiny and his own future were one and the same. Anything that jeopardized his control over the political process jeopardized the nation. Thus, the solidification of his authority remained Thieu's primary goal. To "foster a better understanding of national policies," as one of his supporters put it, and to cement his control over the civilian bureaucracy, he launched a so-called administrative revolution that sent thousands of reluctant civil servants into the countryside as visible symbols of presidential power. To retain his control of the National Assembly, Thieu manipulated the laws governing the biannual Senate elections in August, guaranteeing his supporters a majority at the polls. And to bolster his own position even further, he pushed through the assembly in January 1974 an electoral bill allowing him to run for a third time and extending the presidential term from four to five years. The next month, as if to demonstrate that his political control was unassailable, Thieu reshuffled his cabinet, appointing parliamentary opposition leader Tran Van Don vice premier, a position Don soon discovered had neither function nor authority.

By the winter of 1973 Thieu had frozen every potential political opponent beneath a solid sheet of ice. Those who looked closely, however, could see cracks in the surface. One of the most persistent criticisms leveled at the South Vietnamese government during the post-cease-fire period had to do with the issue of political prisoners. During 1972 Saigon authorities rounded up thousands of known or suspected dissidents, a crackdown that showed little sign of abating once the Paris agreements were signed. The Communists charged that more than 200,000 political prisoners were being held in South Vietnamese jails, a figure

most observers regarded as a considerable exaggeration. But Ambassador Martin's insistence that the embassy could not verify a single political prisoner was equally far-fetched. Even the State Department acknowledged that the government had detained between 500 and 1,000 people for "non-violent, non-Communist opposition to the present government," a definition that ignored the fact that the GVN identified almost everyone it arrested as a Communist. More independent estimates ranged between 40,000 and 60,000 people incarcerated for political reasons.

However many there actually were, their numbers were large enough to provoke heated attacks against the government both internationally and among the South Vietnamese themselves. "Thieu sees everyone who opposes him as a Communist," contended Ho Ngoc Nhuan, an opposition deputy. "There are all kinds of people in prison—monks, priests, students, teachers, politicians, old men, women, even children." More scandalous still were the widespread reports of mistreatment and torture meted out inside the prison walls: a young girl hung by her wrists from the ceiling while police burned her breasts with cigarettes; a twenty-three-year-old student forced to drink soapy water, then beaten on the stomach until he vomited; a sixteen-year-old boy tortured with electric shocks; a fourteen-year-old girl repeatedly stripped by guards who placed sandbags across her body then beat her until she vomited blood. During six months of imprisonment no formal charges were ever filed against her. One former longshoreman whose confinement in the infamous tiger cages of Con Son Island left him so crippled he could move about only by dragging himself across the ground on his hands, told American reporter Ron Moreau why he finally signed a statement saying he worked for the Communists. "I felt if I hadn't signed they would have killed me."

Stories like these fueled American opposition to continuing aid for South Vietnam. At the same time, the brutality of its methods and the willingness of the government to throw young Vietnamese into cells with hardened Communists, inevitably produced the very "radicalization" it sought to stamp out. "The cadres were nice to us," reported one university student after his release from Con Son Island. "When we were sick and injured they helped us. They didn't ask us to join the NLF, only to struggle against foreign aggression and the Thieu regime when we were released."

The ill will Thieu created by political repression, however, was nothing compared to the loss of support he suffered as a result of economic distress and government corruption. The misery and graft not only enraged ordinary

Suspected NLF sympathizers, arrested during the Diem regime and not released until 1973, are unable to walk after imprisonment in the tiger cages of Con Son Island.

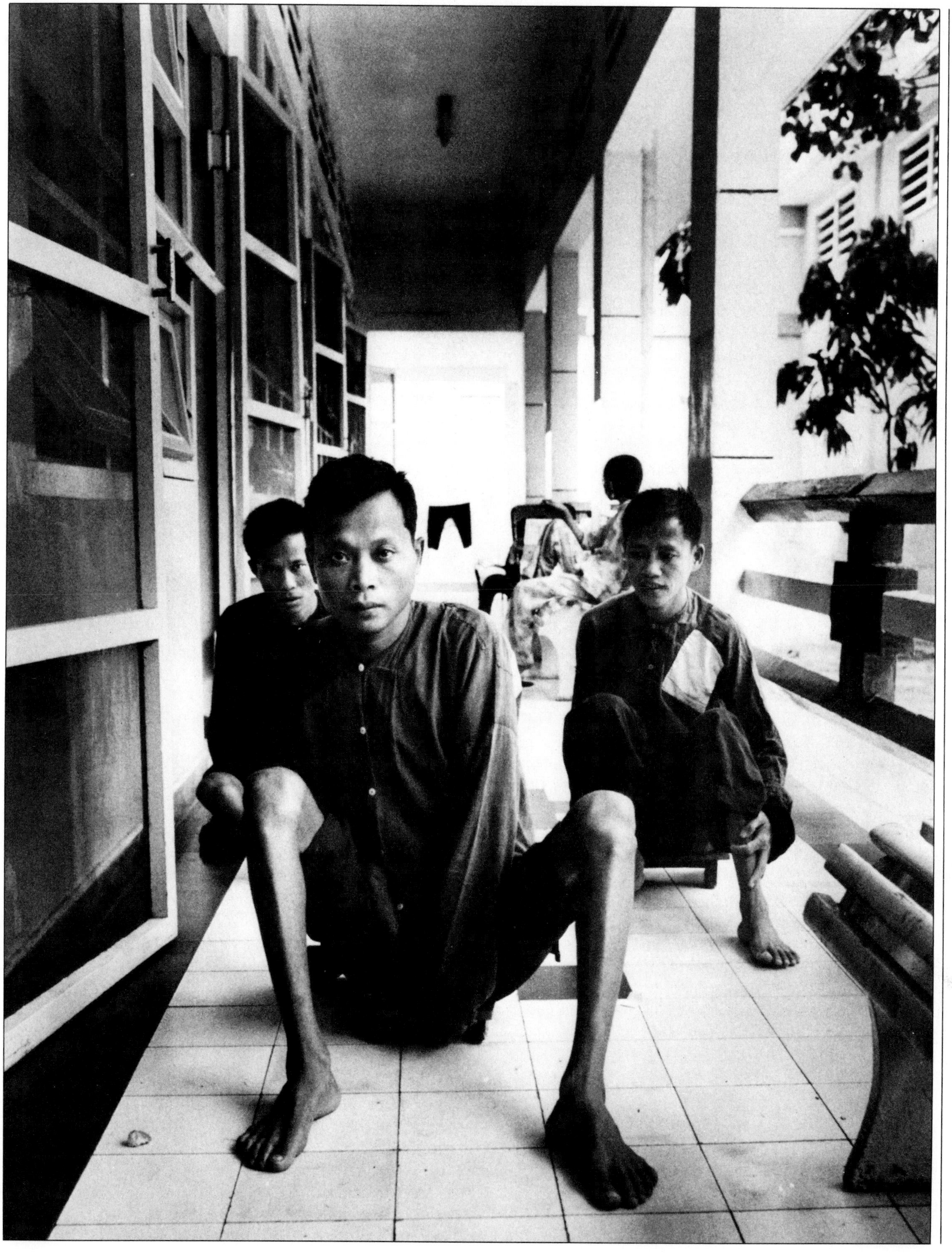

citizens in their own right, but seemed more and more to reflect a regime whose only interest was the protection of a privileged minority. "Corruption always engenders social injustice," said one military commander.

In Vietnam corruption had created a small elite which held all the power and wealth, and a majority of middle-class people and peasants who became poorer and poorer and who suffered all the sacrifices. It was these people who paid the taxes to the government, the bribes to the police, who had to buy fertilizer at exorbitant prices and sell their rice at a price fixed by the government, and it was also these people who sent their sons to fight and die for their country while high government officials and wealthy people sent their sons abroad.

Thieu's failure to take forceful steps against official misconduct was made more serious by his inability to extract sufficient U.S. aid to stem economic collapse. His authority had always rested, more than anything else, on his claim of being the favored conduit of American largesse. As the tap began to run dry, the president's prestige steadily declined.

Indeed, the American connection had become a liability for Thieu in a number of ways. Although they applauded his willingness to stand up to Washington, many Vietnamese blamed the provisions of the hated peace accords on the president. He also suffered from the growing public perception, fostered by government propaganda, that the United States had abandoned them to their enemies. "Time and again," remembered one DAO officer, "I heard South Vietnamese military men and civilians bemoan their fate at having been cursed with a faltering ally while the Communists basked in the luxury of two faithful sponsors each vying to outdo the other in generosity." They were bewildered at the lack of American response to Communist violations of the agreements, which they saw as a direct challenge thrown down by Hanoi to test U.S. commitment. And they resented the charges of administration opponents in Washington that the South Vietnamese were to blame for the enormous sums of money the United States had already spent on the war. It had not been the Vietnamese who demanded hot meals supplied to combat units in the field, stocked PXs with thousands of expensive cameras and tape recorders, or sent their troops to cities all over the Orient for rest and relaxation. To them it seemed that "if the Americans could only have saved part of the cost of just a few weeks of their stay in Vietnam and used the saving for aid," commented Bui Diem, the former GVN ambassador to the United States, South Vietnam would not have found itself in such dire straits.

But most of all the South Vietnamese resented the dependency of the government on the Americans. It was all too clear that senior political and military officials had come to rely on U.S. advice and support to such an extent that when it was removed they did not know what to do. "The ranks of South Vietnamese leadership, who here-tofore had proved readily amenable to U.S. wishes, now found themselves hopelessly vulnerable, unable to stand on their own feet, and utterly incapable of pulling the nation together," wrote Generals Nguyen Duy Hinh and Tran Dinh Tho. Their failure to do so reinforced the common belief that the Saigon government was little more than a puppet of the United States, as one senior military commander admitted, "deprived of all national prestige, lacking in national mandate and thus being untrustworthy." Since to most Vietnamese Thieu's selection as president had been itself an American decision, he became the primary focus of a pervasive national self-contempt.

Nothing revealed Thieu's waning stature more vividly than the curious rehabilitation of former South Vietnamese president Ngo Dinh Diem. Reviled by his countrymen at the time of his assassination in 1963, Diem suddenly became a symbol, a source of nostalgia for a time of strong leadership and personal integrity. The contrast with his predecessor was hardly flattering to the current occupant of the presidential palace. "Mr. Thieu paled beside Mr. Diem in personal prestige," observed one high-ranking officer. "He did not have the necessary background as a leader of the people. He lacked what was termed as revolutionary virtue which the people in the South or North wanted to see in a national leader." Ten years after his death, 3,000 Diem supporters marched through Saigon to attend a memorial service in honor of the first president of the Republic, then moved on to a nearby cemetery where Diem lay buried under an inconspicuous concrete slab. Thieu, who had actively supported Diem's overthrow, defrayed the costs of the commemoration with a personal contribution of $1,000. It was a gesture that won him little credit. In the chill winter of South Vietnam's discontent, the king sat uneasy on his throne.

Portents of disaster

By the second anniversary of the "cease-fire," South Vietnam was a nation of disbelievers. In the villages of the central coast visitors discovered a ubiquitous anxiety; in the towns of the delta a sense of weariness and despondency. In the countryside, where after the Tet offensive of 1968 the GVN had made significant gains, there was again a measuring of sides and a withdrawal of commitment. And in Saigon, where government horror stories of massive North Vietnamese military preparations and imminent Communist offensives blared constantly from radios and propaganda banners, there was fear. Over the entire country, like the gray clouds of the monsoon, hung a grim fatalism.

"The people seem indifferent, they seem ready to bear all that happens," said Nguyen Van Huyen. "In fact, the people are very angry." Under the impact of economic hardship and official corruption, the nation's fragile social cohesion began to give way. As the NVA build-up continued, frightened merchants abandoned their property in the highlands and fled southward toward Saigon. Alongside newspaper reports of stepped-up Communist military activity were the lengthening columns of RVN casualties. In 1973 over 24,000 had lost their lives. By the early summer of 1974, RVNAF combat deaths exceeded 500 a week. Except for the period of the North Vietnamese 1972 Easter offensive, it was the highest rate of South Vietnamese deaths recorded at any time during more than twenty years of armed conflict.

Writing after the war Generals Hinh and Tho described a nation on the brink of disaster:

> In the midst of these difficult times, South Vietnamese society, which had never been united in the anti-Communist struggle, was sinking deeper into division and selfishness. Internal strife and the threat of collapse were also aggravating. The authority of government and national leaders as well as popular faith sank to an all-time low. It was no longer possible to mobilize the masses, and the survival strength of South Vietnam was visibly on the decline with each new Communist attack.

Worst of all, thought the DAO's Captain Stuart Herrington, was "the erosion of the people's confidence in ultimate victory. There was a growing sense that one was sitting on a time bomb, and that the North Vietnamese were adding new sticks of dynamite to that bomb every day." Without leadership, without purpose, without sustenance, almost without hope, through the remaining months of 1974 the people of South Vietnam watched their future march inexorably toward them.

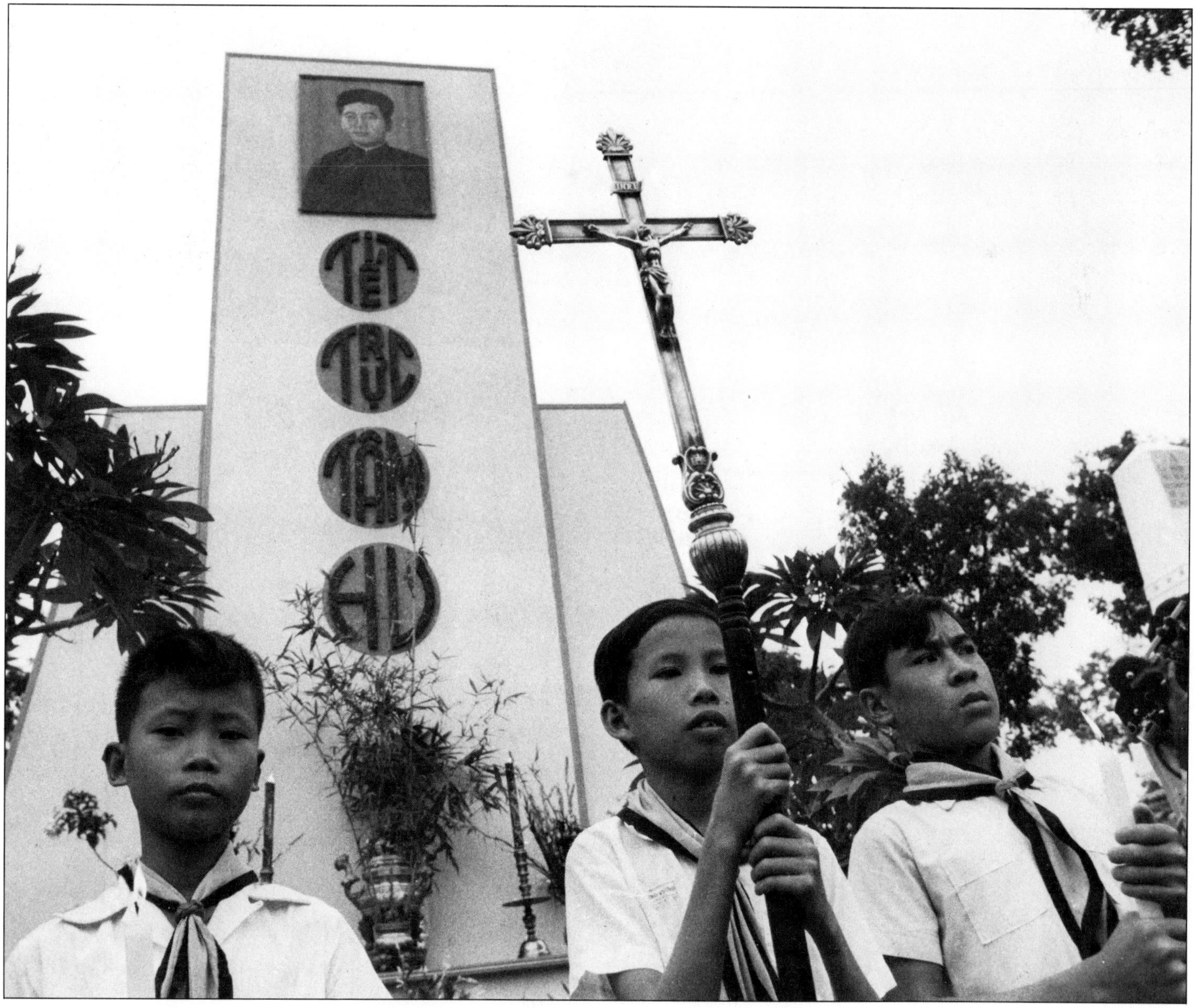

South Vietnamese Boy Scouts participate in a memorial service for the late President Ngo Dinh Diem on November 2, 1973, ten years after the military coup in which Diem and his brother were assassinated.

The Year of the Tiger

"In the spring of 1974, after the New Year of the Tiger, a high level conference of military cadres met at 33 Pham Ngo Lao Street in Hanoi. Included were representatives from all the battlefronts, all services and branches, all corps and divisions, as well as representatives of all agencies of the office of the General Command."

The gathering of the Communist military leadership described by General Van Tien Dung was an outgrowth of the Central Committee's deliberations the previous October. They met to study the Resolution of the 21st Plenum "and to discuss concrete plans for its implementation on the military front." The conference reaffirmed that the Vietnamese revolution could "only gain victory through revolutionary violence." If Saigon persisted in its refusal to implement the provisions of the Paris agreements, wrote General Dung, there would be "no other course for us but to conduct revolutionary warfare, destroy the enemy, and liberate the South." Their plans approved by the

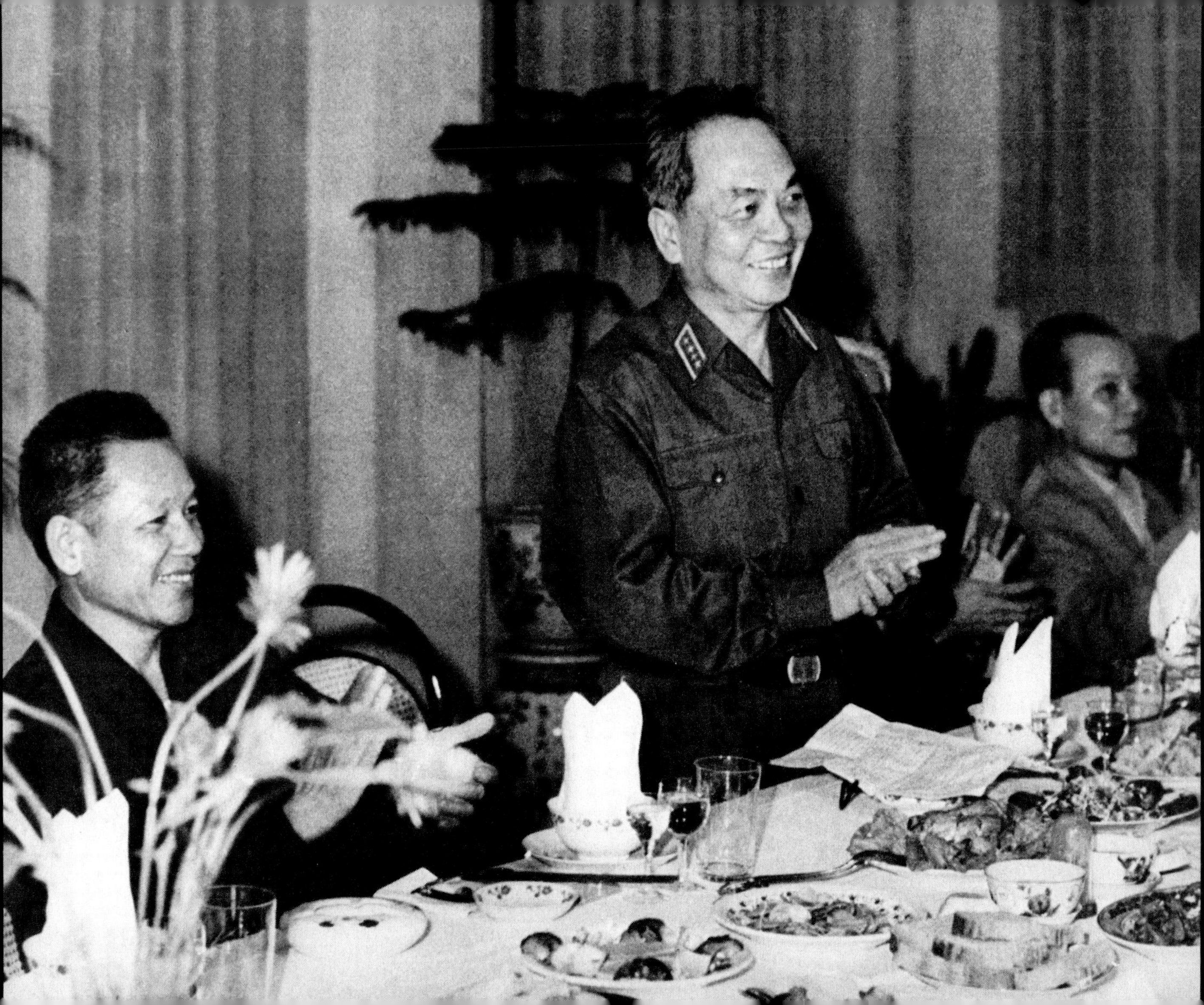

Politburo, orders went out to "all battlefields to step up activities, carry out offensives and uprisings, preserve and develop the strategic initiative, and change the situation on all fronts, thereby creating conditions for widespread, large-scale offensives in 1975." The watchwords for the new offensive were "counterattack and attack."

Counterattack and attack

The strategy conceived by the military command was essentially an enlargement of the strategic raids campaign under way since the last months of 1973. In addition to attacks against economic targets like roads, storage facilities, and airfields, operations would be mounted to inflict casualties, overextend and demoralize ARVN forces, regain territory lost since the cease-fire, and capture strategic positions favorable for future large-scale attacks. While the level of military activity would be carefully calibrated to remain below the estimated threshold that would provoke U.S. intervention, the NVA would exert pressure not only against remote outposts and isolated hamlets but also against major population centers and district towns. The graduated offensive would provide an opportunity to try out new tactics and refine command and control arrangements in preparation for larger operations the following year. Convinced that the balance of forces had begun to shift in their favor, the Communists would test the resistance of the South Vietnamese army and the readiness of their own troops for the protracted struggle that lay ahead.

During the first week of May, NVA units struck ARVN bases and outposts throughout Quang Tin Province. The eruption of ground attacks and rocket bombardments signaled the opening of a campaign that for the remainder of the summer would sweep like a giant wave back and forth across Military Region 1 from Quang Ngai to Thua Thien. On May 4 elements of the NVA 1st and 2d Divisions attacked Tien Phuoc District Town and the village of Ky Tra, a minor road junction in the hills west of Chu Lai. By the fifth Ky Tra had fallen, along with one of the outposts guarding Tien Phuoc. Meanwhile, NVA rockets pounded 2d ARVN Division headquarters at Chu Lai and the airfield at Tam Ky. As the fighting continued around Tien Phuoc, claiming mounting casualties on both sides, 2d ARVN Division commander Brigadier General Tran Van Nhut also had to contend with NVA thrusts into the coastal regions of Quang Ngai Province and heavy enemy pressure against the town of Gia Vuc near the Quang Ngai-Kontum border. Despite repeated attempts to break through ARVN defenses, the Communists were unable to take Tien Phuoc. But by mid-June, when enemy units began leaving the area, three battalions of the 2d ARVN Division had been rendered ineffective due to casualties and equipment losses.

As the NVA withdrew from Tien Phuoc, the Communists were preparing a coordinated offensive in Quang Nam Province under the operational command of the newly activated 3d Corps. The focus of the campaign was the strategic Khe Le Valley, southwest of Da Nang, control of which would give easy access to the populated regions of the coast. Shortly after midnight on July 18 NVA artillery, rockets, and mortar rounds slammed into the Nong Son Ranger base and an ARVN camp at Da Trach. Initial ground attacks were driven back, but during the night an RF outpost at Ap Ba, midway between the two garrisons, was overrun. Tanks and artillery continued to pound Da Trach until at midafternoon on the nineteenth a five-battalion infantry assault finally routed the defenders whose bunkers and firing positions had been demolished by the enemy bombardment. The following day Nong Son also succumbed. As NVA infantry and antiaircraft units took up positions in the hills above the valley, rocket and mortar fire crashed into Duc Duc subsector headquarters and the Da Nang air base. ARVN and VNAF efforts to dislodge the NVA from around Da Trach provoked fierce resistance and heavy casualties. Meanwhile, the Communists continued to batter Duc Duc as well as ARVN rear areas, sending eleven battalions into the Quang Nam coastal plain where they attacked government positions, shelled district towns, and destroyed bridges along Highway 1.

For 3d ARVN Division commander Major General Nguyen Duy Hinh, the enemy he now faced in Quang Nam posed unexpected and formidable problems.

His combat tactic was clearly a model of mobile conventional warfare. Enemy forces attacked only during daylight and with the support of artillery and armor. The deadly enemy artillery firepower, the increase in other types of fire, and in particular the use of AA guns for direct ground support were factors that caused some concern to our troops. Enemy bodies displayed new equipment, modern first-aid kits, and modern combat rations.

By the end of the month Communist forces totaling more than three divisions were besieging ARVN positions throughout eastern Quang Nam. Potential reinforcements had been tied down by widespread NVA attacks in Quang Ngai Province timed to coincide with the opening of the enemy drive around Da Nang. While General Hinh attempted to regroup his scattered units and halt the Communist advance, on July 29 the 29th NVA Regiment struck Thuong Duc District Town, the westernmost ARVN position remaining in the province.

Taken completely by surprise, the men of the 79th Ranger Battalion manning the post at Thuong Duc huddled in their bunkers under a furious barrage. "The intensity of enemy artillery firepower came as a shock to friendly troops," wrote General Hinh. "Never before had

---

Preceding page. *General Vo Nguyen Giap (standing) speaks at a reception honoring General Tran Van Tra (at left) commander of Communist forces south of the central highlands.*

they encountered such a powerful enemy fire. The Ranger artillery section was overwhelmed by it and ceased firing within a few hours. Enemy antiaircraft fire, meanwhile, made VNAF observation and support ineffective." Repeated infantry assaults penetrated so far into Thuong Duc's defenses that on the thirty-first the garrison commander had to ask for artillery fire directly on his command post. Miraculously, the Rangers held on. But casualties continued to mount and by August 5, with a relief column stalled miles from the camp, ammunition and food supplies had been all but exhausted. On the following night the NVA hurled more than a thousand rounds of artillery and mortar fire against the beleaguered outpost. At dawn, waves of infantrymen poured into the shattered camp as the remnants of the 79th Rangers abandoned Thuong Duc, the first district capital lost to the Communists since the cease-fire.

Throughout the rest of August and into September fighting raged in the Que Son Valley, along Hai Van Ridge separating Quang Nam and Thua Thien Provinces, where the South Vietnamese Airborne Division failed in a bloody attempt to retake Thuong Duc, and in the hills overlooking the Phu Bai air base south of Hue. On August 17 Minh Long District Town in southern Quang Ngai Province was captured by the 52d NVA Brigade. One month later the same unit overran the Gia Vuc Ranger camp. The Communists, who lost thousands of men during the campaign in MR 1, suffered setbacks as well as victories. But as one position after another fell to short, violent enemy assaults, South Vietnamese commanders found themselves without reserves to stem the tide or regain lost ground. Only with the onset of the winter monsoon in October was the ARVN able to stabilize its battered lines of defense and gain some respite from four months of continual combat.

While the NVA bulled its way toward the coastal lowlands of MR 1, other Communist forces embarked on a campaign to isolate the central highlands cities of Kontum and Pleiku, eliminate the remaining GVN outposts along their expanding logistical corridor, and exhaust the two ARVN divisions in MR 2 by forcing them to respond to attacks all over the vast mountain region.

At first government forces were able to meet the test. A key element in Communist plans was the construction of two roads—one north of Kontum, one south of Pleiku—running easterly from the main north-south infiltration route and meeting on National Route 19. With their completion the two main population centers in the highlands, as well as II Corps headquarters located at Pleiku, would be completely encircled. In April, two regiments of the 320th NVA Division attacked Outpost 711 blocking the southern branch of the twin roads. But the small garrison held out long enough for the 22d ARVN Division, reinforced with a Ranger group, to come to the rescue. After several weeks of fighting the government task force drove the attackers back, preventing completion of the southern route.

Outpost 711 had benefited from its proximity to the substantial ARVN forces garrisoned at Pleiku. More isolated government positions in the highlands proved far more vulnerable to Communist attack. At Dak Pek, for example, the 360 men of the 88th Ranger Battalion and some 300 Popular Forces soldiers manning the mountain outpost astride Route 14 were supplied entirely by air and had only the camp's own small artillery battery with which to defend themselves. Besieged on May 12 by a regiment of the 324B NVA Division, the camp endured four days of punishing artillery, mortar, and rocket attacks with little support from the VNAF, which was unable to penetrate intense enemy antiaircraft fire. On the sixteenth the government troops finally gave way before a combined infantry and tank assault. Ten days after the fall of Dak Pek two NVA infantry battalions overran the Tieu Atar frontier post 248 kilometers to the south, leaving Communist logistical operations unimpeded from the major sup-

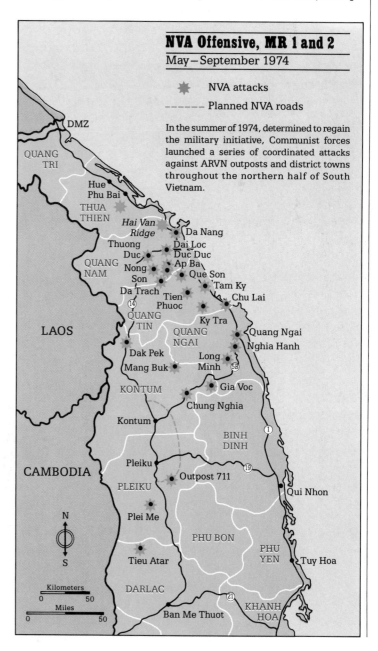

NVA Offensive, MR 1 and 2
May–September 1974

★ NVA attacks

------ Planned NVA roads

In the summer of 1974, determined to regain the military initiative, Communist forces launched a series of coordinated attacks against ARVN outposts and district towns throughout the northern half of South Vietnam.

DMZ

QUANG TRI

Hue
Phu Bai
THUA THIEN

Hai Van Ridge

Da Nang
Thuong Duc
Dai Loc
Duc Duc
Ap Ba
QUANG NAM
Nong Son
Que Son
Tam Ky
Da Trach
Chu Lai
Tien Phuoc
QUANG TIN
Ky Tra
LAOS
Quang Ngai
Nghia Hanh
QUANG NGAI
Dak Pek
Long Minh
Mang Buk
Gia Vuc
KONTUM
Chung Nghia
Kontum
BINH DINH
Pleiku
CAMBODIA
Outpost 711
PLEIKU
Qui Nhon
Plei Me
PHU BON
N
PHU YEN
Tuy Hoa
S
Tieu Atar
Kilometers
0   50
DARLAC
Miles
0   50
Ban Me Thuot
KHANH HOA

ply center at Duc Co all the way to Ban Don, 32 kilometers northwest of Ban Me Thuot. The next target of the campaign was Mang Buk, a weakly manned outpost located near a Communist supply route connecting Kontum with Quang Ngai and Binh Dinh Provinces. First attacked on July 25, the camp came under heavy fire on August 18. Without artillery, and denied air support because of bad weather, the defenders withdrew the following day and headed for Chuong Nghia.

In the face of the widespread Communist challenges, II Corps commander Lieutenant General Nguyen Van Toan had neither the manpower nor the mobility to nullify the enemy's advantages of initiative and surprise. On those rare occasions when outside help could be rendered, as in the case of Plei Me, the Communists were repulsed. A well-fortified post midway between Pleiku and Tieu Atar, Plei Me was attacked on August 4 by seven battalions of the 320th NVA Division supported by two 130MM guns, three 120MM mortars, 85MM field guns, 82MM mortars, twelve heavy antiaircraft machine guns, and recoilless rifles.

Over the next ten days two outlying positions fell, but the main camp held on. Unlike Dak Pek and Tieu Atar, the 410 men of the 82d Ranger Battalion manning Plei Me were backed by ARVN howitzer batteries at Outpost 711 and by 175MM guns covering the camp's entire perimeter. As a result, despite twenty ground assaults and over 10,000 rounds of artillery and mortar fire, the enemy was forced to retreat on September 2 with losses of at least 350 men.

Plei Me, however, was an exception. Even when attacks could be anticipated, Communist firepower had grown so formidable that without quick reinforcement and supporting artillery isolated garrisons were doomed. Aware of Communist movements toward Chuong Nghia after their capture of Mang Buk, II Corps headquarters reinforced the base with a battalion of Regional Forces soldiers, bringing the garrison up to 600 men. Defenses were bolstered to include a ring of outposts six kilometers from the camp, intermediate positions three kilometers away, and an inner ring 1,000 meters out. But artillery support still consisted of only the camp's own two 105MM howitzers. When the NVA attacked the outposts on September 30, they had little difficulty in overrunning the outlying positions one by one. By October 2 five outposts had fallen and the main camp was under heavy bombardment. Two

NVA troops use a 76MM recoilless rifle to attack the town of Minh Long in Quang Ngai Province during the Communist summer offensive of 1974.

175MM guns sent from Kontum to support Chuong Nghia moved at a tortuous pace due to poor road conditions, while enemy fire on the camp's airstrip prevented the airlift of reinforcements from the province capital. On October 3, with the 175MM guns still out of range, the Communists mounted their final assault. Under withering artillery fire a battalion of NVA infantrymen broke through the last of Chuong Nghia's defenses and seized the camp. Few of the original 600 defenders survived. The last major outpost in Kontum Province had fallen.

The offensive in the south

The loss of the highlands outposts posed a serious threat to the GVN's overall defense strategy. Even more ominous, however, was the NVA offensive in Military Region 3, where from early spring to late summer Communist units tested Saigon's defenses in a wide arc west, north, and east of the capital.

During the first week of April the 7th NVA Division overran the small firebase of Chi Linh forty-eight kilometers north of Saigon, severing Route 13 and jeopardizing government control over the important Saigon-Phuoc Long axis. Ten days later, after a siege of nearly fifteen months, the Ranger outpost at Tong Le Chan on the Tay Ninh-Binh

South Vietnamese forces defend their position in the mountains outside of Kontum during the mid-1974 North Vietnamese offensive.

Long border finally capitulated. Savage bombardments and unrelenting sapper attacks had reduced the garrison's effective strength to less than 250 men. As Tong Le Chan's defenders struggled through the jungle toward An Loc, the 5th NVA Division attacked the Duc Hue Ranger outpost near the Vam Co Dong River in Hau Nghia Province. Although the attackers failed to dislodge the government battalion, over the next weeks they succeeded in occupying and fortifying most of the territory between the Vam Co Dong and the Cambodian border. Meanwhile, on May 16 the 9th NVA Division captured three government outposts on the northern edge of the Iron Triangle. As III Corps commander Lieutenant General Pham Quoc Thuan rushed reinforcements into the strategically crucial region only thirty-two kilometers northwest of Saigon, elements of the 7th NVA Division moved south from Chi Linh to attack the bridge over the Song Be River at Phu Giao.

Struggling to contain the Communist attacks north and west of the capital, General Thuan was also forced to give his attention to the eastern provinces of the military region where the strategic raids campaign threatened to sever

163

Highway 1, Saigon's principal connection to the central coast. During April two NVA regiments assaulted Regional Forces outposts along the Long Khanh–Phuoc Tuy border, halting the flow of commerce along Route 2 and successfully tying down the 18th ARVN Division. No sooner had government forces dispersed the two regiments, allowing General Thuan to redeploy the 18th Division north of Saigon, than local VC units, supported by NVA Main Force regiments, resumed their campaign. On May 24 the Communists overran Bao Binh Village near the vital road junction of Xuan Loc, then seized the Rung La refugee settlement to the east on June 11, effectively cutting Highway 1. Although a government task force managed to clear the road by June 17, insufficient manpower prevented a counterattack against Bao Binh, from which the Communists continued to harass Rung La and periodically block traffic along Highway 1.

Through June and July the primary focus of military activity in MR 3 remained the Iron Triangle, where repeated ARVN counterattacks inched forward against entrenched NVA positions producing horrendous casualties on both sides. But in August General Thuan had once again to contend with new enemy drives north and west of the capital. A rocket attack against the giant Bien Hoa Air Base on August 10 marked the beginning of coordinated assaults against Hoa Da, Dat Cuoc, and Ba Cam outposts a few kilometers to the north. Manned only by Regional Force soldiers, all three were overrun in the space of a day by the 165th NVA Regiment, which virtually destroyed an entire RF battalion in the process. Since Communist control of the outposts would put the enemy within easy rocket range of Bien Hoa, government troops mounted a strong counterattack that by the end of the month had succeeded in recovering all the lost positions.

The intensity of the fighting was even greater in Tay Ninh Province, where the 6th NVA Division attempted to push Communist control eastward from the Cambodian border. On August 14 the blow fell simultaneously on three outposts guarding the approaches to Tay Ninh City, while diversionary attacks were made against the Suoi Da and Ben Cau outposts to the west and south. Despite brutal artillery bombardment and tank assaults, the ninety-seven RF defenders at Luoc Tan held off the NVA for six days. Meanwhile, Communist rockets crashed into a civilian hospital in Tay Ninh City, killing one patient and wounding sixteen others. At Luoc Tan casualties reduced the garrison's effective strength by more than half. Attempts to relieve the outpost faltered. On August 20 an NVA battalion finally breached the camp's perimeter and captured the remaining defenders.

Facing a much higher concentration of government forces than in either of the two northern military regions, the Communists were unable to make substantial territorial gains around Saigon during the summer campaign. Moreover, they suffered heavy casualties that forced the temporary withdrawal of several major units from the battlefield. Yet the government's military situation had scarcely improved as a result of the fighting. Whipsawed back and forth across the region by constant enemy attacks, compelled to abandon several important positions, ARVN and Territorial Forces had endured serious losses of their own in men and morale. The Communist thrusts in MR 3 had simply opened too many wounds for the RVNAF to heal.

The same slow bleeding afflicted government fortunes in the delta. Attempts by the NVA 5th Division to in-

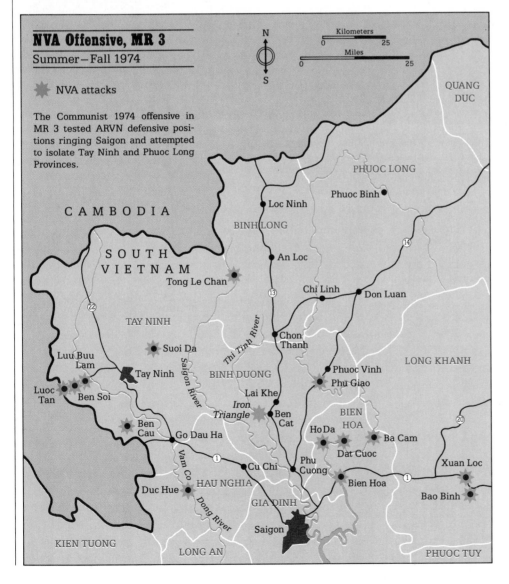

NVA Offensive, MR 3

Summer–Fall 1974

⭐ NVA attacks

The Communist 1974 offensive in MR 3 tested ARVN defensive positions ringing Saigon and attempted to isolate Tay Ninh and Phuoc Long Provinces.

CAMBODIA

SOUTH VIETNAM

QUANG DUC

PHUOC LONG

Phuoc Binh

Loc Ninh

BINH LONG

An Loc

Tong Le Chan

Chi Linh

Don Luan

TAY NINH

Suoi Da

Chon Thanh

LONG KHANH

Luu Buu Lam

Tay Ninh

BINH DUONG

Phuoc Vinh

Phu Giao

Lai Khe

Luoc Tan

Ben Soi

Iron Triangle

Ben Cat

BIEN HOA

Ho Da

Ba Cam

Ben Cau

Go Dau Ha

Dat Cuoc

Xuan Loc

Phu Cuong

Bien Hoa

Cu Chi

Bao Binh

Duc Hue

HAU NGHIA

GIA DINH

Saigon

KIEN TUONG

LONG AN

PHUOC TUY

Thi Tinh River

Saigon River

Vam Co

Dong River

Battle of the Iron Triangle

In the bloody year of 1974 no single operation or campaign was longer, more ferocious, or more costly than the Battle of the Iron Triangle. Pitted by countless bomb and shell craters, undermined by a network of abandoned tunnels, the Triangle bore the scars of thousands of skirmishes, firefights, and full-scale attacks that had raged across the flat, scrub-covered plain for more than twenty years. What made the area so valuable was apparent from one glance at the map. Like the head of an arrow pointed straight at the heart of South Vietnam, the wedge of land lying to the west of Ben Cat was no more than forty kilometers northwest of the capital. NVA control of the region would put Communist artillery within range of Tan Son Nhut Air Base and threaten vital ARVN defensive positions at Phu Cuong, Cu Chi, and Lai Khe.

On May 16 two regiments of the 9th NVA Division, backed by a small contingent of tanks, overwhelmed Rach Bap and Hill 82, two outposts guarding the northern leg of the Triangle. By the evening of the seventeenth, as artillery and rocket fire drove some 4,500 civilians from Ben Cat, Communist troops from the 95C Regiment took possession of An Dien while the 272d Regiment pushed south along Highway 14 toward Phu Cuong.

With government forces clinging only to a narrow bridge connecting Ben Cat and An Dien, MR 3 commander Lieutenant General Pham Quoc Thuan deployed the 18th ARVN Division in a multipronged counterattack designed to recapture all of the lost positions by May 22. The 43d Infantry supported by the 322d Armored Task Force attacked from the south toward Rach Bap and Hill 82. Task Force 318 advanced from the east toward An Dien, while three battalions of the 7th Ranger Group struck from the north toward Hill 82. None of these efforts met with success. By May 28, with the counterattack bogged down, Thuan decided to regroup for a fresh assault.

A renewed push began on June 1 spearheaded by the 52d Infantry, which crossed the Thi Tinh River south of Ben Cat then turned north toward An Dien, while other elements of the 18th Division attacked the village over the semi-repaired An Dien bridge. Over the next two days Communist and government forces traded heavy blows that decimated the 52d Regiment. On June 4 government troops battling enemy tanks finally entered An Dien. Although captured NVA soldiers reported terrible casualties among their comrades, the Communists launched a furious counterattack on the night of June 5 to 6 with two reserve battalions. But the ARVN held, and General Thuan predicted that the remaining two outposts would be recaptured within three weeks.

In fact, it would take four months before government soldiers regained Hill 82, only three kilometers west of An Dien. The dense brush and cratered terrain obscured the enemy's entrenchments and concealed reserve positions. ARVN armor, restricted to a narrow dirt road surrounded by high grass that reduced the attackers' visibility to no more than a few meters, were picked off by hidden enemy soldiers wielding B41 antitank grenade launchers and Soviet 82MM recoilless rifles. Meanwhile, Communist defenders occupying the high ground had the advancing government columns in full view. Dug into the thick jungle and rubber plantations north of Hill 82, concentrations of enemy artillery pounded the only avenues of approach as soon as ARVN soldiers came within range. Instead of concentrating on neutralizing the Communist artillery, government soldiers were lured into pretargeted artillery zones, then cut to pieces by heavy fire. Making matters worse was the onset of the summer monsoon that, combined with Communist antiaircraft barrages, virtually eliminated VNAF air support.

Between June 7 and July 1 the men of the 18th ARVN Division along with supporting armored task forces repeatedly attacked NVA positions east, south, and north of Hill 82, only to be driven back by enemy artillery and antitank fire that claimed thousands of government casualties. By the end of the month the troops he had originally committed had been so roughly handled that General Thuan abandoned the attempt to retake Hill 82 until new plans could be devised.

When the ARVN counterattack resumed on September 7, the initial results were no better than they had been two months earlier. A new government task force swiftly reached the enemy perimeter but could not penetrate the mines and barbwire that ringed the base of the hill. Driven back through pouring rain by fierce artillery fire and tank assaults, the task force was replaced by three battalions of the 9th Regiment, which began still another assault on September 19. Using effective counterbattery fire and small assault teams, the 1st and 3d Battalions inched forward, eliminating enemy bunkers one by one. Joined on October 2 by a battalion of the 25th ARVN Division, the attackers pounded NVA defenses with salvos of 155MM howitzer fire that forced the remaining enemy soldiers from their shattered earth and log fortress. Finally, on the afternoon of October 4, government soldiers placed their flag atop Hill 82.

Another six weeks passed while ARVN regrouped and reinforced its battered units before driving the NVA from its last foothold in the Triangle, Rach Bap. In the interim the southern Communist command received instructions from Hanoi to prepare for the offensive strikes to begin at the end of the year. Withdrawing most of its units to base areas farther north, the enemy left behind only token forces. On November 20, after a firefight that left forty ARVN soldiers wounded, GVN troops entered Rach Bap unopposed. The Battle of the Iron Triangle was over.

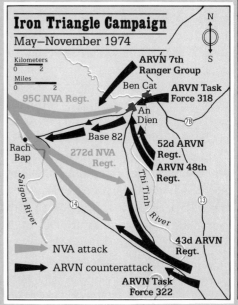

Iron Triangle Campaign
May–November 1974
N
S
Kilometers
0
2
Miles
0
2
ARVN 7th
Ranger Group
Ben Cat
ARVN Task
Force 318
95C NVA Regt.
An
Dien
7B
Base 82
Rach
Bap
272d NVA
Regt.
52d ARVN
Regt.
ARVN 48th
Regt.
Saigon River
Thi Tinh River
13
14
NVA attack
ARVN counterattack
43d ARVN
Regt.
ARVN Task
Force 322

filtrate Kien Tuong Province from its base in Cambodia were driven back on each occasion by the 7th and 9th ARVN Divisions. Farther south, however, the Communists were more successful. Government forays against the Tri Phap provoked vigorous reaction, wrote JGS Chairman General Cao Van Vien. "The three organic divisions of IV Corps were constantly tied up either in combat operations or in providing support and assistance to the Regional and Popular Forces." The weakness of the territorial units created a vacuum in the southern delta that the Vietcong was quick to fill, gaining control over villages and hamlets in Kien Giang, An Xuyen, and Chuong Thien Provinces and capturing the town of Hung Long, the first district seat in MR 4 ever lost to the enemy. Meanwhile, Communist units moving out of their base in the U Minh Forest raided hamlets, seized rice, and assassinated uncooperative village officials. The summer of 1974 witnessed no spectacular initiatives in the delta, no stunning victories or defeats, just a steady weakening of resistance and an insidious erosion of government control.

It was a development of "grave concern" to a Saigon command equally troubled by the ever-increasing supply of new and more deadly weapons that local enemy forces in the delta continued to receive. For behind the front lines of battle the Communist logistical network pushed constantly southward, daily expanding to meet the demands of escalating military operations and to pave the way for the final onslaught.

Strong ropes

In the mountainous regions stretching along the Laotian and Cambodian borders, in the forests of northern Tay Ninh, Binh Long, and Phuoc Long Provinces, the Communists were building a mighty military force: constructing logistical installations; stockpiling weapons, ammunition, and supplies; reorganizing the expeditionary army; training replacements; building hospitals; improving roads and bridges. "It was a picture to be proud of," wrote General Dung. "In that region of our Fatherland were more than 20,000 kilometers of strategic roads running north to south, with campaign roads running west to east—strong ropes inching gradually, day by day, around the neck, arms, and legs of a demon, awaiting the order to jerk tight and bring the creature's life to an end."

According to DAO estimates, by September 1974 the Communist order of battle in South Vietnam consisted of ten divisions (not including the seven reserve divisions north of the DMZ), with an overall combat strength of more than 200,000 men. This growing force was supported by some 700 tanks and up to 450 artillery pieces, primarily 122MM and 130MM guns far outranging the RVNAF's

Vietcong soldiers on parade. By September 1974 Communist combat strength in South Vietnam exceeded 200,000 men.

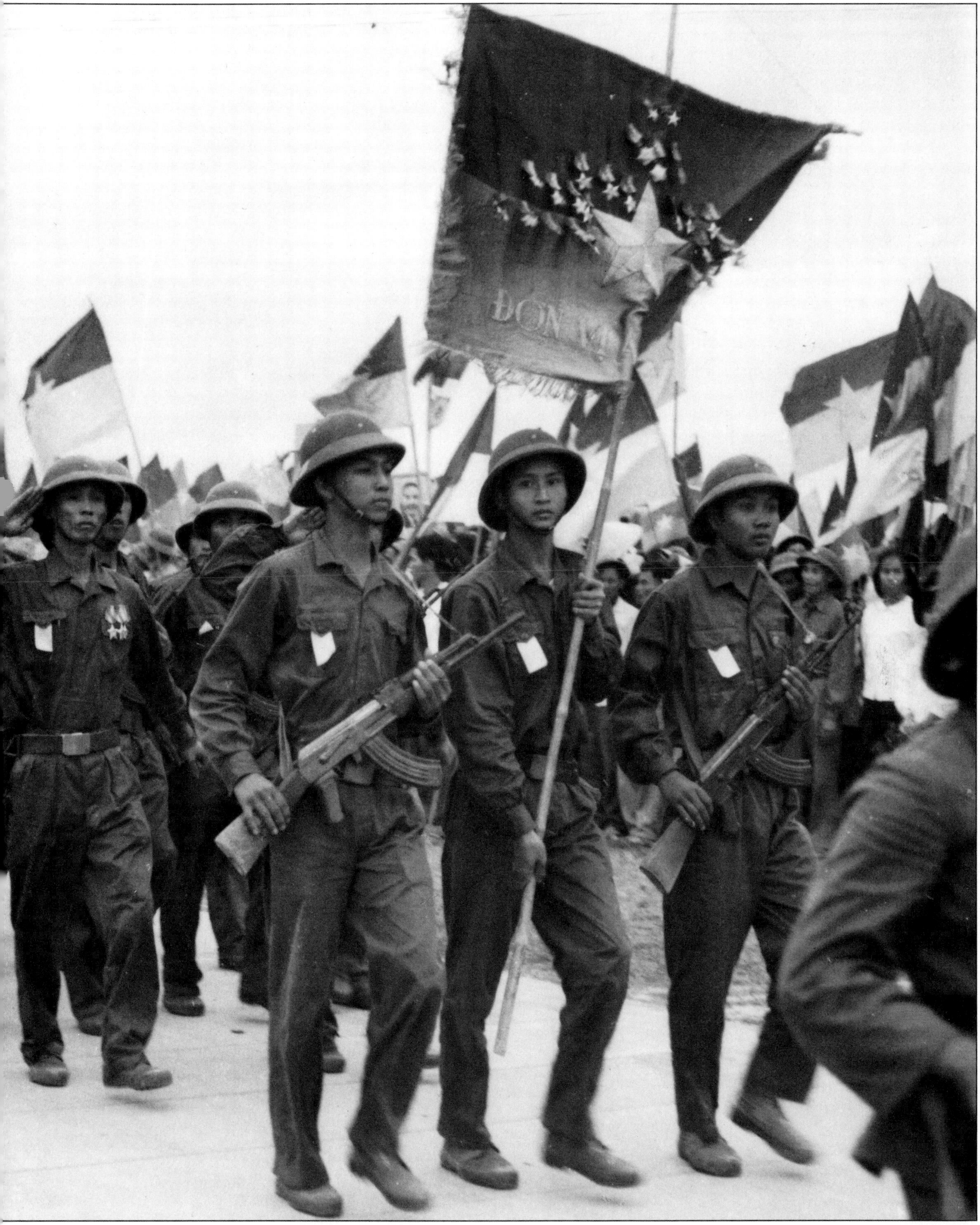

105MM and 155MM howitzers. Among the enemy units were twenty antiaircraft regiments now armed with an improved version of the Soviet SA-7 Strela missile. Earlier, Communist marksmen had averaged one hit for every five Strelas fired. The ratio now was virtually one for one with some hits recorded as high as 13,000 feet.

Out of their growing manpower pool the Communist command created additional units like the 26th Armor Brigade, the 75th Artillery Division, the 477th Antiaircraft Division, the 25th Engineer Division, and the 25th Sapper Division. To consolidate their forces along more conventional lines, four new infantry divisions were organized out of existing NVA regiments in Military Regions 3 and 4. And to meet the planning and coordination requirements of multidivisional operations, three new corps commands were activated: the 2d Corps, responsible for the region north of Da Nang; the 3d Corps, in command of units in southern MR 1 and the central highlands; and the 301st Corps, headquartered near Saigon.

In all, the summer offensive had accomplished a great deal. The expansion of their increasingly sophisticated logistics network permitted the Communists to move regular units, tanks, and artillery to the front lines of battle within a matter of hours. During the campaign the NVA had tested new tactics and command arrangements, achieving for the first time localized fire superiority. The fighting disrupted transportation and communications throughout the country, weakened the South Vietnamese economy, and generated hundreds of thousands of new refugees, effectively reversing the gains made by the government resettlement program since the cease-fire.

In the delta, the Communists had penetrated deep into contested territory, gaining control over virtually all but the province and district capitals in the central and southern part of the region. In Military Region 3 they had nibbled away at Saigon's defenses, threatening to isolate entirely Tay Ninh and Phuoc Long Provinces. To the north, the NVA had driven to the very edge of the coastal plains—its artillery now within range of nearly every major RVNAF installation and population center—and steadily eroded the defensive screens around Hue and Da Nang.

Although Communist casualties were high, the wide-ranging NVA attacks had cost the ARVN dearly. Government casualty lists included a disproportionate number of experienced junior officers and NCOs. Replacements were sufficient in neither training nor numbers, while the

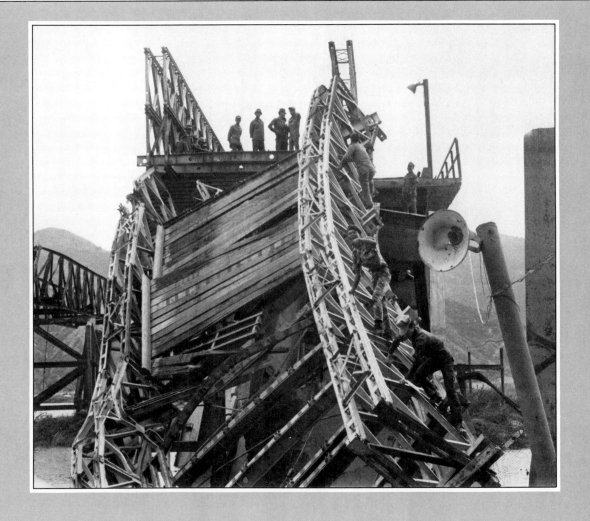

The Communist offensive of 1974 left much of South Vietnam battered and bloody. Right. ARVN engineers survey the damage after Vietcong sappers brought down a bridge in Binh Dinh Province. Far right. An ARVN soldier pulls three wounded comrades from a delta firefight.

Communists continued to fill their ranks from an unimpeded flow of men pouring out of North Vietnamese training camps. Exhausted and overextended ARVN units had completely surrendered the initiative, retreating to static defensive positions scattered all across the northern provinces. Outside the government perimeters, Communist troops ranged at will, gathering their forces in superior numbers to overwhelm vulnerable South Vietnamese positions. By the fall of 1974, as the enemy moved from strength to strength, the armed forces of South Vietnam sank into a passivity from which they would never recover.

A posture of defeat

As the military situation deteriorated, South Vietnamese leaders made no significant strategic adjustments. Instead, they looked hopefully to the restoration of U.S. aid as the principal solution to their problems.

A joint study conducted by the DAO and the South Vietnamese General Staff in May 1974 concluded that due to changing battlefield circumstances and inflationary pressures, the $1.45 billion military aid package proposed by Saigon the previous September for fiscal year 1975 would be insufficient in the event of a major Communist offensive. The $1.126 billion limit recently set by the House of Representatives for fiscal year 1975 was at best marginal. Anything less would "seriously affect both the capabilities and morale" of the armed forces. Transmitting this assessment to Washington on June 1, General Murray warned: "You can roughly equate cuts in support to loss of real estate." If aid fell to the $750 million level, Hanoi would have no inducement to negotiate, and South Vietnam would be forced to abandon large segments of the country. Below that figure the United States could "write off RVN as a bad investment and broken promise. GVN would do well to hang on to the Saigon and Delta areas."

Convinced of their helplessness without substantial increases in American assistance, laboring under a command structure that left individual Corps commanders answerable only to the presidential palace, prevented from redrawing defensive lines by Thieu's unwillingness to surrender territory, the JGS did little more than wait and hope. Some outposts in the delta were shut down under a "consolidation" program; and during the latter part of 1974 the GVN began organizing some territorial units into Mobile Regional Forces Groups. But the vast majority re-

mained committed to static local security. There were also discussions among JGS staff officers about withdrawing military assets from the northern half of the country to strengthen defenses in the more populated and economically vital regions to the south. But no serious planning was undertaken, no decisions reached.

Meanwhile, scattered outposts continued to be overrun at a depressing rate, and a staggering cost. When the garrison at Gia Vuc fell into Communist hands, after permission to withdraw the battalion had been denied, only 20 of the 400 Rangers guarding the insignificant village were ever accounted for. Of the approximately 1,000 men who manned Da Trach, only 174 made it out alive. "The final result was that the RVNAF was a giant chained in place," wrote General Nguyen Duy Hinh. "The enemy, entirely unafraid of retaliation, just concentrated on the offensive, and thereby enjoyed a great advantage."

The one tangible response of the South Vietnamese command to the growing crisis was an intensification of draconian measures designed to husband the nation's dwindling military resources. About one-fifth of the Vietnamese Air Force was grounded. By September helicopter flights had been cut in half, including medical evacuation. Fighter-bomber sorties and reconnaissance flights were also drastically curtailed, reducing fire support by as much as 50 percent and gravely affecting the ability of the VNAF to keep track of enemy movements. Flying hours and contractor support were slashed, and over 1,000 airmen-trainees were turned into infantrymen, a development having what one senior officer called "a most adverse psychological effect in the Vietnamese Air Force." The deactivation of more than 600 boats and twenty-one of the forty-four riverine units reduced naval operations in the delta by more than 70 percent, compromising the defense of remote outposts, threatening the security of the Saigon-Vung Tau artery, and sharply restricting the number of vessels available to escort supply convoys. Artillery ammunition expenditures dropped to an average of three rounds per weapon per day. Infantrymen now made do with eighty-five rifle bullets a month.

The impact of the shortages was everywhere apparent: in the thousands of trucks placed on blocks for lack of fuel; in radios silent for lack of batteries; in bandages and surgical dressings washed and reused for lack of adequate medical supplies; in outposts protected by bamboo stakes for lack of barbed wire; in perimeters strung with grenades for lack of mines; and in wounded who died for lack of aerial medical evacuation. "Faced with an enemy whose firepower and resources were constantly upgraded, our troops had to make do with increasing austerity," despaired one ARVN division commander. "They were taught single-shot firing while the enemy rained on them an outpour of deadly fire. Grenades were used sparingly because resupply did not come in sufficient quantities. While the enemy moved his troops to combat by trucks, our troops were trained to march. Medical evacuation, meanwhile, was slow and ineffective." Thanks to lavish air power and abundant artillery support, every South Vietnamese KIA from 1970 to 1972 accounted for five enemy killed. In 1973 the ratio dropped to 1:2; in 1974 it was only 1:1.5.

In the first eight months of 1974 South Vietnam lost 20,000 men in combat. Between July and October more than 4,700 men had been killed, wounded, or were missing in action from the fighting in Quang Nam Province alone. The immensity of the sacrifice came home to Captain Stuart Herrington when he attended the funeral of a young Vietnamese friend killed in action. The burial took place at Bien Hoa national cemetery, one of four sites set aside in each of the military regions for those who had perished in defense of their country.

During Tinh's graveside service, I stood near two long rows of open graves, each more than one hundred meters from end to end. Next to them were three more rows of fresh graves, each grave a mound of earth covered by a red and yellow South Vietnamese flag. One week later, I returned for a traditional second graveside service and noticed with horror that all of the graves had been filled, and that workers were busily digging three more rows. I counted almost four hundred new graves.

As serious as such losses were, in terms of pure manpower they paled beside a desertion rate that by the last quarter of 1974 reached an all-time high of nearly 240,000 men a year. The total for one division during 1974 was 523 men killed, 3,328 deserted, leaving battalions averaging only 277 men each, approximately half their assigned strength. Nor was this an exceptional case. The 3d Division's maneuver battalions had shrunk by 200 men apiece since July. Replacements sent to make up the difference were neither adequate nor inspiring: 60 of the officers were former deserters; most of the enlisted men were ex-convicts. According to DAO assessments, of the thirteen ARVN divisions, six were rated either ineffective or only marginally fit for combat.

As he marched into battle during the last months of 1974, the South Vietnamese soldier had neither the means nor the leadership to sustain himself. Faced with battle-field defeats, mounting casualties, and materiel shortages, the military command withdrew into what one historian has called "a psychology of accommodation and retreat." Fearful that the United States was preparing to sell them out, they grasped at the hope that, in the end, Washington would come to the rescue. "For the first time in the war," wrote General Cao Van Vien, "our armed forces were in the decided position of underdog. It now became clear that the most [we] could hope to achieve was a delaying action pending restoration of U.S. military aid to its former level." But there would be no restoration of aid, no sudden reversal of America's waning concern. Saigon was running out of friends, and her friends were running out of time.

A loss of control

Throughout its twenty-year history South Vietnam had looked to Washington for counsel and support. Always in times of crisis the White House had responded. But neither the current occupant of the Oval Office nor his associates could any longer muster the clarity of purpose necessary to act effectively. Its authority compromised by the ongoing Watergate investigations, its policies chained to commitments it was unwilling to abandon, the administration was unable to substantially influence either its foreign allies or its domestic opponents. By the summer of 1974 Richard Nixon had lost control of the presidency, the Congress, and the course of events in Indochina.

In Saigon, Ambassador Martin maintained a laissez-faire approach toward the Thieu government. His lack of interference nourished the South Vietnamese president's hopes for continuing American support. Despite Congressional prohibitions against the use of U.S. military forces in Indochina, despite reductions in aid and the escalating political crisis in Washington, Thieu clung tenaciously to the written promises he had received from President Nixon that the United States would stand by its ally. The embassy did nothing to shake Thieu's confidence by repeating assurances that Congress could be persuaded to grant additional funds and by minimizing the political ramifications of the Watergate hearings.

Some of Thieu's advisers, alarmed by General Murray's warnings to abandon indefensible positions, and seeing all too clearly that Richard Nixon's days were numbered, took steps to prod the president into action. During an inspection tour in August, Prime Minister Khiem alerted MR 1 commander Lieutenant General Ngo Quang Truong that territory might have to be surrendered in order to buy time in the event of a major Communist assault. Meanwhile, Thieu's cousin, Hoang Duc Nha, conducted a study to determine how the 3 million people of the northern provinces would be safely transferred south should truncation become necessary.

For Thieu, however, the idea of giving up a large part of South Vietnam had only one utility. With no intention of seriously considering such a move, he used the threat of retrenchment in an attempt to pry more aid from the United States. Showing them a JGS plan based on Murray's ominous projections, Thieu sadly told visiting U.S. lawmakers: "This is what will happen if Congress is not more forthcoming." His cynicism angered his closest supporters, who wished the president would deal more forcefully with the reality of his country's predicament. But Thieu would not be moved, his limited capacity for action held firmly in place between the Americans who were telling him his situation was grave and the Americans who were telling him he had nothing to worry about.

The same conflicting signals hamstrung U.S. policy in Cambodia. When Ambassador John Gunther Dean ar-

rived in Phnom Penh in March 1974, he quickly concluded that whatever role the United States still had to play there was little likelihood of reversing the government's failing military fortunes. The only hope lay in a "non-military solution" that would halt the fighting and allow the Americans a graceful exit. Warning the State Department that "time is against us," Dean recommended that a new approach be made to Khmer Rouge leader Khieu Samphan.

But Secretary of State Henry Kissinger rejected the proposal out of hand. He would not treat with the insurgents from a position of weakness. Nor did he embrace Graham Martin's suggestion that Washington sever its ties with the Lon Nol government and allow Prince Sihanouk to return to Phnom Penh as the basis for a cease-fire. To Kissinger, Lon Nol was a bargaining chip that would only be given away if substantial concessions could be wrung from the Khmer Rouge. Thus, United States policy in Cambodia remained immobile. When Dean persisted in his search for a political settlement he was sharply reprimanded. "I don't want to hear about Laos-type compromises," Kissinger told him tartly. "Your job is to strengthen the military position so we can negotiate from strength."

It was a hopeless task. Government forces managed to stave off the insurgents' dry season offensive primarily because the Khmer Rouge lacked sufficient ammunition to push home their advantage. This obstacle was overcome in April when Khieu Samphan visited Peking. At a formal banquet the Khmer Rouge leader denounced all "such maneuvers as sham ceasefire, sham talks and sham peace" and presented China's Premier Chou En-lai with a grenade launcher. When Chou took the weapon and aimed it at the ceiling he symbolized a decisive turning point in Chinese policy toward Cambodia. The unwillingness of the United States to seek a political solution to the war left only one alternative. During their talks with Samphan the Chinese made a commitment to furnish the military hardware necessary to finish the job. The weapons and ammunition that soon flowed from Peking enabled the Khmer Rouge to maintain their punishing attacks through the monsoon season and to prepare for the final offensive.

In the meantime, Cambodia suffered a torment that seemed to have no end. Along with the continuing fighting came reports from Khmer Rouge territory of wholesale political assassinations, brutal "psychological reorientation," and the forced relocation of entire villages amid a reign of terror almost incomprehensible in its savagery. In those areas still controlled by the government, the economic crisis had reached catastrophic proportions. Food was so costly that most of the refugees crowded into Phnom Penh could afford no more than one day's supply of rice a week. By the summer of 1974, reported the British journalist William Shawcross, most of the people in the cities were slowly starving to death.

Dean did what little he could to keep Lon Nol afloat, forcing the government to restrict the import of such ex-

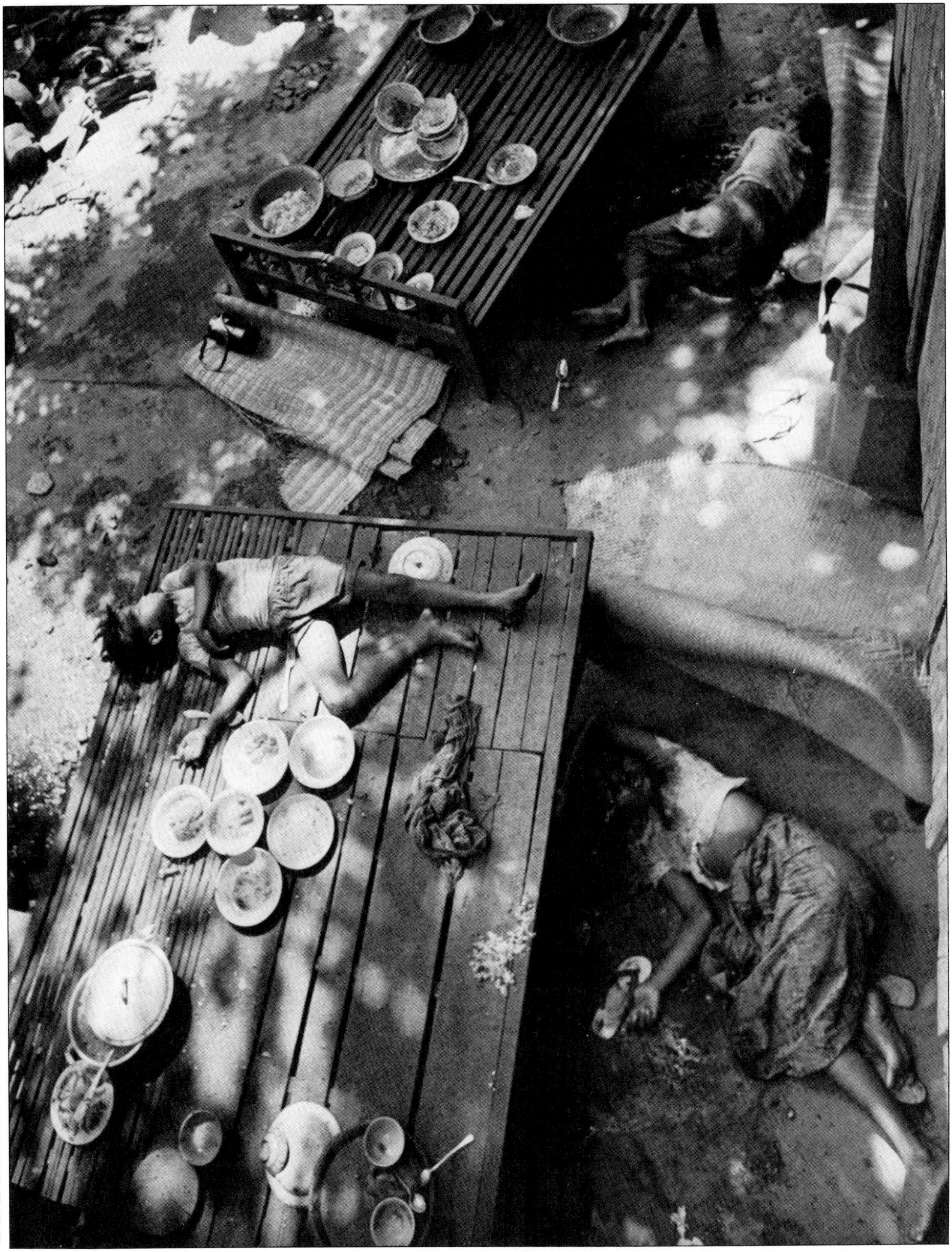

travagant luxuries as televisions, canned asparagus, and Mercedes automobiles; lecturing ineffective commanders; and insisting upon the removal of the most corrupt of the marshal's associates. But Washington's continuing support of the Phnom Penh regime undercut his efforts at every step. Emotionally committed to Cambodia as the "Nixon doctrine in its purest form," the American president assured Lon Nol that the United States "remains determined to provide maximum possible assistance to your heroic self defense and will continue to stand side by side with the republic in the future as in the past." Against such inertia Dean struggled in vain.

If the field of battle was less bloody, the stakes were just as high when Washington lawmakers began their deliberations in May on military assistance to Vietnam for fiscal year 1975. Despite the losses suffered during the debate over the 1974 military aid budget, the White House was optimistic about the prospects for FY '75 funding. Congress, annoyed by the frozen Strategic Arms Limitations Talks and suspicious of the ongoing Soviet arms build-up, was in no mood to make drastic cuts in overall defense spending. As the original $1.6 billion Vietnam proposal was slashed first to $1.4 billion, then $1.126 billion, and finally $1 billion between early May and late July, however, administration officials descended on Congress in a futile attempt to plug the dike.

Focusing on the "moral obligation" of the United States to "provide our friends with the minimum required to defend themselves and to deter a renewed North Vietnamese offensive," Secretary of State Kissinger warned that American credibility hung in the balance. "Failure to sustain our purposes," he argued, "would have a corrosive effect on [U.S.] interests beyond the confines of Indochina." Kissinger insisted that if adequate funds were supplied for the next two years, a "substantial reduction" could thereafter be achieved. Once the North Vietnamese became convinced that military victory was not within their grasp, they would accept the Saigon government and accede to a political settlement. All that was needed to sustain "the achievements of recent years" were sums "small in proportion to the total effort that has been made." After all, Kissinger reminded the congressmen, the entire military aid package the administration sought for FY '75 was approximately "what we spent in a single month in 1968 at the height of U.S. involvement."

But the administration seemed incapable of getting its act together. While Secretary of Defense James Schlesinger was assuring Congress that "the armed forces of South Vietnam were giving an excellent account of themselves," precluding an all-out North Vietnamese offensive in the near future, Ambassador Martin stumped Capitol Hill armed with General Murray's warning that anything

less than $1 billion in aid "would mean the end of South Vietnam as we now know it." Yet Martin also insisted that the South Vietnamese government was "stronger than ever." If provided with adequate aid the RVNAF could contain the military threat on its own, said the ambassador, because the Communists had put aside their hopes of victory through force of arms alone. "It is now crystal clear," he told one group, "that the North Vietnamese cannot conquer the South militarily."

Instead, the aging Hanoi leaders are still trying to seize full power in the South through a combination of military, political and economic pressure. They are also attempting to achieve a cutback in U.S. military and economic assistance to the South, which they hope would accelerate the collapse of the structure of South Vietnamese society.

Torn between his desire to convince skeptical lawmakers that Saigon was making progress against its enemies, and his need to persuade Congress that the danger of collapse remained acute, the ambassador tried to refute "the assertion made frequently in recent months that eliminating or sharply cutting our aid to South Vietnam will bring peace by forcing the South Vietnamese to negotiate a settlement." The only peace such action would win, he declared, would be "that of abject surrender to Communist aggression, or the peace which would follow a bloody Communist victory."

Despite Martin's dire predictions, many members of Congress believed that a severe funding reduction would secure an end to the fighting. Representative John Flynt of Georgia told the House that the $700 million aid package he proposed would "go further to achieve peace and to maintain peace in that tragic and unfortunate part of the world than if we give the entire $1 billion." Some administration opponents argued, as one put it, that U.S. aid only propped up a "self-perpetuating dictatorship" that kept thousands of political prisoners "under barbarous conditions." Others were simply bewildered by the conflicting testimony. After sitting through days of appropriations hearings, five House members complained: "No one knows precisely what the appropriate level of support should be."

But most Congressional opposition reflected a more profound hopelessness. Optimistic scenarios of economic recovery and military success were simply not credible to the majority. Like Senator Hubert Humphrey, few were convinced that additional funding would do any good. "The money may buy time," said the Minnesotan, "but it won't buy peace." Concerned that a disproportionate share of U.S. aid was being swallowed up in Indochina, Republicans and Democrats alike insisted that the United States had other commitments around the world that deserved attention. Beyond these considerations, however, more central for most congressmen than complicated fiscal projections or contradictory assessments of U.S. interests was the overriding conviction that America had been

Victims of the savage fighting that engulfed Cambodia during the summer of 1974.

Metaphors of Misconception

The American involvement in Southeast Asia was marked from the beginning by two striking characteristics: an indefatigable optimism and a fascination with the quantification of "progress." These same traits, which had served U.S. interests in Vietnam so poorly in the past, continued to obscure the vision of U.S. policymakers during the crucial summer of 1974.

Even as multiplying Communist victories, economic chaos, and public protest staggered the Saigon government, Secretary of State Henry Kissinger was telling Congressional committees of "the gains for peace and stability" since the cease-fire that the United States now intended to "consolidate." Kissinger's assertions of South Vietnamese military strength were echoed by Secretary of Defense James Schlesinger. "To many who observed the ARVN of six or seven years ago," said Schlesinger, "the account they are now giving of themselves is splendid."

No one, however, was more relentless in his optimism than Ambassador Graham Martin. Admitting that the "immediate, short-range economic picture may look unfavorable," Martin insisted in testimony before the Senate Foreign Relations Committee that "its very severity has, up to this point, contributed to the political unity, as all Vietnamese have tightened their belts. There has been no panic, no political unrest, but a steadfast, pervasive determination to surmount this latest obstacle to their goal of a better life, in freedom, for themselves and their children."

Although such statements were meant for public consumption, the private reports Washington received from Saigon also painted a rosy picture of South Vietnamese confidence and resolve. More than anything else, the glowing accounts were the product of a fortress mentality whose chief architect was Ambassador Martin. Dogged by a skeptical press corps, the embassy "compensated for sometimes misleading media coverage by presenting information on Vietnam in a positive light," one former DAO intelligence staffer told a Congressional inquiry after the war. "The net result of this policy was to lull Washington level officials into a false sense of security concerning Vietnam."

Attempts to overcome embarrassing stories filed by "negative" reporters were matched by a thoroughgoing internal censorship within the U.S. Mission. After comparing reports made by U.S. province representatives with those ultimately passed on to Washington, Senate investigators concluded that "the thrust of information submitted from the field to Saigon is sometimes altered and ... on occasion significant information is withheld altogether."

The ambassador's fears that criticism of the GVN would bolster Congressional opposition to increased military aid also infected the CIA. In late 1974, Chief of Station Tom Polgar declared there was "no strong evidence that the morale factor has at this stage significantly affected ARVN's combat performance." His emphatic assertions that the government had the situation well in hand, that the people were "coping" well with economic difficulties, and that the continuing increase in population suggested "both physical prowess and a hopeful view of the future" were so ludicrous that CIA headquarters refused to pass the report along.

Among the U.S. agencies in Saigon, only the Defense Attaché Office regularly provided Washington with critical assessments of the deteriorating state of South Vietnam's armed forces. DAO reports were unsparing in their description of the economic hardship, social injustice, and corruption under which ordinary soldiers labored, candidly discussing the effects of logistical mismanagement, heavy casualties, and disintegrating morale. In a postwar interview DAO intelligence chief Colonel William Le Gro denied that sensitive material had been "edited out" of his department's reports. The problem was not in Saigon, the colonel insisted, but in Washington. "I have the impression that policy makers at the highest level in Washington didn't want to hear, didn't want to believe what we were telling them."

Yet it was the Defense Attaché Office that unintentionally transmitted to Washington the most egregious example of misinformation of the post-cease-fire period. Among the material the DAO provided the Pentagon on a regular basis were casualty figures taken from the daily operational reports of South Vietnamese units in the field. For nearly two years no one realized that these were only preliminary statistics. Because of the confusion of battle, administrative inefficiencies, and the reluctance of commanders to acknowledge heavy losses, the full count was made available only in revised reports that were never checked against the original lists.

The disparity was enormous. Instead of the 13,786 battle deaths reported by the DAO for 1973, 25,473 had actually been killed according to official records. During the first eight months of 1974 South Vietnamese KIA were not 9,606, as the DAO believed, but 19,375. The mistake, wrote the American journalist Arnold Isaacs, seemed a metaphor of American misconceptions in Vietnam. "For years, U.S. civilian and military officials had tried to show success by reducing the war to statistics and computer tape, ignoring all its many intangibles. Now, it turned out, for the most emotionally telling statistic of all, numbers that literally meant life and death, the Americans hadn't even managed to count correctly in the first place."

By the time the error was finally caught in October 1974, the administration had used the original figures to support its claim that the cease-fire had resulted in a significant decrease in hostilities, and Congress had debated two aid bills under the mistaken impression that South Vietnamese losses were substantially below pre-cease-fire levels. Whether the correct information would have made any difference in the decisions reached in Washington is impossible to say. That the White House and the Congress were badly informed of the reality of what was happening in Vietnam is certain.

involved in Vietnam too long. "When are we ever going to get it through our heads that we have gotten out of South Vietnam?" demanded Connecticut Representative Robert Giaimo. "We not only have gotten out because of the will of the Congress or the Administration, we have gotten out because of the demands of the American people."

Before the Flynt amendment came to a vote, opponents of the measure made a last-ditch effort to sway their colleagues. "I say that to reduce the funds for South Vietnam from [the $1 billion ceiling] would be tantamount to abandonment," declared Representative William Minshall on the House floor. Robert Sikes of Florida also took up Saigon's cause. The South Vietnamese "are fighting well, the government is strong," he asserted. "The older [DRV] leaders are getting out of the picture. The young leaders are wondering whether it is worth the effort." Reminding the members of the damage that Watergate had already done to the nation abroad, conservatives pleaded for a show of strength. "Do not in a time of crisis let people believe that the United States is now too weak to respond to a challenge," thundered Louisiana's Joe Waggonner. "Do not force a challenge."

Their appeals were to no avail. On August 6 the House passed the Flynt amendment by a vote of 233 to 157. Two weeks later the Senate followed suit, only after narrowly defeating a measure introduced by Senator William Proxmire of Wisconsin to reduce the level of aid still further. In the event, the Vietnamese did not even receive the full $700 million. Since DAO operations, shipping costs, and certain undelivered FY '73–74 equipment would be covered under the appropriation, the South Vietnamese armed forces were left with only $450 million.

Two days after the fateful House vote, Richard Nixon resigned. The new president, Gerald Ford, immediately sent Thieu a personal letter reassuring him of continued support. "I know you must be concerned by the initial steps taken by Congress on the current fiscal year appropriations for both economic and military assistance," wrote Ford. "Our legislative process is a complicated one and it is not yet completed. Although it may take a little time, I do want to assure you that in the end our support will be adequate on both counts." Drafted by Martin with Kissinger's approval, the explicit reassertion of commitment in the face of the obvious intention of Congress to end American involvement was a measure of the disarray into which U.S. policy had fallen.

"It was a stupid letter and a commitment," General Murray later remarked. Stung by the Congressional action, the outgoing defense attaché publicly charged that the United States had set a "sadistic and racist" standard that left the South Vietnamese to "substitute bodies, bone and blood for bullets." Against Martin's direct order, Murray met with the JGS for a final time, begging the South Vietnamese high command to withdraw military units to more defensible positions as a last hope of protecting their

dwindling resources. General Vien and army Chief of Staff General Dang Van Khuyen agreed with Murray's rationale but told him they could not act. As long as Thieu accepted the American promises of assistance, such a move remained politically impossible.

The glass is full

The twin shocks of the House vote and the Nixon resignation were devastating blows to the South Vietnamese president. Beset by military reverses and economic crises, Thieu's eroding authority had come to depend more and more on the mandate of American support. The stunning departure of the man who symbolized that special relationship, and the inability of the new American president to restore the aid funds cut by Congress, convinced critics of the Saigon government that Thieu's last claim to leadership had disappeared. Within weeks the beleaguered president faced the most serious political challenge of his career.

The crisis exploded on September 8 when a group of Catholic lay and religious leaders led by Father Tran Huu Thanh, a fifty-nine-year-old anti-Communist militant, issued "Indictment No. 1." Focusing squarely on the scourge of corruption as the fundamental symptom of South Vietnam's ill health, the daring public manifesto left no doubt who was to blame for the country's miseries: "The present terrible state of corruption can exist only because the nation's leader himself has protected and initiated it. Corruption robs the people down to their bones, it stabs the soldiers' backs, it undermines the national economy, and it destroys the people's strength to resist." The document not only accused members of Thieu's family by name of skimming profits from hospital construction, illegal speculation in fertilizer, and the theft of funds from government rice-transport subsidies, it also charged Thieu himself with involvement in heroin trafficking and questionable real estate manipulations that had netted the president a personal fortune. Whatever validity there was to the specific allegations, they were less important than the cumulative portrait of a man who had forfeited any claim to moral leadership. Didn't the commander in chief "feel ashamed before his conscience," the indictment demanded angrily, "when combatants are lacking rice to eat, clothes to wear and houses to live in—and whose wives sometimes have to sell their bodies in order to feed their children?" The "present rotten, dictatorial family regime" was "a national disaster and a national shame, a betrayal of all those who have been sacrificing themselves for the hard, protracted struggle of our people and army for more than a quarter of a century."

In the political tinderbox that South Vietnam had become by the fall of 1974, the accusations sparked a roaring fire of public protest. Defying government censors, three Saigon dailies published the full text of the in-

Protest and Repression

In the fall of 1974, public demonstrations mounted against corruption in Thieu's adminstration and family. That August in Hue, a protest held by the People's Anti-Corruption Movement, a Catholic group alleging that even President Thieu himself engaged in illegal activities, had been broken up by police with tear gas and clubs. That only set the stage for what was to happen in September and October in Saigon, where Thieu answered serious charges of corruption by first removing from positions of authority some of the accused and then using censorship and force against his detractors.

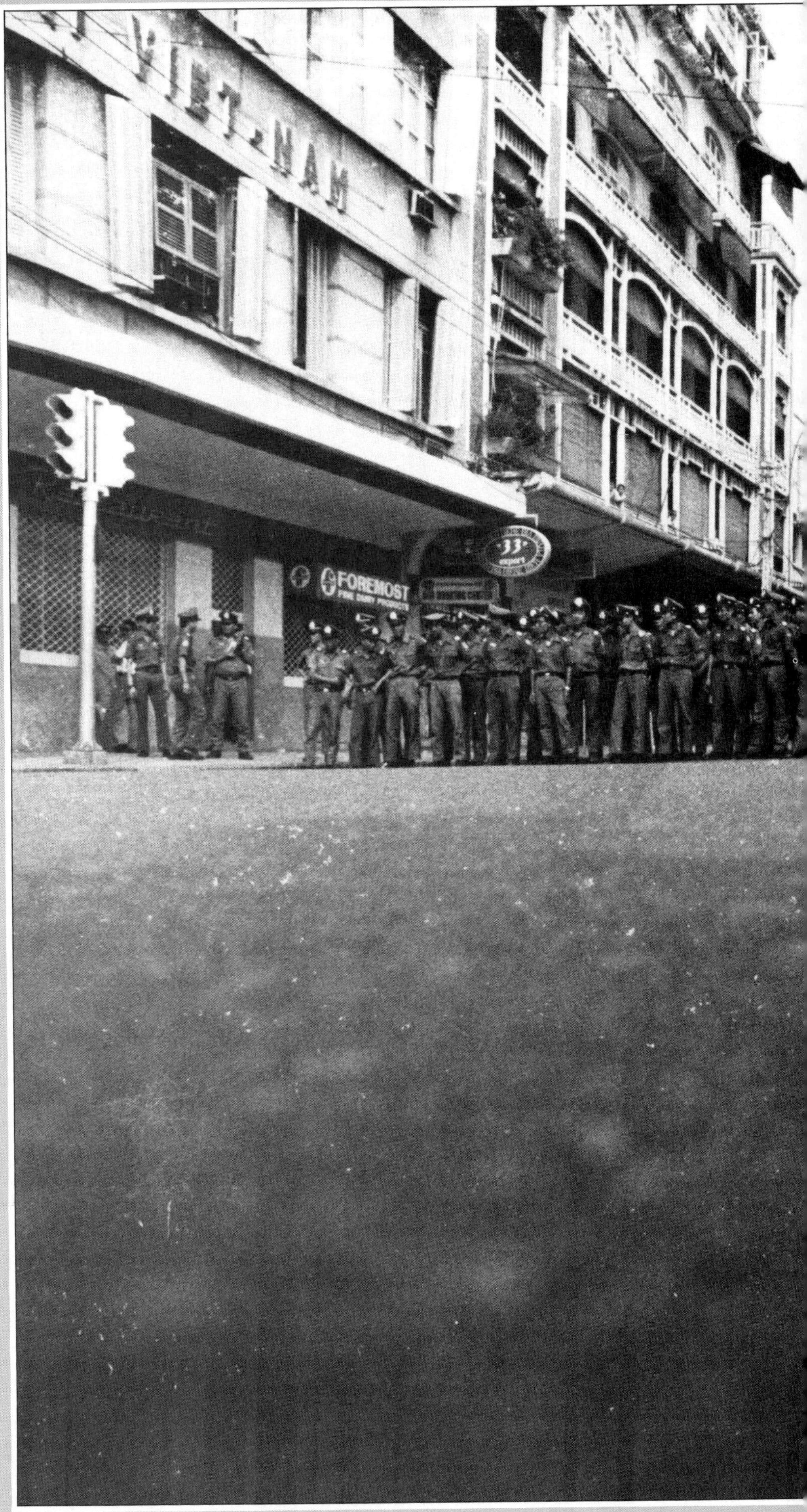
VIET-NAM
FOREMOST
33

Police form a human wall preventing anticorruption marchers from reaching downtown Saigon on October 10, 1974.

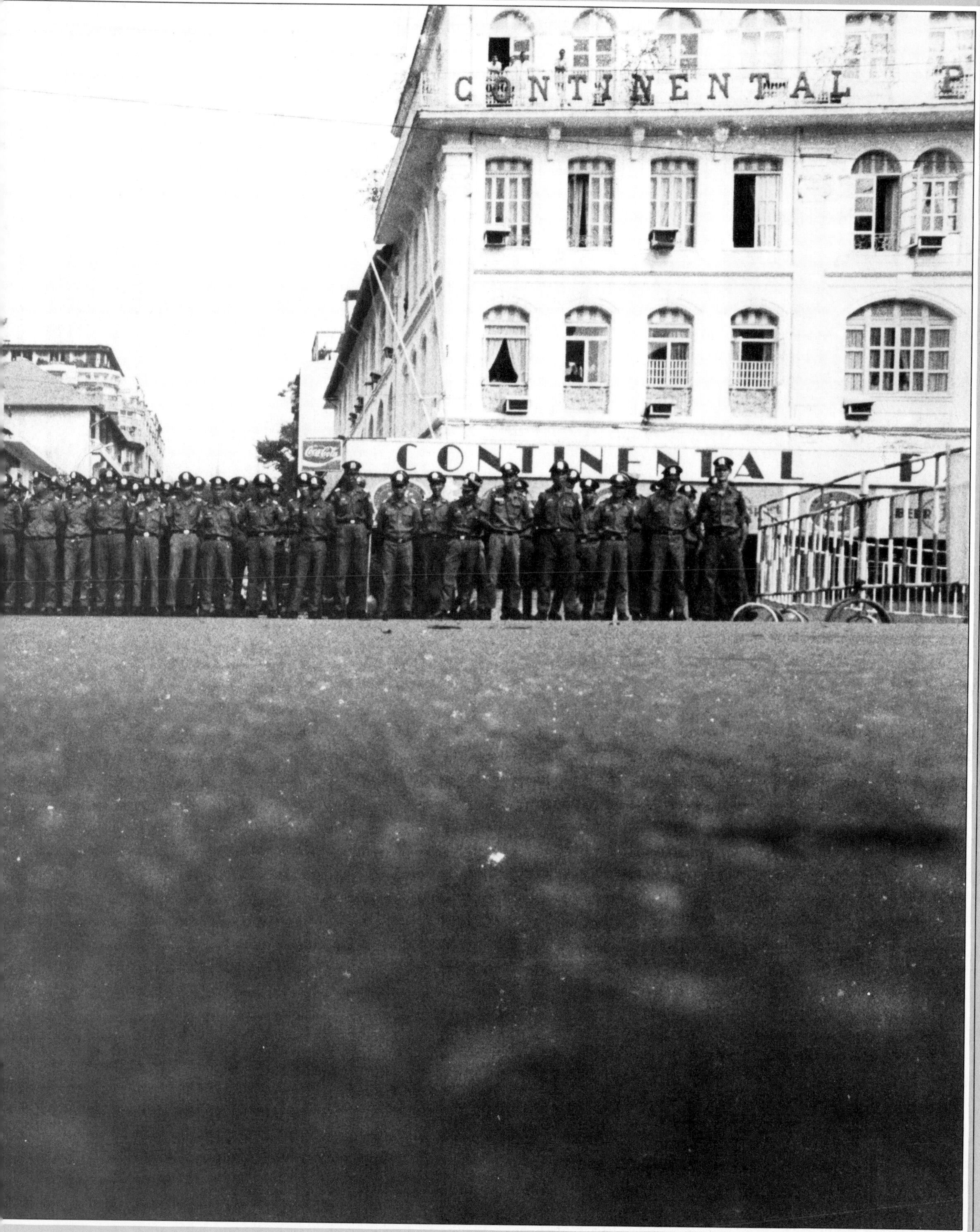
CONTINENTAL
CONTINENTAL

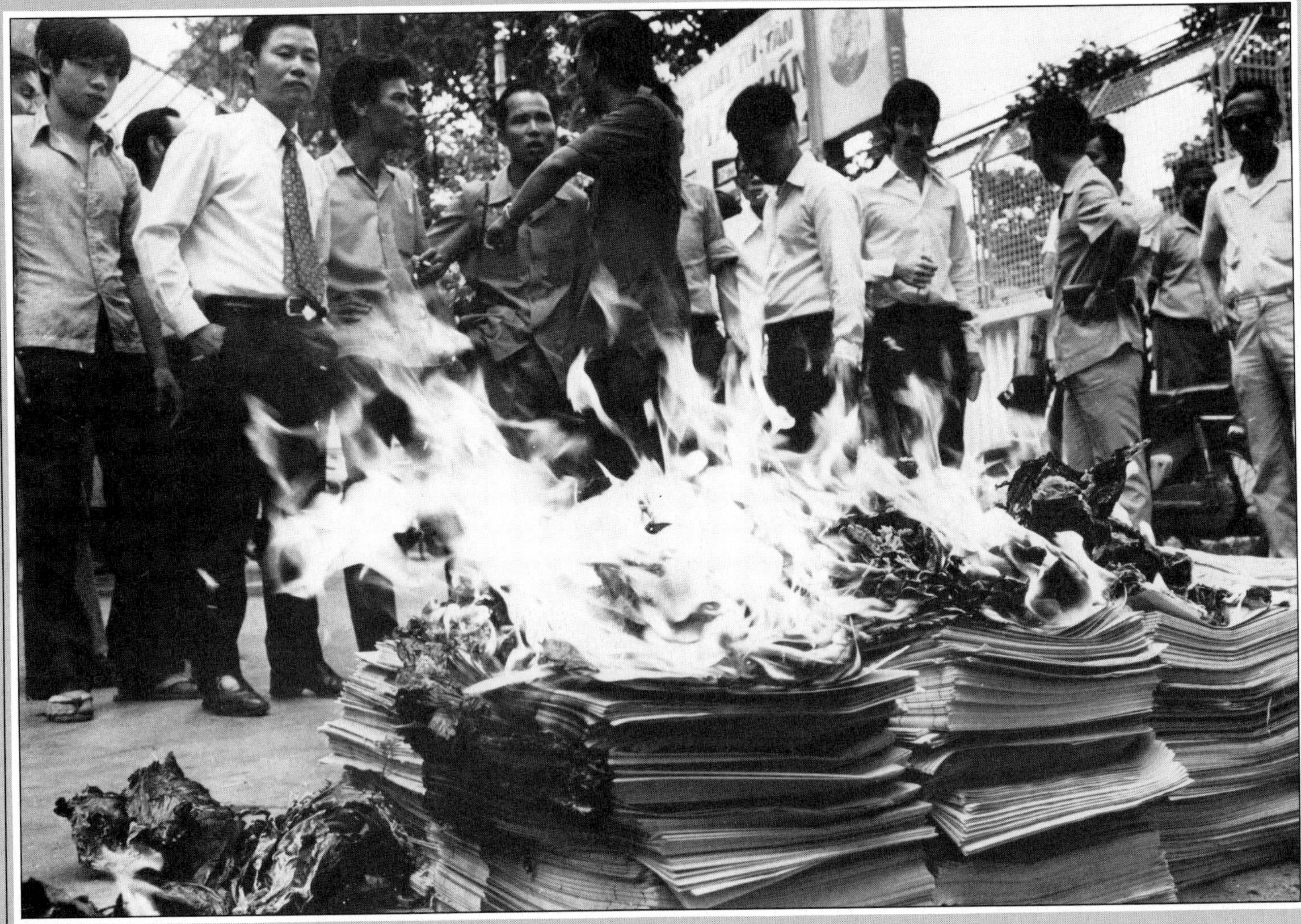

Above. *In a public protest of press censorship on September 19, the publisher of* Song Than *burns 10,000 copies of the daily newspaper after government censors ordered the edition confiscated.*

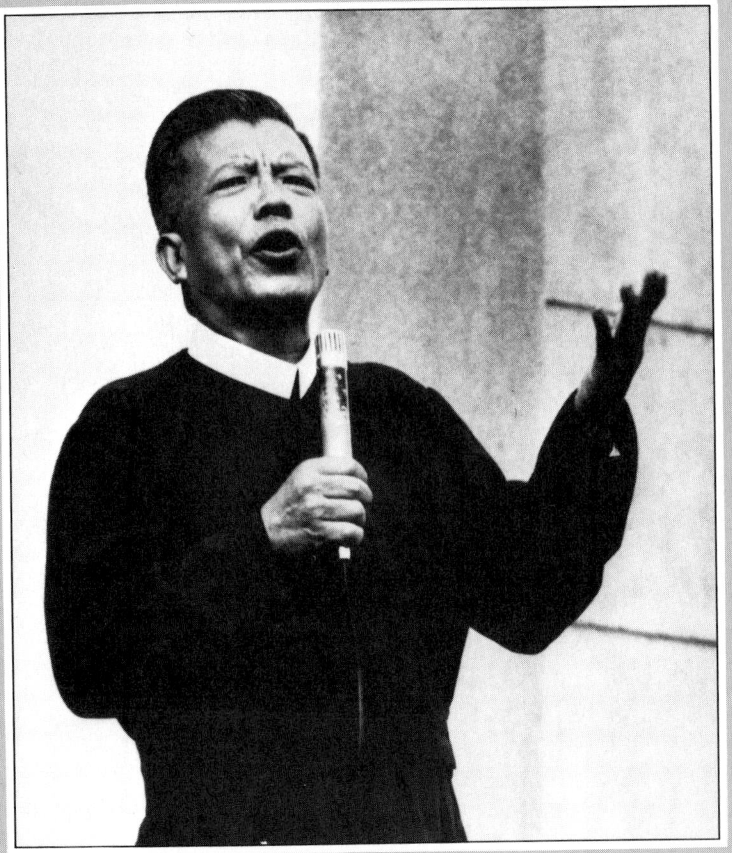

Left. *Father Tran Huu Thanh, the leader of the anticorruption movement, calls President Thieu to task before a crowd in Saigon.*

Right. *Catholic demonstrators and police clash in the streets of the capital, October 30. The attempt to break through government barricades left sixty demonstrators and thirty police seriously injured.*

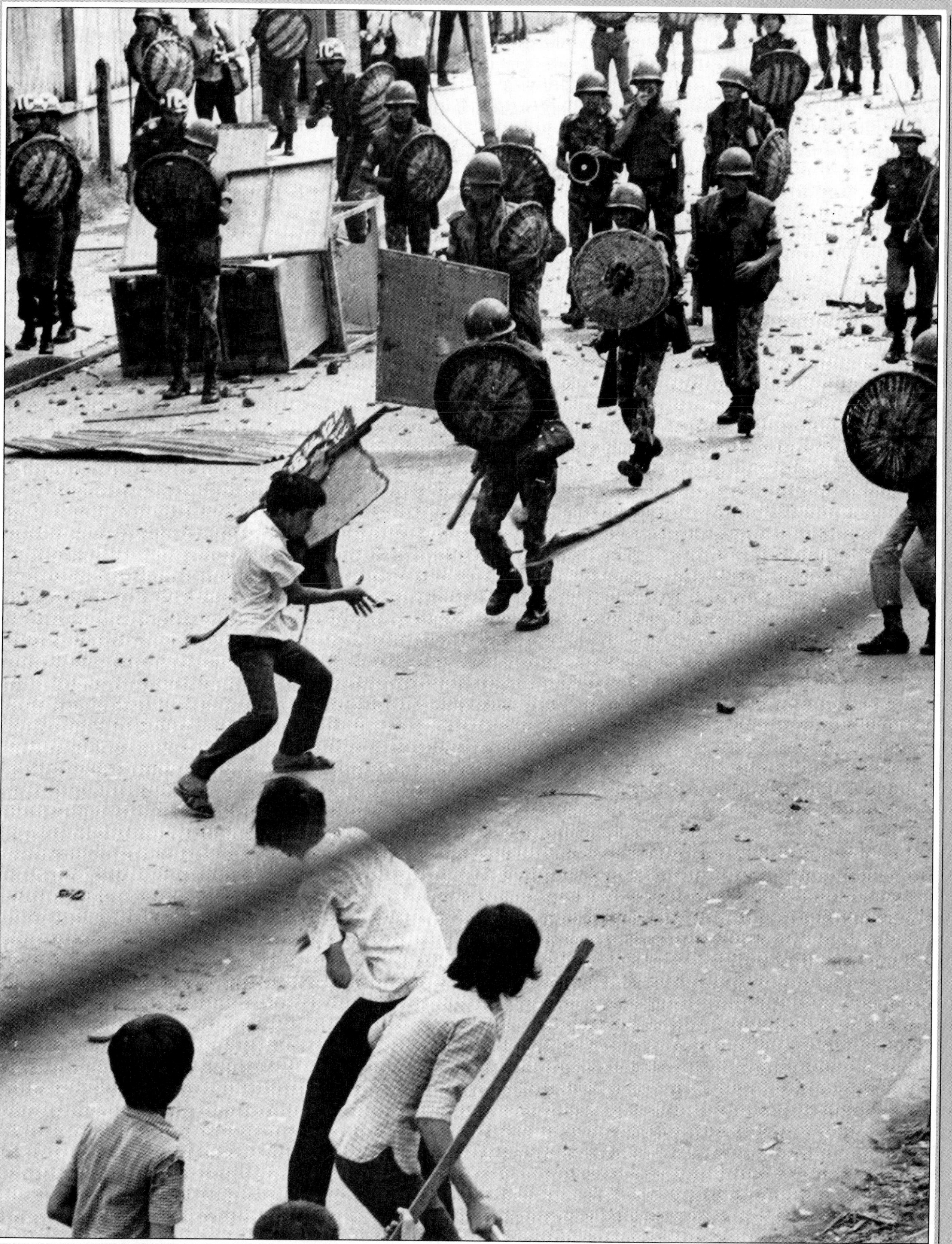

dictment. Although the offending editions were immediately confiscated, the government's attempts at repression only provoked more public outcry. Newspaper editors banded together to protest press censorship. A group of Buddhist politicians and religious leaders formed the "National Reconciliation Force" to demand implementation of the Paris agreement. An "Anti-Famine Movement," a "Women's Movement for the Right to Life," and a campaign for the release of political prisoners emerged out of nowhere to compete for public attention.

Government charges that some of the swelling protest had been instigated by the Communists were undoubtedly true. But the fever of discontent was so widespread that within a matter of weeks Father Thanh's anticorruption movement had generated what one of Thieu's advisers called "a vast anti-government crusade." The long-suppressed anger of ordinary South Vietnamese had erupted in a torrent of denunciation directed at the one man they held responsible above all others for their country's distress. "There have always been charges of corruption," said Tran Van Tuyen, an opposition leader in the National Assembly, "but the open charges were just the last drop of water that makes the full glass overflow. President Thieu just has to make an answer."

When Thieu did respond, three weeks later, he conspicuously avoided mention of any of the specific accusations made against him in the indictment. "Let me say from the time I was a lieutenant until I became a president," he told a nationwide radio audience on September 30,

let you, compatriots and combatants, feel free to point out to me any corrupt practice on my part, any bribe that I accepted, any time that I traded my prestige, any time I pressured people to pay me in exchange for a promotion. ... If my relatives or my wife or children are corrupt or violate the law, let the law deal with them. I will not take up their defense or condone them. That is the answer to the charge that I am corrupt and condone corrupt elements among my relatives.

Neither the president's ambiguous defense nor his vague promises to remove restrictions on political activity and root out corruption satisfied anyone. As sporadic demonstrations broke out and criticism over his continuing inaction mounted, Ambassador Martin urged the South Vietnamese leader to diffuse the situation or risk what credit he still possessed in Washington.

On October 24 Thieu bowed to the growing pressure and dismissed four cabinet members, including Information Minister Hoang Duc Nha. The next day the Ministry of Defense announced the firing or demotion of nearly 400 field grade officers. The cabinet shuffle and military discharges only fed fuel to the flames. Father Thanh vowed that demonstrations would continue. "Personnel changes are not important. We want a change of stance and policy." One National Assembly deputy was more explicit: "Dropping a few technocrats will not change things," he

declared. "The man at the top must be changed." With few options remaining, Thieu made the most substantial concessions of his seven-year presidency. On October 30 he removed three of his four regional commanders, Lieutenant Generals Nguyen Van Toan, Pham Quoc Thuan, and Nguyen Vinh Nghi. The sacrifice of key members of the military hierarchy on which his power ultimately rested was a stark reflection of the gravity with which Thieu viewed the political crisis that swirled around him. But it also left those clamoring for reform only one remaining target: the president himself.

The campaign "is only beginning," declared Father Thanh. That night thousands of demonstrators held a huge torch-light parade through the predominantly Catholic Tan Linh District north of the capital. But the South Vietnamese president had gone as far as he was going to go in the direction of conciliation. When anticorruption ralliers attempted to march into downtown Saigon on the morning of October 31, police halted the protesters in a melee of swinging clubs, flying rocks, and burning cars. Hastily erected barbwire barriers went up around the National Assembly, the central market, and other possible demonstration sites. They were still there the following day when Thieu took once more to the radio to deliver his annual National Day address.

Warning that the combination of political attacks against the government and North Vietnamese military pressure could "lead the country into the hands of Communism," Thieu declared that he would no longer permit his opponents "to propagate groundless news, to create religious divisions, to slander the government, to calumnify government officials, and to undermine the economy." Although promising to ease restraints on the press and political parties, and pledging not to run for reelection the following October, he vowed that the government would "preserve security and public order to the maximum." If anyone had any doubts about the president's intentions they were quickly dispelled. By week's end more demonstrators had been injured in clashes with police. Eleven opposition legislators were beaten and arrested, along with twenty-eight newsmen rounded up during a police raid on the Viet Nam Press Club.

In the face of the government's show of force, protest subsided. Buddhist spokesmen continued to refer to "deep discontent" among the population, and former General Duong Van Minh denounced the "impotence and corruption" of a regime that prolonged its existence only by means of "repression, bribery, division and suppression of truth." But the violence had fragmented opposition groups already divided along religious and political lines and dissuaded ordinary citizens from participating in public demonstrations. If the people had for the moment been cowed, however, they had not been convinced. A public opinion survey conducted by the GVN revealed that popular confidence in the performance of the government and its ability to defend the country from the Communists was at its lowest ebb since 1968.

The beginning of the end

The developments out of Washington in early August precipitated a different sort of turmoil in North Vietnam. The departure of Richard Nixon, the man who less than two years earlier had sent American B-52s to ravage Hanoi and Haiphong, was cause for elation among the members of the Politburo. But what could be expected from the new administration? Would Ford be able to persuade Congress to restore military aid to Saigon? Would Congress give the new president a freer hand in Vietnam than it had been willing to grant his predecessor? Although some in Hanoi advised caution, others quickly concluded that the change of power had created "new opportunities" only waiting to be grasped.

The ensuing debate found the hawks within the leadership once more calling for all-out war. Pointing out that the latest aid cuts had condemned the South Vietnamese to waging a "poor man's war," they argued that U.S. pressure for territorial demarcation would only increase as Saigon's forces grew weaker. It was thus more important than ever that the NVA pursue the military advantage it had gained during the summer campaign. After two years of arduous labor the logistical network in the South had been completed, materiel stockpiled, and combat units brought up to offensive strength. They now had the means to ensure that if negotiations resumed, the DRV would come to the conference table in a position of unquestioned strength. Against these arguments the moderates again referred to the uncertainty of support from Moscow and Peking. Both superpowers continued to urge Hanoi to concentrate on economic development, and neither had shown any willingness during recent meetings to significantly increase military assistance. The priorities of the government, declared Premier Pham Van Dong, must remain "balanced" between revolution and reconstruction.

What brought the debate to a close was the outburst of public protest against the Thieu regime in late September. Not only was the unrest proof that popular confidence in the Saigon government had plummeted, it also reduced the likelihood of U.S. intervention to save Thieu from defeat. Seizing the opportunity, the Provisional Revolutionary Government announced on October 8 that it would no longer negotiate with Saigon "as long as Nguyen Van Thieu and his gang remain in power." Only when the current government was overthrown could "serious negotiations" resume. Although talks between the two sides had actually broken off five months earlier, the PRG declaration marked the formal end of the Paris agreement.

Thus, the joint meeting of the Politburo and the Central Military Committee in early October was an unambiguous council of war. As the General Staff presented its strategic combat plan, two questions assumed special importance: What was the state of the South Vietnamese armed forces, and what were the intentions of the Americans? Reviewing the gains of the summer offensive the conferees noted that during the fighting enemy morale had fallen, the number of combat troops had sharply decreased, Saigon's limited reserve forces had bogged down, and the steady reduction in American aid had so reduced mobility and fire support that the ARVN had completely abandoned offensive operations. "We paid particular attention to the battle which knocked out the district town of Thuong Duc," wrote General Dung.

This was a test of strength with what were said to be the enemy's best-trained troops. When we knocked out Thuong Duc, the enemy sent a whole division of paratroops for days of continuous counterattacks to take it back. But we inflicted heavy casualties on them, held Thuong Duc, and forced the enemy to give up.

The conclusion was inescapable: "As we increasingly took the initiative and grew stronger, the enemy grew weaker and more passive every day."

More difficult to answer, and more heatedly debated, was the second question. "Did the Americans have the ability to send troops back into the South when our large attacks led to the danger of the Saigon army's collapse?" What the North Vietnamese leadership saw when it looked at the United States was what their Chinese neighbors liked to call a "paper tiger." Reeling from the political nightmare of Watergate, a divided Congress confronted an untested president with little experience in foreign affairs. Still feeling the effects of the worldwide oil crisis, Americans struggled with economic recession and increasing inflation. Preoccupied with superpower confrontations and quarreling allies, the United States was more confused about its role in the world than ever before. There was no doubt that Washington still possessed the means to "punish" the North in the event of major GVN setbacks. But it no longer had either the confidence in its ally or the certainty of purpose to bring that power to bear. The consensus of the conference was put in the form of a resolution by First Party Secretary Le Duan: "Now that the United States has pulled out of the South, it will be hard for them to jump back in. And no matter how they may intervene, they cannot rescue the Saigon administration from its disastrous collapse."

What emerged from the political and military deliberations of October was a statement of policy known as the "Resolution for 1975." In that document, and in summaries of its conclusions and recommendations that were distributed to the military commands in the South, the leadership affirmed an historic judgment. The war had moved into "its final stage." The NVA had achieved a superiority on the battlefield that should and must be exploited. In a phased, two-year offensive to begin in mid-December, Communist forces would move out of the jungles and

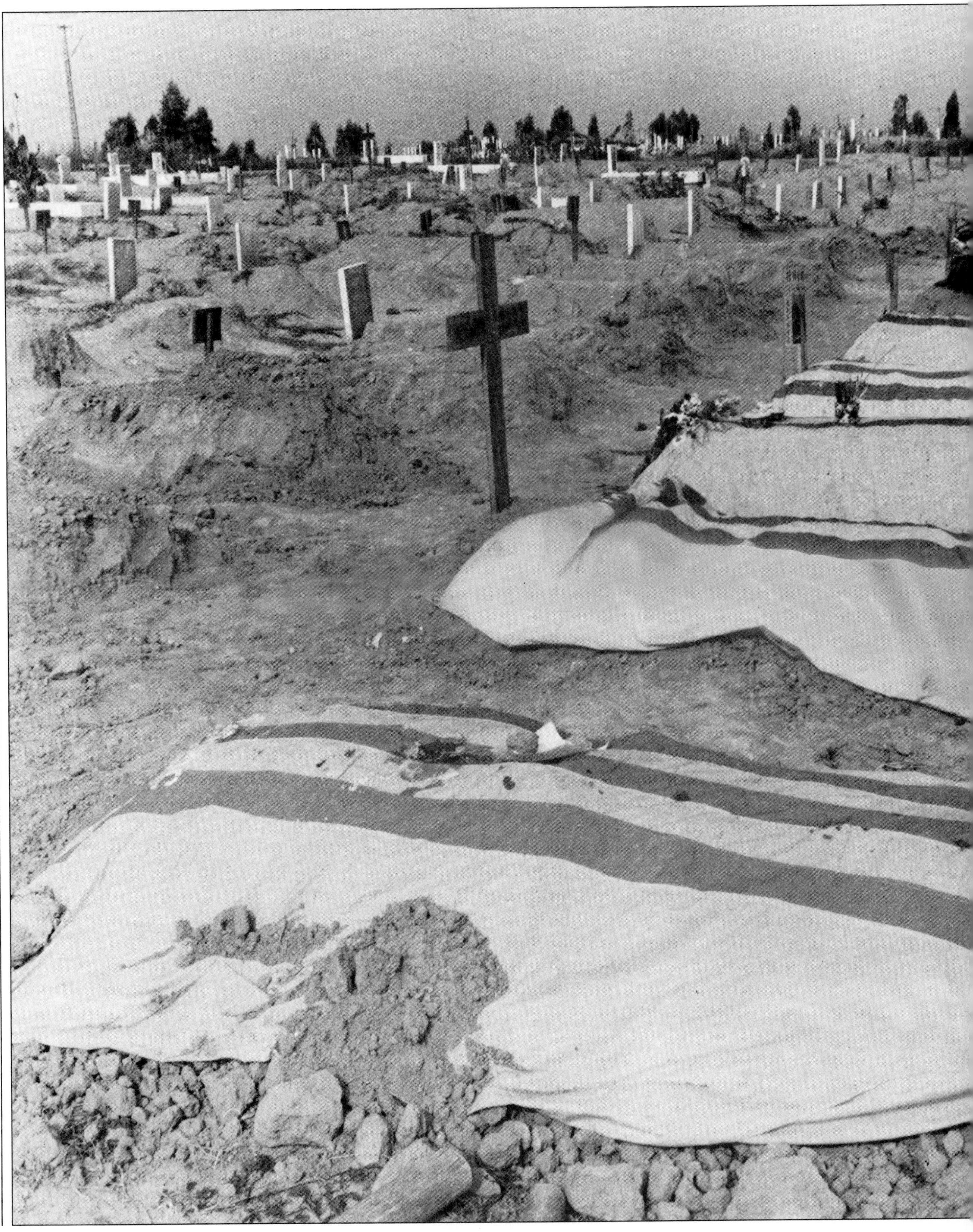

mountains into the populated areas, destroying the RVNAF, creating conditions for the overthrow of the Thieu regime, and paving the way for the capitulation of the South Vietnamese government. The first objective of the new offensive would be the vast, lightly defended region the Vietnamese called Tay Nguyen and the Americans knew as the central highlands.

As the Year of the Tiger drew to a close, VNAF reconnaissance flights sighted enemy convoys numbering more than 200 vehicles moving men and supplies to forward positions in Military Regions 1 and 2. Recruit training centers north of the DMZ were instructed to cut down their programs to two weeks, the same orders they had received in 1968. According to U.S. intelligence estimates, the Communist Main Force army in the South now consisted of nineteen divisions numbering over 300,000 men. In early December heavy fighting broke out in the delta provinces of Kien Tuong and Dinh Tuong, in Long Khanh and Binh Tuy east of Saigon, and in Tay Ninh, where Communist mortar and artillery attacks around Nui Ba Den Mountain drove thousands of terrified refugees into the province capital. During the second week of the month the South Vietnamese army reported 706 men killed and 2,758 wounded, the highest weekly casualty toll since the cease-fire took effect.

During 1974 the armed forces of South Vietnam lost nearly 31,000 men killed in action. As a percentage of the country's overall population, the 56,000 combat deaths suffered by the RVNAF since January 1973 represented proportionally more than one-and-a-half times the total number of U.S. losses in all of World War II. The intensity of the new Communist attacks, the inability of the government to ease the crushing burden of economic hardship, and the shattering realization of declining American support produced an unprecedented crisis of morale. "After nearly thirty years of war," wrote General Nguyen Duy Hinh, "South Vietnam was exhausted materielly and worn out spiritually. Its inherent weaknesses and difficulties were still not overcome, but its means to carry on the fight were drastically reduced."

On December 13, 1974, the North Vietnamese 7th Division, supported by tanks and artillery, attacked the small garrison town of Don Luan in southern Phuoc Long Province. By January 6 the provincial capital of Phuoc Binh had fallen. For the embattled people of South Vietnam, the final agony had begun.

Left. *Freshly dug graves at a military cemetery near Bien Hoa bear silent testimony to a nation's torment.*

Following pages. *In late 1974 a North Vietnamese armored unit prepares for the final offensive.*

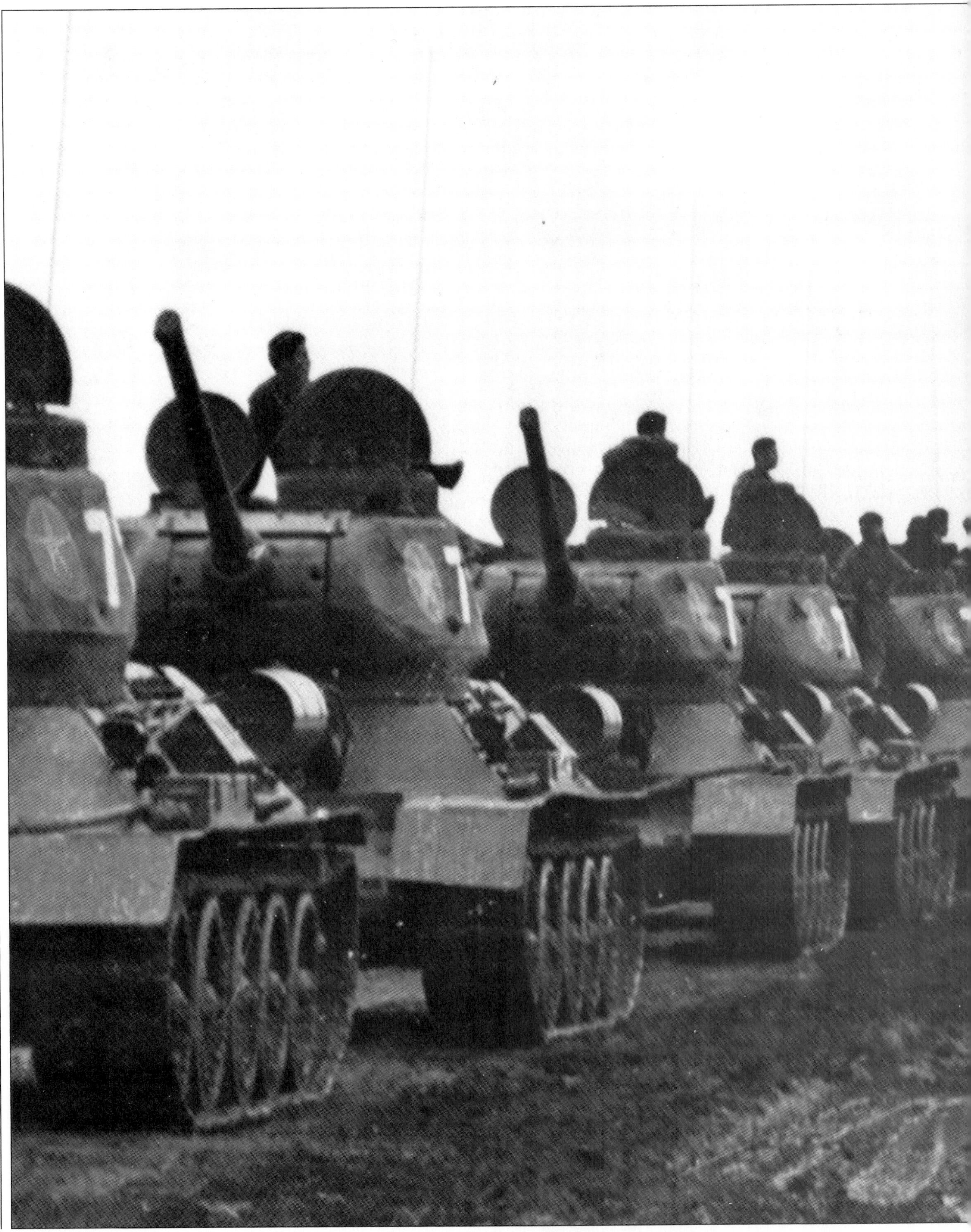

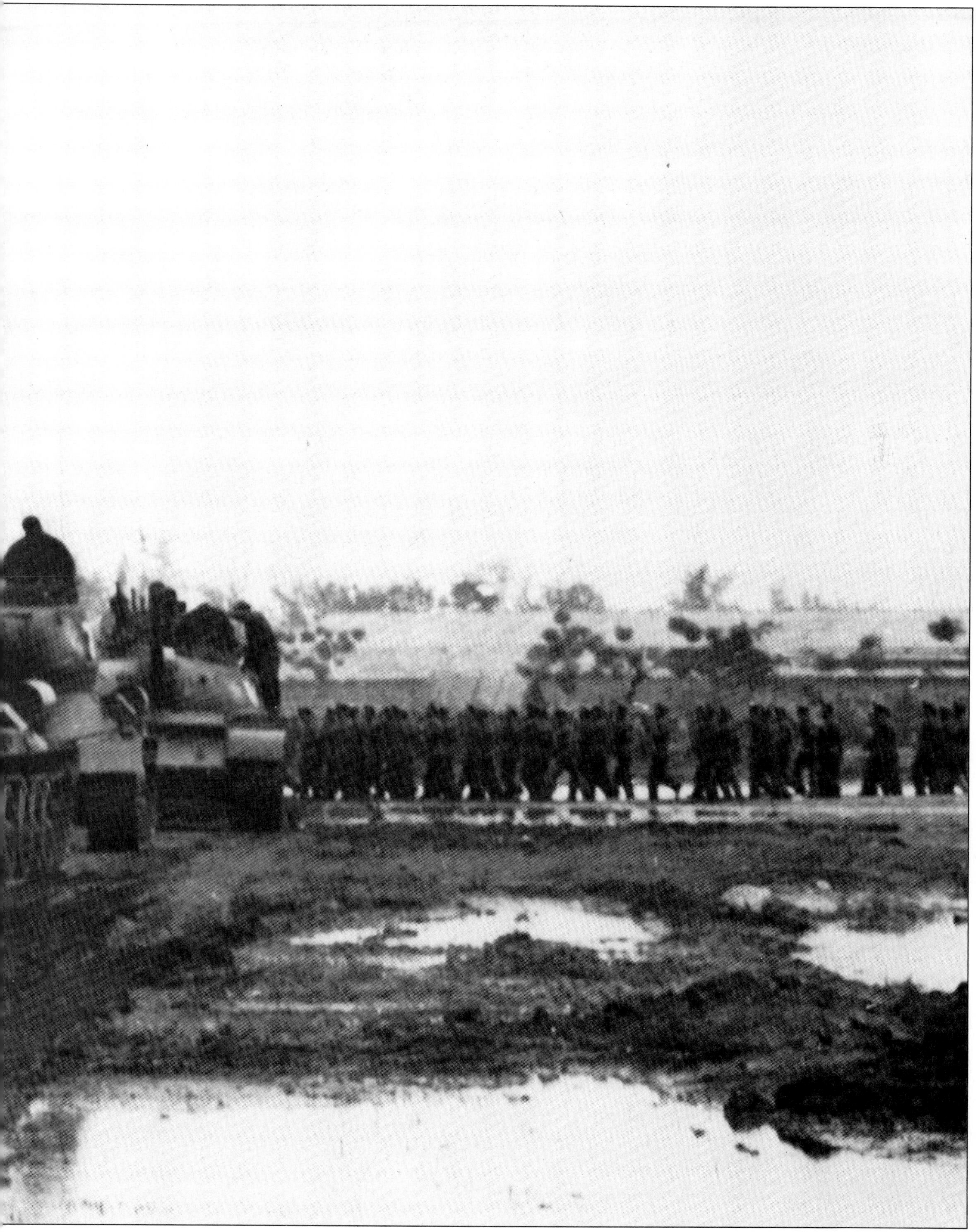

Bibliography

I. Books and Articles

"Aid to Thieu: A Strategy of Deception." *Thoi-Bao Ga*, July/August 1974.

Amter, Joseph A. *Vietnam Verdict*. The Continuum Publishing Corp., 1982.

Bernstein, Carl, and Bob Woodward. *All the President's Men*. Simon & Schuster, 1974.

Blakey, Scott. *Prisoner at War: The Survival of Commander Richard A. Stratton*. Doubleday, 1978.

Blum, John M. et al. *The National Experience, Fourth Edition*. Harcourt Brace Jovanovich, 1977.

Branfman, Fred. "Indochina: The Illusion of Withdrawal." *Harper's*, May 1973.

Burchett, Wilfred. *Grasshoppers & Elephants: Why Vietnam Fell*. Urizen Bks., 1977.

Buttinger, Joseph. *Vietnam: The Unforgettable Tragedy*. Horizon Pr., 1977.

Chanda, Nayan. "A Permanent State of Misery." *Far Eastern Economic Review*, October 11, 1974.

———. "Thieu's Foes: Back to Reality." *Far Eastern Economic Review*, December 27, 1974.

Chesley, Capt. Larry. *Seven Years in Hanoi*. Bookcraft, Inc., 1973.

Chomsky, Noam. "Endgame: The Tactics of Peace in Vietnam." *Ramparts*, April 1973.

Chomsky, Noam and Edward S. Herman. "The Search for an Honest Quisling." *Ramparts*, December 1974.

Collins, Peter. "Thieu's Eleventh Hour." *Far Eastern Economic Review*, November 1, 1974.

"The End and the Beginning." *Airman*, June 1973.

Fellowes, Commander Jack H. "Operation Homecoming." *U.S. Naval Institute Proceedings*, December 1976.

FitzGerald, Frances. "Vietnam: The Cadres and the Villagers." *Atlantic Monthly*, May 1974.

———. "Vietnam: Reconciliation." *Atlantic Monthly*, June 1974.

Gallup Organization. *Gallup Opinion Index*. Gallup, 1973–1974.

Goodman, Allan E. *The Lost Peace: America's Search for a Negotiated Settlement of the Vietnam War*. Hoover Inst. Pr., 1978.

———. "South Vietnam: War Without End?" *Asian Survey*, January 1975.

Grant, Zalin B. "Vietnam without GI's." *New Republic*, May 19, 1973.

Haldeman, H. R. *The Ends of Power*. New York Times Bks., 1978.

Herring, George C. *America's Longest War: The United States and Vietnam, 1950–1975*. Wiley, 1979.

Herrington, Stuart A. *Peace with Honor?* Presidio Pr., 1983.

Hersh, Seymour M. *The Price of Power: Kissinger in the Nixon White House*. Summit Bks., 1983.

Hubbell, John G. et al. *P.O.W.* Reader's Digest Pr., 1976.

Isaacs, Arnold R. *Without Honor: Defeat in Vietnam and Cambodia*. The Johns Hopkins Univ. Pr., 1983.

Jensen, Lt. Col. Jay R. *Six Years in Hell: A Returned POW Views Captivity, Country, and the Nation's Future*. Horizon Publishers, 1974.

Jones, James. *Viet Journal*. Delacorte Pr., 1973.

Kalb, Bernard, and Marvin Kalb. *Kissinger*. Little, Brown, 1974.

Karnow, Stanley. *Vietnam: A History*. Penguin Bks., 1983.

Kirk, Donald. *Tell It to the Dead: Memories of a War*. Nelson-Hall, 1975.

Kissinger, Henry. "The Vietnam Negotiations." *Foreign Affairs*, January 1969.

———. *The White House Years*. Little, Brown, 1979.

———. *Years of Upheaval*. Little, Brown, 1982.

Krich, Claudia A. "Vietnam: The Sickness." *The Progressive*, November 1974.

Landau, David. "Peace Is at Hand." *Ramparts*, March 1973.

Le Hoang Trong. "Survival and Self-Reliance." *Asian Survey*, April 1975.

Lewy, Guenter. *America in Vietnam*. Oxford Univ. Pr., 1978.

Lukas, Anthony. *Night-Mare*. Viking Pr., 1976.

McArthur, George. "South Vietnam—A Crisis Swells Amid the Bustle." *Vietnam Report*, July 1, 1974.

Markham, James M. "Not 10, Not 15, but 50 Rounds." *New York Times Magazine*, April 14, 1974.

Morris, Roger. *Uncertain Greatness*. Harper & Row, 1977.

Murray, Gen. John E. "The Politics of Logistics: Or How to Lose a War." Manuscript, August 16, 1984.

———. "Vietnam Logistics: Who's to Blame?" *Military Logistics Forum*, September/October 1984.

Nguyen Cao Ky, Gen. *Twenty Years and Twenty Days*. Stein & Day, 1976.

Nguyen Nam Phong. "A Rather Disturbing Sign." *Vietnam Report*, October 15, 1974.

Nguyen Ngoc Ngan. *The Will of Heaven*. E.P. Dutton, 1982.

Nguyen Van Thieu, Gen. "The Four Issues of the Day." *Vietnam Report*, October 15, 1974.

Nixon, Richard. *RN: The Memoirs of Richard Nixon*. Grosset & Dunlap, 1978.

Palmer, Gen. Bruce, Jr. *The 25-Year War*. The Univ. Pr. of Kentucky, 1984.

Papp, Daniel S. *Vietnam: The View From Moscow, Peking, Washington*. McFarland & Co., 1981.

Parker, Maynard. "Vietnam: The War That Won't End." *Foreign Affairs*, January 1975.

Plumb, Charlie. *I'm No Hero*. Independence Pr., 1973.

Porter, Gareth. *A Peace Denied*. Indiana Univ. Pr., 1975.

———. "Does Thieu Continue the War to Avoid Political Defeat?" *Christian Century*, April 25, 1973.

"POW Escort." *Airman*, June 1973.

Pratt, John Clark, comp. *Vietnam Voices: Perspectives on the War Years, 1941–1982*. Penguin Bks., 1984.

Roberts, Chalmers. "Foreign Policy Under a Paralyzed Presidency." *Foreign Affairs*, July 1974.

Schell, Jonathan. *The Time of Illusion*. Vintage Bks., 1975.

Schellhorn, Kai M. *Vietnam ohne Amerika: Die Strategie Hanois*. Tudov Buch, 1975.

Shaplen, Robert. "Letter From Indochina." *The New Yorker*, June 2, 1973.

———. "Letter From Indochina." *The New Yorker*, January 28, 1974.

———. "Letter From Saigon." *The New Yorker*, January 6, 1975.

———. "Letter From Vietnam." *The New Yorker*, February 24, 1973.

Shawcross, William. "Report from Saigon: An Economy Near Collapse." *Ramparts*, July 1974.

———. *Sideshow*. Simon & Schuster, 1979.

Snepp, Frank. *Decent Interval*. Random, 1977.

Szulc, Tad. "How Kissinger Did It: Behind the Vietnam Ceasefire Agreement." *Foreign Policy*, Summer 1974.

———. *The Illusion of Peace*. Viking Pr., 1978.

Thuong Duc. "The New Political Scene." *Vietnam Report*, October 15, 1974.

Timmes, Major Gen. Charles J. "Military Operations After the Cease-Fire Agreement, Part I." *Military Review*, August/September 1976.

Tran Van Don, Gen. *Our Endless War: Inside Vietnam*. Presidio Pr., 1978.

Van Tien Dung, Gen. *Our Great Spring Victory*. Monthly Review Pr., 1977.

Wacker, Stephen G. "The Interface Between Beliefs and Behavior: Henry Kissinger's Operational Code and the Vietnam War." *Journal of Conflict Resolution*, March 1977.

Warner, Denis. *Not With Guns Alone*. Hutchinson of Australia, 1977.

White, Theodore H. *Breach of Faith: The Fall of Richard Nixon*. Atheneum, 1975.

II. Government and Government-Sponsored Published Reports

Cao Van Vien, Gen. *The Final Collapse*. Indochina Monographs. U.S. Army Center of Military History, 1983.

———. *Leadership*. Indochina Monographs. U.S. Army Center of Military History, 1981.

Cao Van Vien and Lt. Gen. Dong Van Khuyen. *Reflections on the Vietnam War*. Indochina Monographs. U.S. Army Center of Military History, 1983.

Dillard, Walter Scott. *Sixty Days to Peace: Implementing the Paris Peace Accords, Vietnam 1973*. National Defense Univ. Pr., 1982.

Dong Van Khuyen, Lt. Gen. *The RVNAF*. Indochina Monographs. U.S. Army Center of Military History, 1980.

Hoang Ngoc Lung, Col. *Intelligence*. Indochina Monographs. U.S. Army Center of Military History, 1983.

Hosmer, Stephen T. et al. *The Fall of South Vietnam*. Rand Corporation, 1978.

Le Gro, Col. William E. *Vietnam from Cease-Fire to Capitulation*. U.S. Army Center of Military History, 1981.

McCubin, Hamilton I., ed. *Family Separation and Reunion: Families of Prisoners of War and Servicemen Missing in Action*. GPO, 1974.

Momyer, William W. *The Vietnamese Air Force, 1951–1975: An Analysis of Its Role in Combat*. Vol. 3, Monograph 4, USAF Southeast Asia Monograph Series, Office of Air Force History, 1975.

Nguyen Duy Hinh, Maj. Gen. *Vietnamization and the Ceasefire*. Indochina Monographs. U.S. Army Center of Military History, 1980.

Nguyen Duy Hinh and Brig. Gen. Tran Dinh Tho. *The South Vietnamese Society*. Indochina Monographs. U.S. Army Center of Military History, 1980.

Sutsakhan, Lt. Gen. Sak. *The Khmer Republic at War and the Final Collapse*. Indochina Monographs. U.S. Army Center of Military History, 1984.

Tran Van Tra, Sr. Gen. *Vietnam: History of the Bulwark B-2 Theatre*. Vol. 5, Concluding the 30-Years War. GPO, 1983.

U.S. Congress. House. Committee on Appropriations. *Department of Defense Appropriations—Oversight of Fiscal Year 1975 Military Assistance to Vietnam*. 94th Congress, 1st sess., 1975.

———. *Foreign Assistance and Related Agencies Appropriations for 1974, Part 2*. 93d Congress, 1st sess., 1973.

———. *Foreign Assistance and Related Agencies Appropriations for 1975, Part 2*. 93d Congress, 2d sess., 1974.

———. Committee on Armed Services. *Hearing on H.R. 12565—Supplemental Authorization for FY 74.* 93d Congress, 2d sess., 1974.

———. Committee on Foreign Affairs. *Fiscal Year 1975 Foreign Assistance Request.* 93d Congress, 2d sess., 1974.

———. *U.S. Aid to Indochina.* Report of a staff survey team to South Vietnam, Cambodia, and Laos. 93d Congress, 2d sess., 1974.

———. *Vietnam—A Changing Crucible.* Report of a study mission to South Vietnam. 93d Congress, 2d sess., 1974.

———. Committee on Government Operations. *U.S. Assistance Programs in Vietnam.* 92d Congress, 2d sess., 1972. H. Rept. 92-1610.

———. "Second Supplemental Appropriations Bill, 1973." *Congressional Record,* June 29, 1973.

U.S. Congress. Senate. Committee on Appropriations. *Department of Defense Appropriations for Fiscal Year 1976.* 94th Congress, 1st sess., 1975.

———. *Foreign Assistance and Related Programs Appropriations for Fiscal Year 1975.* 93d Congress, 2d sess., 1974.

U.S. Congress. Senate. Committee on Armed Services. *Military Procurement Supplemental—Fiscal Year 1974.* 93d Congress, 2d sess., 1974.

———. *Southeast Asia.* Report by Senator Dewey F. Bartlett. 94th Congress, 1st sess., 1975.

U.S. Congress. Senate. Committee on Foreign Relations. *Foreign Assistance Authorization.* 93d Congress, 2d sess., 1974.

———. *Thailand, Laos, Cambodia and Vietnam.* 93d Congress, 1st sess., 1973.

———. *Vietnam: May 1974.* Staff Report. 93d Congress, 2d sess., 1974.

U.S. Congress. Senate. "Continuing Appropriations, 1974." *Congressional Record,* June 29, 1973.

———. "Department of Defense Appropriation Act, 1975." *Congressional Record,* August 21, 1974.

———. "Military Procurement Authorization, 1974." *Congressional Record,* May 6, 1974.

———. "War Powers Act." *Congressional Record,* July 18, 1973.

U.S. Veterans Administration, Office of Planning & Programs. *Study of Former Prisoners of War.* GPO, 1980.

III. Unpublished Government and Military Sources
Department of the Army, Office of the Adjutant General, Defense Attaché Office, Saigon. DAO Final Assessment, June 1975.

———. DAO Quarterly Assessment, Nos. 1–7, July 1973–February 1975.

IV. Newspapers and Periodicals Consulted by Authors:
Far Eastern Economic Review (1972–1974); *New York Times* (1972–1974); *Newsweek* (1972–1974); *Time* (1972–1974); *U.S. News and World Report* (1972–1974).

V. Interviews
Stuart A. Herrington, Colonel, Negotiations Staff Officer, Four-Party Joint Military Team, 1973–1975; Hoang Ngoc Lung, Colonel, former Deputy Chief of Intelligence, South Vietnamese Joint General Staff; William E. Le Gro, Colonel, U.S. Defense Attaché Office, Saigon, 1972–1975; Graham Martin, former U.S. Ambassador to South Vietnam, 1973–1975; John E. Murray, General, former U.S. Defense Attaché to South Vietnam, 1973–1974.

Map Credits

All maps prepared by Diane McCaffery. Sources are as follows:
p. 21—Snepp, Frank, *Decent Interval,* Vintage Bks., 1978, p. 54; Le Gro, Col. William, *Vietnam from Cease-Fire to Capitulation,* U.S. Army Center of Military History, GPO, 1981, p. 22.

p. 104—"The New Look" map in "And Now, a Third Vietnam," *Newsweek,* July 16, 1973; Vo Bam, Gen., "The Legendary Ho Chi Minh Trail," *Vietnam Courier* 20, no. 5, p. 11.

p. 112—Le Gro, Col. William, *Vietnam from Cease-Fire to Capitulation,* U.S. Army Center of Military History, GPO, 1981, p. 57.

p. 122—Le Gro, Col. William, *Vietnam from Cease-Fire to Capitulation,* U.S. Army Center of Military History, GPO, 1981, p. 92.

p. 161—Le Gro, Col. William, *Vietnam from Cease-Fire to Capitulation,* U.S. Army Center of Military History, GPO, 1981, p. 111.

p. 164—Le Gro, Col. William, *Vietnam from Cease-Fire to Capitulation,* U.S. Army Center of Military History, GPO, 1981, p. 97.

p. 165—Le Gro, Col. William, *Vietnam from Cease-Fire to Capitulation,* U.S. Army Center of Military History, GPO, 1981, p. 100.

Photography Credits

Cover Photograph:
Dennis Brack—Black Star.

Peace Is at Hand
p. 7, Genvieve Chauvel—Sygma. p. 8, Claude Lafontan/Gamma-Liaison. p. 11, UPI/Bettmann Newsphotos. p. 12, John Giannini—Sipa. p. 17, UPI/Bettmann Newsphotos. p. 19, AP/Wide World. p. 22, Goksin Sipahioglu—Sipa. p. 23, Eastfoto. p. 25, J. P. Laffont/Gamma-Liaison. pp. 26–27, © Harry Benson. p. 29, UPI/Bettmann Newsphotos. p. 31, Goksin Sipahioglu—Sipa. p. 33, AP/Wide World.

Cease Fire!
p. 35, Dieter Ludwig—Camera Press. p. 36, Barr Gallup Ashcraft—Black Star. p. 39, UPI/Bettmann Newsphotos. p. 40, left, Dieter Ludwig/Gamma-Liaison; right, Percy Dumas—Camera Press. p. 41, Dieter Ludwig/Gamma-Liaison. p. 42, Courtesy of the Asia Resource Center. p. 44, Jean-Claude Labbe/Gamma-Liaison. pp. 45–49, UPI/Bettmann Newsphotos. p. 52, top, AP/Wide World; bottom, Philip Jones Griffiths—Magnum. p. 53, Ali Nun—The New York Times. p. 55, UPI/Bettmann Newsphotos. p. 57, Sarah Webb Barrell—Camera Press. p. 59, Genvieve Chauvel/Gamma-Liaison. p. 60, Abbas/Gamma-Liaison.

The Word War
pp. 62–63, Roger Pic. pp. 64–65, Marc Riboud. pp. 66, 67, top, Ian Berry—Magnum. p. 67, bottom, Keith Brinton. p. 68, Rene Burri—Magnum.

America at Peace
p. 71, Ed Grazda—Magnum. p. 73, Gamma-Liaison. pp. 74–75, Charles Bonnay—Black Star. p. 76, David Hume Kennerly—TIME Magazine. p. 77, UPI/Bettmann Newsphotos. p. 78, AP/Wide World. p. 80, Jean-Claude Labbe—Gamma-Liaison. p. 81, AP/Wide World. p. 83, John Sotomayor—The New York Times. p. 85, AP/Wide World. pp. 86–87, J. P. Laffont—Sygma. p. 88, Sygma. p. 91, Nixon Project/National Archives. p. 93, Major General John E. Murray Collection. p. 94, AP/Wide World.

Home at Last
p. 96, Ray Cranbourne—Black Star. p. 97, Eddie Adams—TIME Magazine. p. 98, Dennis Brack—Black Star. p. 99, top, Carl Mydans—TIME Magazine; bottom, Jarrold Cablock—TIME Magazine. pp. 100–101, Nixon Project/National Archives.

The Third Indochina War
p. 103, Goksin Sipahioglu/Gamma-Liaison. p. 107, Bert Pfeiffer, courtesy of the Asia Resource Center. p. 109, Courtesy of the Asia Resource Center. p. 110, Eastfoto. p. 111, top, Hilmar Pabel; bottom, Sovfoto. p. 113, UPI/Bettmann Newsphotos. p. 114, Le Minh—TIME Magazine. p. 117, UPI/Bettmann Newsphotos. p. 119, St. Louis Post-Dispatch/reprinted with permission. p. 120, Gamma-Liaison. p. 125, AP/Wide World.

Eye of the Storm
p. 127, Christine Spengler—Sygma. p. 128, Sylvain Julienne/Gamma-Liaison. p. 129, UPI/Bettmann Newsphotos. p. 131, AP/Wide World. p. 132, Slyveine/Gamma-Liaison. p. 133, Sou Vichith/Gamma-Liaison.

Portents of Disaster
p. 135, Le Minh—TIME Magazine. p. 137, left, Agence France-Presse; center, Jean-Claude Francolon/Gamma-Liaison; right, Major General John E. Murray Collection. p. 138, Charles Bonnay/Gamma-Liaison. p. 139, UPI/Bettmann Newsphotos. p. 141, Charles Bonnay/Gamma-Liaison. p. 143, Nguyen Ngoc Luong—The New York Times. p. 145, Raymond Depardon/Gamma-Liaison. p. 147, Charles Habib/Gamma-Liaison. p. 150, Alain Dejean—Sygma. p. 152, AP/Wide World. p. 153, Major General John E. Murray Collection. p. 155, Charles Bonnay—TIME Magazine. p. 157, AP/Wide World.

The Year of the Tiger
pp. 159–62, Courtesy of the Asia Resource Center. p. 163, Alain Dejean—Sygma. p. 167, Courtesy of the Asia Resource Center. p. 168, AP/Wide World. p. 169, Barr Gallup Ashcraft. p. 172, Sylvain Julienne—Sygma. p. 176, © 1974, John Spragens, Jr. p. 178, top, UPI/Bettmann Newsphotos; bottom, Le Minh—TIME Magazine. p. 179, UPI/Bettmann Newsphotos. p. 182, John Giannini/Gamma-Liaison. p. 184, Courtesy of the Asia Resource Center.

Boston Publishing Company wishes to thank the following Time-Life Books correspondents for their assistance in acquiring the pictures for this book: Ann Natanson (Rome), Dick Berry (Tokyo), Elizabeth Kraemer-Singh (Bonn) and Dorothy Bacon (London).

Index

Names, Acronyms, Terms

Air America—a CIA-sponsored airline, based in Taiwan, that was often used for secret operations throughout Asia.

ARVN—Army of the Republic of (South) Vietnam.

Chieu Hoi—"open arms," the program promising clemency and financial aid to guerrillas who stopped fighting and returned to live under South Vietnamese government authority.

COSVN—Central Office for South Vietnam. Communist party headquarters in the southern portion of South Vietnam.

DAO—Defense Attaché Office. Part of the U.S. Mission to South Vietnam, this office replaced MACV in 1973 after the cease-fire and administered the program of military assistance to South Vietnam.

DMZ—demilitarized zone. Established by the Geneva accords of 1954, provisionally dividing North Vietnam from South Vietnam along the seventeenth parallel.

DOD—U.S. Department of Defense.

DRV—Democratic Republic of (North) Vietnam.

Enhance Plus (Operation Enhance)—massive influx of military equipment from the U.S. to RVNAF in 1972-73 to demonstrate support for President Thieu and to raise the level of allowable aid that would be permitted under the Paris agreement.

FANK—Forces Armées Nationales Khmères. The army of the government of Cambodia.

IV Corps (MR 4)—fourth allied combat tactical zone encompassing the Mekong Delta region.

GAO—General Accounting Office. Congressional body that studies the effectiveness and efficiency of government programs.

GVN—Government of (South) Vietnam.

Ho Chi Minh Trail—a network of roads and pathways through the jungles and mountains of Laos and Cambodia that prior to 1973 served as the principal NVA infiltration route of men and materiel into South Vietnam.

ICCS—International Commission of Control and Supervision. Assigned the task of monitoring the implementation of the Paris agreement, the commission consisted of representatives from Canada (later replaced by Iran), Hungary, Indonesia, and Poland.

JGS—Joint General Staff. South Vietnamese counterpart to the U.S. Joint Chiefs of Staff.

JMC—Joint Military Commission. Consisting of representatives of North Vietnam, the PRG, the U.S., and RVN, its purpose was to ensure that the concerned parties implemented and abided by the agreement's provisions.

JMT—Joint Military Team. Consisting of representatives of North Vietnam, the PRG, the U.S., and RVN, its purpose was to account for prisoners and MIAs on all sides.

Joint Casualty Resolution Center—established as a successor to MACV's Personnel Recovery Center, the JCRC worked to recover Americans still missing in action from its Thailand headquarters.

Khmer Rouge—name given by Prince Sihanouk to Cambodian Communists.

KIA—killed in action.

Landgrab '73—attempts on the part of both Communist and Saigon forces to gain control of strategic points in 1973 before the cease-fire went into effect.

Linebacker I—code name for U.S. bombing of North Vietnam resumed under President Nixon in April 1972.

Linebacker II—code name for Christmas 1972 bombing of North Vietnam.

MACV—Military Assistance Command, Vietnam. U.S. command over all U.S. military activities in Vietnam, originated in 1962.

MIA—missing in action.

MR—Military Region. Term that replaced Corps Tactical Zone in latter part of the war. One of four geographic zones into which South Vietnam was divided for purposes of military and civil administration.

NCNRC—National Council of National Reconciliation and Concord. Charged by the Paris peace accords to organize general and local elections for a new South Vietnamese government. Composed of the two combatants and a mutually agreeable "third force."

NCO—noncommissioned officer.

NLF—National Liberation Front. Officially the National Front for the Liberation of the South. Formed on December 20, 1960, it aimed to overthrow South Vietnam's government and reunite North and South Vietnam. The NLF included Communists and non-Communists.

NVA—North Vietnamese Army. Also called the People's Army of Vietnam (PAVN).

I Corps (MR 1)—"Eye" Corps. First allied combat tactical zone encompassing the five northernmost provinces of South Vietnam.

Operation Homecoming—Pentagon code name for procedures aimed at easing the transition of American POWs from Communist prison camps to their homes in the United States.

Pathet Lao—Laotian Communist guerrillas under the leadership of Prince Souphanouvang.

PF—Popular Forces. South Vietnamese village defense militia.

piaster—South Vietnamese unit of currency.

POW—prisoner of war.

PRG—Provisional Revolutionary Government. Established in 1969 as the government of the NLF.

RF—Regional Forces. South Vietnamese provincial defense militia.

RVN—Republic of (South) Vietnam.

RVNAF—Republic of (South) Vietnam Armed Forces.

SA-7—"Strela missile." An antiaircraft missile used by the NVA after 1972. Carried by a single man and fired from the shoulder, the weapon incorporated an infrared homing system that proved effective against slow-moving aircraft and helicopters.

SA-2—a Russian-built, surface-to-air missile with effective altitude of 59,000 feet and speed of Mach 2.5.

SAM—surface-to-air missile.

sapper—originally, in European wars, a soldier who built and repaired fortifications. NVA/VC sappers were commando raiders adept at penetrating allied defenses.

III Corps (MR 3)—Three Corps. Third allied combat tactical zone encompassing the area from the northern Mekong Delta to the southern central highlands.

II Corps (MR 2)—Two Corps. Second allied combat tactical zone encompassing the central highlands and the adjoining central lowlands.

Vanguard Youth—volunteer North Vietnamese youth organization mobilized into road-building brigades in the post-cease-fire years.

VC—Vietcong. Common reference to the NLF, a contraction of Vietnam Cong San (Vietnamese Communist).

VCI—Vietcong infrastructure. NLF local apparatus, responsible for overall direction of the insurgency including all political and military operations.

VNAF—(South) Vietnamese Air Force.